Springer Texts in Business and Economics

Springer Texts in Business and Economics (STBE) delivers high-quality instructional content for undergraduates and graduates in all areas of Business/Management Science and Economics. The series is comprised of self-contained books with a broad and comprehensive coverage that are suitable for class as well as for individual self-study. All texts are authored by established experts in their fields and offer a solid methodological background, often accompanied by problems and exercises.

Robert Rieg • Ute Vanini • Werner Gleißner

Enterprise Risk Management

A Modern Approach

Springer

Robert Rieg
Faculty of Business
Aalen University
Aalen, Germany

Werner Gleißner
Future Value Group AG
Leinfelden-Echterdingen, Germany

TUD Dresden University of Technology
Dresden, Germany

Ute Vanini
Kiel University of Applied Science
Kiel, Germany

ISSN 2192-4333 ISSN 2192-4341 (electronic)
Springer Texts in Business and Economics
ISBN 978-3-031-86424-7 ISBN 978-3-031-86425-4 (eBook)
https://doi.org/10.1007/978-3-031-86425-4

This Springer imprint is published by the registered company Springer Nature Switzerland AG
The registered company address is: Gewerbestrasse 11, 6330 Cham, Switzerland

Preface

Risk is everywhere! Without uncertainty about the future, managing organizations would be easy but boring, and managers would not be able to become more successful in the future. With an uncertain future comes risk—but also opportunity. Hence, coping with risk and opportunity is the main challenge facing managers. Both factors must be considered together, but while opportunities are often discussed in strategic and operational management, the topic of risk is not always considered appropriately.

Management is always about managing opportunities and risks. Especially in the recent past, many companies have faced various political and economic challenges: the COVID-19 pandemic, political crises, supply chain disruptions, and inflation, to name a few. The fact that managing risk is a necessary task for all organizations, managerial levels, and decisions underlies the concept of **Enterprise Risk Management** (ERM).

This textbook is primarily intended for business students, but it is also suitable for students in executive education programs and organizational practitioners interested in the topic. We take an applied approach, putting theories, methods, and tools into practice and showing both how to use them and how to avoid pitfalls. These aspects comprise the main differences between this book and other textbooks on risk management, which focus exclusively on financial risks, include prohibitively mathematical elaborations, or adopt a "just-do" approach without carefully combining theory and practice.

Compared to previous books on ERM, this one has several special features. In particular, it presents methods that are required to support business decisions; this aspect of risk management is also addressed in the COSO Enterprise Risk Management Framework (COSO ERM) published in 2017. As decisions are dependent on the overall scope of risk, this book explains in detail the methods used to perform risk aggregation based on corporate planning using Monte -Carlo simulation—methods that are rarely considered in ERM literature. In addition, the link between risk management and value-based management is outlined because an enterprise value is a suitable decision criterion for corporate management as it summarizes return and risk in one key figure. Due to specific legal regulations, some methods (e.g., for risk aggregation or the recording of insolvency risk) have only been discussed in German-language publications. This previous research (and the related practical knowledge) is presented here for the first time, categorized and related to the international context of ERM. In addition, the book addresses increasingly important new developments in ERM, including sustainability risks, which have financial and non-financial implications, and the positioning of ERM as a building block for two comprehensive concepts, resilience and robust corporate strategies, to ensure the future viability and sustainable success of a company.

Similarly, previous literature reviews and meta-studies have also failed to take into account the topics addressed in this book. The summarized presentation of ERM and the related research agenda outlined by Naik and Prasad (2022) do not include these topics, and they lack a discussion of risk aggregation and the link to valuation theory in particular [see also Lechner and Gatzert (2018) and González et al. (2020)].

Even a textbook on risk is at risk of including errors, so readers are more than welcome to comment on them and suggest improvements. Life is a journey into the unknown, but with a little help and some perseverance, it gets better step by step.

Aalen, Germany — Robert Rieg
Kiel, Germany — Ute Vanini
Leinfelden-Echterdingen, Baden-Württemberg, Germany — Werner Gleißner

Acknowledgments

Over the years, many people have supported our work and given us food for thought on this topic. We learned from many of them. Foremost are our students at our respective universities, who challenged us to explain concepts better and provide applications for theories. Additionally, the practical exchanges with risk managers sharpened our understanding of ERM.

This textbook grew out of our other textbooks on ERM published in German as well as a variety of journal articles, conference participations, and trade publications. We thank all readers and discussants for their valuable feedback and insights that have helped to improve our understanding of the subject.

Competing Interests The authors have no competing interests to declare that are relevant to the content of this manuscript.

About the Book

The Why and How of Using this Book

Enterprise Risk Management for All Types of Organizations and (Future) Managers

Enterprise Risk Management (ERM) helps managers weigh expected returns against associated risks when making important decisions. This is necessary, for example, when making investment decisions or changing corporate strategy, as different strategies typically involve different risks. ERM techniques are necessary for the further development of management accounting, corporate finance, and value-based management systems.

ERM creates transparency with regard to planning and risk and identifies the most important risks that determine the overall risk exposure of a company. In this way, it creates the conditions for initiating appropriate ERM measures to help stabilize the company's earnings (cash flows) and reduce the probability of corporate crises. Hence, it makes a decisive contribution to securing companies' continued existence.

To gain transparency about a company's risks and initiate appropriate ERM measures, a company must develop and expand its ability to identify, quantify, aggregate, monitor, and control risks. The purpose of this book is to present the methodological principles, procedures, and tools necessary to do this and to show how ERM can be implemented in an organization.

Curated Content

The text covers all aspects of ERM that are necessary for business students and ERM practitioners. We have divided the content into two parts. The first, called "Foundation," covers the general concepts of risk, decision-making under risk, and risk modeling with Monte-Carlo simulation, which is the main workhorse of quantitative ERM. The second part, "Application," follows the main management process, covering strategic and operational management of risks and opportunities, organizational aspects of implementing ERM, and new developments and current trends. The book concludes with extensive case studies and worked examples. An appendix with a glossary and further information completes the text.

Although we discuss financial risk in the text, this is not a textbook that focuses on the financial industry (e.g., banks and insurance companies). The financial industry has specific business models that are highly specialized and regulated. While the fundamentals are the same, the applications in financial organizations are so different from those in other businesses that it would be difficult to integrate all of this into a single textbook.

The content and exposition of our textbook surpasses those in other textbooks:

- We integrate ERM with general management concepts, methods, and instruments, especially those concerning corporate finance and management accounting. This happens and should happen in the real business world, but it is often not covered in other textbooks.
- The legal environment has changed, and in many countries, modern management is liable for inappropriate decisions that do not include and document risk considerations. For every management decision, the so-called Business Judgment Rule requires a documented report that includes a discussion of decision alternatives and a quantitative examination of their risks and benefits. In our textbook, the reader learns about key decisions, which risks to include in such a report, and how to do so. In this way, the link between risk management, value-based management, and simulation-based valuation is established.

Support Material

A cornerstone of our textbook is the application of concepts and theories to practice and the demonstration of tool and instrument use. This is achieved through illustrative examples and worked examples for quantitative methods. Additionally, we include questions at the end of each chapter to repeat and discuss content; more extensive and comprehensive case studies are provided in Chap. 13.

Who Is This Book for?

The textbook works well as a **complete semester-long course** on ERM at the advanced undergraduate or graduate level of studies. It introduces students specializing in business or related studies to the fundamentals and application of ERM. The background knowledge on which we build includes general management, financial and managerial accounting, financing and capital budgeting, and basic descriptive statistics. The mathematical level does not go beyond what is typically taught at the beginning of a bachelor's program.

The textbook's 13-chapter structure is designed for a 12–14-week semester with one session per week. Depending on the level of students' background knowledge, instructors may choose to teach two chapters per session in the beginning; this would allow them to accompany later chapters with extensive case preparation and discussion, include additional lectures with practical or academic insights, and incorporate modeling exercises with Monte-Carlo simulation.

The textbook can serve as a reference or complementary text for other courses that do not focus exclusively on risk but need some input on it or for students of all types and levels who are interested in the topic. Finally, the textbook can serve as a handbook for practitioners to guide them through the process of implementing and applying ERM.

What Are the Main Ideas of the Book?

In the world of business, uncertainty is a constant companion. As future entrepreneurs and business leaders, understanding how to navigate this uncertainty is crucial for your success. This is where risk management comes into play. Let's explore the key concepts:

1. What is Risk?

   Risk is inherent in every business decision. It encompasses both potential dangers and opportunities that arise from uncertainty. When we make plans, risk represents the possibility that actual outcomes may differ from our expectations. Understanding risk is the first step in managing it effectively.
2. Types of Risks

   Businesses face various types of risks. Strategic risks threaten a company's long-term success and competitive position. Economic risks arise from uncertainties in key business factors like demand or prices. Operational risks challenge day-to-day business operations and efficiency. Sustainability risks pose long-term threats to the company's viability and social responsibility. Recognizing these different risk categories helps in developing comprehensive risk management strategies.
3. Enterprise Risk Management (ERM)

   ERM is a holistic approach to managing risk across an entire organization. It involves systematically identifying, assessing, aggregating, and managing risks. The goal of ERM is to create transparency about risks and identify potential threats to the company's existence early on. By implementing ERM, businesses can make more informed decisions and better protect their assets and reputation.

4. Risk Analysis and Aggregation
   Effective risk management requires thorough analysis. Risks are often described using probability distributions to capture their potential impact. However, risks rarely occur in isolation. Risk aggregation combines multiple risks to understand their overall impact on the business. This comprehensive view helps in prioritizing risk management efforts and allocating resources effectively.
5. Decision-Making and Strategy
   Risk management is integral to strategic decision-making. It helps in weighing potential returns against risks when evaluating business opportunities. By incorporating risk assessment into strategy formulation, businesses can develop more robust plans. This approach leads to strategies that are better equipped to withstand uncertainties and capitalize on opportunities.
6. Building a Resilient Business
   A successful company needs three key elements to thrive in an uncertain environment. First, it requires a robust strategy that can be adapted to changing conditions. Second, it needs financial sustainability to weather unexpected challenges. Third, it must have the ability to deal with uncertainty through effective risk management practices. These elements combined create a resilient business model.
7. Risk Management Culture
   Effective risk management is not just the responsibility of a single department. It should be embedded in the organization's culture. Everyone in the organization should consider risks in their decision-making process. This "embedded ERM" approach helps in both day-to-day operations and long-term planning. By fostering a risk-aware culture, businesses can proactively address challenges and seize opportunities.

   By understanding these concepts, you'll be better prepared to navigate the complex world of business, make informed decisions, and build resilient organizations that can thrive in uncertain environments.

Contents

About the Authors

Robert Rieg is a professor of management accounting and control at Aalen University, Germany. He earned a doctorate from the University of Hohenheim, Germany, and a habilitation from Sopron University, Hungary. He teaches managerial accounting and risk management and pursues various endeavors in business analytics, allowing him to indulge his passion for statistics and quantitative methods. His recent scientific work has focused on the relationship between digitalization and management accounting, as well as on the roles and tasks of risk managers in practice.

Ute Vanini is a professor of management accounting and control at Kiel University of Applied Sciences. She received a doctorate from the University of Kiel, Germany. In addition, she is a member of various company supervisory boards as well as the Schleswig-Holstein Doctoral College and author of numerous publications on ERM and sustainability controlling. Her research focuses on the integration of ERM and management accounting as well as the inclusion of sustainability goals in corporate management.

Werner Gleißner is Chairman of the FutureValue Group AG, Germany, and Honorary Professor at the Technical University of Dresden, Germany (Business Administration, esp. Risk Management), as well as Chairman of the EACVA (European Association of Certified Valuators and Analysts) and the German Society for Crisis Management (DGfKM). He is also a member of the advisory board of the RMA Risk Management & Rating Association e.V. and a member of the International Controller Association (ICV) and the Schmalenbach Society.

He is a proponent of a new research approach that integrates risk management, rating, and valuation methods, which have been largely separated in the past. He uses simulation methods to study value-based management through corporate valuation models of imperfect capital markets that take into account corporate risk information and appropriate risk measures.

His research and work focus on risk management, rating and strategy development, method development for risk aggregation and value-based management, and investment and portfolio management. He has published many specialist publications and is a lecturer at several universities.

List of Symbols and Abbreviations

β	Beta (Factor for systematic risk in the CAPM)
b	debt limit (%)
BJR	Business Judgment Rule
C	cost of capital
c_D	cost of debt
c	cost of capital (rate)
c_{EQ}	cost of equity
c^0_D	contractually agreed interest rate on debt capital
CAPM	Capital Asset Pricing Model
CE	capital employed
C.E.	certainty equivalent
CF	cash flow
COV	covariance
CSR	Corporate Social Responsibility
CV	coefficient of variation
CVaR	Conditional Value at Risk
D	debt capital
d	diversification factor
DCF	discounted cash flow
DVaR	Deviation Value at Risk
E	earnings
e	expected (e.g., expected EBIT : $EBIT^e$)
E(…)	expected value
EaR	earnings at risk
EBIT	earnings before interest and taxes
EBITDA	earnings before interest, taxes, depreciation, and amortization
EBITM	EBIT-Margin
EBT	earnings before tax
ECR	Equity Capital Requirement
EL	expected Loss

EQ^M	Market value of equity capital
EQ	equity capital
EQR	equity ratio
ES	expected shortfall
ESG	Environmental, Social, and Governance
EVA	Economic Value Added
F(…), f(…)	function of
fCF	free cash flow
g	growth rate (also: w)
GRC	Governance Risk and Compliance
H	target value
HARA	Hyperbolic Absolute Risk Aversion
I	investment
λ	lambda = Market price of the risk (e.g., Sharpe Ratio)
LPM	Lower partial moments
m	multiplier (for valuation)
MCS	Monte-Carlo simulation
MRP	market risk premium
NPV	net present value
P	profit (Earnings), Payout
p	probability (of insolvency)
p.a.	per annum
PD	probability of default or probability of insolvency
P&L	profit and loss
P/E Ratio	price-earnings ratio
π	(absolute) risk premium
R(…)	risk measure
r_E^e	expected return on equity
r_f	risk-free interest rate
r_m^e	expected return of the market portfolio or stock market index ($=E(\widetilde{r}_m)$)
RAC	risk-adjusted capital
RAVA	risk-adjusted value added
RBC	risk-bearing capacity
RC	risk capital
ROA	return on assets (%)
ROCE	return on capital employed (%)
RORAC	return on risk-adjusted capital (%)
rp	risk premium (%)
rr	recovery rate (%)
S	sales
s	tax rate
ρ	correlation coefficient
σ	Sigma, standard deviation

σ^2	Sigma squared, variance
$U(\ldots)$	utility function
V	value
VAR	variance (σ^2)
VaR	Value at Risk
W	wealth
w_x	proportion of security x in the portfolio
WACC	Weighted Average Cost of Capital
X, Y	quantity (Volume)

Chapter 1
Risks, Opportunities, and Enterprise Risk Management

Abstract Corporate success is not possible without risk-taking. Risks and opportunities result from the unpredictable future and lead to either negative or positive deviations from planned corporate targets. The extent of risks and opportunities depends on numerous factors such as the volatility of relevant market prices, which must be identified, analyzed, and controlled using enterprise risk management (ERM). In many countries, companies are required by law to implement risk management (RM) approaches. Therefore, this section discusses the need for enterprise-wide RM, defines key terms, and introduces the concept of ERM in detail.

Keywords Enterprise risk management (ERM) · Quantifiability of risks · Risk categories · Risk definition · Uncertainty

Questions
- Why is ERM necessary in corporate practice?
- What is the "risk paradox"?
- How are the terms "uncertainty," "risk," "opportunity," "losses," and "crises" defined and differentiated from each other?
- How can risks be categorized?
- Which objectives and tasks are associated with ERM?

1.1 The Need for ERM and the Risk Paradox

1.1.1 Increasing Exposure to Risks

In general, all business activities cause risks because not all relevant developments in the business environment can be fully anticipated and the impact of many management decisions on business objectives is uncertain. For example, the price of

Supplementary Information The online version contains supplementary material available at https://doi.org/10.1007/978-3-031-86425-4_1.

R. Rieg et al., *Enterprise Risk Management*, Springer Texts in Business and Economics, https://doi.org/10.1007/978-3-031-86425-4_1

necessary resources may increase more than predicted, a new competitor may unexpectedly enter the market, or a pandemic may cause a global lockdown that disrupts the supply chain. There is also risk associated with the development and launch of new products (product innovation risk), which is exemplified by the case of the Airbus A380 aircraft.

Example: Development and Market Launch of the A380 by Airbus
The Airbus A380 is the largest aircraft in civil aviation. The basic version seats 555 passengers on two floors. The A380 is used by airlines including Singapore Airlines, Quantas, Emirates, and Lufthansa. In total, the development of the A380 costs more than €12 billion, about €4 billion more than originally planned. Throughout the development period, technical problems arose in the engines as well as in the cabin electronics. This meant that the start of production, the first delivery to Singapore Airlines, and the first flight all had to be postponed several times. Compared to the original plan, the delivery of the A380 was delayed by 22 months. The delivery delays cost Airbus €4.8 billion in net profit between 2006 and 2010. Due to further production and delivery delays, the breaking-even point rose to around 420 aircraft sold, from the 250 originally calculated.

Other technical glitches, particularly with the engines, fuel tanks, and power cables, further hampered the A380's operations. In addition, Airbus' decision to use a global supply chain to assemble various parts of the A380 created a logistical nightmare. The diversity of suppliers and the complexity of the components caused significant delays. Another critical issue was the incompatible software used by the French and German engineering teams, which led to significant errors in the design of the aircraft's wiring. These technical and logistical challenges led to severe delays and cost overruns. In addition, Airbus misjudged the market demand for very large aircraft; the aviation market was moving toward smaller, more fuel-efficient models—a trend that Airbus underestimated.

In 2019, Airbus finally announced that production would cease in 2021. Despite receiving a total of 251 orders, the program's ability to reach the break-even point was hindered by the high production costs, lower-than-expected demand, and reduction in production rate. The market shift toward smaller, more fuel-efficient aircraft and the lack of new orders for the A380 further compounded the financial challenges faced by the program (source: https://www.handelsblatt.com/unternehmen/industrie/riesenjet-der-a380-war-eine-fehlentscheidung-fuer-airbus-und-europa/23986680.html (19.12.2023)).

The case of the Airbus A380 clearly shows that unmanaged risks can lead to major economic losses for companies. Failure to identify and manage risks at an early stage can even lead to the **insolvency** of companies if the damage caused is sufficiently great. The following figure shows the change in the number of corporate insolvencies in selected European countries between 2018 and 2022 (Fig. 1.1).

Overall, firms have been experiencing an increasing need for implementing ERM (Hunziker, 2021; Vanini & Rieg, 2021). Seven arguments speak in favor of ERM:

First of all, many countries have established **legal requirements** for implementing ERM. For example, the Sarbanes Oxley Act (SOX) of 2002 must be applied not only by all companies listed on US stock exchanges but also by their foreign subsidiaries. Section 404 requires the establishment of an internal control

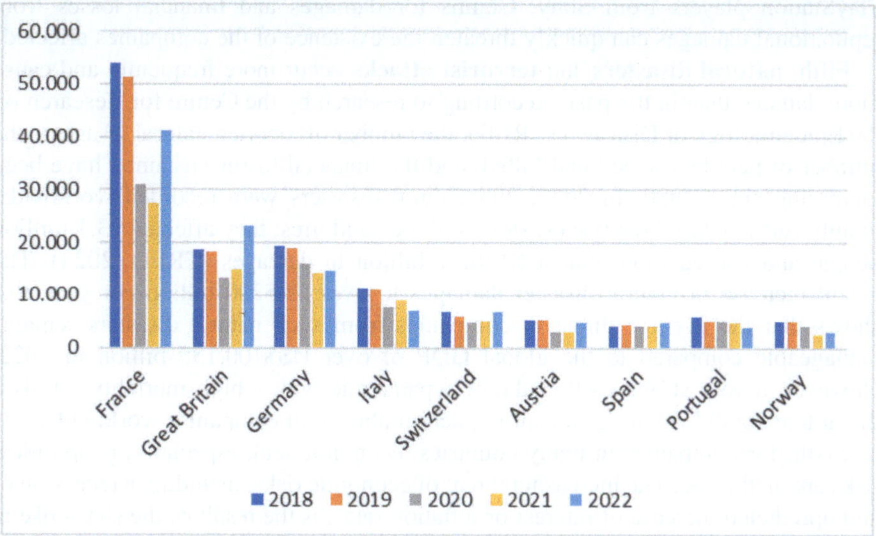

Fig. 1.1 The number of corporate insolvencies in selected European countries from 2018 to 2022 (source: https://de.statista.com/statistik/daten/studie/3752/umfrage/unternehmensinsolvenzen-in-westeuropa-seit-2007/)

system to ensure the financial reporting of companies. In addition, there are further legal requirements for certain industries, such as banks and insurance companies (e.g., equity capital regulations; Basel II, Basel III, and Basel IV).

Second, due to increased international competition, the growing interdependence of these markets, and geopolitical conflicts, the **prices and volumes** of raw materials and components in many sourcing and supply markets have become much more **volatile** and therefore less predictable. This trend has been and will continue to be exacerbated by strong interdependencies in the supply chain, as demonstrated by the pandemic crisis. Demographic changes in many developed countries will make skilled labor an increasingly scarce resource.

Third, **technological progress** such as digitalization has not only improved production efficiency but also accelerated the development of new products or even completely new business models. However, the opportunity to benefit from technological progress not only brings with it the danger of technological risks but above all requires **considerable investment** from firms and thus leads to an increase in fixed costs. Unfortunately, fixed costs cannot be reduced easily in the event of a crisis, and they endanger the solvency of companies. In addition, technological progress leads to a shortening of technology and product life cycles in many industries, which makes a faster amortization of investments necessary and further increases the risk of bad investment.

Fourth, the rapid development of information and communication technologies promotes market transparency, but it also leads to increased risks with regard to **data and IT system security** in many companies. For example, cybercriminals obtained addresses, passwords, and possibly credit card numbers of several million

PlayStation players from Sony. Claims for damages and financial losses from reputational damages can quickly threaten the existence of the companies affected.

Fifth, **natural disasters** and **terrorist attacks** occur more frequently and cause more damage than in the past. According to research by the Centre for Research on the Epidemiology of Disasters (CRED), the number of reported natural disasters, the number of people affected and killed, and the financial losses sustained have been increasing since 1980. In 2023, 399 natural disasters were recorded worldwide, mainly earthquakes, heat waves, storms, floods and fires; they affected 93.1 million people and caused more than US$202.7 billion in damages (CRED, 2024). The recent increase in natural disaster damages to over US$200 billion per year also shows that the average threat to companies from such natural disasters remains manageable compared to the global GDP of over US$100,135 billion in 2022. However, a very strong earthquake or a pandemic with a high mortality rate is a threat that could have a significant impact on almost all companies worldwide.

Sixth, for companies in many countries, economic and, especially, geopolitical risks are on the rise. The increasing threat of economic risks, including a recession or an unpredicted increase of interest or inflation rates, is the result of the sharp rise in global corporate and government debt in recent decades (consider the economic and financial crisis of 2008–2010 and the currency crisis in the eurozone). Geopolitical risks are the result of long-standing conflicts, as in the Middle East, or the global policies of countries such as Russia and China, which are associated with increasing economic, political, and military power. The reduction in the influence of Western countries tends to increase the risks for companies.

Finally, many companies are exposed to threats from **white-collar crime**, which can come in the form of embezzlement, balance sheet manipulation, damage to assets, corruption offences, and other compliance violations perpetrated by employees (fraud) or individuals outside the company. A prominent example is the case of Wirecard, a payment processor and financial services provider headquartered in Munich, Germany, that was part of the German DAX index. In 2020, the company went bankrupt due to a series of corrupt business practices and fraudulent financial reporting. The former CEO and other top executives have been arrested or have been on trial since 2023 (https://en.wikipedia.org/wiki/Wirecard, 08.01.2024).

Overall, the examples above show the wide variety of potential risks and sources of risk that companies face. A systematic and institutionalized management approach to potential risks therefore appears to be absolutely essential for corporate survival and value creation. Given the crucial importance of ERM, the frequency of empirical studies on risk management has increased significantly in recent years (Horvey & Odei-Mensah, 2023), particularly, p. 785). The predominant focus of the published studies in this area is the USA, followed by the United Kingdom, Canada, and Australia (Horvey & Odei-Mensah, 2023), p. 786).

1.1.2 Risk Paradox

Firms are increasingly exposed to a large variety of risks, but there are biased risk perceptions in corporate practice that are not based on facts and may lead to an over- or underestimation of risk. For example, individuals tend to overestimate the likelihood of unlikely events like winning a lottery or experiencing a natural disaster and underestimate the risk of more probable events like car accidents (Gleißner, 2022).

An **underestimation of risk** happens in several business contexts. For example, most start-ups overestimate their chances of success and income prospects. For example, only about half of newly founded companies are still on the market 5 years after founding and just a fifth last 8 years (vgl. Luo & Mann, 2011; Åstebro et al., 2014). The median income of self-employed individuals is often lower than that of employees, although the self-employed face a higher economic risk and therefore have to earn a risk premium as compensation (vgl. Åstebro & Elhedhli, 2006). Nearly two-thirds of all mergers and acquisitions transactions fall short of their expectations (vgl. Gerds & Schewe, 2013). Mega-mergers such as those between BMW and Rover in the 1990s or between Daimler and Chrysler at the beginning of the 2000s have caused the loss of many billions of euros in capital (vgl. Kutschker & Schmid, 2011). However, an **overestimation of risk** is strongly associated with individual risk perception. As risks such as natural disasters, terrorism, and civil wars dominate media, people are more aware of them and overestimate their impact (Gleißner, 2022).

Risks must therefore be correctly described based on their probability of occurrence and their potential for damage or opportunity and assessed using suitable risk measures in order to support rational management decision-making processes.

1.2 Uncertainty, Risk, and Opportunity

The term **risk** is defined inconsistently in the literature (for a broad discussion, see Bromiley et al., 2015). Generally, risk refers to the possibility of an undesirable outcome. It is the potential of losing something of value, whether physical (like property), emotional (such as well-being), or financial (Aven & Thekdi, 2020). It is the consequence C (effect) of a future activity or event A (threat, hazard, price development, etc.) due to the associated uncertainties U (Aven & Thekdi, 2020) (Fig. 1.2). Consequently, risks can be measured by their consequences and the associated uncertainties (Aven & Thekdi, 2020, pp. 10–12):

$$\text{Risk} = f\,(A, C, U) \tag{1.1}$$

The various definitions and concepts of risk differ primarily in terms of the extent of the consequences C that are considered (Bromiley et al., 2015).

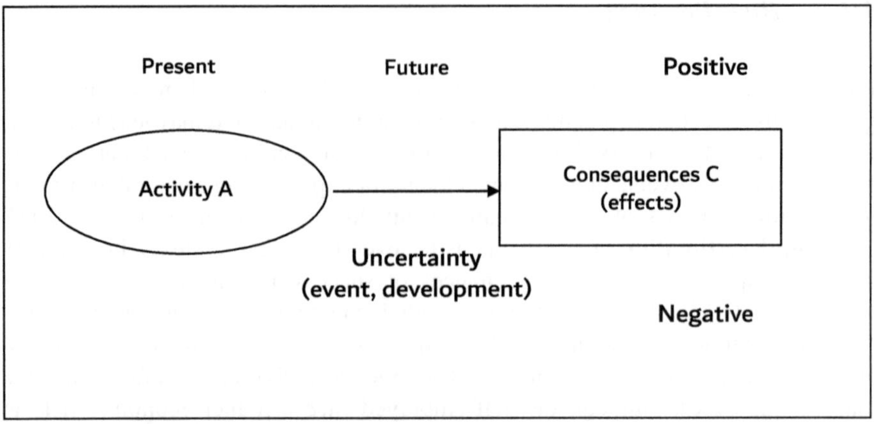

Fig. 1.2 The basic features of the risk concept (Aven & Thekdi, 2020)

- **Narrow perspective**: Overall, there is disagreement among authors as to whether only existence-threatening consequences should be considered, whether the extent to which positive consequences in the sense of opportunities should also be included, and whether risks only affect financial value or should also be measured along other dimensions. In our view, risks should also include non-existential consequences, since the simultaneous occurrence of several non-existential risks can also lead to the insolvency of a company. Opportunities should also be integrated in the risk concept, as good risk management should not only fulfill legal requirements and avoid excessive risks but should also contribute to the value creation of the company. We therefore favor a broad understanding of risk.
- **Reference to Specific Planned Objectives**: C Can Be Evaluated in either Absolute or Relative Numbers. For Example, Hubbard (2020) Defines Risk without Referring to a Planned Target as "a potential loss, disaster, or other undesirable event measured with probabilities assigned to losses of various magnitudes." in our Opinion, this Definition Is Too Narrow, as Risks Do Not Only Result from Potential Losses but Also from the Company's Inability to Achieve its Planned Targets. Similar to our Opinion, Other Authors Define Risks in Relation to Previously Defined Corporate Objectives. For Example, Hunziker (2021) Points out:

[A] key risk is a risk that exceeds a significance threshold - for example a business objective or benchmark, set by the firm. Many risks can have an upside potential (opportunity) and a downside potential (risk), risk a possible positive or negative deviation from an expected or planned outcome. (p. 5)

As a consequence, the following definition of risk is applied in this textbook:

Definition Risks are potential positive or negative deviations from planned business objectives that result from the uncertainty of the future. Positive deviations are also referred to as opportunities, while negative deviations are downside risks.

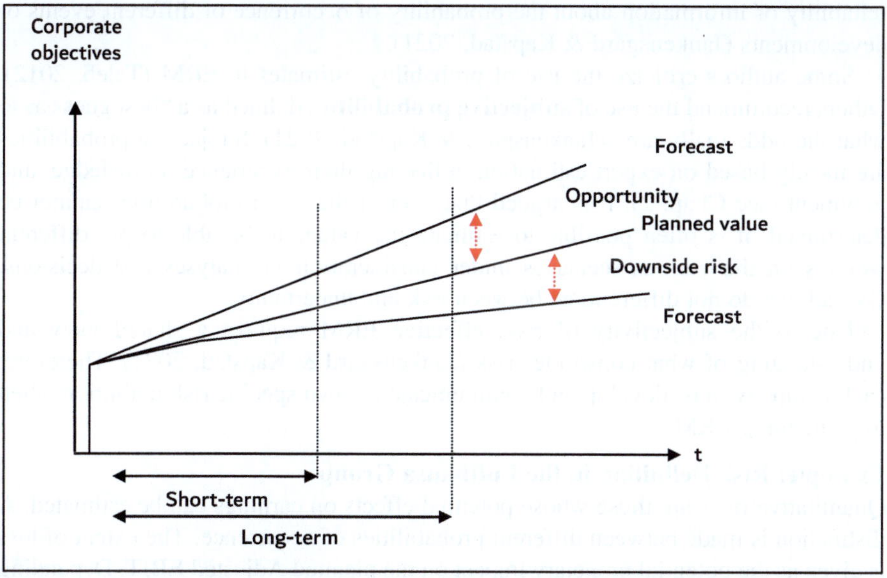

Fig. 1.3 Elements of the business risk concept in ERM (adapted from Vanini & Weinstock, 2006)

Deviations arise from unforeseen changes in relevant environmental factors or management decisions (risk factors). Business objectives include financial outcomes, such as net income, operating profit, or cash flows, and non-financial objectives, such as corporate image or carbon footprint. Risks can be described by their likelihood of occurrence and the magnitude of the loss or gain, and they can be measured over different time periods. In the following text, risks are always considered to include both opportunities and downside risks.

The elements of the risk definition are summarized in Fig. 1.3.

The above definition recognizes that risks are consciously taken to realize opportunities. Neglecting opportunities carries the risk of excessive risk avoidance. This can lead to opportunities not being recognized and thus not being seized, which can jeopardize future success and, thus, the existence of the company. In addition, the definition focuses on the quantification of risks, as risk assessment based on the probability of occurrence and the extent of damage is an important prerequisite for risk management.

Uncertainty

Some authors distinguish between risk and **uncertainty,** using the former only for identifiable and quantifiable future events and developments for which objective probabilities of occurrence can be calculated and the latter for unforeseeable and thus unquantifiable events and developments (Knight, 1921). For example, a dice roll can be described as a situation under risk since an objective probability of one-sixth can be derived for each dice result. In business, however, objective probabilities are rare. Thus, the main difference between uncertainty and risk is the availability and reliability of information about the probability of occurrence of different events or developments (Jankensgård & Kapstad, 2021).

Some authors criticize the use of probability estimates in ERM (Taleb, 2012). Others recommend the use of **subjective probabilities** defined as a "best guess as to what the odds really are" (Jankensgård & Kapstad, 2021). Subjective probabilities are mostly based on expert estimation, reflecting their experience, knowledge, and judgment (see Chap. 2). It is argued that even if the exact probabilities cannot be determined, it is often possible to estimate the values to be able to put different weights on the various scenarios under consideration in analyses and decisions. Overall, we do not differentiate between risk and uncertainty.

Due to the subjectivity of risk, effective ERM requires a shared view and understanding of what constitutes risk (Jankensgård & Kapstad, 2021). Therefore, each company must develop and communicate its own specific risk definition when implementing ERM.

Example: Risk Definition in the Lufthansa Group
Quantitative risks are those whose potential effects on earnings can be estimated. A distinction is made between different probabilities of occurrence. The extent of loss is given as the potential monetary impact on the planned Adjusted EBIT. Depending on the type of risk, this may relate either to relatively infrequent event risks, such as IT failure following a cyberattack, or to risks from deviations from planned business developments, due to fuel price volatility, for instance. Quantitative risks therefore form the basis for the overarching verification of potential deviation from plans and forecasts. The thresholds for classifying the monetary Adjusted EBIT effect are defined centrally for the Lufthansa Group and for the Group companies according to standardized criteria. (Source: Annual Report Lufthansa Group, 2022).

Losses and Risks
If risks occur and have negative financial consequences, they may be realized as losses. Risks always refer to potential deviations from targets in the future and can still be managed accordingly. Losses (or gains), on the other hand, are always realized values that can no longer be influenced. Moreover, losses and gains are often calculated in relation to historical or current comparative values (e.g., previous year's values or purchase prices), while risks refer to planned values.

Example: Difference Between Losses and Risks
A company plans a net profit after tax of US$45 million for the following year. Due to quality problems in production, there is a decline in sales and turnover. In the middle of the year, the company forecasts that if the quality problems cannot be solved in the short term through suitable measures, the turnover could drop by 20%, and the net profit for the year would be US$ − 5 million. The company's profit risk is US$-50 million. The quality problems can be solved by the end of the year through staff training and a change of suppliers, but both measures require further costs. At the end of the year, the company achieves a net profit after tax of US$10 million. Despite missing the planned net profit for the year by US$35 million, there is no loss because no negative result was achieved for the year.

Crises and Risks

If risks are not recognized and managed adequately, they can cause corporate crises. A **crisis** is a highly negative corporate condition often associated with a strong destruction of company value and threatens its existence. Crises arise due to various factors, such as failures of internal control processes. They can also have external causes, such as the COVID-19 pandemic of 2020. A corporate crisis thus results from unforeseen losses or an unplanned high liquidity requirement. This term refers to the actual situation of a company, whereas risks represent future potential dangers and opportunities. Crisis management deals with the prevention of, preparation for, handling of, and recovery from crisis events (Jankensgård & Kapstad, 2021).

1.3 Categorization of Risks

The above examples illustrate that there are many risks to which companies are exposed. These risks have very different characteristics, which are important for their identification, quantification, and management. Risks should therefore be categorized according to these characteristics (Table 1.1).

Risks must be categorized because they are identified, quantified, and controlled using different methods and measures. For example, the probability of occurrence of external risks cannot be reduced using internal control measures. Risk categorization requires the selection of appropriate criteria and the development of a company-specific risk register. A risk classification illustrates the purpose of risk management to employees and thus supports risk identification (Jankensgård & Kapstad, 2021).

Symmetry of Risk Profile

Based on the symmetry of the risk profile, a distinction is made between **symmetric risks**, where the downside risk is accompanied by an opportunity, and **asymmetric risks,** which lack opportunities. For example, share price risks are symmetric because the share value can decrease or increase relative to the entry price. The fire risk in a production plant is an example of an asymmetric risk because it is not associated with an opportunity. Asymmetric risks are referred to as "pure risks" and symmetrical risks as "speculative risks."

Table 1.1 Categorization of risks (adapted from Vanini & Rieg, 2021)

Criteria	Characteristics			
Symmetry of risk	Symmetric risks		Asymmetric risks	
Corporate objective	Profit risks	Liquidity risks	Value risks	Non-financial risks
Quantifiability	Quantifiable risks		Non-quantifiable risks	
Source	Hazard risks	Strategic risks	Financial risks	Operating risks
Control approach	Preventable risks	Strategy risks	External risks	

Corporate Objectives

Depending on the company's objectives, risks can be categorized as profit, liquidity, value, and non-financial risks. Profit, liquidity, and value risks are all financial risks because they relate to a company's financial objectives and are measured in monetary units. **Profit risks** affect a company's financial performance, for example, its net income or earnings before interest and taxes (EBIT). **Liquidity risks** relate to cash flow and threaten a company's solvency. **Value risks** affect the value of the company.

In recent years, stakeholders such as customers, employees, and NGOs have become increasingly influential in corporate management decisions, as companies must meet the expectations of their stakeholders. Thus, non-financial objectives such as corporate image, customer satisfaction, and carbon footprint have been increasingly integrated into companies' target and incentive systems. As a result, **non-financial risks**, which are potential deviations from non-financial objectives, must be considered in corporate ERM. Non-financial risks are measured in non-monetary units such as tons (carbon footprint) or subjective scores (customer satisfaction), but they often lead to profit, liquidity, or value risks (COSO, 2017).

Non-financial risks also include environmental, social, and governance **(ESG) risks**, which are threats to a company's ESG objectives. These risks are gaining in importance due to the increasingly stakeholder-focused orientation of many companies and the relevance of factors such as corresponding sustainability ratings for financial investors. They can lead to large-scale damage to a company's reputation, as well as economic consequences such as lost sales. There are already approaches to integrate these risks more strongly into companies' risk management approaches (COSO, wbcsd 2018).

Quantifiability of Risks

Quantifiable and non-quantifiable risks can be differentiated according to their measurability. **Quantifiable risks** can be described by their probability of occurrence and the extent of the damage or opportunity they present relative to a corporate objective. Often, these risks are well-known, and we have historical data or valid expert experience to describe them. **Non-quantifiable risks** are often unknown events or developments for which the data basis for quantifying their target effect is lacking. Non-quantifiable risks are sometimes named qualitative risks. Qualitative risk assessments are at least partially based on subjective risk assessments made by individuals, but risks are ultimately always quantified, even if this is done implicitly when estimating their subjective relevance (Hunziker, 2021; Romeike & Stallinger, 2021). However, risks that are not quantified are not unquantifiable in the narrower sense because quantification based on the best available information, possibly subjective expert estimates, is always possible (Sinn, 1980; Höse & Huschens, 2022).

Quantifiable risks can be differentiated into event risks and distribution risks. **Event risks** result from single events such as natural disasters or pandemics that occur relatively rarely, have an asymmetric risk profile, and often have a high negative impact on one or more corporate objectives. Therefore, these risks are also referred to as **low probability-high impact risks** and are mapped by discrete distribution functions such as the binomial distribution. **Distribution risks** result from the uncertainty of corporate business activities and are caused by unforeseen developments of relevant external factors such as a spike in the price of raw materials. The effects of distribution risks on corporate objectives can be positive or negative depending on the development of the external factor. Distribution risks therefore usually have a symmetric risk profile. In addition, the number of possible changes is infinitely large, so these risks are often described by continuous distribution functions (Romeike & Stallinger, 2021).

Black swan risks are classified as unique and thus almost unpredictable events or developments such as geopolitical crises and disruptive technologies with a massive and transformative impact on companies. They are outliers that surpass regular expectations, but they can be explained after their occurrence (Taleb et al., 2009). Therefore, there have been controversial discussions surrounding whether they can be quantified (Aven & Thekdi, 2020). The processes that determine the effects of black swan risks are often non-linear and complex, with large discontinuities as inherent features. Due to their uniqueness, it is very difficult to quantify black swan risks (Jankensgård & Kapstad, 2021). There has been some discussion about whether COVID-19 was a black swan risk, but most have denied the event this status because pandemics and epidemics have occurred regularly in the past and various governmental and non-governmental organizations warned of the danger and possible effects of a pandemic (Gleißner, 2020).

Sources of Risk

The source of a risk is named a **risk factor**, which is defined as any random event or uncertain development of a relevant factor that might lead companies to deviate from their planned or target corporate objectives. The categorization of risks according to their sources is relevant for ERM because early warning indicators should be defined for each relevant risk factor. In addition, transparency about potential risks is necessary for the development of adequate control measures (Aven & Thekdi, 2020).

Risks can be roughly divided into external and internal risks. **External risks** result from changes in legislation, social developments, and events such as natural disasters. They can be further differentiated into hazard risks, strategic risks, and financial risks. **Hazard risks** are those that have traditionally been addressed by insurers, including fire, theft, windstorm, liability, business interruption, pollution, health, and security. **Strategic risks** include, for example, threats to a company's strategic success potential (such as brands or expertise in research and development). Planning risks can be derived directly from corporate or project planning. Every uncertain planning assumption indicates a planning risk (uncertain planning assumption). **Financial risks** are an important special case of planning risks. They cover potential losses due to changes in financial markets, including interest rates, foreign exchange rates, commodity prices, liquidity risks, and credit risks. **Operational risks** result from internal operating processes, including customer satisfaction, product development, product failure, trademark protection, corporate leadership, information technology, management fraud, and information risk (D′ Arcy & Brogan, 2001).

Hazard risks are often asymmetric, meaning that their occurrence has only negative impacts and is not linked to an opportunity, whereas the other risks can be mostly described as symmetric. Hazard risks are often insurable, but the damage they cause is not fully covered by insurance. For example, fire insurance does not cover the risk of qualified staff leaving, a loss of confidence among customers, or a loss of creditworthiness among investors and banks.

Control Approach

According to the underlying control approach, Kaplan and Mikes (2012, p. 49 ff.) developed the following categorization (Kaplan & Mikes, 2012):

- **Preventable risks** are internal risks that are controllable. Depending on their potential damage impact, preventable risks should be either tolerated, reduced, or completely eliminated through means of active prevention such as monitoring operational processes and guiding people's behavior. The risk management tactics for preventable risks require a compliance-based control approach and an intense collaboration with the audit function.
- **Strategy risks** result from a company's business model and must be accepted by a company within its risk-taking capacity in order to generate business performance. These risks are necessary for corporate success as they also offer opportunities. They cannot be managed through a rule-based control model.
- **External risks** arise from outside the company and are therefore beyond its influence or control (e.g., natural disasters or geopolitical conflicts). ERM must concentrate on their identification and assessment, for example, through stress-testing and scenario planning and the mitigation of their impact on corporate objectives, as companies cannot prevent such events from occurring.

It is important to understand that the categorization of risks ultimately supports the effectiveness of ERM, especially the process of risk identification. For many of the central tasks relevant to ERM, such as the derivation of equity requirements for covering risks or the evaluation of alternative courses of action, the total scope of the risks to be determined by risk aggregation is relevant (see Sect. 5.5).

1.4 Concept, Objectives, and Tasks of Enterprise Risk Management

Historically, firms have managed the various risks discussed above separately—financial risks have been managed by treasury departments and hazard risks by the insurance functions. Such a silo risk management leads to fragmentation of the ERM function and neglects potential interdependencies as well as diversification effects between the different risks. Over the last few years, it has become clear that a more holistic approach to ERM that controls the different risks on a portfolio level leads to enhanced effectiveness and efficiency (Bromiley et al., 2015). Overall, this holistic, integrated approach to risk management is called ERM (D′ Arcy & Brogan, 2001).

There are numerous conceptualizations and definitions of ERM in theory and practice (for an overview, see (Bromiley et al., 2015) and a "plethora of guidelines, frameworks, and tools for ERM" (Mikes & Kaplan, 2015).

Overall, there has been some **consensus** on the following points (Bromiley et al., 2015; COSO, 2017; Hunziker, 2021; Hardy & Saunders, 2022):

- ERM includes all types of risks, including traditional risks, such as product liability of accidents and currency risks, and strategic and other business-related risks. ERM must give an overview of all relevant risks, opportunities, and the interdependencies between them as a foundation for evaluating a company's risk-taking capacity.
- ERM is holistic. Business units do not manage their risks independently of each other. Due to diversification effects, risks should be aggregated across the organization and managed on an aggregated level.
- ERM is value-creating. Not only should it ensure the survival of a company, but it should also generate value for all stakeholders. Thus, it has developed from a primarily compliance-based approach into a management tool with a value-adding function that considers risks not only as dangers to mitigate but also as opportunities to take, given an adequate risk-return profile and staying within the firm's risk-taking capabilities.
- ERM supports managerial decision-making. ERM must be linked to the managerial decision-making processes in an organization so that managers can evaluate and choose the decision alternative with the most favorable risk-return profile.
- ERM is a continuous and integrated enterprise-wide process of identifying, assessing, and managing the key risks of an organization. The ERM process considers all risks together, recognizing the interdependencies of different risks and the differing impacts of distinct areas of the business.
- ERM is applied in a top-down/bottom-up approach. It is a primary responsibility of the supervisory board of a firm, and corporate governance is a key component of ERM. The broad risk appetite of a company is set by the supervisory board and is then translated into more detailed risk tolerance limits that are applied in the operations of the organization. The supervisory board is also responsible for developing a strong risk culture as a foundation for ERM. The implementation of ERM also involves a bottom-up approach, especially since the identification of risks involves the contributions of operative management.

The following table compares the main characteristics of a modern ERM understanding to a more traditional risk management approach (Table 1.2).

Thus, in the context of this textbook, the following definition of ERM is applied:

Definition Enterprise risk management (ERM) consists of all organizational regulations and activities for the systematic, continuous, and company-wide identification, assessment, reporting, and management of all key risks of a company and its

Table 1.2 Characteristics of TRM vs. ERM

Traditional risk management (TRM)	Enterprise risk management (ERM)
Silo view of risk. Deals with risks independently. No systematic understanding of interdependencies and correlation among risks	Portfolio view of risk. Deals with risks holistically. Interdependencies and correlation among risks analyzed and understood. Natural hedges recognized and exploited. Understands internal/external contexts in evaluating risk portfolios
Limited strategic scope or influence. Technical and tactical rather than strategic. RM is not an important element in decision-making by supervisory board and top management and is not considered important in corporate governance. Middle management function	Considers the entity's risk appetite/ criteria in evaluating strategic alternatives for achieving objectives. Supervisory board and CEO are strongly involved with ERM, which plays an important role in corporate governance. Risk management is an essential consideration in strategic decisions
No consideration for the allocation of capital	Economic capital view. Allocating capital to achieve the highest risk-adjusted return
Negative, cost-based, and narrowly focused on downside only	Positively value-based, broadly focused. Risk management is not only related to potential downside risk but is also used to exploit opportunities to create value
Ambiguous ownership of some types of risk	All risks assigned ownership with accountability
Focus is only on measurable risks such as hazard and financial risks. Ill-defined operational or strategic risks such as supply chain, cyber, and reputation risks may be acknowledged but ignored	Adopts a single comprehensive risk oversight structure and risk culture for dealing with all types of risks. Particular focus on identifying and prioritizing top/critical risks and understanding root causes

Source: McShane (2018)

support through suitable, adequate methods and tools. ERM aims to secure the company's long-term existence and support managers' decisions to ensure improved value creation through the achievement of planned corporate objectives, reduction of risk and capital costs, and capitalization on opportunities within the firm's risk-taking capacity. The implementation of ERM is the responsibility of the company's management.

The ERM **tasks** that are essential to achieve these objectives are as follows (Diederichs, 2018; Vanini & Rieg, 2021):

- Creation of a company-wide **risk culture** to strengthen the risk awareness of managers and employees and to guide them toward risk-adequate decisions and behavior.
- Formulation and implementation of a **risk strategy** and **risk policy principles** as concrete guidelines for all actions in the company.
- Integration of **risk targets** into the company's incentive and remuneration system as well as into target agreement and performance measurement.

- Implementation of an **operational ERM process** for the systematic and continuous management of risks, including their identification, assessment, communication, control, and monitoring.
- Establishment of **risk governance**, including clear responsibilities.
- Implementation of measures for **risk assessment and control** based on the risk profile and risk-taking capacity of the company.
- Documentation and further development of the entire ERM system.
- Establishment of a procedure for risk aggregation based on corporate planning to determine the overall scope of risk (capital requirements).
- Alignment of risk management decision-oriented that means it considers the risk/return profile of options for action in business decisions (e.g., via investments). This leads to a link with value-based management via the value drivers, cost of capital, and probability of default (value-based risk management (Gleißner, 2019).

Figure 1.4 summarizes the relationships between corporate objectives and ERM tasks and objectives.

1.5 Summary

- There are various reasons for ERM implementation in firms, including legal requirements such as SOX, environmental uncertainty caused by intense price or cost competition, and external threats from pandemics, natural disasters, terrorist attacks, and economic crime.
- Risks result from unforeseen environmental developments and non-target management decisions.
- Risks are potential deviations from planned corporate objectives.
- A distinction is made between downside risks, which represent negative deviations from corporate objectives, and opportunities, which refer to positive deviations. Both terms are included in a broad understanding of risk.
- Risks can be categorized according to many different criteria, such as the affected corporate objective. Risk categorization is the basis of risk identification.
- Risks that occur can lead to losses. If the company's earnings and liquidity situation are sustainably impaired by losses, corporate crises and insolvency may result.
- ERM is a holistic and integrated approach for company-wide identification, quantification, communication, disclosure, and handling of risks. It should support managerial decision-making.
- The relevant ERM tasks are as follows: the implementation of an adequate risk culture and risk strategy, the integration of risks in management control systems, and the implementation of a company-wide, operational ERM process.

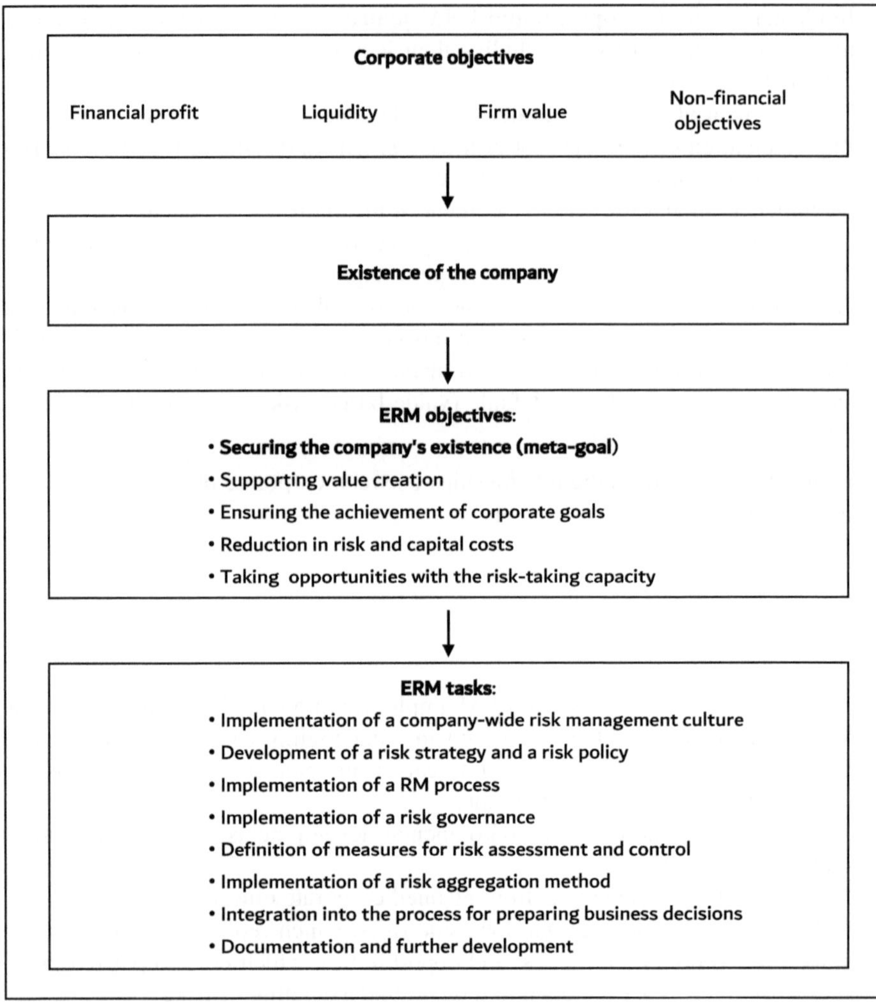

Fig. 1.4 Relationship between corporate goals and ERM tasks and objectives (adapted from Diederichs, 2018)

1.6 Exercises and Questions

1. Explain the risk paradox.
2. How can the terms "uncertainty," "risk," "opportunity," "loss," and "crisis" be distinguished from each other? Give an example for each term.
3. How can risks (and opportunities) be categorized?
4. Differentiate event risks from distribution risks. Why is this distinction important for risk management?

5. What are the goals and tasks of ERM?
6. Explain five of the main reasons for the increasing need for ERM in companies.

References

Åstebro, T., & Elhedhli, S. (2006). The effectiveness of simple decision heuristics. Forecasting commercial success for early-stage ventures. *Management Science, 52*, 395–409.

Åstebro, T., Herz, H., Nanda, R., & Weber, R. A. (2014). Seeking the roots of entrepreneurship: Insights from behavioral economics. *The Journal of Economic Perspectives, 28*, 49–69.

Aven, T., & Thekdi, S. (2020). *Enterprise risk management: Advances on its foundation and practice*. Routledge, Taylor & Francis Group.

Bromiley, P., McShane, M., Nair, A., & Rustambekov, E. (2015). Enterprise risk management: Review, critique, and research directions. *Long Range Planning, 48*, 265–276. https://doi.org/10.1016/j.lrp.2014.07.005

COSO (2017). Enterprise Risk Management – Integrating with Strategy and Performance.

CRED (2024). 2023: Disasters in Numbers. Brussels.

D'Arcy, S. P., & Brogan, J. C. (2001). Enterprise risk management. *Journal of Risk Management of Korea, 12*, 207–228.

Diederichs, M. (2018). *Risikomanagement und Risikocontrolling* (4th ed.). Vahlen.

Gerds, J., & Schewe, G. (2013). *Post merger integration: Unternehmenserfolg durch Integration Excellence* (5th ed.). Springer.

Gleißner, W. (2019). Cost of capital and probability of default in value-based risk management. *Management Research Review, 42*, 1243–1258.

Gleißner, W. (2020). Die Corona-Krise: Fakten, Prognosen und Risiken. *Corporate Finance, 11*, 121–130.

Gleißner, W. (2022). *Grundlagen des Risikomanagements: Handbuch für ein Management unter Unsicherheit* (Management competence) (4th ed.). Verlag Franz Vahlen.

Hardy, M. R., & Saunders, D. (2022). Quantitative enterprise risk management. *International series on actuarial science*, 2022: 1. Cambridge University Press.

Horvey, S. S., & Odei-Mensah, J. (2023). The measurements and performance of enterprise risk management: A comprehensive literature review. *Journal of Risk Research, 26*, 778–800.

Höse, S., & Huschens, S. (2022). The risk of the unseen. In T. Klein, S. Loßagk, M. Straßberger, & T. Walther (Eds.), *Modern finance and risk management: Festschrift in honour of Hermann Locarek-Junge* (pp. 173–196). World Scientific.

Hubbard, D. W. (2020). *The failure of risk management: Why it's broken and how to fix it* (2nd ed.). Wiley.

Hunziker, S. (2021). *Enterprise risk management: Modern approaches to balancing risk and reward* (2nd ed.). Springer.

Jankensgård, H., & Kapstad, P. (2021). *Empowered enterprise risk management: Theory and practice*. Wiley.

Kaplan, R. S., & Mikes, A. (2012). Managing risks: A new framework. *Harvard Business Review, 90*, 48–60.

Knight, F. H. (1921). *Risk, uncertainty and profit* (Vol. 31). Houghton Mifflin.

Kutschker, M., & Schmid, S. (2011). *Internationales Management* (7th ed.). Oldenbourg Wissenschaftsverlag.

Luo, T., & Mann, A. (2011). Survival and growth of Silicon Valley high-tech businesses born in 2000. *Monthly Labor Review*, 16–31.

McShane, M. (2018). Enterprise risk management: History and a design science proposal. *The Journal of Risk Finance, 19*, 137–153.

Mikes, A., & Kaplan, R. S. (2015). When one size doesn't fit all: Evolving directions in the research and practice of enterprise risk management. *Journal of Applied Corporate Finance, 27*, 37–40.

Romeike, F., & Stallinger, M. (2021). *Stochastische Szenariosimulation in der Unternehmenspraxis: Risikomodellierung, Fallstudien, Umsetzung in R*. Springer.

Sinn, H.-W. (1980). *Ökonomische Entscheidungen bei Ungewißheit. Die Einheit der Gesellschaftswissenschaften* (Vol. Bd. 28). J.C.B. Mohr (Paul Siebeck).

Taleb, N. N. (2012). *The black swan: The impact of the highly improbable* (2nd ed.). Random House.

Taleb, N. N., Goldstein, D. G., & Spitznagel, M. W. (2009). The six mistakes executives make in risk management. *Harvard Business Review, 87*, 78–81.

Vanini, U., & Rieg, R. (2021). *Risikomanagement: Grundlagen -- Instrumente -- Unternehmenspraxis* (Lehrbuch) (2nd ed.). Schäffer-Poeschel Verlag Stuttgart.

Vanini, U., & Weinstock, M. (2006). Risikoinventur bei der HSH N Real Estate AG. *CON, 18*, 379–386.

Chapter 2
Theories of Decision-Making Under Risk

Abstract Enterprise risk management (ERM) should support managerial decision-making to increase firm performance and firm value. Although decisions are made every day, few people realize that decisions are fundamentally structured in terms of cost and benefits and risks and opportunities. These factors must be analyzed to understand how decisions are made and how they can be improved. The underlying structure is not always visible in risk decisions and risk models in practice, so it is important to be aware of it when individuals in organizations build risk models and make decisions under risk. Such decisions should consider expected values, risk attitudes, and risk diversification which are explained in this chapter.

Keywords Beta factor · Capital Asset Pricing Model (CAPM) · Capital market line · Certainty equivalent · Decision-making · Diversifying risks · Enterprise risk management (ERM) · Expected utility · Principal-agent theory · Portfolio theory · Risk attitude · Risk premium

Questions
- Why are theories and models important in enterprise risk management (ERM)?
- What are the fundamental concepts of expected utility theory, and how is it applied in risk decisions?
- How do various approaches to probability differ, and what is their relevance in risk assessment?
- What are the key principles of portfolio theory, and how does diversification benefit risk management?
- What is the Capital Asset Pricing Model (CAPM), and what limitations does it face in practical applications?
- Which alternative approaches exist for estimating risk-adjusted returns, and what are their implications for ERM?

Supplementary Information The online version contains supplementary material available at https://doi.org/10.1007/978-3-031-86425-4_2.

R. Rieg et al., *Enterprise Risk Management*, Springer Texts in Business and Economics, https://doi.org/10.1007/978-3-031-86425-4_2

- How can concepts of risk-adjusted discount rates, risk premiums, and certainty equivalents be applied in decision-making?
- What is the relationship between risk assessment and value-based management in ERM?

2.1 A Need for Theories and Models in Enterprise Risk Management

Whether they are aware of it or not, when people in organizations make decisions in an uncertain world or build a risk model to analyze and aggregate risks in a quantitative way, they employ a theory. A **theory** is basically the what, how, and why of the world around us (Whetten, 1989). The "what" defines the phenomenon of interest, the variables, parameters, and assumptions we have, the "how" relates these to each other to produce an outcome, and the "why" tells us about the underlying principles that are employed to explain the former.

We will see, for example, that people undertaking risky decisions do not consider their monetary value but the expected utility that an option might offer.

Closely related to the concept of a theory is the concept of a **model**. Models are tools to concretize theories; to formalize them, if necessary; to understand their consequences for practice; and to verify them. Models contain necessary simplifications. They do not and should not represent everything, but only those aspects that are considered relevant for research or practice. The image of a landscape is not the landscape itself, as this would be unmanageable (Rodrik, 2016). In ERM, a risk model is often used to quantitatively aggregate financial risks. Such risk models, which we will discuss in detail in Sect. 5.6, do not include, for example, the body size of managers, although this seems to have an impact on the career path and thus also on the financial success of a company (Judge & Cable, 2004).

Students and practitioners alike may be confused by the lack of a singular, comprehensive ERM theory or model. Instead, there is a multitude of different theories and models, even for the same phenomenon. The variety of models is easily explained because (a) models have a purpose, so different purposes lead to different models, and (b) a modeler can choose from a large toolbox of modelling techniques and approaches, such that individual modelers may differ in their approaches to the same problem (for an overview Page, 2018). Nonetheless, it seems important to build models in an operational way that reflects reasonable and plausible mechanisms and assumptions (see Sect. 5.6).

While there are many theories on and in risk management, there are two interlinked theoretical perspectives on ERM (for the following Jankensgård, 2019): **information processing** and agency problems. First, given that information on risk and opportunities are not just there but have to be identified, evaluated, and aggregated, ERM has to deal with a problem of information provision which can be based on information processing theory (Tushman & Nadler, 1978). This theory stresses the need to match information needs, capacity, and supply. Concerning ERM in organizations, this means to align the process of gathering, processing, and presenting risk-related information. A second theoretical stance is the **principal-agent problem** of firms with separated ownership and management. This is discussed further in Sect. 2.4 of this chapter.

2.2 A Short History of Decision-Making Under Risk

Decision-making is challenging because the future is uncertain. Historically, simple heuristics like the Max-Min rule were initially used to evaluate risks in decision-making. The first scientific foundation came with the **expected utility theory**, which provided a metric for assessing decision options. However, its practical relevance was limited due to the difficulty in determining utility functions and the inability to aggregate them across individuals.

In 1952, Markowitz's "Portfolio Selection" established a systematic approach to balancing risk against expected return. His work laid the foundation for capital market theory and investment theory. Building on this, the **Capital Asset Pricing Model** (CAPM) by Sharpe, Lintner, and Mossin connected risk to returns, simplifying decision-making under uncertainty by combining expected value with a measure of risk. However, these models are based on restrictive assumptions, such as the notion of perfect capital markets.

Later models, such as the three- and five-factor models by Fama and French, expanded on these concepts but continued to rely on stock return fluctuations. Due to the limitations of these models, investment-theoretic and simulation-based valuation models were developed. These models do not require the assumption of perfect capital markets and directly incorporate the results of risk analyses. By combining market data with risk management information, these approaches provide a more comprehensive basis for making informed decisions under uncertainty (Jensen & Smith, 2000; Mishra, 2014; further reading Sapre, 2021).

2.3 Expected Value and Expected Utility

People usually are not interested in money itself but in the potential uses and benefits it can offer or what economists call "utility." The difference is relevant for decisions under risk as the following example shows.

Example

One possible rule for comparing decision alternatives is to determine the expected outcome and the variance or spread of possible outcomes.

Suppose you are offered three alternative games:

- Alternative 1: You receive US$10.
- Alternative 2: You toss a coin and receive US$25 for heads and pay US$0 for tails.
- Alternative 3: You toss a coin and receive US$40 for heads and pay US$10 for tails.

The probabilities of heads and tails are 50% each. What are the expected values and standard deviations of the possible values in each case?

In Alternative 1, the expected value is US$10 and the dispersion of the possible values is zero. In Alternative 2, the expected value is 50% * US$0 + 50% * US $25 = US$12.50. The standard deviation around this value is €12.50. Alternative 3 has a higher expected value of US$15, but the standard deviation is US$25. Obviously, both the expected return and the risk increase from alternatives one to three.

In this example, most people would probably choose the safe Alternative 1; some may choose Alternative 2, but people rarely choose Alternative 3. The exceptions are people who are very risk-averse and like to gamble. Without knowing an individual's risk attitude, it is not clear which decision they will make.

In addition, people do not value every possible outcome of a decision in the same way; they may assign value to the individual utility of an outcome differently depending on their preferences. The relationship between the expected value and the utility of a decision was first formulated by the mathematician Bernoulli and formalized as expected utility theory (Damodaran, 2008). The **St Petersburg Paradox** below illustrates that point. It follows that the simple decision rule resting on expected values and variances does not reflect how people decide in reality.

Example: St Petersburg Paradox

David Bernoulli developed the idea of expected utility based on a game of chance: a fair coin is tossed until it comes up heads. If the first toss comes up heads, you get US $2; if the second toss comes up tails, you get US$4, and so on. The payout doubles each time tails comes up on consecutive tosses. However, if heads come up, you get nothing. The payout P is therefore $P = 2^{i-1}$ for each roll i. Weighting these payouts by the 50% probability per toss, the expected total payouts $E(P)$ up to a series of n tosses is.

$$E(P) = \sum_{i=1}^{n} \frac{1}{2^i} 2^{i-1} = \frac{1}{2} n \tag{2.1}$$

With an infinite number of coin flips, the expected payoff would also be infinite. All players would have to immediately sell their houses and farms as a stake to participate in the game, but no one would do that. Bernoulli's insight was that players do not evaluate money in terms of the expected monetary value itself but rather its utility. The expected value must therefore be transformed to a utility function $U(x)$, where U is the utility and the expected utility is given by $U(E(P))$. Players typically give very low weight to expected value, resulting in low stakes of a few euros (Jerger, 1992).

2.4 Risk Attitude, Risk Premium, and Certainty Equivalent

The utility function of expected values can be used mathematically as an indicator of the risk attitude of a decision-maker. If the second derivative is less than zero, which is $U'' < 0$, the marginal utility decreases as the expected value of the outcome increases. This relationship is also known as Gossen's first law in microeconomics. In game and decision theories, this relationship is referred to as **risk aversion** (Jerger, 1992). Besides to risk aversion, there are also risk neutrality and risk appetite. Each one of these **risk attitudes** has its own utility function. In the case of risk neutrality, the outcome utility increases proportionally to the risk taken. In other words, a risk-neutral decision-maker does not want to be overcompensated for taking increasing risks. For risk-averse decision-makers, on the other hand, the decision utility increases disproportionately, so these decision-makers are more likely to seek risks. A risk-averse utility function is expressed in a concave curve and a risk-averse utility function in a convex curve.

By measuring risk attitude, one can determine what additional compensation a decision-maker would have to receive to take a certain risk. This additional compensation is the **risk premium**. It is the difference between the expected value of an uncertain event and a utility-equivalent certain value, namely, the **certainty equivalent** (Eisenführ & Weber, 2010) as is illustrated in the following example.

Example: Risk Premium and Certainty Equivalent
The size of the certainty equivalent gives us information on an individual's risk attitude. Assume a logarithmic utility function that leads to a decreasing marginal utility for increasing risk and thus a decision-maker expecting a monotonically increasing risk premium (Damodaran, 2008). In other words, the individual is risk averse (Table 2.1):

According to this logic, the risk premium is zero for risk-neutral decision-makers, positive for risk-averse decision-makers, and negative for risk-seeking decision-makers. Consequently, risk-averse decision-makers would be willing to be paid/ receive a risk premium for taking risks. In the example above, the risk premium indicates risk aversion.

Table 2.1 Example certainty equivalent

Assumptions	Risk adverse decision maker with log utility utility function = ln(expected value)	
Lottery	Win 10 € or 100 € p each with 50%	
Expected value (EV) of Lottery	50% * 10 € + 50% * 100 € =	$55.00
Utility of EV	U(55) = ln(55) =	4.007
Utility of separate possible events	50% * ln(10 €) + 50% * ln(100 €) =	3.454
Certainty equivalent for these $e^{U(A) + U(B)}$ (C.E.)		$31.62
Risk premium = E(lottery)–C.E.		$23.38

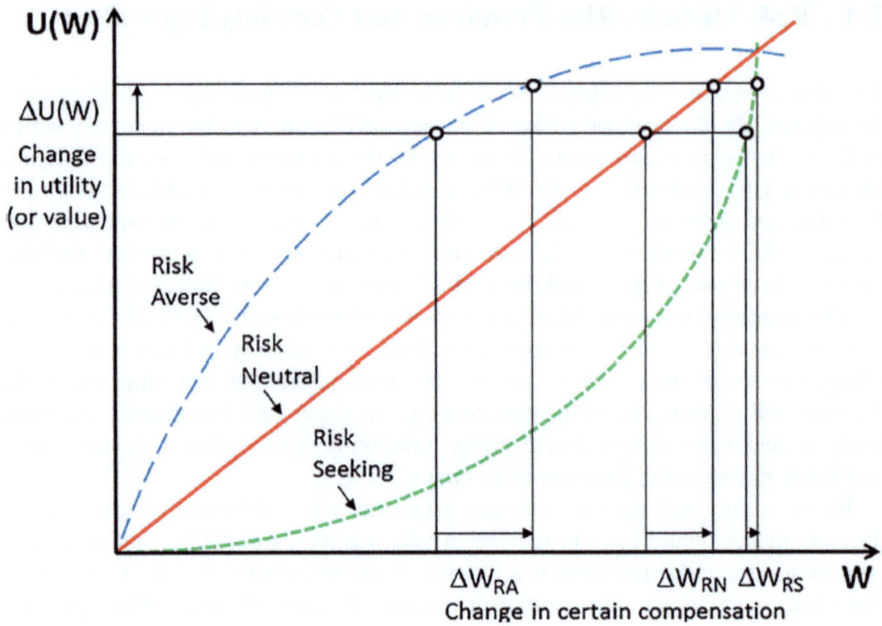

Fig. 2.1 Risk propensities. Source: Harris and Wu (2014)

Most economic models assume that decision-makers are risk-averse or at least risk-neutral (Bamberg et al., 2019) (Fig. 2.1).

To capture risk aversion in such models, Arrow and Pratt developed a metric. It is based on the plausible assumption that decision-makers consider how their initial utility would change in a decision made under uncertainty. One could directly use the slope of the risk preference curve which is the first derivative of the utility function. However, the risk preference curve depends on the individual. Instead, Arrow and Pratt suggest using the second derivative to determine the change in the change in wealth as a function of the wealth level (i.e., $W =$ wealth):

$$-\frac{U''(W)}{U'(W)} \tag{2.2}$$

This is the absolute risk aversion, meaning the change in risk aversion with an absolute change in wealth. The relative risk aversion can also be determined for a percentage change in wealth. This is calculated via (Schoemaker, 1982; Damodaran, 2008):

$$-\frac{W * U''(W)}{U'(W)} \tag{2.3}$$

Table 2.2 Empirical results for risk preferences (Vanini, 2016)

Study	Empirical risk attitudes					Participants
	Risk Taking	Risk neutral	Risk averse	Irrational	Others	
Holt and Laury (2002)	7.1%	23.0%	58.3%		13.2%	Students
Anderson and Mellor 2009	4.7%	20.8%	74.5%			Students
Mascalet et al. (2009)	2.7%	10.2%	87.1%			Students, self-employed persons, and employees
Pennings and Smidts (2000)	61.0%	4.0%	35.0%			Company owners
Bellemare and Shearer (2006)	17.6%	13.7%	37.3%		3.4%	Employees of a timber company
Günther and Detzner (2009)	18.7%	17.0%	29.4%	35.0%		Managing director
Günther and Detzner (2012)	18.0%	27.0%	26.0%	29.0%		Management accountants

Highest rating highlighted in gray

In the case of absolute risk aversion, the amount one is willing to risk changes with the absolute change in wealth, so an increase in wealth of US$100 leads to an increase in the risk premium by US$x. In the case of relative risk aversion, the reference point is the relative change in wealth, meaning that a 5% increase in wealth leads to a change in the risk premium by US$y.

Individual Risk Attitude

The risk attitude varies from individual to individual, which empirical studies show very clearly. This phenomenon can be explained by the various factors influencing individual risk attitudes (also Mishra, 2014; Vanini, 2016). For example, Hartog et al. (2002) found that risk aversion decreases with increasing income and wealth. Moreover, entrepreneurs are less risk averse than employees, civil servants are more risk averse than employees, and women are more risk averse than men. There is also evidence that individuals inherit their risk aversion from their parents (de Paola, 2013).

The extent to which risk aversion can be identified for an entire organization is not entirely clear. While many models have assumed a uniform risk aversion for all decision-makers in an organization, there are only a few relevant empirical findings in the existing literature (e.g., Bickel, 2006). In general, it can be assumed that risk attitude is a basic personality trait but that it is moderated in concrete situations by numerous factors such as risk perception (Slovic, 2010) (Table 2.2).

Pros and Cons of Expected Utility Theory

The general validity of expected utility theory was questioned early on, and various situations, often called paradoxes, were pointed out in which individuals do not decide as the theory recommends. As a result, the theory is not considered sufficient to describe all decisions under risk in reality (Schoemaker, 1982). However, it seems to provide a useful description for less extreme decisions that means those with probabilities of occurrence that are not close to zero or one. It seems also appropriate when decisions are repeated and decision-makers can reasonably calculate with expected values (Jungermann et al., 2005). Therefore, expected utility theory can be seen as a general benchmark for how one should rationally approach a decision under risk (Klein & Scholl, 2012; Laux et al., 2018). However, some argue that expected utility, including all its variants and refined models, is unable to explain risky decisions in a consistent way (Friedman et al., 2017).

These difficulties in modelling human decision-making point to fundamental assumptions about decision-making. For example, expected utility theory assumes that individuals (can) apply complex mathematical-statistical procedures (Baddeley, 2019). However, since decision-makers are always confronted with temporal and cognitive constraints and should consider boundary conditions and contextual factors, real decision-making behavior can rather be described as limited by bounded rationality (Simon, 1990). If individuals then make another optimal decision under constraints, it is the same rational perspective, but with a different name. This applies, for example, to the principal-agent theory (PAT), in which several decision-makers, information asymmetry, and different interests are assumed as constraints. What Simon, the founder of the idea of bounded rationality, wants to express, however, is that individuals are subject to external constraints as well as cognitive limitations and therefore do not pursue optimization in the mathematical sense, but rather settle for a sufficiently high level of aspiration (satisficing). Therefore, decision-making procedures should always be examined to see in which context they function better or worse. Their adequacy thus also depends on the context, meaning that there are no generally applicable methods of decision-making. If individuals have little time or want to expend little effort, they usually rely on very simple decision rules, called heuristics. These rules can be applied in situations, if no distortions occur (Gigerenzer, 2008).

2.5 New Institutional Economics, Agency Problems, and Risk

Expected utility theory (EUT) only considers decisions made by one individual. It is more realistic to assume that there are multiple actors for whom exchanges and cooperation can be economically beneficial. In a market economy, exchange, cooperation, and risk-taking are stimulated and organized through the price mechanism, and EUT fits here—often well. However, most people in developed countries are not active in markets but work within organizations which poses new challenges.

The starting point for such organizational challenges is employment contracts that are incomplete in terms of the performance outcome to be achieved because the performance outcome cannot be verified and enforced by third parties such as courts.

Goals such as the commitment to the company or the development of company-specific knowledge (human capital) cannot be fully represented by contract clauses. Both the employer and the employee may then be tempted to evade their obligations and act opportunistically. The employer may refuse to pay because of a lack of results, and the employee may fail to deliver the promised results. This creates organizational and personnel-related risks for firms. The literature on **institutional economics** suggests solutions to such problems, such as sharing the expected benefits of interaction, efficiency wages that are higher than market wages, or performance tournaments between employees (Kräkel, 2015).

A second type of organizational challenge arises from participation and delegation, when a principal, typically an owner of the firm or higher-level manager, assigns a task to an agent, for example, a lower-level manager or employee, and promises compensation for the agent's performance. Typically, such vertical relationships are characterized by asymmetric information: The agent has more and better information about his labor input and chances of success. The principal either does not have this information or can only obtain it at a prohibitively high cost. Such questions are often treated under the heading of **principal-agent theory** (PAT) (synonym: agency theory). Positive PAT tries to explain the existence of real-world contract structures and institutions, while normative PAT tries to derive optimal contract structures and institutions on the basis of formal mathematical models. Jensen and Meckling (1976) are important representatives of the positive agency theory, while Holmström (1982) is regarded as a representative of the normative approach.

PAT explores the relationship dynamics between two parties: the principal, who delegates tasks, and the agent, who executes them. This theory addresses the inherent issues of **information asymmetry** and **conflicting interests**, where the principal and the agent have different states of information and goals, respectively. Both parties aim to maximize their utility, which introduces potential conflicts, especially under conditions of uncertain futures and varying risk appetites.

Contractually, the principal engages the agent to perform specific duties, compensating the agent for task execution while aiming to maximize his own utility, which is the benefits from the agent's activities minus costs and agent compensation. These costs include contract initiation and enforcement expenses, known as agency costs, which also cover welfare losses due to typically achieving suboptimal (second-best) outcomes.

Before closing the contract, the principal faces uncertainty about the agent's suitability and the quality of anticipated services, raising the risk of adverse selection. Strategies to mitigate this risk include the agent's signaling of service quality, the principal's screening efforts, and self-selection mechanisms through differentiated contract offers to reveal true agent capabilities.

After closing the contract, the issue of **moral hazard** emerges, with the agent possibly engaging in unobservable actions (hidden action) or withholding information (hidden information) that affect outcomes. Remedies include constraining the agent's actions, enhancing transparency through reporting systems, and implementing incentive schemes to align the agent's efforts with the principal's interests.

Ultimately, PAT advocates designing contractual and incentive structures to minimize **agency costs** while balancing optimal incentive settings and risk-sharing between the principal and the agent. The agent's compensation often links to performance measures influenced by uncontrollable factors, necessitating risk premiums by risk-averse agents, which can reduce the principal's profits.

Several implications of the principal-agent approach for ERM are apparent: There are fundamental conflicts of interest between principals and agents with respect to the risk situation and tits management. Conflicts of interest may arise if the owners do not manage the firm themselves and instead delegate the management of the firm to outside managers. Managers are usually poorly diversified, having invested their human capital and some of their financial capital in only one firm. They act in a risk-averse manner to reduce the volatility of the firm's earnings and the likelihood that the firm will become insolvent. Thus, managers have an incentive to use ERM to manage their own income uncertainty. Conflicts of interest with shareholders may arise because, for example, too much diversification or too little leverage may mean that the firm's risk is too low relative to the shareholders' **risk appetite**. The issue of inadequate entrepreneurial risk can be countered by employing an appropriate incentive design, such as one with a convex relationship between compensation and performance under risk, as well as by selecting managers with an appropriate risk appetite.

On the other hand, ERM measures, for example, for assessing the risks caused by the agent's activities, serve to monitor the agent and are thus a tool for overcoming hidden information and hidden action problems. This applies to the principal-agent relationships between owners and management, management and decentralized business unit management, and managers and employees in individual organizational units.

Agency theory also provides an analytical framework for understanding legal regulations such as the requirement to set up an ERM system or the Business Judgment Rule. Since the shareholders of a stock corporation have hardly any direct influence and control options, statutory regulations at least partially fill this gap and reduce agency costs for shareholders. The design of **incentive and compensation systems** for managers can also be understood from this agency perspective: Bonus systems should be designed in such a way that managers also consider the long-term and not only the short-term consequences of their decisions.

The economic and financial crisis of 2008/2009 demonstrated the consequences of an uneven distribution of risks and rewards and inappropriate short-term incentives. The financial industry relied on short-term bonus contracts to attract and retain talented employees, losing sight of the long-term consequences. Lack of regulation of the financial industry and increased risk-taking in the not unfounded hope that the taxpayer, and thus others, would ultimately cover the risks further fueled this process of excessive risk-taking. The crisis is a textbook case of problems of information asymmetry, lack of oversight, and the resulting incentives to take advantage of poorly informed and poorly hedged market participants (Tirole, 2019).

2.6 Probabilities as the Foundation of Risk Quantification

Risks arise from uncertain future events. To quantify risks, information is needed not only about their impact but also about the probability of their occurrence. In this context, the term **probability** should first be clarified. It refers to random events and the description of the degree of certainty or uncertainty of their occurrence. Four probability concepts are distinguished: (1) the axiomatic, (2) the classical, (3) the statistical, and (4) the subjective concept of probability (Rudas, 2004):

1. The **axiomatic concept of probability** can be traced back to Kolmogorov. His axioms show that a probability is a real number in the interval [0;1]. An impossible event has a probability of zero; a certain event has a probability of one.
2. The **classical concept of probability**, founded by Laplace, derives the probability p (A) from the frequency of event A with respect to a total number of events (Stigler, 1975). A textbook example is a coin toss or a roll of the dice, where ideally each event is equally frequent and therefore equally probable.
3. A direct transition can be made here to the concept of **statistical probability (also called frequentist probability)**, which infers the probability of an event from its observed frequency. This is based on the law of large numbers, but sometimes you need a lot of data to get a sufficiently accurate probability estimate.
4. Finally, the **subjective concept of probability** is the assessment of probability by one or more individuals based on experience or knowledge. Since many events occur rarely and their probability is therefore difficult to determine logically or statistically, probabilities must often be estimated subjectively. They then reflect a degree of (personal) belief and are not an objectively measurable quantity (Lindley, 2014). Is the degree of one's own conviction necessarily and inevitably arbitrary and therefore ultimately worthless? Certainly not. For one thing, probabilities cannot be objectively determined for many decisions and events. For another, subjective probabilities can be biased, but they can be improved by a broader information base as well as by the involvement of several individuals (Hubbard, 2014). A central concept for improving probability estimation and learning from new information is based on **Bayes' theorem**.

The Bayes' theorem, developed by Thomas Bayes, allows us to re-evaluate previous judgments and assessments based on new information or data. Formally, this means:

$$p(\theta|\text{data}) = \left(p(\text{data}|\theta)^{*} p(\theta)\right) / (p(\text{data})) \tag{2.4}$$

where $p(\theta)$ is the a priori probability of a conjecture θ (theta), $p(\text{data}|\theta)$ is the conditional probability of getting exactly the data if the conjecture θ is correct, and $p(\theta|\text{data})$ is the a posteriori probability that the conjecture is true given the observed data. Thus, a change in the original conjecture (i.e., a belief update) occurs as a result of the data, where $p(\theta)$ is multiplied by the conditional probability, called the

Table 2.3 Example for Bayes' theorem with belief update (based on Lambert, 2018)

	A	B	c = a*b	d = a*b/e
Assumption about number of red balls	A priori probability	Likelihood	A priori * likelihood	A posteriori = a priori * likelihood p(data)
0	1/6	0/5	0	0
1	1/6	1/5	1/30	1/15
2	1/6	2/5	1/15	2/15
3	1/6	3/5	1/10	3/15
4	1/6	4/5	2/15	4/15
5	1/6	5/5 = 1	1/6	5/15
Totals	1	3	0.5	1
E: *p*(data) = *p*(red ball) = total c = 0.5				

likelihood, $p(\text{data}|\theta)$. The parameter $p(\text{data})$ is used to normalize the likelihood since it is not a probability in the interval [0,1], but the result $p(\theta|\text{data})$ must be a probability. Therefore, a posteriori probability = likelihood of the (new) data * a priori probability.

Suppose we know that there are five balls in an urn. Each ball is either red or white, meaning that if we draw a ball, the probability of getting a red ball is p (ball = red) = 0.5. The possible number of red balls is between zero and five, but we have no information about how many there actually are. However, all states are equally likely, so the probability for each of the six possible states is 1/6. If we now draw a ball and it is red, the expected probabilities change. It becomes more likely that there will be several red balls in the urn. The a posteriori probability is higher the more balls you assume a priori because if you assume more red balls, the frequency of drawing a red ball is also higher. In other words, the probability of drawing a single red ball when there are three red balls is 3/5. By drawing a single red ball, the a posteriori probability that there are three balls in the urn increases from 1/6 to 3/15 = 20% according to Bayes' theorem. The following table shows this for all possible states. A likelihood is not a probability, since the sum of the likelihoods is greater than one (Table 2.3).

The importance of Bayes' theorem for ERM lies in the fact that new knowledge can be used to systematically improve previous risk assessments (Gleißner, 2014):

- A customer's risk of non-payment is increased (he pays only after reminders) or decreased (he pays on time over a longer period) by his former payment behavior.
- The risk of launching a new product on the market can provide insights into the prospects of the new product on the overall market (a posteriori) via the previous experience of new product launches (a priori) combined with the testing of the new product on a small market (Zhou, 2005).

The challenge is to quantify the probabilities. In general, the **quantification of probabilities** is necessary when making important decisions to limit reliance on vague and imprecise statements such as "relatively low" or "in rare cases." While statistical probabilities can be determined with some degree of accuracy if the number of observations in a sample is large enough and the origin of the sample is known, this is more difficult in the case of subjective probabilities. You can ask individual decision-makers for their assessments, either directly as probabilities ("What is your estimate of the risk of default in %?") or indirectly as a kind of bet ("Would you bet US$10 that the customer will pay?"), either as individual values or according to the type of distribution ("Do you think defaults are normally distributed?"). Since all individuals have certain judgment and decision biases (see Chap. 3), often have insufficient information, or simply find their own opinions very convincing, there is often little reliance on a subjective probability judgment. Therefore, several people with different levels of experience and knowledge should be interviewed independently, and their assessments should be averaged (Makridakis et al., 2009). Quantified probabilities are the basis for risk assessment and risk measurement (for application see Chap. 8).

2.7 Effects of Diversifying Risks: Portfolio Theory

In corporate practice, there is often more than one risk. The total risk is only the sum of a list of individual risks if they occur independently. Suppose that the average risk of non-payment by customers of a mail-order company is 1%. However, if an economic recession affects many customers and causes them to become unemployed, the overall risk increases, and the expected default rate becomes larger than 1%. Here, the individual risks depend on each other.

Yet, such interdependent risks can also be reduced; this is called **risk diversification**.

Example: Rolling Dice
The probability for any number on an ideal die is 1/6, so the probabilities are evenly distributed. When you roll two dices at the same time, the frequencies of results of both dices are combined. Certain sums of the dots, specifically those in the middle of the range of possible values, occur more frequently. For instance, there are more chances of getting a seven than a two. The distribution becomes more normal. The probabilities of "extreme" outcomes, such as two and twelve, decrease significantly. This is the effect of diversification (Fig. 2.2).

The idea of risk diversification is also reflected in the **Portfolio Theory** developed by Harry M. Markowitz in the 1950s. Portfolio theory is concerned with the selection of securities, especially stocks, for an optimal portfolio. Markowitz's basic idea is to select securities that do not behave identically in terms of their price development, meaning their risks and opportunities. The main assumptions and propositions of portfolio theory are (Francis & Kim, 2013) as follows:

- Each security can be described in terms of its expected return *R* of security *I*, $E(r_i)$, and the respective variance of its returns, $\sigma^2\ (r_i)$ or $VAR\ (r_i)$. Here, the expected

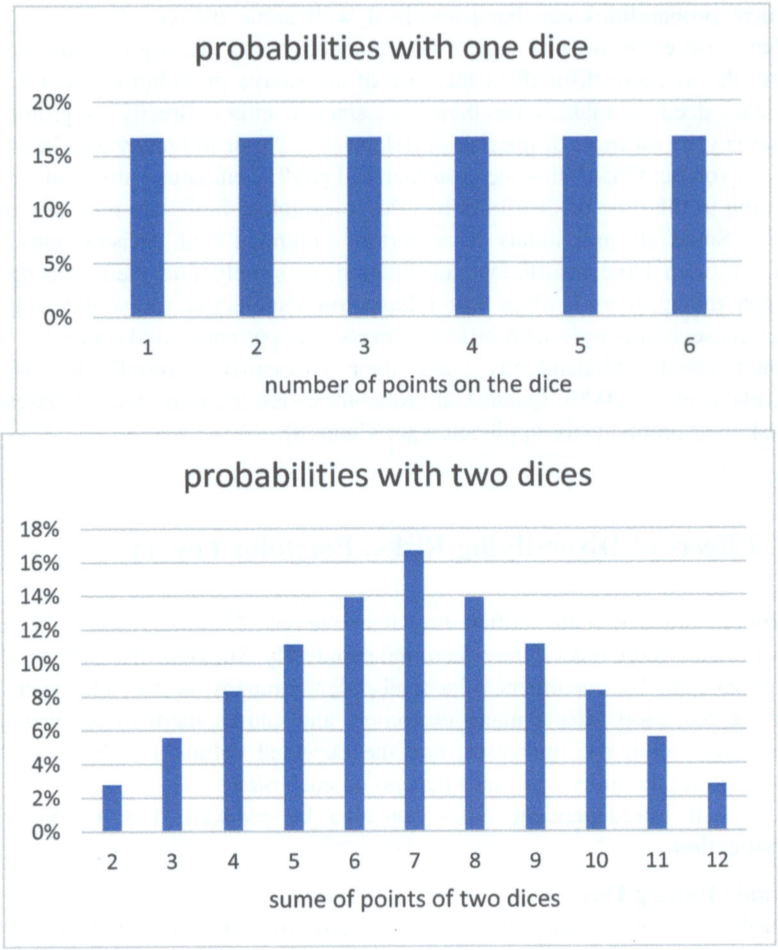

Fig. 2.2 Distribution of eyes for one die and two dice (see also Savage, 2012)

return is a measure of the future uncertain return of the security; the variance is the variation of returns and therefore is a measure of the risk of the security.

- Investors make investment decisions based on the expected return and the risk of a security.
- Investors are risk-averse, meaning that they will only accept higher risk if the expected return increases disproportionately.
- There are no transaction costs or taxes.
- All securities are arbitrarily divisible.
- The observation period is one period (two-point model).

The optimal portfolio p follows from portfolio theory that if two securities i and j are included in a portfolio, the expected return of the portfolio results from the addition of the weighted expected returns of both securities i and j:

$$E(r_p) = w_i * E(r_i) + w_j * E(r_j) \tag{2.5}$$

with
$E(r_p)$ = expected return of portfolio p
$E(r_i)$ = expected return of security i
$E(r_j)$ = expected return of security j
w_i = proportion of security i in the portfolio
w_j = proportion of security j in the portfolio
Note that the risk of the portfolio is not simply the sum of the individual risks; it also includes the covariance between the returns of the two securities:

$$VAR(r_p) = w_i^2 VAR(r_i) + w_j^2 VAR(r_j) + 2w_i w_j COV(r_i, r_j) \tag{2.6}$$

with
$VAR(r_p)$ = variance of expected return of portfolio p
$VAR(r_i)$ = variance of expected return of security i
$VAR(r_j)$ = variance of expected return of security j
$COV(r_i,r_j)$ = Covariance of expected returns of securities i and j
The following example illustrates the concept. Two stocks, A and B, are to be combined in a portfolio; their returns data are given. While the individual stocks have returns of 11.50% and 8.00%, respectively, the expected return of the whole portfolio is intermediate at 9.50%. The weights depend on the variance and covariance of both stocks. In this case, Stock A is riskier and should be assigned a weight of 42% in a portfolio. The variance of the overall risk is lower than the variances of each stock individually, so the right combination reduces risk, as suggested by modern portfolio theory (Table 2.4).

To assess the statistical association of the returns of securities, most practitioners use correlation coefficients instead of the covariance. The former is simply a standardized covariance restricted to the range of −to +1. Depending on the correlation between the expected returns of securities i and j, it is possible to reduce the risk of a portfolio of both securities There are four cases:

Case 1: The expected returns of the two securities i and j are fully positively correlated, with a correlation of +1. In this case, the risk of the portfolio is the sum of the individual risks of the two securities, and risk reduction by mixing the two securities is not possible.

Case 2: The expected returns of the two securities i and j are uncorrelated; hence, the risk of the portfolio is lower than the risk of the individual securities.

Table 2.4 Modern portfolio theory example

Returns of	Stock A	Stock B
	10%	7%
	12%	9%
	14%	6%
	9%	10%
	13%	8%
Statistics		
Expected return	**11.60%**	**8.00%**
Standard deviation	**2.07%**	**1.58%**
Variance	0.00043	0.00025
Covariance	−0.0002	
Weight of stock	41.67%	58.33%
E(Return p)	**9.50%**	
Variance portfolio	0.0000625	
Stddev portfolio	**0.79%**	

$$\sigma_P = \sqrt{w_i^2 \sigma_i^2 + w_j^2 \sigma_j^2} \tag{2.7}$$

Case 3: The expected returns of the two securities i and j are completely negatively correlated. Here, maximum diversification effects can be achieved, since the risk can be completely reduced to zero:

$$\sigma_P = \left| w_i \sigma_i - w_j \sigma_j \right| \tag{2.8}$$

Case 4: The expected returns of the two securities i and j are not perfectly correlated. Depending on the strength of the correlation, there are diversification effects:

$$\sigma_P = \sqrt{w_i^2 \sigma_i^2 + w_j^2 \sigma_j^2 + 2 \cdot w_i \cdot w_j \cdot k_{ij} \cdot \sigma_i \cdot \sigma_j} \tag{2.9}$$

For more than two risky securities, the expected portfolio return and its variance are calculated as follows:

$$E\left(r_p\right) = \sum_{i=1}^{I} w_i E(r_i) \tag{2.10}$$

$$VAR\left(r_p\right) = \sum_{i=1}^{I} \sum_{j=}^{J} w_i w_j COV\left(r_i, r_j\right) \tag{2.11}$$

The **efficient portfolios** can be identified by plotting all possible mixtures or portfolios of securities according to expected return and standard deviation. A portfolio is efficient if there is no other portfolio of securities with lower risk for

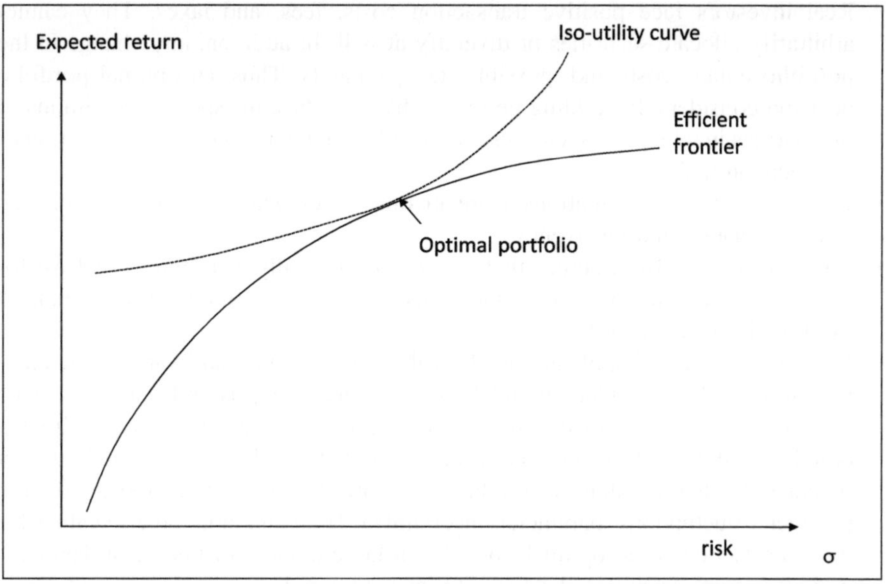

Fig. 2.3 Efficiency curve and optimal portfolio

the same expected return, higher expected return for the same risk, or both higher expected return and lower risk. The set of all efficient portfolios can then be plotted as an efficiency curve (Fig. 2.3).

An investor chooses the portfolio on the efficiency curve that matches his **risk attitude**. An investor's risk attitude is determined by his utility function, which represents the trade-off between expected return and risk and is graphically described by an iso-utility curve. All points on an iso-utility curve have the same value for a (risk-averse) investor. An investor's optimal portfolio lies at the tangent point of the iso-utility curve with the highest utility and the efficiency curve of the portfolios.

Portfolio theory is important because it can provide a quantitative answer to the question of how best to diversify different investment opportunities to balance risk and return. It can therefore be used to advise on the management of financial assets (Spremann, 2010). However, it does not explain how asset prices and price fluctuations occur; it is merely an algorithm that combines the returns and risks of given securities in a way that is optimal for a decision-maker (Hubbard, 2009; Siegel, 2010). For this reason, it was criticized quite early on (Michaud, 1989; Jorion, 1992; Chopra & Ziemba, 2012). Accordingly, a simple transfer into practice is not as easy as it is made out to be in the business press because the selection of assets is crucial for the success of diversification.

Regarding the assumptions of portfolio theory, it must be acknowledged that some **assumptions** are **problematic**:

- Real investors face positive transaction costs, fees, and taxes. They cannot arbitrarily allocate securities or diversify at will. In addition, any change in the portfolio entails costs and, possibly, tax payments. Thus, an optimal portfolio decision considers the holding period of the securities, the specific conditions of the markets in which the securities are traded, and the income and tax situation of the decision-maker.
- In addition to price fluctuations, there are other risks to an investor's wealth, such as expropriation and insolvency.
- Portfolio theory also assumes that returns are normally distributed. At least for equities as one of the most important asset classes, this assumption does not hold (Makridakis et al., 2009).
- Finally, for practical applications, the values of the return and variance parameters must be known. One should know the future returns and variances since investments are made for the future. Often, however, they are simply estimated based on historical data, and it is assumed that they will hold true in the future. In practice, this is often done with relatively short time series, which leads to large parameter fluctuations (parameter uncertainty). To obtain more precise values for the construction of an optimal portfolio, a large amount of historical data over periods ranging from decades to centuries is required.

Due to the unrealistic assumptions and practical problems of implementing the model, alternatives were developed. However, they cannot be explained in detail here.

2.8 Risk and Return in Decision-Making

2.8.1 Capital Asset Pricing Model

Portfolio theory forms the basis of the **capital asset pricing model (CAPM)** developed by William F. Sharpe, John Lintner, Jan Mossin, and Jack L. Treynor in the 1960s (for an overview Rossi, 2016). The following additional assumptions are introduced to the premises of portfolio theory: (a) there is a risk-free interest rate at which investors can borrow or invest any amount of money at any time, and (b) all investors have homogeneous expectations about the return and risk of all securities. The following basic statements can be derived from the CAPM:

- Investors can mix their individual securities portfolios with the risk-free opportunity R_f.
- The combination of this risk-free investment opportunity and the efficient portfolios creates a **capital market line**. The efficient portfolio, which dominates all other security portfolios and is structured the same for all investors, regardless of their risk appetite (Tobin separation), is found where the capital market line touches the efficiency line (tangent point M). This portfolio contains all available securities of a market in proportion to their capitalization (market portfolio).

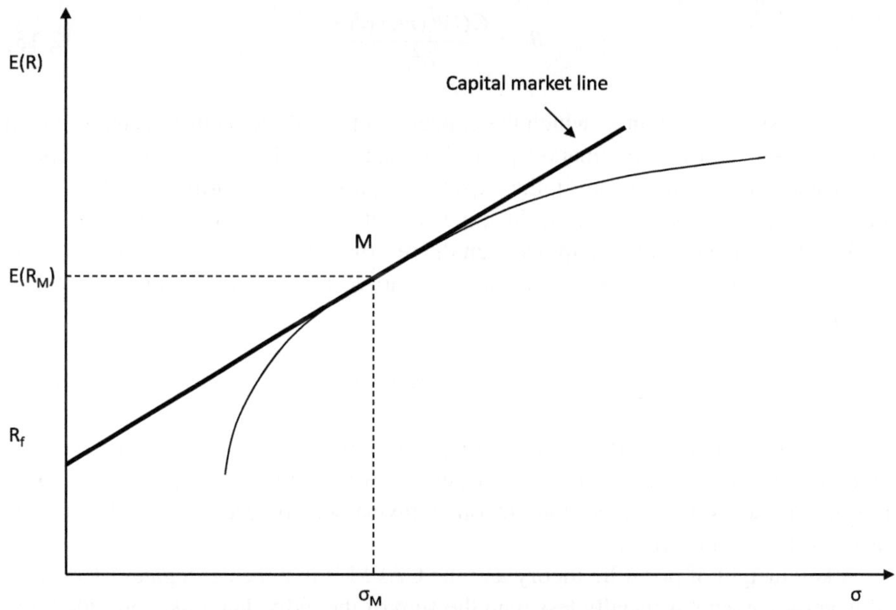

Fig. 2.4 Capital market line and optimal portfolio M

Determining the optimal combination of the risk-free investment with the market portfolio results in the tangent point on an investor's respective iso-utility curve (Fig. 2.4).

The expected return is derived as follows:

$$E(R_p) = R_f + \frac{E(R_m) - R_f}{\sigma_m} * \sigma_p \tag{2.12}$$

where
$E(R_p)$ = expected return of portfolio p
$E(R_m)$ = expected return of market portfolio
σ_p = standard deviation of expected return of portfolio p
σ_m= standard deviation of expected market portfolio
R_f = return of risk-free investment

The second term of Eq. 2.12 (= $E(R_m)-R_f$) can be interpreted as the **risk premium** and includes the return over and above the risk-free return that an investor receives for taking on the risk of the portfolio p.

CAPM models distinguish between the systematic and unsystematic risk of a security. The **systematic risk** β is rewarded by the market and cannot be eliminated by diversification, while unsystematic risk can be in theory eliminated by diversification. Systematic risk is also known as the **beta factor**. The beta of a security i is calculated in the following way:

$$\beta_i = \frac{COV\,(r_i, r_M)}{\sigma_M^2} \tag{2.13}$$

It expresses the extent to which the expected return of the security changes when the expected return of the market portfolio changes by 1%. With a beta factor of 1 (greater than 1 or less than 1), the expected return of the security fluctuates to the same (greater or lesser) extent as the expected return of the market portfolio.

There is a linear relationship between the return of a security i and its risk β_i. The return on a security consists of a risk-free part R_f and a risk premium $[E(R_m) - r_f] * \beta_i$:

$$E(R_i) = r_f + \left[E(r_m) - r_f\right] * \beta_i \tag{2.14}$$

Portfolio theory and the CAPM are particularly relevant to the financial risk assessment and management of securities. However, they also attempt to apply risk diversification considerations to other investment objects such as businesses or markets and their risks.

A key insight of portfolio theory and the CAPM is that the aggregate risk of a set of uncertain events is usually less than the sum of the individual risks, provided that there are negative correlations between these events. This diversification effect applies both to a set of similar or largely homogeneous risks, such as securities in a portfolio, and to a portfolio of more heterogeneous investments. The diversification effect must be considered in both risk assessment and risk management. If the overall risk position of a company is to be determined quantitatively, the single risks cannot simply be added together since this would lead to misinterpretation. Instead, risk interdependencies must be taken into account. The diversification effect plays an important role in risk management as the overall risk of a company can be reduced by an appropriate combination of negatively correlated business areas.

The CAPM also shows that an investor's expected return on an investment consists of a minimum return in the form of a risk-free interest rate and a risk premium. The **risk premium** is largely determined by the individual risk factor β (beta) of an investment. In principle, this has implications for financial risk assessment and management. It can be argued that the risk of any investment can be measured by its beta factor. However, outside the securities markets, beta factors are very difficult to determine due to a lack of data. Moreover, the beta factor reflects only the systematic, non-diversifiable risk of an investment. However, it is believed that the portion of **unsystematic risk** due to company-, business-unit- or product-specific risk factors accounts for 70% of the total risk of an investment and cannot be fully diversified outside the securities markets. Beta is therefore an incomplete measure of risk. Regarding risk management, the CAPM allows the risk premium of an investment to be taken into account in the profitability scales used to evaluate investments and in the allocation of equity to cover risk.

Since its inception, the CAPM has been subject to theoretical and empirical criticism. We summarize some of the **criticisms** (Dempsey, 2013):

- The CAPM assumes that all investors have the same information. If this were the case, there would be no point in buying or selling shares because the capital market would be in equilibrium. The financial valuation of the company would also be superfluous because the value of the company would already be known.
- The hypothesis derived from the CAPM that stock returns can be explained or predicted by the beta factor can be considered empirically refuted. Other factors are much more highly correlated with stock returns, such as market capitalization, the market-to-book ratio, and many others.
- Other assumptions, such as the absence of transaction costs, taxes, and bankruptcy costs, do not hold in reality and should not be ignored when making decisions and valuations.
- The stock market, which is often dominated by short-term commitments, does not appear to be a suitable benchmark for longer-term investments in companies and also for value-based management.
- Since the future is unknown, valuation practice mostly uses past values of stock returns. This not only raises the fundamental question of whether the comparison is meaningful. It is also unclear which comparable portfolios should be used over which time periods.

In practice, such criticism is often ignored and an adapted version of CAPM is used. It is based on historical data instead of expected returns and assumes that historical returns reflect the company-specific risk in the future. The implication for ERM is that risks are mostly underestimated when using this sort of CAPM. The approach presented in the following section seems to be more appropriate.

2.8.2 *Alternative Approaches to Estimating Risk-Adjusted Returns*

While the Capital Asset Pricing Model (CAPM) provides a theoretical framework for understanding risk and return, it has limitations in its practical application, particularly for non-public companies or specific investment projects. Alternative approaches have been developed to estimate risk-adjusted returns using internal company data and forecasts. These methods aim to provide a more tailored assessment of risk and return for decision-making purposes.

Two general approaches to estimating risk-adjusted returns are particularly relevant in the context of enterprise risk management (ERM) (Gleißner, 2022):

Earnings Volatility Approach

This method focuses on the variability of expected earnings as a measure of risk. It assumes that the volatility of a company's or project's earnings is a key indicator of its risk profile. The basic premise is that higher earnings volatility implies higher risk, which should be reflected in higher required returns.

Key aspects of this approach include the following:

a. Estimation of expected earnings: This involves forecasting future earnings based on historical data, market trends, and company-specific factors.
b. Calculation of earnings volatility: This can be done using statistical measures such as standard deviation or coefficient of variation.
c. Risk adjustment: The expected return is adjusted based on the level of earnings volatility, typically by adding a risk premium that increases with volatility.

The risk-adjusted return (*R*) could be expressed as (Gleißner & Ernst, 2023):

$$R = Rf + \lambda^* \, SD(E)/E(E) \tag{2.15}$$

with
Rf is the risk-free rate
λ is a factor representing the market price of risk
SD(*E*) is the standard deviation of earnings
E(*E*) is the expected value of earnings

This approach has the advantage of being relatively straightforward to implement and interpret. However, it assumes that all deviations from expected earnings, both positive and negative, contribute equally to risk, which may not always be the case.

Potential Loss and Capital Requirement Approach

This approach concentrates on the downside risk, particularly the potential for losses that could threaten a company's financial stability. It considers the amount of capital required to cover potential losses, often referred to as economic capital. This method aligns closely with risk management practices, as it directly addresses the question of how much capital a company needs to withstand adverse scenarios.

Key components of this approach include the following:

a. Estimation of potential losses: This involves modeling various scenarios that could lead to financial losses.
b. Determination of capital requirements: Based on the potential loss scenarios, the amount of capital needed to maintain financial stability is calculated.
c. Risk-adjusted return calculation: The required return is adjusted based on the capital requirements, with higher capital requirements leading to higher required returns.

Yet, this approach requires usually more advanced risk management methods, like **Monte Carlo simulation** to estimate the amount of capital required to cover potential losses. We discuss this in Chap. 5.5.

This approach has the advantage of focusing directly on downside risk, which is often of primary concern in risk management. But as we said, it can be more complex to implement and may require sophisticated modeling techniques.

Both approaches share some common elements:

- They rely on company-specific data and forecasts rather than market-based information.

- They attempt to quantify risk in a way that is meaningful for internal decision-making.
- They can be adapted to various types of companies and projects, including those not traded on public markets.

In the context of ERM, these alternative approaches offer several advantages: first, they allow for a more nuanced understanding of company-specific risks; second, they can be integrated with existing risk assessment and management processes; third, they provide a basis for linking risk considerations directly to strategic decision-making; and finally, they can be tailored to reflect the specific risk factors most relevant to a particular company or industry.

However, these methods also have limitations: They rely heavily on the quality of internal data and forecasts, which can be subject to biases or errors. They may not fully capture external market perceptions of risk, which can be important for publicly traded companies, and the complexity of these models can make them challenging to communicate to stakeholders who may not have a strong financial or risk management background.

In practice, many companies use a combination of CAPM and these alternative approaches to get a more comprehensive view of risk-adjusted returns. The choice of method often depends on the specific decision-making context, the available data, and the company's overall risk management framework.

It's important to note that while these approaches provide valuable insights for decision-making under risk, they should not be used in isolation. They should be part of a broader decision-making process that considers both quantitative and qualitative factors and aligns with the company's overall strategy and risk appetite.

In later chapters, we will explore these methods in more detail, including specific calculation techniques, practical implementation challenges, and their application in various ERM contexts. For now, understanding the basic principles and trade-offs of these alternative approaches provides a foundation for more advanced discussions of risk-adjusted decision-making in ERM.

2.8.3 Incorporating Risk into Decision-Making

Once we have estimated the risk associated with a decision or investment, the next step is to incorporate this risk assessment into the decision-making process. This section introduces key concepts that allow us to adjust our decision criteria to account for risk.

Concept of Risk-Adjusted Discount Rates

Risk-adjusted discount rates are a fundamental tool for incorporating risk into financial decision-making. The basic idea is to adjust the discount rate used in present value calculations to reflect the level of risk associated with future cash flows.

In general, the risk-adjusted discount rate (r) can be expressed as:

$$r = rf + rp \tag{2.16}$$

where

rf is the risk-free rate

rp is the risk premium

The risk-free rate represents the time value of money, while the risk premium compensates for the uncertainty of future cash flows. Higher risk is reflected in a higher-risk premium, which leads to a higher discount rate. This higher discount rate reduces the present value of future cash flows, reflecting the principle that riskier cash flows are worth less to risk-averse decision-makers.

Introduction to Risk Premiums and Certainty Equivalents

Risk premiums and certainty equivalents are two related concepts that help us quantify the impact of risk on decision-making.

1. **Risk Premium**: This is the additional return an investor expects to receive for taking on additional risk. It's the *rp* in the risk-adjusted discount rate formula above. The risk premium can be thought of as the "price of risk"—how much additional return is required to compensate for a given level of risk.
2. **Certainty Equivalent**: This is the guaranteed amount that a decision-maker would consider equally desirable to a risky prospect. It's typically less than the expected value of the risky prospect for a risk-averse decision-maker. The difference between the expected value and the certainty equivalent is another way to quantify the risk premium.

Mathematically, if CE is the certainty equivalent and $E(X)$ is the expected value of a risky prospect, it follows:

$$CE = E(X) - RP \tag{2.17}$$

where RP is the risk premium.

Applying these Concepts in Decision-Making under Risk

These concepts can be applied in various ways to support decision-making under risk:

1. **Project Evaluation**: When evaluating investment projects, using risk-adjusted discount rates in net present value (NPV) calculations ensures that riskier projects are held to a higher standard. This helps prevent the selection of projects that may have high expected returns but excessive risk.
2. **Comparison of Alternatives**: Certainty equivalents can be used to compare options with different risk profiles. By converting each option to its certainty equivalent, decision-makers can make apples-to-apples comparisons.
3. **Risk-Return Trade-offs**: By explicitly quantifying risk premiums, decision-makers can assess whether the additional return offered by a riskier option is sufficient compensation for the additional risk.

4. **Setting Hurdle Rates**: Organizations can use risk-adjusted discount rates to set appropriate hurdle rates for different types of investments or business units, ensuring that each is evaluated against a benchmark that reflects its specific risk profile.
5. **Portfolio Decisions**: When making decisions about a portfolio of projects or investments, these concepts can help in achieving the desired overall risk-return profile.

It's important to note that while these quantitative tools are valuable, they should be used in conjunction with qualitative assessments and sound judgment. The process of estimating risk premiums and determining appropriate discount rates involves both art and science, requiring a deep understanding of the specific context and potential future scenarios. Moreover, these concepts should be applied consistently within an organization's overall ERM framework. They provide a way to translate high-level risk assessments and risk appetite statements into concrete decision criteria, helping to ensure that day-to-day decisions align with the organization's overall risk strategy.

In the following chapters, we will delve deeper into practical methods for estimating risk premiums and applying these concepts in various business contexts. We will also explore how these ideas can be integrated with other risk management tools and processes to support comprehensive, risk-informed decision-making.

2.8.4 Implications for Enterprise Risk Management

The concepts of risk-adjusted returns and their incorporation into decision-making processes have significant implications for enterprise risk management (ERM). This section explores how these ideas inform risk management decisions and briefly touches on their connection to value-based management.

How Understanding Risk-Adjusted Returns Informs Risk Management Decisions

1. **Risk Quantification**: The methods for estimating risk-adjusted returns provide a quantitative framework for assessing and comparing risks across different parts of an organization. This allows risk managers to prioritize risks more effectively and allocate resources to risk mitigation efforts where they will have the greatest impact.
2. **Risk Appetite Alignment**: By translating risks into financial terms through risk-adjusted returns, organizations can more easily align their risk-taking activities with their stated risk appetite. For instance, a company might set limits on investments or projects based on their risk-adjusted returns, ensuring that the overall risk profile remains within acceptable bounds.
3. **Performance Evaluation**: Risk-adjusted performance measures allow for fairer comparisons between business units or investment strategies that operate under

different risk conditions. This can lead to more balanced incentive structures that discourage excessive risk-taking and reward effective risk management.

4. **Strategic Decision-Making**: Understanding risk-adjusted returns enables more informed strategic decisions. For example, when considering expansion into new markets or product lines, decision-makers can weigh the potential returns against the associated risks in a structured manner.
5. **Capital Allocation**: Risk-adjusted return metrics can guide more efficient allocation of capital within an organization. By directing resources to areas that offer the best risk-adjusted returns, companies can optimize their overall risk-return profile.
6. **Risk Transfer Decisions**: When evaluating risk transfer options (such as insurance or hedging), the concept of risk-adjusted returns provides a framework for assessing whether the cost of transfer is justified by the reduction in risk.
7. **Scenario Planning and Stress Testing**: The methods used to estimate risk-adjusted returns often involve modeling various scenarios. This aligns well with scenario planning and stress testing exercises in ERM, providing a consistent approach to assessing the impact of potential future events.

Link Between Risk Assessment and Value-Based Management

The concepts of risk-adjusted returns create a natural bridge between risk management and value-based management (see Chap. 10). This link is crucial for integrating risk considerations into overall business strategy and decision-making. While we will explore this connection in greater depth in later chapters, it's worth noting a few key points:

1. **Value Creation**: Both ERM and value-based management ultimately aim to increase the long-term value of the organization. Risk-adjusted return metrics provide a common language for discussing how risk management activities contribute to value creation.
2. **Holistic Decision-Making**: By incorporating risk adjustments into return calculations, organizations can make more holistic decisions that consider both the potential upside and downside of various options. This aligns with the principles of value-based management, which emphasizes long-term value creation over short-term gains.
3. **Shareholder Communication**: Risk-adjusted performance measures can help in communicating the company's risk management efforts and their impact on value to shareholders and other stakeholders.
4. **Strategic ERM**: The integration of risk assessment and value-based management supports a more strategic approach to risk management, moving beyond compliance and loss prevention to viewing ERM as a value driver.
5. **Resource Allocation**: Both disciplines inform how resources should be allocated within an organization. Risk-adjusted return metrics can help ensure that this allocation optimizes value creation while keeping risks within acceptable limits.

In conclusion, the concepts of risk-adjusted returns and their application in decision-making processes are fundamental to modern ERM practices. They provide a quantitative basis for integrating risk considerations into strategic planning, operational decisions, and performance management. As we delve deeper into ERM practices in subsequent chapters, we will continue to build on these foundational ideas, exploring how they can be applied in various contexts and combined with other risk management tools and techniques to support comprehensive, value-driven risk management.

2.9 Summary

- Theories and models play a crucial role in Enterprise Risk Management by providing frameworks to structure and simplify complex risk scenarios. They help in understanding, quantifying, and managing risks effectively. However, it's important to recognize that models often contain necessary simplifications and should be adapted to specific contexts to remain relevant and effective.
- Expected utility theory forms the basis for understanding how individuals make decisions under risk. This theory explains that people base their choices not on monetary value alone, but on the expected utility derived from outcomes, which can vary significantly based on personal risk preferences. Concepts such as risk aversion, risk neutrality, and risk appetite are central to this understanding.
- Various approaches to probability—axiomatic, classical, statistical, and subjective—are fundamental in risk assessment. Bayes' theorem is particularly important as it allows for updating risk assessments based on new information, providing a dynamic approach to risk management.
- Portfolio theory demonstrates how constructing a diversified portfolio can help manage and mitigate risks. By spreading investments across various assets, the impact of individual investment risks can be significantly reduced, achieving a balance between risk and return. This principle can be extended beyond financial investments to various business operations.
- The Capital Asset Pricing Model (CAPM) provides a framework for understanding the relationship between risk and return. However, it has limitations in practical applications. Alternative approaches to estimating risk-adjusted returns, such as earnings volatility and potential loss methods, offer more tailored risk assessments for ERM, particularly for non-public companies or specific projects.
- Concepts such as risk-adjusted discount rates, risk premiums, and certainty equivalents are key to incorporating risk considerations into decision-making processes. These tools allow for more informed project evaluations, comparisons between alternatives with different risk profiles, and setting appropriate hurdle rates for investments.
- Understanding risk-adjusted returns has significant implications for ERM, including improved risk quantification, better alignment with organizational risk appetite, and more informed strategic decision-making. Moreover, there's a crucial link between risk assessment and value-based management in ERM, supporting a

holistic and strategic approach to risk management that goes beyond compliance to drive long-term value creation.

2.10 Exercises and Questions

1. What insights does new institutional economics provide for organizational problems? What are the implications for ERM?
2. Compare and contrast risk aversion and risk neutrality. How do these concepts affect decision-making in ERM? Provide an example for each.
3. Discuss the role of Bayes' theorem in updating risk assessments. Provide a detailed example of how it might be applied in a business context, such as updating the probability of a project's success based on new market information.
4. Explain the principal-agent problem and its implications for corporate governance and ERM. How can organizations design incentive structures to align the interests of managers (agents) with those of shareholders (principals) in the context of risk management?
5. Describe the fundamental principles of portfolio theory. How does diversification help in managing risks? Provide an example of how a company might apply these principles to its business operations or investment strategy.
6. What are the limitations of common risk models discussed in the chapter? How can these limitations be addressed in practice? Discuss potential solutions for at least three limitations.
7. How do frequentist and subjective probability differ? In what situations might each approach be more appropriate for risk assessment in ERM?
8. Explain how learning from experience occurs in the sense of Bayes' theorem. Provide a step-by-step example of how a risk manager might update their beliefs about a particular risk based on new data.
9. Critically analyze the main features of the CAPM and the criticisms against it. How do these criticisms impact its applicability in ERM?
10. Discuss possible reasons for the widespread use of the practitioner CAPM despite its limitations. What alternatives might be more suitable for ERM purposes?
11. Compare the risk discount method and the risk premium method in terms of determination effort, flexibility, and transparency of assumptions and calculations. Which method would you recommend for a medium-sized manufacturing company, and why?
12. A project has an expected cash flow of US\$10 million. The scope of risk is expressed by the standard deviation of the cash flow and is US\$3 million. What is the certainty equivalent used to evaluate the project if $\lambda = 0.3$ is used as a measure of risk aversion? Should one invest in the project under these conditions if an investment of US\$9.5 million would be required? Show your calculations and explain your reasoning.

13. Explain how the concepts of risk-adjusted returns can be applied to improve strategic decision-making in a multinational corporation. Provide a specific example.
14. How does the integration of risk assessment and value-based management support a more strategic approach to ERM? Provide examples of how this integration might influence decision-making at different levels of an organization.

References

Anderson, L. R., Mellor, J. (2009). Are risk preferences stable? Comparing an experimental Measure with a validated survey-based measure. *Journal of Risk and Uncertainty, 39*(2), 137–160.

Baddeley, M. (2019). *Behavioural economics and finance*. Routledge, Taylor & Francis Group.

Bamberg, G., Coenenberg, A. G., & Krapp, M. (2019). *Betriebswirtschaftliche Entscheidungslehre* (16th ed.). Verlag Franz Vahlen.

Bellemare, C., & Shearer, B. S. (2006). Sorting, incentives and risk preferences: Evidence from a field experiment; IZA Discussion Papers, No. 2227, July 2006, IZA Bonn.

Bickel, J. E. (2006). Some determinants of corporate risk aversion. *Decision Analysis, 3*, 233–251. https://doi.org/10.1287/deca.1060.0080

Chopra, V. K., & Ziemba, W. T. (2012). The effect of errors in means, variances, and covariances on optimal portfolio choice. In L. C. Maclean & W. T. Ziemba (Eds.), *Handbook of the fundamentals of financial decision making* (Vol. 4, pp. 365–373). World Scientific. https://doi.org/10.1142/9789814417358_0021

Damodaran, A. (2008). *Strategic risk taking: A framework for risk management*. Wharton School Pub.

de Paola, M. (2013). The determinants of risk aversion: The role of intergenerational transmission. *German Economic Review, 14*, 214–234. https://doi.org/10.1111/j.1468-0475.2011.00561.x

Dempsey, M. (2013). The CAPM: A case of elegance is for tailors? *Abacus, 49*, 82–87.

Eisenführ, F., & Weber, M. (2010). *Rationales Entscheiden* (5th ed.). Springer.

Francis, J. C., & Kim, D. (2013). *Modern portfolio theory: Foundations, analysis, and new developments + website. Wiley finance series*. Wiley.

Friedman, D., Isaac, R. M., James, D., & Sunder, S. (2017). *Risky curves: On the empirical failure of expected utility*. Routledge.

Gigerenzer, G. (2008). *Rationality for mortals: Risk and rules of thumb. Evolution and cognition*. Oxford University Press.

Gleißner, W. (2014). Wahrscheinlichkeiten, Bayes Theorem und statistische Analysen: Was ist dran an "Never change a winning team!". *Controller Magazin, 39*, 68–74.

Gleißner, W. (2022). *Grundlagen des Risikomanagements: Handbuch für ein Management unter Unsicherheit* (Management competence) (4th ed.). Verlag Franz Vahlen.

Gleißner, W., & Ernst, D. (2023). The simulation-based valuation of companies and their strategies: Classification, methodology and case study. *The European Business Valuation Magazine (EBVM), 2*, 4–16.

Günther, T., Detzner, M. (2009). Risikoverhalten von managern — ergebnisse empirischer controllingforschung. *CFO aktuell, 24*(Juni), 124–129.

Günther, T., Detzner, M. (2012). Sind manager und controller risikoscheu? ergebnisse einer empirischen untersuchung. *Controlling, 24*(4/5), 247–254.

Harris, C., & Wu, C. (2014). Using tri-reference point theory to evaluate risk attitude and the effects of financial incentives in a gamified crowdsourcing task. *Journal of Business Economics, 84*, 281–302. https://doi.org/10.1007/s11573-014-0718-4

Hartog, J., Ferrer-i-Carbonell, A., & Jonker, N. (2002). Linking measured risk aversion to individual characteristics. *Kyklos, 55*, 3–26. https://doi.org/10.1111/1467-6435.00175

Holt, C. A., & Laury, S. K. (2002). Risk aversion and incentive effects. *American Economic Review, 92*(5), 1644–1655.

Holmstrom, B. (1982). Moral hazard in teams. *The Bell Journal of Economics, 13*, 324–340.

Hubbard, D. W. (2009). *The failure of risk management: Why it's broken and how to fix it*. Wiley.

Hubbard, D. (2014). *How to measure anything: Finding the value of "intangibles" in business* (3rd ed.). Wiley.

Jankensgård, H. (2019). A theory of enterprise risk management. *Corporate Governance: The International Journal of Business in Society, 19*, 565–579.

Jensen, M. C., & Meckling, W. H. (1976). Theory of the firm: Managerial behavior, agency costs and ownership structure. *Journal of Financial Economics, 3*, 305–360.

Jensen, M. C., & Smith, J. C. W. (2000). The theory of corporate finance: A historical overview. *SSRN Journal*. https://doi.org/10.2139/ssrn.244161

Jerger, J. (1992). Das St.-Petersburg-Paradoxon. *WiSt - Wirtschaftswissenschaftliches Studium*, 407–410.

Jorion, P. (1992). Portfolio optimization in practice. *Financial Analysts Journal, 48*, 68–74. https://doi.org/10.2469/faj.v48.n1.68

Judge, T. A., & Cable, D. M. (2004). The effect of physical height on workplace success and income: Preliminary test of a theoretical model. *The Journal of Applied Psychology, 89*, 428–441. https://doi.org/10.1037/0021-9010.89.3.428

Jungermann, H., Pfister, H.-R., & Fischer, K. (2005). *Die Psychologie der Entscheidung: Eine Einführung* (2nd ed.). Elsevier, Spektrum, Akad.-Verl.

Klein, R., & Scholl, A. (2012). *Planung und Entscheidung: Konzepte, Modelle und Methoden einer modernen betriebswirtschaftlichen Entscheidungsanalyse* (Vahlens Handbücher der Wirtschafts- und Sozialwissenschaften) (2nd ed.). Franz Vahlen.

Kräkel, M. (2015). *Organisation und management*. Mohr Siebeck, Tübingen. https://doi.org/10.1628/978-3-16-153976-3.

Lambert, B. (2018). *A student's guide to Bayesian statistics*. Sage.

Laux, H., Gillenkirch, R. M., & Schenk-Mathes, H. Y. (2018). *Entscheidungstheorie* (10th ed.). Springer.

Lindley, D. V. (2014). *Understanding uncertainty. Wiley series in probability and statistics*. Wiley.

Makridakis, S. G., Hogarth, R. M., & Gaba, A. (2009). *Dance with chance: Making luck work for you*. Oneworld.

Mascalet, D., Colombier, N., Denant-Boemont, L., Lohéac, Y. (2009). Group and individual risk preferences: A Lottery-choice experiment with self-employed and salaried workers. *Journal of Economic Behavior & Organization, 70*, 470–484.

Michaud, R. O. (1989). The Markowitz optimization enigma: Is 'optimized' optimal? *Financial Analysts Journal, 45*, 31–42. https://doi.org/10.2469/faj.v45.n1.31

Mishra, S. (2014). Decision-making under risk: Integrating perspectives from biology, economics, and psychology. *Personality and Social Psychology Review, 18*, 280–307. https://doi.org/10.1177/1088868314530517

Page, S. E. (2018). *The model thinker: What you need to know to make data work for you*. Basic Books.

Pennings, J. M. E., & Smidts, A. (2000). Assessing the construct validity of risk attitude. *Management Science, 46*(10), 1337–1348.

Rodrik, D. (2016). *Economics rules: The rights and wrongs of the dismal science*. W. W. Norton.

Rossi, M. (2016). The capital asset pricing model: A critical literature review. *Global Business and Economics Review, 18*, 604–617.

Rudas, T. (2004). *Probability theory: A primer. Quantitative applications in the social sciences* (Vol. 142). Sage.

Sapre, N. (2021). *Munich personal RePEc archive revisiting the expected utility theory and the consumption CAPM*. Working paper, LMU.

Savage, S. L. (2012). *The flaw of averages: Why we underestimate risk in the face of uncertainty*. Wiley.

Schoemaker, P. J. H. (1982). The expected utility model: Its variants, purposes, evidence and limitations. *Journal of Economic Literature, 20*, 529–563.

Siegel, L. B. (2010). GUEST EDITORIAL: Black Swan or Black Turkey? The state of economic knowledge and the crash of 2007–2009. *Financial Analysts Journal, 66*, 6–10.

Simon, H. A. (1990). Invariants of human behavior. *Annual Review of Psychology, 41*, 1–19.

Slovic, P. (2010). *The feeling of risk: New perspectives on risk perception*. Earthscan risk in society series.

Spremann, K. (2010). *Finance* (4th ed.). IMF. https://doi.org/10.1524/9783486720266

Stigler, S. M. (1975). Studies in the history of probability and statistics. XXXOV.: Napoleonic statistics: The work of Laplace. *Biometrica, 62*, 503–517.

Tirole, J. (2019). *Economics for the common good*. Princeton University Press.

Tushman, M. L., & Nadler, D. A. (1978). Information processing as an integrating concept in organizational design. *Academy of Management Review, 3*, 613–624. https://doi.org/10.2307/257550

Vanini, U. (2016). Risikoneigung und Unternehmenssteuerung–Ergebnisse empirischer Studien. In L. Nadig & U. Egle (Eds.), *CARF Luzern 2016 Konferenzband* (pp. 319–362). Verlag IFZ.

Whetten, D. A. (1989). What constitutes a theoretical contribution? *Academy of Management Review, 14*, 490–495. https://doi.org/10.2307/258554

Zhou, S. (2005). Auf dem falschen Dampfer?: Anwendung des Bayes-Theorems zur Risiko-Abschätzung in der strategischen Unternehmensplanung. *RISKNEWS*, 71–74.

Chapter 3
Heuristics and Biases in Enterprise Risk Management

Abstract This chapter explores the pivotal role of heuristics and biases in ERM. It provides an in-depth examination of how cognitive shortcuts or heuristics, while beneficial for quick decision-making, can also introduce significant biases that potentially skew judgment and lead to suboptimal outcomes. The chapter delves into various types of biases, including motivational, cognitive, and group-specific, elucidating how they influence decisions in business environments. One key focus of the chapter is prospect theory, which articulates how individuals evaluate potential losses and gains from a specific reference point, thereby impacting their risk assessments and decisions. This theory is illustrated through practical examples demonstrating its application in real-world business decisions. Additionally, the chapter discusses strategies to mitigate the adverse effects of these biases, emphasizing the importance of structured decision-making processes, continuous education on cognitive biases, and a risk-aware culture within organizations. Through this comprehensive analysis, the chapter aims to equip business administration students with the necessary tools and understanding to apply psychological insights effectively in ERM and beyond, fostering better decision-making practices in their professional careers.

Keywords Biases · Heuristics · Prospect theory · Risk sensitivity

Questions

- What are the fundamental concepts of heuristics and biases, and how can these cognitive shortcuts facilitate efficient decision-making while also leading to systematic errors that affect business outcomes?
- How does prospect theory explain decision-making under risk, particularly in terms of reference points, loss aversion, and the diminishing sensitivity to gains and losses?
- What are the various types of biases, including motivational, cognitive, and group-specific ones, and how do these biases influence individual and collective decision-making within organizations?

Supplementary Information The online version contains supplementary material available at https://doi.org/10.1007/978-3-031-86425-4_3.

R. Rieg et al., *Enterprise Risk Management*, Springer Texts in Business and Economics, https://doi.org/10.1007/978-3-031-86425-4_3

- What strategies can be employed to mitigate the negative effects of cognitive biases in enterprise risk management (ERM), focusing on implementing structured decision-making processes, promoting bias awareness, and fostering a risk-aware culture?
- How can the theoretical concepts of heuristics, biases, and prospect theory be applied to real-world business scenarios to enhance the ability to make informed and rational decisions in complex, uncertain environments?

3.1 Introduction to Real-World Decision-Making and Heuristics

People make numerous decisions every day, many of which occur quickly and unconsciously. While this approach generally serves us well in daily life, it can become problematic when the stakes are high or when decision-making processes are influenced in ways that lead to suboptimal outcomes. This is particularly relevant in organizational contexts and enterprise risk management (ERM) decisions, as these are ultimately made by individuals rather than by the organization itself (Slovic, 2000).

The way humans make decisions is often based on **heuristics**. Heuristics in decision-making are mental shortcuts or rules of thumb that simplify complex problem-solving and decision processes. They allow individuals to make efficient decisions with minimal cognitive effort, particularly in uncertain and ambiguous situations. Heuristics enable rapid judgments by focusing on salient information while ignoring less relevant data.

While heuristics can be beneficial for streamlining decision-making, they often introduce biases that can skew judgments and lead to suboptimal outcomes. Motivational biases, such as wishful thinking, occur when emotions influence perceptions. For example, an entrepreneur might overestimate a venture's success probability due to personal attachment and optimism, ignoring realistic assessments of market challenges. **Cognitive biases** such as the availability heuristic create errors in processing and recalling information. This is evident when individuals judge the frequency of events based on how easily examples come to mind, potentially leading to misjudgments about the likelihood of recent but rare events. Finally, **group-specific biases** such as groupthink emerge within collective decision-making processes. These biases arise from the desire for harmony and conformity in a group and result in irrational or dysfunctional decision-making outcomes. For instance, a board may underestimate risks in a business strategy to preserve group consensus if members suppress dissenting viewpoints. Each of these biases underscores the limitations of heuristics, highlighting their potential to misdirect judgments across various contexts.

The following sections apply real-world heuristic decision-making for risky decisions. The discussion begins with prospect theory, a concept frequently cited in the literature to describe real-world risk-related decisions. After that, the discussion turns to discussion biases in greater detail before concluding with an examination of the circumstances under which heuristics may or may not be effective.

3.2 Prospect Theory

Prospect theory, developed by Kahneman and Tversky (1979) provides a descriptive model of how decisions are made under conditions of risk. The theory posits that individuals engage in a two-phase process when making decisions: the **editing phase**, in which options are simplified and narrowed down, is followed by the evaluation phase, in which decisions are assessed based on a reference point (Kahneman & Tversky, 1979).

During the **evaluation phase**, any change in the value of an option, such as a stock price, is perceived relative to this reference point, classifying outcomes as gains or losses. This distinction is crucial because prospect theory introduces the concept of loss aversion, where losses are perceived as more impactful than an equivalent gain. Moreover, the theory suggests a diminishing marginal utility, indicating that the utility function curves downward as gains increase, illustrating a saturation effect where further gains contribute less to overall utility (Laux et al., 2018).

Several key insights emerge from **prospect theory**:

1. Decision-makers are highly influenced by their reference points and generally prefer avoiding losses to acquiring equivalent gains.
2. Individuals exhibit risk-averse behavior toward gains and risk-seeking behavior toward losses. This often leads to realizing gains too prematurely and potentially exacerbating their losses (Wenig, 2009).
3. People react more intensely to changes in utility rather than to absolute levels of utility (Baddeley, 2019).

To illustrate prospect theory in action, consider a company deciding whether to invest in a new manufacturing system that could significantly improve productivity but carries risks of malfunctions and unexpected maintenance costs. The decision-makers in this scenario are likely influenced by their current productivity and costs, which serve as reference points for evaluating the new investment. Due to loss aversion, they might be more focused on the potential for malfunctions and additional costs, considering these risks as losses relative to their current stable operations. This can lead them to overemphasize the downside risk and underweight the potential gains.

Decision-makers often react more intensely to changes in utility rather than absolute levels. This concept suggests that if the company's perceived change from the current system to the new one is positive, they might be inclined to invest. However, if even a small perceived change is negative, they might resist due to the strong emotional impact of loss, regardless of the absolute benefits of the investment.

While prospect theory has been instrumental in modeling decision-making behavior in experimental settings, its applicability in real-world scenarios can be limited. Real-life decision environments often involve complex alternatives with uncertain outcomes and probabilities that are not clearly defined. Such environments necessitate repeated decisions or collaborative decision-making, complicating the predictability of actions based on prospect theory alone (Bromiley, 2010).

It is crucial to recognize that while prospect theory offers a descriptive framework, it does not inherently explain why individuals make riskier decisions when confronting potential losses, nor does it delve into the detailed processes of decision-making under risk. Prospect theory underscores the **importance of heuristics** in understanding real-life decisions and refining decision-making strategies where necessary (Gigerenzer, 2008).

Case Study: Implementing Prospect Theory in Business Decisions at TechnoWidget Inc.

Background: TechnoWidget Inc., a leading technology firm specializing in consumer electronics, is facing critical strategic decisions regarding its expansion into emerging markets. The management team, while experienced, has encountered challenges in aligning its decision-making processes with the inherent risks and uncertainties of new market territories.

Objective of this case: To apply prospect theory to improve decision-making processes by addressing biases and enhancing the understanding of gains versus losses, thereby optimizing strategic investments and minimizing irrational risk-taking behavior.

Application of Prospect Theory:

Scenario Development: TechnoWidget Inc. plans to launch a new line of smart home devices in Southeast Asia. Two investment options are considered:

- Option A: Moderate investment of US$5 million with a 75% probability of moderate success and a 25% probability of failure.
- Option B: High investment of US$15 million with a 50% chance of high returns and a 50% chance of significant losses.

Editing Phase (Prospect Theory): The CFO of TechnoWidget Inc. simplifies these options based on their potential impacts on the company's financial health, considering the current economic stability as the reference point. Loss aversion is identified where the fear of losing US$15 million in Option B heavily weighs against its potential higher returns.

Evaluation Phase: Reference Dependence—The reference point is set at the company's current market position without the new product line. Any gain is viewed relative to this position, and any loss is a deviation below it.

- Loss aversion: The decision-makers are disproportionately avoiding Option B—not due to its inherent risk/reward profile, but because the potential losses loom larger than the equivalent gains.
- Diminishing sensitivity: As the investment amount increases, the sensitivity to further gains decreases, making the high returns from Option B less appealing compared to the secure, though lower, returns of Option A.

Decision Outcome: The management decides to proceed with Option A, the moderate investment approach. This decision is influenced by their higher sensitivity to losses and a desire to maintain stability in new markets without risking significant capital.

Review and Analysis: After the decision, the company conducts a review session in which they analyze the impact of cognitive biases on their decision-making process. They recognize that while prospect theory helped them understand their aversion to losses, it also highlighted the need for a balanced approach that does not overly penalize high-potential opportunities.

Strategic Adjustments: To counteract loss aversion in future decisions, TechnoWidget Inc. has implemented a structured decision-making framework incorporating scenario analysis and risk assessment tools to quantify and mitigate biases.

3.3 Types of Cognitive Biases Relevant to ERM

3.3.1 Heuristics and Biases

The seminal paper by Kahneman and Tversky (1979) initiated a vast body of research into biases inherent in heuristics-based decision-making. In response, a counter-movement has emerged that argues that heuristics are often beneficial and, in many cases, equally or more effective than analytical decision-making (Gigerenzer et al., 2011).

To understand why such **biases** occur, two aspects must be considered. First, humans have limited cognitive abilities and capacities as well as unstable and possibly inconsistent preferences. Thus, they cannot always perform mathematical operations and optimizations consistently, at least not in their head and under time constraints (Simon, 1990; Klein, 2002; Mishra, 2014). Human cognition comprises three interlinked cognitive systems:

- Perception (the automatic reception of sensory impressions and stimuli).
- Intuition.
- Logical thinking or reasoning (cognitive processing).

Many factors influence all three cognitive systems. For example, a person's judgment and decision-making process is based on an internal model of the environment that determines what information the person considers relevant to a particular decision. In addition, due to a person's limited information processing capacity, the search for and processing of information can be expected to generate cognitive load, to which the individual responds with appropriate heuristics.

3.3.2 Motivational Biases

In Sect. 3.1, three categories of biases were introduced: motivational, cognitive, and group-specific (Montibeller & von Winterfeldt, 2015; following Hunziker, 2021).

Motivational biases occur when the desirability or undesirability of events, consequences, outcomes, or choices influences judgments. Examples include the following:

- **Affect heuristic**: People show an emotional reaction in a given situation without further deliberating. If an option is valued as positive, people immediately decide in favor of it, although it might not be in their best interest. Managers might pursue a merger or acquisition based solely on the perceived prestige and growth opportunities associated with the expansion, without adequately considering the integration challenges, cultural mismatches, or financial strain such moves often entail.
- **Confirmation bias:** A well-known distortion that enables people to select information that fits their existing opinion and to disregard conflicting evidence. Like the previous example, the managers would seek information supporting their merger decision while ignoring or downplaying conflicting evidence about the firm's weak performance or customer complaints to be acquired.
- **Optimism (wishful thinking)**: Individuals tend to overestimate their capabilities, status, and performance, assuming they are above average. Despite the knowledge that many mergers fail, the managers in the example above believe their decision will be successful due to their superior expertise and anticipated good fortune.

3.3.3 Cognitive Biases

Cognitive biases in decision-making refer to systematic errors in thinking that affect how individuals process and interpret information, often leading them away from the logical or rational decision paths typically expected in formal decision-making frameworks. Some typical cognitive biases are (for these and more, see Hunziker, 2021) as follows:

- **Anchoring bias**: This bias occurs when individuals rely heavily on an initial piece of information (the "anchor") to make subsequent judgments. For instance, in risk assessment, if a risk manager is initially told that a project's estimated loss is US$100,000, they might anchor to this figure and underestimate the potential for greater losses, even when presented with contrary evidence.
- **Availability bias**: This refers to the tendency to base decisions on information that is most readily available, often influenced by recent events or prominent examples. In ERM, if a recent cyber-attack has been widely reported, a risk manager might overestimate the likelihood of similar attacks, potentially overlooking other critical risks like physical security breaches.
- **Status quo bias**: This bias leads an individual to prefer things to remain as they are, resisting change even when it may be beneficial. In an enterprise, a risk manager may continue using outdated risk assessment methods simply because

that is how it has always been done, missing opportunities to adopt more effective methods.

- **Framing**: The framing bias occurs when the way information is presented influences decision-making. For example, in risk communication, if a risk manager frames an issue in terms of potential gains ("you could save 10% on insurance") instead of potential losses ("you could lose 10% of your assets without insurance"), it could affect stakeholders' risk perceptions and decisions.
- **Hindsight bias**: This is the inclination to see past events as having been more predictable than they actually were. In ERM, a common example is after a major incident, where stakeholders claim they "knew it would happen," potentially leading to misplaced confidence in future predictions and overlooking the inherent uncertainty in risk assessment.
- **Overconfidence**: This bias reflects a tendency to overestimate one's abilities or knowledge. A risk manager might assume they understand all the potential risks in a project without thoroughly analyzing data or consulting experts, leading to significant oversights and increased risk exposure.

3.3.4 Group-Specific Biases

Group-specific biases focus on decision-making involving several individuals. Although such group decision-making can have many advantages, distorted decision-making can also arise, and groups are prone to several biases (also Sunstein & Hastie, 2015), including the following:

- **Authority bias** occurs when individuals in a group give undue weight to the opinions or decisions of an authority figure, often overlooking other valuable input. For example, in a risk management meeting, the CEO suggests implementing a new risk mitigation strategy; because the CEO holds authority, team members might agree without critically evaluating the risks and benefits of the strategy. This bias can lead to missed opportunities for alternative approaches and increase the risk of a flawed decision.
- **Conformity bias** is the tendency of individuals to align their beliefs or behavior with those of the group, even when they disagree with the prevailing opinion. For instance, an ERM team discusses whether to adopt a new cybersecurity protocol. If the majority of the group supports it, other members may conform to avoid conflict or criticism, despite having reservations about its effectiveness. This bias can prevent important dissenting opinions from surfacing, potentially leading to security vulnerabilities.
- **Groupthink** occurs when the desire for group harmony or consensus leads to irrational or dysfunctional decision-making, with members suppressing dissenting viewpoints to maintain cohesion. Suppose a company's risk management team is tasked with developing a disaster recovery plan. The team leader suggests a plan that most members internally doubt. However, the team members suppress

their concerns to maintain group cohesion and avoid conflict, leading to an inadequate recovery plan that might fail during an actual disaster.

- **Hidden profile bias** refers to a situation in which certain information critical to decision-making is known by some group members but not shared with the entire group, leading to decisions based on incomplete data. As an example, consider a risk assessment meeting; one team member knows about a recent security breach at a competitor's facility but does not mention it because it seems irrelevant to the current topic. Unaware of this information, the rest of the group decides to focus on other risks, leading to a potentially significant oversight in their risk management strategy.
- **Social loafing** occurs when individuals in a group put in less effort because they believe others will pick up the slack, leading to reduced productivity and accountability. Suppose a risk management team is assigned to create a risk mitigation report. As it is a group task, some members contribute minimally and assume that others will do the work. This leads to an incomplete or low-quality report, increasing the risk of overlooking critical issues and compromising the company's risk management approach.

Case Study: Rapid Decision-Making in Crisis Management at SafeHarbor Insurance

Background: SafeHarbor Insurance, a mid-sized insurance company, faces frequent decisions related to assessing and responding to claims, especially during natural disasters like hurricanes or floods. The Claims Department often relies on heuristics, or mental shortcuts, to expedite decision-making during these high-pressure situations.

Situation: In the wake of Hurricane Delta, SafeHarbor Insurance was overwhelmed with claims. The Claims Department needed to quickly assess the validity and extent of damages to allocate resources efficiently. The team utilized two common heuristics: the availability heuristic and the affect heuristic.

Application of Heuristics

1. **Availability Heuristic.**
    - **Application:** Claims adjusters often judge the likelihood of claim veracity based on similar past claims that are easily recalled.
    - **Benefits:** This heuristic allowed adjusters to swiftly process routine claims by comparing them to common cases from recent storms, thus speeding up the approval process.
    - **Problems:** However, this led to biases where less common but severe claims were underestimated or misjudged because they did not match the typical examples in the adjusters' memories.
2. **Affect Heuristic.**
    - **Application:** Adjusters made quick judgments about the claims based on their emotional reactions to the claimants' stories or circumstances.

- **Benefits:** This enabled faster decision-making when claimants' distress was evident, prompting quicker payouts and support to those visibly in dire situations.
- **Problems:** Decisions influenced by emotions led to inconsistent claim evaluations, where similar cases received different treatments based on the adjusters' emotional responses rather than the facts of the case.

Outcome: Following the hurricane, SafeHarbor Insurance faced criticism for inconsistent claim resolutions and a lack of fairness in the process. This led to customer dissatisfaction and tarnished the company's reputation for reliability and fairness in handling claims.

3.4 Evolutionary and Adaptive Perspectives on Heuristics and Biases

Drawing on insights from Mishra (2014), we can understand heuristics and biases from an evolutionary and adaptive perspective. This approach suggests that many of our decision-making tendencies, including those that appear irrational, may have evolved to solve recurrent problems in our ancestral environments.

Risk-sensitivity theory, as described by Mishra (2014), posits that decision-makers should elevate risk acceptance in situations of need, when low-risk options are unlikely to meet one's needs. This theory provides a functional explanation for why individuals might engage in what appears to be irrational risk-taking behavior.

From this perspective, many cognitive biases can be reframed as adaptive responses to environmental challenges. For example, loss aversion may reflect the greater importance of avoiding critical losses (e.g., starvation) compared to acquiring equivalent gains in ancestral environments.

The evolutionary approach also helps explain why certain biases persist despite their potential for negative outcomes in modern contexts. These biases may have been adaptive in ancestral environments but may not always serve us well in the complex, rapidly changing business world. Understanding this evolutionary context can help risk managers develop more effective strategies for mitigating these biases in organizational settings.

3.5 The Positive Role of Heuristics in Decision-Making

While much attention has been given to the potential pitfalls of heuristic-based decision-making, researchers like Gerd Gigerenzer have highlighted the positive aspects of heuristics. The **fast and frugal heuristics approach** takes a more positive view of human decision-making and action.

Due to the complexity of the environment, the time pressure of many decisions, and their limited information processing capacities, people use heuristics to arrive at sufficiently good evaluations of complex alternatives and thus to make decisions efficiently (i.e., with a justifiable cognitive and temporal effort). Judgment heuristics are rules of thumb based on intuition. They simplify the process of judgment and decision-making but carry the risk of systematic biases, as illustrated by the many biases that can occur.

This shows that in reality, individuals often make decisions emotionally and intuitively (Haidt, 2001) and follow other decision-makers without deeper reflection (Sloman & Fernbach, 2017). However, decision-makers do not act completely irrationally, and the abovementioned biases do not always lead to wrong decisions (Arkes et al., 2016; Gigerenzer, 2018). Studies show that some of these biases are no longer biases when the decision context is taken into account (Gigerenzer, 2008). Overoptimism and a limited overestimation of the chances of success can be productive in some cases, such as if one wants to motivate people to get involved and try the seemingly impossible.

The **fast and frugal heuristics** approach takes a more positive view of human decision-making and action (Gigerenzer, 2008). It assumes that people mostly apply simple rules of thumb (heuristics) that are based on only a few pieces of information (frugal). However, to function appropriately, they must fit the context of the decision (so-called ecological rationality). Heuristics are neither better nor worse than complex algorithms per se but are only suitable for certain types of situations. For example, the portfolio theory by Markowitz for the risk diversification of investments works very well if all the necessary information about investments, their returns, and return fluctuations is available. In real investment cases, however, such information is often lacking, and a simple 1/N rule that recommends simply allocating an investment amount can beat more complex methods like Markowitz's portfolio theory (Gigerenzer, 2008). The "1/N rule" in portfolio formation is particularly helpful because Markowitz portfolio formation has many problems due to restrictive assumptions.

In sum, for heuristics to function appropriately, they must fit the context of the decision. This concept, known as **ecological rationality**, suggests that the effectiveness of a heuristic depends on its match with the environment in which it's applied.

3.6 Risk Sensitivity Theory and Its Application to Organizational Decision-Making

Risk-sensitivity theory, as outlined by Mishra (2014), provides a framework for understanding how and when individuals and organizations might engage in risky behavior. This theory suggests that risk-taking is an adaptive response to situations of high need, where safe options are unlikely to meet necessary goals.

In organizational contexts, this theory can help explain why companies might engage in risky ventures when facing financial difficulties or competitive pressures. It also provides insights into how different levels of resource availability might influence risk-taking behavior across an organization.

Risk-sensitivity theory posits that need motivates decision-making behavior. Need describes disparity between a present state and a goal or desired state. If the disparity between a goal state and a present state increases, individuals should make decisions that seek to bridge that disparity. This is the fundamental mechanism underlying risk-sensitivity theory: if an organism cannot meet its needs with a safe, low-risk behavioral option, then it should choose a high-risk behavioral option that at least offers a chance of meeting that need.

In the context of ERM, risk-sensitivity theory can provide valuable insights into how organizations might respond to different levels of financial pressure, competitive threats, or resource scarcity. For instance, a company facing a significant market share loss might be more inclined to take risks in product development or marketing strategies compared to a company in a stable market position.

3.7 Balancing Heuristics and Analytical Approaches in ERM

Effective ERM requires a balance between heuristic-based decision-making and more formal analytical approaches. Heuristics can be particularly useful in situations requiring quick decisions, when dealing with incomplete information, or in highly complex environments where formal analysis may be impractical. For example:

- In crisis management scenarios where rapid response is crucial.
- When assessing novel risks with limited historical data.
- Under dynamic market conditions where formal models may lag behind real-time changes.

For **critical decisions** with far-reaching consequences, when dealing with novel situations, or when there's ample time for thorough analysis, more formal and analytical approaches to risk assessment and decision-making may be preferable. This might include:

- Major strategic decisions like mergers and acquisitions.
- Long-term capital investment projects.
- Comprehensive enterprise-wide risk assessments.

The key is to recognize when each approach is most appropriate and to develop organizational capabilities that can leverage both heuristic and analytical decision-making processes effectively. Several strategies to mitigate biases and improve ERM practices can be derived from the discussion above.

1. Develop structured decision-making processes that explicitly account for common biases. This might involve using decision trees, scenario analysis, or other formal decision-making frameworks that force consideration of multiple perspectives and outcomes.
2. Promote ongoing education about cognitive biases and their impacts on decision-making. This can include training programs that teach employees to recognize and mitigate their own biases, as well as those of others.
3. Encourage diverse perspectives and challenge groupthink through techniques like devil's advocacy or red team exercises. These approaches can help surface potential risks or issues that might otherwise be overlooked due to conformity or authority biases.
4. Implement formal risk assessment tools and quantitative analysis methods to complement intuitive judgments. This can include statistical modeling, Monte Carlo simulations, or other quantitative risk assessment techniques.
5. Regularly review and update risk management practices based on outcomes and new insights. This involves creating feedback loops that allow for learning from both successes and failures in risk management.
6. Foster a risk-aware culture that values critical thinking and open discussion of potential risks. This cultural shift can help counteract biases like optimism bias or the tendency to suppress dissenting opinions.
7. Use checklists and standardized procedures to ensure consistent risk assessment across the organization. This can help mitigate the impact of individual biases and ensure that key risk factors are not overlooked.
8. Implement a system of checks and balances, where important risk-related decisions are reviewed by multiple parties or committees. This can help counteract individual biases and provide a more balanced perspective on potential risks.
9. Leverage technology and data analytics to provide objective insights that can complement human judgment. This can include using artificial intelligence or machine learning algorithms to identify patterns or risks that might not be apparent to human observers.
10. Encourage a long-term perspective in decision-making to counteract biases that favor short-term gains over long-term stability. This might involve adjusting incentive structures or implementing longer-term performance metrics.

The role of ERM is to sensitize decision-makers to the risk of misjudgments, to identify typical biases in decision-making, to design the context so that such biases do not occur, and to improve the quality of decision-making through training and tools. Some of the possible measures and tools discussed in this textbook are as follows:

- Establishment of a risk culture (Chap. 7).
- Development of a common understanding of risk within the organization (Chap. 1).
- Risk assessment by managers based, for example, on a checklist.

- Critical discussion of risk assessment by independent people to compensate for personal misjudgments.
- Consistent statistical evaluation of loss data and use of benchmarks.
- Easy-to-understand mathematical or simulation-based procedures for assessing the combined effect of multiple individual risks.
- Understandable documentation of the processes used and assumptions made.

3.8 Summary

- Understanding heuristics and biases is crucial for effective ERM. This involves recognizing both the pitfalls and benefits of heuristic-based decision-making. By doing so, organizations can develop more robust and adaptive risk management strategies.
- Integrating multiple theoretical perspectives enhances decision-making in uncertain environments. Insights from prospect theory, risk-sensitivity theory, and fast and frugal heuristics provide a nuanced understanding of how individuals and groups make decisions. This knowledge can inform the design of risk management processes, training programs, and organizational cultures.
- An evolutionary perspective on decision-making biases provides valuable insights. What may appear as irrational behavior often has adaptive roots. This understanding can help risk managers develop more effective strategies that work with, rather than against, natural human decision-making tendencies.
- Formal analytical tools remain important in mitigating biases. These tools serve as a check on intuitive judgments and help ensure that important risks are not overlooked due to cognitive shortcuts. They are particularly crucial in modern business environments where biases can lead to suboptimal outcomes.
- The balance between heuristic and analytical approaches should be dynamic. Organizations need to adapt their approach to the specific context and nature of the risks being managed. While fast and frugal heuristics may be invaluable in rapidly changing environments or crises, detailed analytical approaches are necessary for long-term strategic decisions or complex risk scenarios.
- Successful ERM requires a holistic approach that leverages both heuristics and formal methods. This involves using the efficiency of heuristics while guarding against their potential biases, supplemented by formal analytical methods where appropriate. Such an approach enhances an organization's ability to navigate complex risk landscapes.
- The ongoing challenge for risk managers and leaders is to create systems and cultures that effectively blend intuitive and analytical decision-making. This involves recognizing the value and limitations of each approach. By doing so, organizations can build more resilient, adaptive, and effective ERM capabilities suited to the complexities of the modern business world.

3.9 Exercises and Questions

1. What are heuristics, and how can they be both beneficial and detrimental in the decision-making process within a business environment?
2. Explain the concept of loss aversion as described by prospect theory. How might this influence a manager's decision to invest in a new business venture?
3. Discuss how the availability heuristic might lead to skewed risk assessments in a company's strategic planning. Can you provide an example from recent events or market changes?
4. What are some strategies that businesses can implement to mitigate the negative effects of motivational biases like wishful thinking in their decision-making processes?
5. How does groupthink potentially affect the outcomes of strategic meetings, and what measures can be taken to prevent it in corporate environments?
6. Describe the role of framing in affecting decision outcomes. How can risk managers use positive framing to influence stakeholders' perceptions and decisions regarding risk management strategies?
7. Discuss the implications of the anchoring bias in financial forecasting and budgeting. How can businesses ensure more accurate predictions and estimations?
8. What are some of the cognitive and group-specific biases that can affect decisions in high-stakes business environments like mergers and acquisitions?
9. How might understanding and applying prospect theory benefit a company in managing its enterprise risks more effectively?
10. Examine a recent business decision made by a well-known company. Identify which heuristics and biases might have played a role in that decision-making process, discussing both positive and negative impacts.

References

Arkes, H. R., Gigerenzer, G., & Hertwig, R. (2016). How bad is incoherence? *Decision, 3*, 20–39. https://doi.org/10.1037/dec0000043

Baddeley, M. (2019). *Behavioural economics and finance*. Routledge, Taylor & Francis Group.

Bromiley, P. (2010). Looking at prospect theory. *Strategic Management Journal, 31*, 1357–1370. https://doi.org/10.1002/smj.885

Gigerenzer, G. (2008). *Rationality for mortals: Risk and rules of thumb. Evolution and cognition*. Oxford University Press.

Gigerenzer, G. (2018). The Bias Bias in behavioral economics. *Review of Behavioral Economics, 5*, 303–336. https://doi.org/10.1561/105.00000092

Gigerenzer, G., Hertwig, R., & Pachur, T. (Eds.). (2011). *Heuristics: The foundations of adaptive behavior*. Oxford University Press.

Haidt, J. (2001). The emotional dog and its rational tail: A social intuitionist approach to moral judgment. *Psychological Review, 108*, 814–834. https://doi.org/10.1037/0033-295X.108.4.814

Hunziker, S. (2021). *Enterprise risk management: Modern approaches to balancing risk and reward* (2nd ed.). Springer.

Kahneman, D., & Tversky, A. (1979). Intuitive prediction: Biases and corrective procedures. *TIMS Studies in Management Science, 12*, 313–327.

Klein, G. (2002). The fiction of optimization. In G. Gigerenzer & R. Selten (Eds.), *Bounded rationality: The adaptive toolbox* (1st ed., pp. 103–121). MIT Press.

Laux, H., Gillenkirch, R. M., & Schenk-Mathes, H. Y. (2018). *Entscheidungstheorie* (10th ed.). Springer.

Mishra, S. (2014). Decision-making under risk: Integrating perspectives from biology, economics, and psychology. *Personality and Social Psychology Review, 18*, 280–307. https://doi.org/10.1177/1088868314530517

Montibeller, G., & von Winterfeldt, D. (2015). Cognitive and motivational biases in decision and risk analysis. *Risk Analysis, 35*, 1230–1251. https://doi.org/10.1111/risa.12360

Simon, H. A. (1990). Invariants of human behavior. *Annual Review of Psychology, 41*, 1–19.

Sloman, S., & Fernbach, P. (2017). *The knowledge illusion: Why we never think alone*. Riverhead Books.

Slovic, P. (2000). *The perception of risk: Risk*. Society and Policy Series.

Sunstein, C. R., & Hastie, R. (2015). *Wiser: Getting beyond groupthink to make groups smarter*. Harvard Business Review Press.

Wenig, C. (2009). Die Prospect-Theorie. In M. Schwaiger & A. Meyer (Eds.), *Theorien und Methoden der Betriebswirtschaft: Handbuch für Wissenschaftler und Studierende* (pp. 193–206). Franz Vahlen.

Chapter 4
Methods of Decision-Making Under Risk

Abstract Most managerial decisions are made under uncertainty about the decisions of other agents as well as about future events. This chapter outlines and explains several methods for dealing with such decisions under risk. All the methods described assume knowledge or at least some expectations about future events and decisions of other agents with some probability. However, this assumption is controversial, and some proponents argue that in a world of "radical uncertainty," other ways of making decisions may be more appropriate.

Keywords Decision-making · Decision tree · Discount rate · Net present value · Radical uncertainty · Real options · Scenario analysis

Questions

- How does understanding the net present value (NPV) and the impact of managerial decisions on shareholder wealth highlight the importance of the time value of money and risk associated with future cash flows?
- How does scenario analysis address NPV's shortcomings by illustrating multiple future scenarios, and how does it help understand uncertainty and risk in decision-making?
- How do decision trees help map and evaluate multi-stage decisions with varying outcomes based on future events?
- What is the concept of real options, and how does it provide flexibility and strategic adaptability in investment decisions?
- What strategies can be used to cope with radical uncertainty, and how do robust decision-making, flexibility, adaptive strategies, pre-mortem analysis, and diversification help manage unpredictability in the business environment?

Supplementary Information The online version contains supplementary material available at https://doi.org/10.1007/978-3-031-86425-4_4.

R. Rieg et al., *Enterprise Risk Management*, Springer Texts in Business and Economics, https://doi.org/10.1007/978-3-031-86425-4_4

4.1 Net Present Value of Future Risks and Opportunities

In a business context, managerial decisions affect shareholders' wealth. Typically, we assume that decisions are beneficial if they increase shareholder wealth. The expected change in shareholder wealth from a decision is essentially the same as the discounted value of future cash flows. Discounting future cash flows takes into account the **time value of money** and the inherent risk of the future. The time value of money describes the idea that an amount of money that is available today is worth more than the same nominal value in the future as it can be used immediately for consumption, earn interest, or be spent otherwise. In contrast, a future sum of money is not yet available and is always subject to unforeseen events that may reduce or eliminate its value.

The **discount rate** represents the opportunity cost of a decision and is related to its riskiness. Opportunity cost refers to the idea that investors can choose between alternative investment opportunities and therefore define a threshold for each alternative. A project is only worth investing in when it offers an expected return equal to or greater than alternative projects. This threshold will increase if the project under consideration is expected to be riskier than others. In general, the higher the risk of a project, the higher the expected return must be to compensate for the additional risk taken (see Chap. 2). The cash flows to be discounted include the projected capital expenditures, future decision-induced changes in operating expenses, and changes in net working capital.

The basic concept of calculating the discounted value of future cash flows goes under different names, like net present value (NPV) or capital budgeting, but they all mean the same thing. The formula reads:

$$NPV = -I_0 + \sum_{t=1}^{T} \frac{CF_t}{(1+r)^t} \quad (4.1)$$

where NPV is net present value, I_0 is initial capital expenditure, CF_t is cash flows per period t, and r is expected discount rate of return.

Example: Calculation of NPV

Assume an investment project with an initial investment of US$1000 and a required return or discount rate of 10%. The expected cash flows for 3 years are listed below. The NPV is the sum of all present values with base year zero or, in other words, the value at the beginning of the investment period. The NPV is US$73.63, meaning that the investment is expected to give a return above the required rate of return of 10% (Table 4.1).

Table 4.1 Example NPV calculation

	Discount rate	10%			
Net present value	Years (t)	0	1	2	3
a	Initial investment	$ – 1000.00			
b	Expected cash flows		$ 400.00	$ 450.00	$ 450.00
c	Discount factors	1	0.9091	0.8264	0.7513
a or b*c	Present value	$ – 1000.00	$ 363.64	$ 371.90	$ 338.09
	Net present value:	$ 73.63			
Discount factor = 1/ $(1 + r)^t$					

4.2 Scenario Analysis

One drawback of the NPV method is that it does not explicitly integrate and illustrate the uncertainty of future cash flows, given that it uses only one value for the cash flow per period and one value for the expected return. The same holds for corporate planning and decision-making in general. They rely on one plan or one value for an expected outcome (Behringer & Gleißner, 2018). However, the dynamics of corporate environment and the complexity of many businesses make it increasingly difficult to determine only one exact value. Assuming a range of possible future values and outcomes seems more appropriate. The range of potential outcomes can be seen as a measure of risk. Scenario analysis attempts to illustrate such risk-related ranges by incorporating multiple scenarios, each one a different materialization of future developments.

In other words, a **scenario** describes a possible future constellation of relevant environmental and corporate factors and their interrelationships. In that sense, it is not a forecast but an image of a possible future. Theoretically, combining environmental and corporate developments can create an unlimited number of scenarios (Postma & Liebl, 2005). Practitioners often apply three scenarios (Damodaran, 2008):

- The **best-case scenario** describes the most favorable of all possible developments.
- The **base, real-case, or trend scenario** describes the most probable development.
- The **worst-case scenario** summarizes the worst of all possible developments.

The range between best case and worst case is called the scenario range. In addition, crash or stress scenarios are sometimes created for extreme risk constellations characterized by abrupt changes, low probability of occurrence, and extreme impact on results.

Table 4.2 Example scenario analysis

Scenario analysis	Discount rate	10%			
Base case	Years (t)	0	1	2	3
	Initial investment	–$1000.00			
	Expected cash flows		$400.00	$450.00	$450.00
	Discount factors	1	0.9091	0.8264	0.7513
	Present value	–$1000.00	$363.64	$371.90	$338.09
	Net present value:	$73.63			
Worst case	Years (t)	0	1	2	3
	Initial investment	–$1000.00			
	Expected cash flows (– 10%)		$360.00	$405.00	$405.00
	Discount factors	1	0.9091	0.8264	0.7513
	Present value	–$1000.00	$327.27	$334.71	$304.28
	Net present value:	–$33.73			
Best case	Years (t)	0	1	2	3
	Initial investment	–$1000.00			
	Expected cash flows (+ 10%)		$440.00	$495.00	$495.00
	Discount factors	1	0.9091	0.8264	0.7513
	Present value	–$1000.00	$400.00	$409.09	$371.90
	Net present value:	$180.99			

Example: Scenario Analysis

Based on the previous example for NPV calculation, we can view the previously defined cash flows as a base case and define two additional scenarios: a worst case with a reduction of cash flows by 10% and a best case with an increase by 10%. The resulting NPVs are now between US$ – 33.73 and US$ + 180.99 (Table 4.2).

Using worst-case, base-case, and best-case scenarios, a transition to a triangular distribution of risk factors and thus the transition to a **Monte Carlo simulation** (MCS) is possible (see for more details in Sect. 8.2.5).

There are several **types of scenarios** (Börjeson et al., 2006):

- **Predictive scenarios**: What will happen based on past trends and/or new events? Examples include trend scenarios based on the extrapolation of past sales and cost trends and a scenario anticipating the impact of losing a major customer.
- **Exploratory scenarios**: What could happen in the event of external events or major new decisions? For example, this type of scenario could be used to explore the impact of a pandemic on sales development or the reorientation of sales from brick-and-mortar to online-only.

- **Normative scenarios:** In what ways can an existing goal be achieved? Such scenarios could identify, for example, alternative lines of business to be used in the event of a pandemic.

Several **shortcomings** of scenario analyses are worth mentioning. First, people tend to underestimate the degree of uncertainty (Bromiley et al., 2015 with further references); hence, they tend to underestimate the scenario range. Second, in complex projects, it is often the case that several interrelated variables are uncertain, making it increasingly difficult to define and calculate scenarios from a practical point of view. Therefore, in more complex application areas, we suggest using a risk model with Monte Carlo simulation (MCS) (see Chaps. 5 and 8).

4.3 Decision Trees

In some cases, risks and opportunities are not simply discrete one-time events; rather, they happen in sequences over time. A typical example is the process of development and testing of a new drug. The new drug must go through various stages and pass several tests before it can be launched on the market. However, while on the market, its success is uncertain and depends on market conditions and competition. A decision may have different effects over time that entail further decisions, and it may also respond to various events that can only be evaluated in advance using probabilities. This leads to a **multi-stage decision** that can be structured and analyzed as a decision tree when combined with uncertain outcomes and events (Damodaran, 2008; Anderson, 2019).

The goal of a decision tree is not only to represent this sequential order but also to assign values to each stage and fork to find the decision **path with the best risk-reward-ratio** or payoff. While a typical scenario analysis also includes events that evolve over time, a decision tree explicitly analyzes the sequence of possible decisions. In this sense, it is more comprehensive and illustrates the willingness to respond to changing situations.

Developing a decision tree requires, first and foremost, a deep understanding of the decision problem and its temporal and sequential structure. In the first step, it is important to distinguish between different **types of nodes**:

- Define a **root node** that represents the beginning of your decision tree for a decision-maker. This root node represents the most important choice, and the goal of decision tree analysis is to evaluate whether an investment at this root node is worthwhile.
- Sequences consist of **event nodes** (circles). These are possible outcomes of uncertain situations, such as high or low demand or passing a drug approval test. For each possible outcome, it is important to determine further possible outcomes and probabilities.
- **Decision nodes** (rectangles) indicate possible choices for decision-makers, such as delaying market entry or investing in a larger facility.

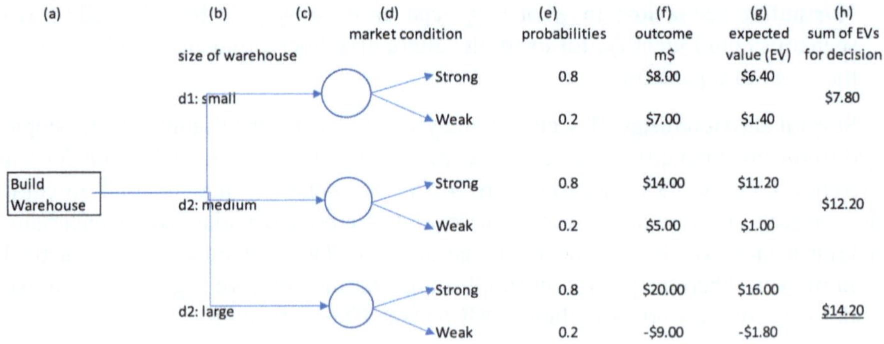

Fig. 4.1 Example decision tree—ACME Retail

- **End nodes** (triangles) are the last step in their respective sequences of event and decision nodes.

Case: Warehouse Construction Decision

ACME Retail Inc. is contemplating building a new logistics warehouse to develop the European market. The size of the warehouse depends strongly on the assumed demand (closely following Anderson et al., 2014). Hence, the optimal decision is one with risks. Since the decision to build the warehouse must be made before the uncertain event evolves, meaning without knowing how the market will react, we develop a decision tree as in Fig. 4.1. The decision can lead to building a small, medium, or large warehouse. The market condition may be strong with high demand or weak with low demand. The management assigns probabilities of 0.8 and 0.2, respectively, to these uncertain events. The possible outcomes (pay-offs) are estimated as in column (f). Multiplying the probabilities with outcomes gives the expected values for each row (g). Adding them up leads to the expected value of the respective decision. For a small warehouse, this gives us 0.8 * US$8 million +0.2 * US$7 million = US$6.4 million + US$1.4 million = US$7.8 million. Performing these steps for each sub-decision leads to d1 = US$7.8 million, d2 = US$12.2 million, and d3 = US$14.2 million. A rational decision-maker would choose the decision with the highest expected value per decision. In this case, that is the decision to build a large warehouse.

The example illustrates the **roll-back method**, which supports optimal decision policy. Starting at the end and working backward toward the root of the tree, a decision-maker stops at each node of every step and chooses the one decision that leads to the highest expected value. In this way, one arrives at the optimal decision policy at the root of the tree.

The management of ACME Retail Inc. may be uncomfortable with this result since the dispersion of possible outcomes for the optimal decision is the largest of all three decision alternatives. So, they consider conducting a market research study. In general, a market research report will not provide "perfect" information or reduce uncertainty to zero, but it will at least provide additional insight and change the

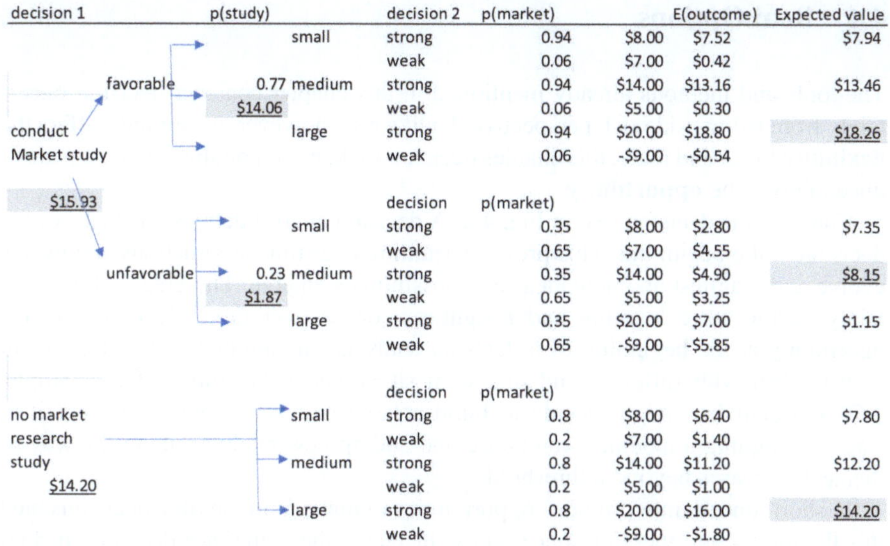

Fig. 4.2 Extended decision tree for ACME Retail Inc.

probabilities of possible market conditions. To keep things simple, the market research report can be favorable, meaning a positive uptick in the probabilities of market conditions, or it can be unfavorable if it provides a gloomier market outlook. With additional information, the decision tree looks different and more complex. The first step is deciding whether to administer a market research study. Also, as mentioned, the probabilities change as a result of a market study, while they stay the same if no market study is done. Figure 4.2 depicts the decision tree and results.

If a favorable market study outcome ($p = 0.77$) is obtained, the best decision is to invest in a large warehouse. Given an unfavorable outcome of the market study ($p = 0.23$), the optimal decision would be a mid-sized warehouse. The expected value of the decision to undertake a market study is, then, 0.77 * US\$18.26 + 0.23 * US\$8.15 = US\$14.06 + US\$1.87 = US\$15.93. This is slightly above the previous result without a market research study, which had a value of US\$14.2.

While simplified, the above example illustrates some of the main challenges of using a decision tree for decision-making. First, it is necessary to structure the sequence of decisions and events appropriately, which means integrating considerable domain knowledge and insight into the decision tree. A decision tree combines experience, formal qualifications, and art. Second, a decision tree requires several predictions for the future, which need to be carefully derived. Third, even with a well-designed decision tree, decision-makers may be reluctant to accept and maintain the recommended decision policy.

This is not to say that decision trees are not useful. They emphasize the idea of sequential decision-making and easily incorporate the uncertainty of decisions and events that opens the black box of many decisions in practice.

4.4 Real Options

The tools and methods already mentioned in this chapter consider decision uncertainty from a downside risk perspective. Unlike risk, however, uncertainty offers the **flexibility** to act and react; this enables decision-makers to capitalize on the upside of uncertainty—the **opportunity**.

Consider the decision tree in Fig. 4.2. A decision analyst defines all stages of the decision at the beginning. This prevents learning over time as situations and events evolve and manifest and new ideas and possibilities emerge. The greater the uncertainty is, the more learning and insight can occur over time. Recognizing this uncertainty at the beginning of a decision analysis can stimulate new ideas about how to deal with different and unknown situations in the future. For example, ACME Retail Inc. might decide to build a large warehouse but implement it in stages, designing a modular warehouse and adding new modules along the way as demand increases beyond a threshold.

In short, uncertainty provides opportunities to make more flexible decisions, and this flexibility, and therefore uncertainty, increases the value of a decision. It does not necessarily decrease it as in NPV or decision trees. The concept to deal with this flexibility is called **real options**. The term is borrowed from financial options, which focus on financial instruments, and applied to real-world situations such as R&D investments.

Real options in decision-making include, for example, (a) delaying or staging an investment, (b) altering its scale (expand or contract), (c) switching to alternatives, or (d) abandoning or exiting an investment. In reality, however, there are more options to be considered (Trigeorgis, 2005; Trigeorgis & Reuer, 2017). As with decision tree analysis, the real options available depend on the specific context, situation, and level of ingenuity of a decision-maker.

The **valuation** of real options is a topic intensively discussed in the literature. Unfortunately, while the basic idea is the same, the results depend heavily on the chosen method (Borison, 2005); also the assumptions of all these methods are often problematic and not easily justifiable. They often use the features of financial options, which would require, for example, tradable security as an asset and certain characteristics of capital markets, such as volatility, that do not exist for real assets and real options (Carmichael et al., 2011). Moreover, the degree of mathematical complexity is often prohibitive.

A first approach is to structure real options as decision options and their consequences as we did in the previous section on scenario analyses. The different options create decision branches that can be valued similarly with NPV. More complex situations need more complex techniques like dynamic programming (Dixit & Pindyck, 1994). The following example illustrates real option valuation in a very simple way.

Table 4.3 Example of real options (I)

	10%		
Risk-adjusted cost of capital	0	1	2
	−$100.00		
		$105.00	
Discount factor	1	0.9091	0.8264
	−$100.00	$95.45	
	−$4.55		

Table 4.4 Example of real options (II)

Split-up & extension	0	1	2
	−$50.00	−$50.00	
		$55.00	$60.00
Net cash flow	−$50.00	$5.00	$60.00
Discount factor	1	0.9091	0.8264
	−$50.00	$4.55	$49.59
	$4.13		
Increase in NPV = option value:			$8.68

Example: Real Option Valuation

We start with a simple investment decision. An investment of US$100 leads to an expected cash flow in the following period of US$105. The investor expects a risk-adjusted return or cost of capital of 10%. The NPV is then as follows (Table 4.3):

Obviously, a negative NPV does not encourage one to invest. Nevertheless, let us assume that there is the possibility of splitting the initial investment up, which would suggest different cash flows for the subsequent two periods (Table 4.4). The same procedure of NPV calculation leads then to US$4.13; the increase in NPV between cases 1 and 2 is the option value of US$8.68. This sounds like a sleight of hand, and one must be careful to base optional plans on solid information and expectations. There might, for example, be additional costs or downsides to splitting up and postponing the investment as well as for expected cash flows beyond the original time horizons.

Real options offer a way to value the benefits of flexibility which is more prevalent in situations with higher uncertainty. Yet, a conclusion would be to seek to invest in highly volatile and uncertain business areas. However, we know from empirical research that the average returns of riskier businesses are lower than those of less riskier ones (Walkshäusl, 2012).

The main difference between the real option approach and scenario analysis is that the former also includes courses of action; the real option approach and decision trees do not seem to differ greatly (Damodaran, 2008).

Real options have several **advantages** for decision-makers in that they give companies the flexibility to delay, expand, contract, or abandon projects based on market conditions and new information. This adaptability is critical in environments characterized by high volatility and uncertainty. By allowing companies to make incremental investments and wait for more information before committing fully, real options represent a reduced risk compared to large upfront expenditures. This phased investment strategy can limit losses on projects that do not perform as expected. The real options approach encourages companies to identify and value future growth opportunities as part of their current investment decisions. This can lead to a more proactive approach to capturing potential market opportunities. Companies that use real options effectively can maintain a competitive advantage by efficiently allocating resources to projects with the highest potential returns, adapting quickly to market changes, and innovating in response to shifts in consumer demands and technology. Real options can help maximize the value of a project by quantifying the value of managerial flexibility in decision-making. This can lead to a more accurate assessment of the true value of the investment.

However, there are several **challenges** for firms using real options which might also explain why not many companies use them (Block, 2007). Valuing real options can be complex and often requires sophisticated financial modelling and a deep understanding of option pricing models. The accuracy of the valuation significantly depends on the assumptions regarding volatility, future returns, and the estimated life of the option. The real options approach is highly sensitive to the input variables used in the models, such as volatility and risk-free rates. Small changes in these inputs can lead to significant variations in the valuation, potentially leading to erroneous strategic decisions. Implementing a real options framework can be resource-intensive, requiring specialized knowledge and tools. Smaller firms might find the cost of developing such capabilities prohibitive. The availability of multiple options and the complexity of the valuation process can sometimes lead to decision-making paralysis, where managers delay decisions excessively in anticipation of more favorable conditions that may never materialize.

4.5 How to Cope with Radical Uncertainty

Radical uncertainty presents a significant challenge in decision-making. In this case, outcomes and their probabilities are not merely unknown but rather unknowable. In such scenarios, traditional tools like net present value (NPV) analysis, decision trees, or real options may not be fully effective due to their reliance on known probabilities and quantifiable risks. Several methods and concepts can help in coping with radical uncertainty. **Robust decision-making** focuses on making choices that are minimally affected by uncertainties. This approach identifies decisions that yield relatively good outcomes across a wide range of scenarios, thus minimizing the downside while capturing potential upsides. It aims to find strategies that are robust under many different future conditions.

Southwest Airlines practices robust decision-making through its business model. By exclusively using Boeing 737 airplanes, Southwest ensures flexibility in crew scheduling and maintenance, while also retaining the ability to switch aircraft between routes as demand changes, thus maintaining operational efficiency under various scenarios.

Flexibility While the traditional real options method uses probabilities, focusing on flexibility allows businesses to adapt their strategy as more information becomes available. This might mean investing in capabilities or technologies that can be pivoted or scaled depending on how uncertainties materialize. This approach treats investments as options that might be exercised in the future when the direction of uncertainty becomes clearer.

Google invests in a wide array of emerging technologies, from artificial intelligence to autonomous vehicles. Each of these investments represents a real option with the flexibility to increase investment as the technology proves viable or to divest if it fails to meet expectations.

Adaptive strategies involve continuous learning and adjustment. Businesses adopting this method remain vigilant to the external environment and internal performance metrics, ready to adapt their strategies based on real-time information and feedback. This iterative process allows businesses to evolve their approaches dynamically as they navigate uncertain terrains.

The fast fashion retailer Zara exemplifies the use of adaptive strategies through its highly responsive supply chain. Zara adapts its clothing designs based on real-time customer preferences and fashion trends, often moving from design to store shelves in just weeks, thereby constantly adapting to the market.

In a **pre-mortem analysis**, stakeholders anticipate the potential failure of a project or strategy and work backward to determine what could lead to such failure. This proactive approach helps in identifying risk factors that are not immediately apparent and prepares the organization to address these risks before they lead to failure (Klein, 2011).

Amazon often conducts pre-mortem sessions before launching major projects. For instance, before launching its Fire Phone, which eventually failed, such a pre-mortem might have highlighted the high competition and the consumer's loyalty to existing brands, potentially prompting a reconsideration of the market entry strategy.

Diversification spreads risk across various assets, products, markets, or investments, reducing dependence on any single source of success or failure. In contexts of radical uncertainty, diversification allows a company to mitigate the impact of adverse events that could not have been predicted.

Berkshire Hathaway, led by Warren Buffett, is a prime example of a diversified company. It holds assets across a broad spectrum of industries, from insurance and utilities to consumer goods and technology. This diversification helps stabilize earnings against sector-specific downturns and unexpected market events.

4.6 Summary

- The chapter began by discussing **net present value (NPV)**, highlighting how managerial decisions impact shareholder wealth through the expected change in shareholder wealth, which is calculated as the discounted value of future cash flows. This section emphasizes the importance of understanding the time value of money and the risk associated with future cash flows.
- **Scenario analysis** is explored as a method to address the shortcomings of NPV by incorporating multiple future scenarios to illustrate the range of possible outcomes. This approach helps in understanding the extent of uncertainty and risk in decision-making.
- **Decision trees** are presented as a tool for mapping out and evaluating decisions that involve sequences of events over time. This method is particularly useful for decisions that require multiple stages and can have varying outcomes based on different future events.
- The chapter introduced the concept of **real options**, which views investment decisions as options and provides the flexibility to adjust decisions based on how actual conditions unfold. This section discusses the value of managerial flexibility and the strategic importance of maintaining the ability to adapt to new information.
- The chapter concludes with strategies on **how to cope with radical uncertainty**, where traditional decision-making tools may be inadequate. It suggests robust decision-making, flexibility, adaptive strategies, pre-mortem analysis, and diversification as methods to handle unpredictability and unknowable factors in the business environment.

4.7 Exercises and Questions

1. How does the net present value method incorporate the time value of money and risk in evaluating investment decisions? Provide an example of how changing the discount rate can affect NPV calculations.
2. Discuss the advantages and limitations of using scenario analysis in business planning. How can scenario analysis help in understanding the risks associated with uncertain future cash flows?
3. Explain how decision trees can be used to improve decision-making in complex projects. What are some of the challenges in constructing and using decision trees effectively?
4. Describe the real options approach to decision-making. What are some examples of real options in business, and how do they provide flexibility in strategic planning?

5. What are the key strategies for coping with radical uncertainty, and how can they be implemented in business practices? Give examples of how these strategies can be applied to different business scenarios.
6. Compare and contrast the effectiveness of scenario analysis, decision trees, and real options in managing risks associated with business decisions. Which method would you recommend for a startup in a high-tech industry and why?

Exercise 1: Ice Cream Investment

Carla Bonafferi has joined a company as a new shareholder and wants to use her capital for a new business field: vegan Italian ice cream. The ice cream is to be sold to retailers in 1 L packs. For production, Carla needs an ice cream machine. There are two models to choose from: ICEMASTER and TURBO-ICE. She first wants to do a net present value calculation under certainty, and she then plans for the investment alternatives by considering uncertainty. The initial data are as follows:

Alternative investments	ICEMASTER	TURBO-ICE	Unit
Expenditures	$650,000	$750,000	[$]
Production capacity p.a.	275,000	300,000	[Liter p.a.]
Maintenance p.a.	$25,000	$10,000	[$ p.a.]
More details for planning these projects			Unit
Rental costs		$48,000	[$ p.a.]
Variable material costs		$1.00	[$ per liter]
Expected sales volume		260,000	[liter p.a.]
Net sales price to retailers		$4.00	[$ per liter]
Number of employees (FTE)		10	[FTE]
Average personnell costs per FTE		$40,000	[$/FTE p.a.]
Planning horizon		4	Years
Cost of capital (required return)		10	[%]
FTE = full time equivalent = full time employed employee			

Prepare an NPV calculation. Which alternative is more profitable?

Exercise 2: Decision Tree

You want to invest in a new product. The development cost is US$100. If the product is marketable, you will sell it, but it is unclear whether the market is favorable for your product. You estimate that there is a 60% probability that the market will be favorable. If it is, you expect a sale price of US$150; if the market is unfavorable, you expect a sales price of US$50. Construct a decision tree and evaluate the net profit.

Exercise 3: SofTech Inc.

SofTech Inc. plans an investment into a new smartphone plant. The CFO Sarah Sunshine uses the following data:

Task 1: Calculate the net present value. Should Sarah decide in favor of investment?

Initial investment	$20,000.00			
Cost of capital	5%			
Years	1	2	3	4
Cash flows per year	$4000.00	$6000.00	$6000.00	$6000.00

The marketing department of SofTech Inc. argues that demand may be stronger after year 1, so Sarah wants to include this uncertainty in her analysis. She assumes that stronger demand will result in a cash flow of US$8000 in each of years 2 through 4 with a probability of 60%. The originally planned cash flows of US$6000 would then have a probability of 40%.

Task 2: Construct a decision tree that considers a stronger or weaker demand with the given probabilities, and calculate the NPV for this decision tree.

Sarah is not happy about this uncertainty because she is risk averse. She has heard about the potential benefits of waiting. What happens to the NPV if Sarah waits until the end of year 1 to decide whether to invest? The initial investment amount will be the same at the end of year 1.

Task 3: Calculate the NPV for the strategy of waiting until the end of year 1, at which point it will be clear whether demand is strong or weak. What is the difference in NPV compared to Task 1? Is there a benefit to waiting for Sarah?

References

Anderson, D. R. (2019). *An introduction to management science: Quantitative approaches to decision making*. Cengage.

Anderson, D. R., Sweeney, D. J., Williams, T. A., & Wisniewski, M. (2014). *An introduction to management science*. Cengage Learning EMEA.

Behringer, S., & Gleißner, W. (2018). Die Unternehmensplanung als Grundlage für die Unternehmensbewertung: Eine empirische Studie. *Die Wirtschaftsprüfung, 71*, 312–319.

Block, S. (2007). Are "real options" actually used in the real world? *The Engineering Economist, 52*, 255–267. https://doi.org/10.1080/00137910701503910

Borison, A. (2005). Real options analysis: Where are the emperor's clothes? *Journal of Applied Corporate Finance, 17*, 17–31. https://doi.org/10.1111/j.1745-6622.2005.00029.x

Börjeson, L., Höjer, M., Dreborg, K.-H., Ekvall, T., & Finnveden, G. (2006). Scenario types and techniques: Towards a user's guide. *Futures, 38*, 723–739. https://doi.org/10.1016/j.futures.2005.12.002

Bromiley, P., McShane, M., Nair, A., & Rustambekov, E. (2015). Enterprise risk management: Review, critique, and research directions. *Long Range Planning, 48*, 265–276. https://doi.org/10.1016/j.lrp.2014.07.005

Carmichael, D. G., Hersh, A. M., & Parasu, P. (2011). Real options estimate using probabilistic present worth analysis. *The Engineering Economist, 56*, 295–320. https://doi.org/10.1080/0013791X.2011.624259

Damodaran, A. (2008). *Strategic risk taking: A framework for risk management*. Wharton School Pub.

Dixit, A. K., & Pindyck, R. S. (1994). *Investment under uncertainty*. Princeton University Press.

Klein, G. (2011). *Streetlights and shadows: Searching for the keys to adaptive decision making* (A Bradford book) (1st ed.). MIT Press.

Postma, T. J., & Liebl, F. (2005). How to improve scenario analysis as a strategic management tool? *Technological Forecasting and Social Change, 72*, 161–173. https://doi.org/10.1016/j.techfore.2003.11.005

Trigeorgis, L. (2005). Making use of real options simple: An overview and applications in flexible/modular decision making. *The Engineering Economist, 50*, 25–53. https://doi.org/10.1080/00137910590917026

Trigeorgis, L., & Reuer, J. J. (2017). Real options theory in strategic management. *Strategic Management Journal, 38*, 42–63. https://doi.org/10.1002/smj.2593

Walkshäusl, C. (2012). Die Volatilitätsanomalie auf dem deutschen Aktienmarkt: Mit weniger Risiko zu einer besseren Performance. *Corporate Finance biz Aufsätze, 3*, 81.

Chapter 5
Risk Quantification, Risk Modelling, Risk Aggregation, and Model Risks

Abstract This chapter introduces the principles and methods of appropriate risk quantification and risk aggregation. In addition to explaining the most important probability distributions for quantification, this chapter discusses typical problems with this task. Within the guidelines of risk quantification, a method is provided that enables the appropriate quantification of different risks. The chapter additionally shows how the overall scope of risk of a company is determined based on corporate planning by means of risk aggregation, especially Monte Carlo simulation.

Keywords Binomial distribution · Monte Carlo simulation (MCS) · Normal distribution · Probability distributions · Risk aggregation · Risk modelling · Risk quantification · Triangular distribution · Uniform distribution

Questions

- How can risks be quantified in enterprise risk management (ERM), and which probability distributions are particularly important for this quantification?
- What are some typical problems encountered in risk quantification, and what strategies can be used to solve them?
- What is a tried-and-tested guideline for risk quantification, and how can it be applied in practice using a case study?
- How does a Monte Carlo simulation (MCS) explain risk aggregation, and how can it be used to determine the overall scope of risk?
- What are the key components of a risk model, and how do they contribute to effective risk management in an enterprise?
- What are the potential risks associated with using models in risk management, and how can these model risks be mitigated?

Supplementary Information The online version contains supplementary material available at https://doi.org/10.1007/978-3-031-86425-4_5.

R. Rieg et al., *Enterprise Risk Management*, Springer Texts in Business and Economics, https://doi.org/10.1007/978-3-031-86425-4_5

5.1 Overview

Economically, the quantification of risks is necessary because only quantified risks can be meaningfully prioritized, aggregated, and assessed in terms of their overall significance for the company (Vose, 2008; McNeil et al., 2015; Blokdyk, 2021). Risks that are not quantified, which means not described in numbers on a cardinal scale, cannot be meaningfully aggregated, so that an overall assessment of the magnitude to which the prospects or the even the existence of a company are threatened by the total risk exposure is not possible. Without risk quantification and risk aggregation which builds on it (Gleißner, 2022), a company's ERM cannot fulfill precisely the two core tasks which are:

- A weighing of expected returns and the associated overall risks as a basis for top management decisions (the measure of risk, in conjunction with a price per unit of risk, the risk premium) can be used to derive a cost of capital rate as a minimum requirement for a risk-adjusted expected return).
- The assessment of the relationship between the total amount of risk and the risk-bearing capacity, in order to avoid a threat to the company's continued existence in the sense of crisis prevention.

From a more formal perspective, one can even argue that a **non-quantification** of risks is not possible at all and that the attempt at a non-quantification inevitably leads to an incorrect quantification. For example, if we look at a company that quantifies, say, five easily quantifiable risks and does not quantify a sixth more difficult to quantify risk, the problem becomes obvious: when assessing the overall magnitude and scope of risk (which should include all six risks), the risk no. 6 is not included. This supposed non-quantification is therefore nothing other than a quantification, namely, a quantification with exactly zero (i.e., either a probability of occurrence of zero or a level of damage of zero).

Planning is always about the future. The fundamental problem of planning is uncertainty about the future. For example, an investment decision using the net present value method requires information about future (free) cash flows. However, these are usually not known with certainty because no one can predict the future exactly. Basically, there are two types of uncertainty (on decisions under uncertainty and risk, see (Gleißner, 2019, 2022 and Chap. 1):

To quantify risks, it makes sense to separate the changes in variables into an expected and an unexpected component, which represents the scope of risk. It is not the extent of change of a variable but the extent of unexpected change of a variable that determines the risk. It is plausible that economic agents form expectations as precisely as possible regarding the future realizations of the variables of interest to them (e.g., interest rates, turnover, or profit) to minimize risks in the sense of unexpected deviations. Rational economic agents will take these expectations into account in their actions. Consequently, an objective quantification of risk depends on the choice of a forecasting method that is as powerful, efficient, and faithful to expectations as possible (Gleißner & Füser, 2000, pp. 933–941; Schosser, 2024).

An unsatisfactory forecast leads to an overestimation of the risk. A forecast model is needed to calculate the expected variable component.

A completely rational expectation formation that would correctly process all available information (Rieg & Gleißner, 2022) is interesting as a thought model, but it can only be expected in reality to a very limited extent. It seems more plausible that in practice only time series analytical procedures (e.g., ARIMA models) will be used. Following the time series analytical approach of Box et al. (2015), a random variable can be X_t as a weighted average of current and q past stochastic shocks μ (MA(q) representation). As an alternative to the MA(q) representation, one can choose a representation as an autoregressive process of order p (AR(p) process) for random variables of a time series. A combination of both approaches is found in ARMA(p,q) models, which can be specified in such a way that the number of parameters (p + q) to be estimated and used for forecasting is minimal.

Accordingly, the changes that cannot be forecasted by means of time series analysis are decisive for the scope of risk. Anything that is predictable is not a risk. According to the previous explanations, the risk of a variable cannot be quantified simply by the standard deviations of the changes in this variable, but rather by the standard deviation of the changes that cannot be predicted (by time series analysis).

5.2 Probability Distributions and Risk Measures

There are many types of probability distributions which are useful in risk modelling. They can be roughly divided into the following (Vose, 2008):

- **Discrete** distributions in which there is a given set of precisely determinable values and their probabilities, for example, the discrete uniform distribution of the values and frequencies of an ideal dice.
- **Continuous** distributions, which can take any value within a defined range of values. For example, sales as a random variable can take any value equal to or greater than zero.
- Discrete distributions have an upper and/or lower **bound**. For example, the number of workplace accidents is always positive, as is sales.
- **Unconstrained** distributions, on the other hand, extend their range of values to infinity. This includes the normal distribution.
- **Parametric** distributions are those for which a mathematical, model-based distribution function exists. We generally assume these in this textbook. A non-parametric distribution could take the form of an empirical frequency distribution, for example, for which no simplifying mathematical function can be specified. Empirical frequency distributions are used, for example, in the context of historical simulation. This allows empirical correlations to be represented very flexibly and often quite simply as random variables.

Continuous distributions are described by a density function *f*(*x*) (probability density function, pdf). The probability that a variable *X* assumes at most the value *a* is then described by the integral of the density function. It is also called the cumulative density function (cdf).

$$p(X \leq a) = \int_{-}^{a} f(x)dx \tag{5.1}$$

A **discrete distribution** is referred to as a probability mass function, which is added up for a certain value *X* to obtain the probability *p* for all $x_i \leq X$:

$$p(x_i \leq X) = \sum\nolimits_{x_i \leq X} f(x_i) \tag{5.2}$$

The **uniform distribution** assigns the same probability to each value within the value range. A discrete uniform distribution contains individual events with identical probability, as is the case with a fair dice, for example. Examples of continuous uniform distributions are the payment defaults of many individuals, similar customers, or cases of damage to a pipeline. The mean value of a uniform distribution is calculated as the minimum and maximum values divided by two.

A **binomial distribution** describes the probability that an event A will occur exactly k times if a Bernoulli experiment is repeated n times. A Bernoulli experiment is characterized by the fact that two events A and B can occur with the probabilities $p(\text{A}) = \text{p}$ and $p(\text{B}) = 1-p$; these do not change, and all repetitions are independent of each other. Classic examples are the coin toss, but also rejects in production. The expected value μ of a binomial distribution is $n * p$; the standard deviation results in $\sigma = \sqrt{n * p * (1-p)}$.

The **triangular distribution** is a very simple discrete or continuous distribution characterized by three values: the minimum value a, the most probable value b, and the maximum value c. It is often used in practice and is very flexible. The mean value of a triangular distribution is $(a + b + c) / 3$.

The **normal distribution** (also known as the Gaussian distribution or bell curve) is particularly important in statistics and risk modelling, not least due to the central limit theorem of statistics. A normal distribution is approximated as the sum of a large number of independent events, each of which makes only an insignificant contribution to the total. For example, quantity deviations from expected sales are approximately normally distributed for a large number of customers with independent purchasing behavior. Other examples are error fluctuations in tests, measurement inaccuracies, and fluctuations in employee performance. The normal distribution has the following properties:

- It is fully described by two parameters: expected value and standard deviation. Distributions with the same parameters are therefore identical.

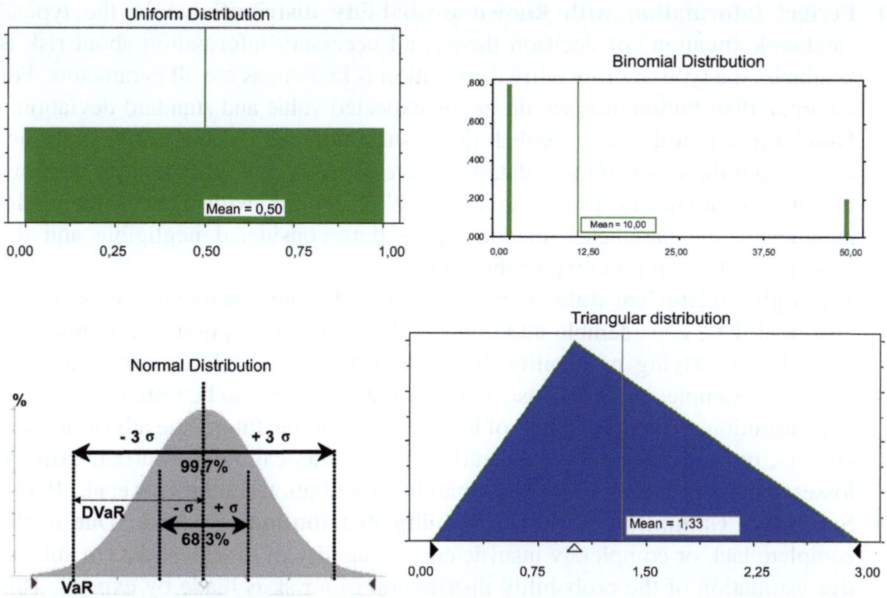

Fig. 5.1 Probability distributions. Source: Gleißner (2022, S. 224)

- Its density function has a bell-shaped curve, hence the name bell curve for the normal distribution.
- The distribution is symmetrical around the expected value.
- The mode, median, and expected value coincide.
- The distribution approaches the x-axis asymptotically to the left and right.

In business practice, several probability distributions are often required in combination to describe a risk appropriately (Fig. 5.1). A binomial distribution can be combined with the triangular distribution, especially in the case of event risks (event-oriented risks). For example, an event risk is described specifically by the probability of occurrence p in conjunction with a triangular distribution. The triangular distribution indicates the impact (damage) that the occurrence of the risk would have. The damage effects are described by the minimum value (a), most probable value (b), and maximum value (c).

5.3 Challenges in Risk Quantification

Risk quantification is the selection of suitable probability distributions to describe a risk and the determination of the parameters required for this. In general, the better the information available, the better the risk quantification. With regard to the level of information in risk quantification, six (idealized) types can be distinguished (following (Gleißner, 2022):

1. **Perfect information with known probability distributions:** In the typical "textbook situation" of decision theory, all necessary information about risk is available; the type of probability distribution is known, as are all parameters. For a normal distribution, this would be the expected value and standard deviation.
2. **Good data quality:** The probability distribution with respect to risk is not known, but there is sufficient data to derive the underlying probability distribution and its parameters. The "estimation risk" (meta-risk) with regard to the model parameters, the parameter uncertainty, is thus considered negligible and the historical data representative of the future.
3. **Incomplete historical data:** Due to the limited representativeness or scope of historical data, considerable additional (subjective) assumptions are required to infer the underlying probability distribution of the risk. Subjective influences arise, for example, in the (pre-)selection of the hypothesis to be tested on the type of distribution, the extrapolation of historical data to the future, the adjustment for outliers, or the additional consideration of hypothetical, non-occurred, extreme losses in the quantification of the probability distribution (Embrechts et al., 1997).
4. **Subjective estimation of the probability distribution of a risk:** Due to the complete lack or completely insufficient availability of historical data, a subjective estimation of the probability distribution of a risk is made by experts. This situation occurs particularly when the current risky situation is considered singular and thus basically no data is available. However, based on theoretical considerations and a high degree of consensus of the estimates of various experts, it is assumed that the subjective estimates are of such high quality that the explicit consideration of an estimation risk (meta-risk) can be dispensed with.
5. **Subjective estimates with estimation risk**: Due to the uniqueness of the risk under consideration and/or considerable differences in expert estimates, there are considerable uncertainties regarding the probability distribution underlying the risk and/or the model parameters (meta-risk), which necessitates the explicit consideration of this second-order risk.
6. **Lack of any robust data and subjective estimates:** In this case, a meaningful application of standard decision-making procedures is not possible, or the risk is to be judged as unacceptable due to this openness of the decision-making situation (implicitly a quantification with infinity).

Even an apparently objective risk quantification has a considerable number of subjective assessments as its basis, which are often overlooked. For instance, the delineation of the data to be evaluated or the temporal scope under consideration is ultimately a subjective determination. There is also considerable latitude for interpretation in the degree of inflation indexation of historical loss data or the treatment of outliers. The selection of hypotheses to be tested, the choice of distribution type, the test procedures employed (e.g., the Kolmogorov-Smirnov test or a chi-square test in the case of normal distribution), and the extent of the examination of the application prerequisites of these tests also leave considerable room for discretion. Consequently, it is not feasible to achieve absolute objectivity in risk quantification.

Therefore, it is more prudent to prioritize intersubjective verifiability and plausibility in risk quantification.

If **historical data** exist, it must be determined whether the available data are sufficient to adequately assess the risk. In principle, the question concerns the amount of data that must be available. However, one must also ask whether more information is always better or whether it is possible that additional information could lead to incorrect conclusions being drawn.

In addition to the statistical analysis of the historical effects of a risk, it is therefore inevitable in risk management practice to derive distributions for risks from **subjective estimates**. The use of subjectively estimated risk information is sensible and permissible, and there are numerous methods to at least significantly reduce possible distortions in the quantification of risks on the basis of expert estimates (Slovic, 2000; Kahneman & Tversky, 1979; Kahneman et al., 2021; Gleißner, 2022).

In the field of risk quantification, the principle of using the most accurate and up-to-date information in the context of the risk analysis and presenting it in a transparent manner is of paramount importance. This also applies when using subjective expert estimates. It is also appropriate to critically question the quality of the risk analysis results and to improve them if necessary. In this context, it is beneficial to be aware of the psychological distortions of risk perception by experts and to implement strategies to counteract these distortions.

Before quantifying a risk, it is necessary to adequately structure the identified risks. To do this, it is necessary to describe a risk precisely in terms of content and to distinguish it from other risks. Risks often have to be restructured (e.g., summarized).

In the first step, it is usually helpful to consider whether individual risks or facets of a risk can simply be summarized. There are some simple and heuristic rules for this, such as (a case example can be found in Gleißner, 2022):

1. Aggregate risks with the same cause: If two or more risks have the same cause, they can be combined into one risk to aggregate the effect (e.g., by adding the damage, namely, the independent individual risks).
2. Aggregate risks with the same effects: If two risks have the same effect, the probabilities of the causes can be aggregated. In the simplest case, this is done by adding the probabilities of occurrence (for independent risks with a small probability of occurrence).

These heuristic rules of thumb already help for the first structuring of risks. It should be noted, however, that it is generally advisable to understand the actual stochastic dependency at the cause-and-effect level of different risks or facets of a risk and then to carry out a (simulation-based) risk aggregation that adequately takes these stochastic dependencies into account. What is always necessary is a deeper understanding of the content and also the causes and effects of all opportunities and dangers (risks) that can trigger deviations from the plan. The basis is the development of a "stochastic model" that adequately describes the existing relationships, such as dependencies or also amplification effects. The risks must be adequately quantified for this.

5.4 Guideline for Risk Quantification: Explained with a Case Study

As an example, this section contains the application of a tried and tested guideline (based on Gleißner, 2022, p. 251 ff.) of audit questions for the quantitative description of risks to an identified (exemplary) risk.

The following describes the risk:

> "Risk: Failure of a manufacturing machine (expected loss EL = US$2 million and probability of occurrence p = 2%)."

In the context of risk quantification, when considering a given individual risk and an aggregation of several individual risks based on it derived using Monte Carlo simulation, the following questions should be addressed:

1. Is the situation at hand an opportunity or a danger (risk)?

Planned future changes that are not due to chance are not a risk.

Application of the Rule in the Case Study
The failure of the production machine is uncertain (and not planned). This is clearly a risk.

2. Is the risk to be quantified clearly described, structured and differentiated from other risks?

Risk descriptions are often open to interpretation to the extent that the scope of the content is unclear and in particular the demarcation from other individual risks of the company is blurred. This can lead to overlaps and double counting, among other issues. In the case of a risk, it is advisable to make clear what clearly belongs to the risk as well as what clearly no longer belongs to the risk but may already fall into the "area" of another risk.

Often one will find that risks have (1) the same causes or (2) the same effects. In these cases, an adequate restructuring of the risks makes sense (Gleißner, 2022, p. 216 ff.).

Application of the Rule in the Case Study
Overall, if no further explanations are available, the risk considered here is somewhat nebulous. Which production machine is involved? Is the risk perhaps part of a comprehensive uncertainty of maintenance costs? A more precise description of the risk is certainly needed here.

3. Which planned value is the reference point for determining possible positive or negative deviations (opportunities and threats)?

Risk always refers to a planned value or state, and a quantitative description of the risks is not possible without knowledge of this reference point.

Application of the Rule in the Case Study
Consultation with corporate planning department is necessary here. An examination of the cost planning for 2024, in particular the item "maintenance costs," shows that nothing has been planned here so far, and no other entry is recognizable in the planning. A correction of the risk quantification is therefore not necessary in this case. If an "expected loss" EL (e.g., in the amount of the expected loss value $EV = EL \times p =$ US\$2 million $\times$ 2% = US\$ 0.04 million) had already been planned, the "pure risk of loss" (hazard) would become a corresponding hazard plus an opportunity (viz., the chance that the loss will not occur with a probability of 98% and impact plus US\$0.04 million).

4. Over what period of time should the potential impact of a risk be considered?

One or five years, for example, should be used consistently.

Application of the Rule in the Case Study
Information on the temporal dimension of the risk is missing. The risk quantification is incomplete if no additional information exists (e.g., in a risk manual). In this case, it is necessary to specify the time period to which the given data refers (e.g., to 1 year or to the entire planned lifetime of the machine).

5. Is one probability distribution sufficient for the quantitative description of a risk, or do we need two?

In practice, one probability distribution is often used to describe the effects of a risk in a planning period (to be specified). A more precise description is sometimes possible if one specifies (1) a probability distribution for the frequency of occurrence of a loss in a period (e.g., the Poisson distribution) and (2) a distribution for the possible effects when the event occurs (uncertain amount of loss).

Application of the Rule in the Case Study
In the case study of the risk, the impression is created that there are only exactly two possibilities here: it occurs within the period under consideration, or it does not. Whether this quantitative description is actually appropriate depends on how many production machines exist. The description is only appropriate if there is exactly one such production machine and it can only fail

(continued)

exactly once within a year. If, for example, n production machines of the same type exist that can fail exactly once within a year, a description of the risk through a Poisson distribution that indicates the frequency of failures within the period under consideration (e.g., 1 year) would make sense. Even if a machine could fail several times a year, a distribution for the frequency would be necessary. In addition, one needs a description of the uncertain amount of damage in the event of a failure (here the specification of a certain amount of damage of US$2 million is already obviously problematic, which will be considered later; see point 7).

6. Is a description of the change of risk over time necessary?

To describe the effects of a risk in one period on the risk of the following period or the existence of "risk factors" (such as currency rates), the use of stochastic processes, which can be understood as a "multi-period probability distribution," should be considered.

Application of the Rule in the Case Study

Understanding the temporal aspect of risk is crucial when working with a multi-year business plan. The risk profile of the manufacturing machine may not remain static over time. Key considerations include potential changes in failure probability and expected loss amounts as the machine ages, as well as replacement scenarios after a failure.

Advanced tools like the Weibull distribution (Vose, 2008) can help model how risk evolves with the machine's age. Regular reassessment of the risk throughout the business plan's duration is advisable. This dynamic approach to risk analysis allows for a more accurate and adaptable risk management strategy, moving beyond a static view to acknowledge the evolving nature of operational risks over time.

7. What probability distribution for the effects of the risk is appropriate in view of the characteristics of the risk?

Many risks cannot be meaningfully described by the method of specifying (1) probability of occurrence and (2) amount of damage, which is common in practice. A suitable probability distribution must be sought (for more on selection principles, see Gleißner, 2022, p. 222 ff.; Wehrspohn & Ernst, 2022).

Application of the Rule in the Case Study

In the response to (5), reference was made to some problems concerning the description of the risk by the chosen probability distribution (binomial distribution). In general, it can be assumed that even in the case of event-oriented risks, the effects (e.g., damages) are uncertain in the event of occurrence. This is also the case in the case study. The quantitative description of the amount of damage by stating the expected amount of damage (US$2 million) is not appropriate. The uncertainty about the amount of damage is not taken into account. It can be useful here, for example, to express the uncertainty of the amount of damage by specifying (a) minimum value, (b) most probable value, and (c) maximum value. In the case study, we now assume $a =$ US$1 million, $b =$ US$2 million, and $c =$ US$9 million, which incidentally leads to an expected loss of EL = US$4 million ($\frac{a+b+c}{3}$). An alternative would be a beta distribution (see Vose, 2008).

8. What is the data basis for estimating the parameters of the selected probability distribution (see 7.)?

If there is sufficient data from the past that is also representative of the future, this provides the data basis for the parameter estimation. The simple principle applies: The best available information in each case should be used for risk quantification—whereby several sources can also be combined.

Application of the Rule in the Case Study

As is so often the case, one finds a (rudimentary) explanation of the content of the risk in the case study, but no explanation of the risk quantification and the underlying data. This is insufficient with regard to the central requirement for transparency. Enquiries with the risk officer often reveal that the only data basis is a subjective expert estimate. In this case, this also seems appropriate (Gleißner, 2019; Holton, 2004) because a manufacturing machine developed specifically for the company is being considered and no sufficient statistical failure data are (yet) available. In the future, the data basis may improve. However, the use of subjective expert estimates is generally not a problem if they are justified in a comprehensible way (and in particular it is shown that the data basis is an expert estimate).

9. Has it been considered that the net risks are decisive for the quantification of risks?

The scope of risk of a company results from the net risks that remain from the company even after taking into account-initiated risk management measures.

Application of the Rule in the Case Study
In the case study, it is necessary to check whether, for example, an insurance company will cover a part of a possible loss. Ultimately, the net risk is always relevant. In the case study, although business interruption insurance exists, the failure under consideration (hopefully) does not lead to a business interruption. There is no specific insurance for the cause of the failure (see 2), which should be more precisely defined. However, this fact should also be mentioned in the quantitative description of the risk.

10. Were possible "extreme Risks" that have never occurred taken into account in the risk quantification?

For the overall risk scope and the early detection of possible crises, very rare extreme risk manifestations in particular must be taken into account (see Gleißner, 2022, p. 127 ff.).

Application of the Rule in the Case Study
With regard to risk, the topic has already been dealt with in Questions 7 and 8. The indication of a quasi-certain amount of damage of EL = 2 million dollars is by no means sufficient. Whether the triangular distribution now proposed—the specification of minimum value, most probable value, and maximum value—appropriately also covers possible "extreme risks" remains open. A discussion of possible loss scenarios concludes that conceivable extreme events with a probability of occurrence of 1% or less have not yet been considered (which is common in subjective expert estimates). In the case study, therefore, it seems sensible to exclude conceivable extreme cases from the usual risk quantification when specifying the range of the triangular distribution. Such extreme cases include situations such as machine failure at a particularly unfavorable time in the year due to a particularly problematic cause, like an explosion. If such an event occurs, it would be necessary to create a separate supplementary "extreme risk" (with a correspondingly low probability and high impact). Such risks are also relevant, as risk management is particularly concerned with the early detection of serious crises with a low probability, referred to as "developments that threaten the existence of the company."

11. How should estimation risks (especially parameter uncertainty) be dealt with in risk quantification?

In principle, the problem with risk quantification is that one cannot assume perfect data availability. In the case of particularly relevant risks, it can make sense to create transparency about the possible extent of misjudgments of the risk. It is important to avoid fictitious inaccuracies.

Application of the Rule in the Case Study
In the case study, meta-risks, such as parameter uncertainty, have not been considered. For example, one does not read any information on the uncertainty of the probability of occurrence p itself. Bandwidths can also be specified for the probability of occurrence p. In the case study, however, the relevance of the risk for the company results in the fact that the significance of this risk with a "medium relevance" appears too low to have to provide for a quantification of parameter uncertainties. Risk quantification without specifying "meta risks" is acceptable.

12. When and how should statistical tests be used to check the quantitative description of a risk (back-testing)?

Data and new findings generally offer the opportunity to check existing risk assessments and improve them if necessary.

Application of the Rule in the Case Study
In this case study, there are no rules on how to proceed with regard to testing and back-testing. The risk owner is given the task to think through suitable regulations to ensure learning from past loss events.

Conclusion: The risk quantification presented at the beginning of the case study is completely inadequate. Many questions remain open. A risk quantification should be transparent, and the transparency and suitability of the risk quantification are also a subject of the risk management audit (e.g., by the internal audit).

5.5 Risk Aggregation and Monte Carlo Simulation (MCS)

5.5.1 Introduction

Risk aggregation is used to determine the overall scope of risk, which can be expressed using suitable indicators like the equity requirement or the probability of a serious crisis. As risks indicate the extent of possible deviations from plans, the basis for risk aggregation is generally planning (project planning or corporate planning). The aggregation of risks described by different probability distributions or stochastic processes with reference to corporate planning is using an analytical formula. In particular, it is not possible to use such a formula to check whether the risk-bearing capacity (equity and liquidity) of a company is sufficient to bear all risks, if possible combination effects are taken into account. In order to assess the overall risk situation on the basis of the analysis of individual risks, a number of procedures are used in companies, whereby a quantitative assessment of the overall scope of risk based on corporate planning is only possible using a Monte Carlo simulation and the other procedures are therefore more of a preparatory and supplementary nature. (Or can be used in special cases, e.g., if all risks are described by normal distributions)

Several procedures for risk aggregation are proposed in the literature (Gleißner, 2022):

- **Scoring models** can be used to aggregate qualitatively assessed risks. However, scoring models allow only a relatively rough aggregation of risks and neglect risk interdependencies. In addition, the calculated total score of all corporate risks cannot be used to monitor the firm's risk-bearing capacity, as this requires a financial valuation of the total risk exposure.
- Alternatively, the **worst case** or the **expected values** of individual risks can be added. Again, both approaches do not consider any risk interdependencies and thus neglect the potential for risk diversification. Overall, a simple addition of individual risks is not reasonable. Instead, the interdependencies between risks should be analyzed by means of a correlation analysis in order to identify and consider potential diversification effects. In addition, only considering worst-case values neglects the probabilities of occurrences of single risks, whereas expected values do not indicate their actual damage potential (see also the example in Hunziker, 2021).
- Normally distributed risks can be aggregated using **analytical methods** such as the variance-covariance approach, taking into account the various correlation coefficients (see Sect. 5.5.2). However, most risks do not follow a normal distribution. Besides, companies often lack the necessary historical data to determine the variances, covariances, and correlations of past times series to estimate such risk parameters. Consequently, this method is only relevant in the financial sector.
- The most suitable method for risk aggregation is the **Monte Carlo simulation.** Here, the impacts of individual risks on the company's relevant target or planned figures, such as profit or cash flow, are simulated. The result is a distribution of the target figure, which can then be evaluated with the known risk measures. Thus, the risk-bearing capacity can be checked for various confidence levels.

It should be noted that the overall scope of risk should always be determined as a result of risk aggregation and the combined effects of risks should be analyzed. In particular, stochastic dependencies between risks must be taken into account, the simplest special case of which is the correlation of risks.

Example: Consideration of Risk Correlations in Risk Aggregation of an Airline
An airline can aggregate its corporate risks using Monte Carlo simulation. The target figure is the deviation from the respective budgeted target. Correlations between individual risks are taken into account. For example, the management assumes a negative correlation between pilot staff turnover and the risk of an economic

downturn, as the market for pilots always collapses abruptly during economic crises. The staff turnover risk assesses the cost of less or additional pilot training and is mapped in the form of a triangular distribution, while the risk of an economic downturn is assumed to be binomially distributed (it occurs or does not occur). An example of a positive correlation is the price change risk for kerosene fuel and the risk of an economic downturn. The central correlations are discussed and fixed by the Executive Board of Austrian Airlines on the basis of empirical analyses and integrated into the corporate risk model by the risk manager.

5.5.2 Analytical Risk Aggregation: The Variance-Covariance Approach

As mentioned, risk aggregation is used to determine the overall scope of risk and the early detection of serious crises, which are usually the result of several risks materializing.

However, as this is only applicable in special cases, where only normally distributed risks are present, risk aggregation using Monte Carlo simulation is the focus of this chapter. It is also shown here how the probability of insolvency of a company (as the basis for a risk-adjusted rating) can be determined directly using Monte Carlo simulation.

The variance-covariance approach is an analytical method for determining the value at risk, an overall risk position made up of various individual risks. The approach is based on the classic assumption in financial theory of normally distributed portfolio returns and normally distributed price changes. The volatilities (standard deviation) of the risk factors are used to determine the value at risk in the individual risk factors and aggregated to the overall risk position via the correlation matrix at the respective risk consolidation level.

The aggregation of financial risks can basically be carried out in two ways, analytically or by simulation. The analytical method requires a distribution assumption. For example, the variance-covariance model is based on a normal distribution. For example, a normal distribution assumption can be made when modelling risk factors on the basis of a random walk.

The variance-covariance approach is simple and quick to implement, but has a frequently criticized disadvantage, as a normal distribution is generally assumed for all risk factors, as mentioned above. It is just as impossible to aggregate risks that follow different distributions as it is to link them to corporate planning. In practice, the variance-covariance model can serve as an initial quick solution, for example, to obtain a rough impression of the current risks. Daily risk monitoring could be carried out using a variance-covariance model, and risk estimates could be checked at certain intervals using more precise but complex and computationally expensive (stochastic) models.

5.5.3 Simulation-Based Risk Aggregation and Monte Carlo Simulation

The objective of risk aggregation is to determine the overall risk position of a company and to determine the relative significance of the individual risks, taking into account stochastic interactions (correlations) between these individual risks (i.e., combination effects are recognized).

Risk aggregation can only be carried out once the effects of the risks have been quantified, taking into account their respective probability of occurrence, their distribution of damage (quantitative impact), and their interactions with each other.

For an ERM system, risk aggregation methods should fulfill several requirements: (a) capture risks described by chosen probability distributions, (b) recognize non-additive (e.g., multiplicative) links and other interdependencies between risks, and (c) relate the results and methods to corporate planning (see Chap. 10).

Only risk simulation (Monte Carlo simulation), which is therefore described in more detail in this section, fulfills the aforementioned requirements. Due to the computing power available today, almost any complex planning model can be processed with the desired accuracy using this risk aggregation method, which can essentially be understood as an analysis of a large representative sample of possible future scenarios for a company.

In risk aggregation, for example, the planning year is "run through" a total of 100.000 times in independent simulation runs of an Excel model, and a characteristic of the P&L statement is calculated in each case. For this purpose, random numbers are generated that obey the probability distributions for the individual risks. These random numbers are used to determine the following:

- The specific characteristics of the corresponding market parameters (e.g., sales prices) for the distribution-oriented risks.
- Whether a specific event-oriented risk became effective within 1 year (of the simulated years) and, if so, what amount of loss occurred.

The realizations of the event-oriented risks calculated in this way and the characteristics of the parameters of distribution-oriented risks are evaluated according to the correlations in a profit and loss account, which ultimately leads to a value for the operating result, profit before tax, and cash flow in each simulation run. The simulation method thus replaces the impossible or very difficult task of analytically aggregating many different probability distributions with a multiple but numerically simple aggregation of specific values of the probability distributions.

Aggregated distributions of these target variables result from the realizations determined in this way for operating profit, profit before tax, and cash flow. The value at risk is then calculated for these target variables in addition to the expected value and the median, particularly as a measure of risk, meaning, for example, it is specified which values of these key figures will not be undercut with a probability of 95%. In this way, the bandwidth of the probable development of the company is

Table 5.1 Illustrating MCS (I)

R_2 \ R_1	−2	−1	0	1	2
−2	−4	−3	−2	−1	0
−1	−3	−2	−1	0	1
0	−2	−1	0	1	2
1	−1	0	1	2	3
2	0	1	2	3	4

determined. Such a simulation is also used to show the main factors influencing this overall risk position.

If they occur frequently enough, random events can be used to answer a wide variety of questions. This idea, which is already very old in science, has gained a new dimension of applicability in the last 20 years with the advance of computers, as it was suddenly possible to generate "random" events with the computer in large numbers and cheaply or, as the experts say, to simulate them. Since the core of such a simulation is the generation of "chance," the name Monte Carlo simulation has become established.

Analytical solutions usually only exist for simple or highly simplified models of reality (and are nevertheless often already very complicated). For most real-world problems, no analytical solutions are available at all, and simulations are the way to go.

The general procedure for carrying out a Monte Carlo simulation can be described in the following phases:

1. Generate the random numbers required for the Monte Carlo simulation.
2. Convert the random numbers into the required distribution.
3. Carry out a step of a Monte Carlo simulation according to the random numbers drawn and the underlying distribution.
4. Repeat steps 1, 2, and 3 until a sufficient number of simulations have been generated to derive stable distributions and statistics.
5. Final evaluation. This includes forming the mean values (distributions) of the measured variables, calculating the value at risk, and determining the statistical errors.

In principle, Monte Carlo simulation can be thought of as a kind of sampling procedure in which, analogous to the procedure used by market researchers in opinion polls, a large, representative sample—in this case of a company's future scenarios—is used to draw conclusions about the population as a whole. The sampling procedure provides a very concrete idea of what the future of the company will look like, taking into account the known risks.

To illustrate this, a simple example of a Monte Carlo simulation is given below. For example, let there be two independent risks R1 and R2, each with a value between −2 and 2. The probability of each discrete value is 20%. The joint effect of the two risks, the total risk R, is in the range from −4 to 4 and is described in the following Table 5.1.

Table 5.2 Illustrating MCS (II)

Value ("damage")	−4	−3	−2	−1	0	1	2	3	4
Frequency	1	2	3	4	5	4	3	2	1
Probability	4%	8%	12%	16%	20%	16%	12%	8%	4%

Table 5.3 Illustrating MCS (III)

Z_i	$0 \le z < 0.2$	$0.2 \le z < 0.4$	$0.4 \le z < 0.6$	$0.6 \le z < 0.8$	$0.8 \le z < 1$
Characterization (value) (R_i)	−2	−1	0	1	2

There are 25 possible scenarios. For example, there is exactly one scenario (combination of R1 and R2) with a loss value for R (= R1 + R2) of −4; but there are five scenarios with a value of 0. A value of 0 for the total risk R is therefore much more likely than a value of −4. The possible values of R with the respective frequencies or probabilities of occurrence are as follows (Table 5.2):

Therefore, the expected value for the total risk is $E(R) = 0$.

In the Monte Carlo simulation, the problem is not solved analytically, but with the help of random numbers. In this case, two random numbers Z1 and Z2 are required for each simulation run, each of which is greater than or equal to 0 and less than or equal to 1. These are used to determine realized values for R1 and R2. To do this, you need to generate a function that assigns a value for a risk to a random number, taking into account the probabilities of occurrence. For the example, such a function is characterized by the following Table 5.3:

If, for example, the random number 0.3584 is drawn for Z1 and 0.8897 for Z2 in a simulation run, R1 has the value −1, and R2 the value 2.

This would have resulted in an overall risk of 1 for R. This procedure is now repeated 1000 times, for example, resulting in 1000 values each for Z1 and Z2 and thus also for R1, R2, and R. From this, for example, the mean value of the 1000 realized values of R can now be determined as an estimator for the actual expected value of R. However, it is also possible to create a histogram for the frequency distributions of the values of the total risk, which thus reflects the estimated probability distribution of R.

A fundamental problem with risk aggregation arises from the fact that the correlations (dependencies) between different risks must always be considered. The relationships between risks are often described using a correlation matrix, but this only captures linear stochastic dependencies. A plausibility check of a developed correlation matrix is possible because it can generally be assumed that risks should be positively correlated if they have common determinant causes. In risk factor models, the dependency of the planning position on exogenous risk factors (e.g., dollar exchange rate) is modelled (which implicitly results in correlations).

While fully correlated risks (correlation = 1) are to be added in the aggregation, the sum of completely uncorrelated risks is calculated according to the "root approach": total risk $= \sum_{i=1}^{n} R_i^2$.

The part of the risk coverage potential not utilized by risks is referred to as (free) risk-bearing capacity.

The assessment of the overall scope of risk enables a statement to be made as to whether the risk coverage potential of a company is sufficient to bear the scope of risk of the company and thus guarantee the continued existence of the company. In most cases, however, it is not over-indebtedness but illiquidity due to a breach of covenants or minimum rating requirements that is the cause of a serious crisis (a development jeopardizing the continued existence of the company). If a company's existing level of risk is too high compared to its risk-bearing capacity, additional risk management measures are required. Knowledge of the relative significance of the individual risks (sensitivity analysis) is important for a company in practice to prioritize risk management measures.

In the simplest case, risk-bearing capacity can thus be summarized as the difference between the company's risk coverage potential and the aggregated total risk exposure (the result of risk aggregation, see Sect. 5.5). Given the dominant importance of illiquidity as a cause of insolvency, it is advisable to operationalize risk-bearing capacity using a (stochastic) rating forecast.

Bandwidth planning can be used for risk aggregation. Here, the effects of the individual risks are first allocated to specific items, such as the budgeted income statement or the budgeted balance sheet: For example, an unplanned increase in raw material prices will affect the "Cost of materials" item. A rare, high product liability claim, for example, will affect the "Extraordinary expenses" item. A prerequisite for determining the "total scope of risk" using risk aggregation is the allocation of risks to corporate planning items. In this way, the possible causes of a deviation from the plan are presented. Risks can be modelled as a fluctuation range around a plan value (e.g., +/−8% sales volume fluctuation). It is important that the planning reference also recognizes the subsequent effects of risk (e.g., a fall in sales volume reduces the variable costs). Figure 5.2 shows the basic principle of aggregating risks and analyzing sensitivity.

Event risks or event-oriented risks (such as a business interruption due to machine damage) can also be included. They then influence profit via the extraordinary result. In addition to the probability of occurrence, a range of damage must be specified here (e.g., by minimum value, most probable value, and maximum value ("triangular distribution")). A look at the various scenarios of the simulation runs illustrates that each simulation run results in different combinations of risk characteristics.

This results in a simulated value for the target value under consideration (e.g., profit or cash flow) in each step. The totality of all simulation runs provides a "representative sample" of all possible risk scenarios for the company.

Aggregated probability distributions (density functions), which are then used for further analyses, result from the determined realizations of the target value.

Based on the profit distribution function determined by the risk aggregation, it is possible to draw direct conclusions about the company's equity requirements (risk-adjusted capital, RAC). To avoid over-indebtedness, at least as much equity is required as there are losses that could reduce it. Similarly, the need for liquidity

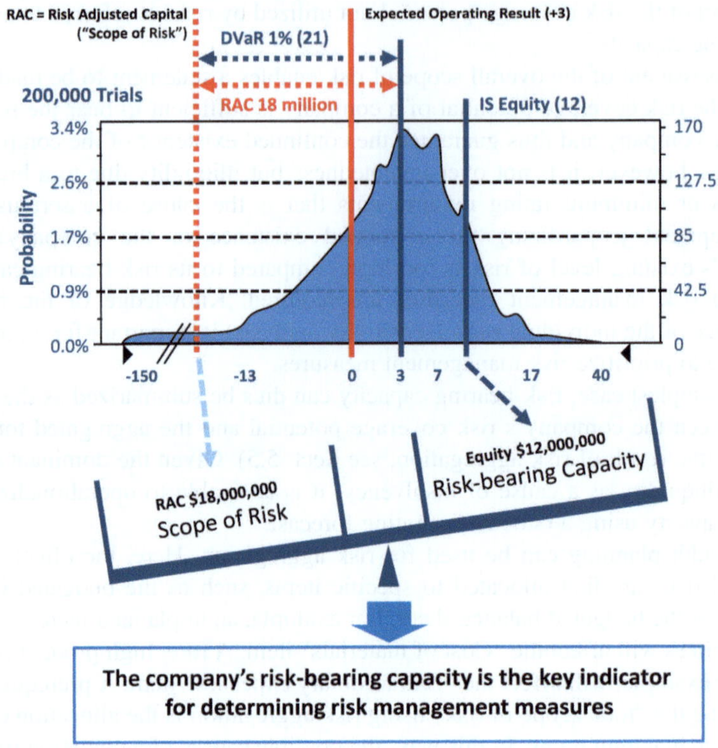

Fig. 5.2 Frequency distribution as a result of risk aggregation. Source: Gleißner and Wolfrum (2019, S. 29)

reserves can be determined using the distribution function of cash flows (free cash flows). Risk ratios can also be derived.

One example is equity cover, which is the ratio of available equity to risk-related equity requirements. Formally, the equity requirement can be operationalized using the risk measure value at risk (VaR) or the expected shortfall or conditional value at risk. The capital requirement is therefore dependent on the aggregated risks and the accepted target rating.

To determine the probability of a crisis, the percentage of all cases in which (a) covenants or (b) minimum rating requirements are breached is also calculated. The probability of insolvency expressed by the rating can be understood as a measure of going concern risk (or insolvency risk). Therefore, the probability of insolvency is the key performance indicator in risk management and an often overlooked value driver (Gleißner, 2019).

In addition to the equity requirement, risk aggregation also results in the standard deviation of profit or earnings. This parameter is often used as the basis for calculate cost of capital (see Chap. 10).

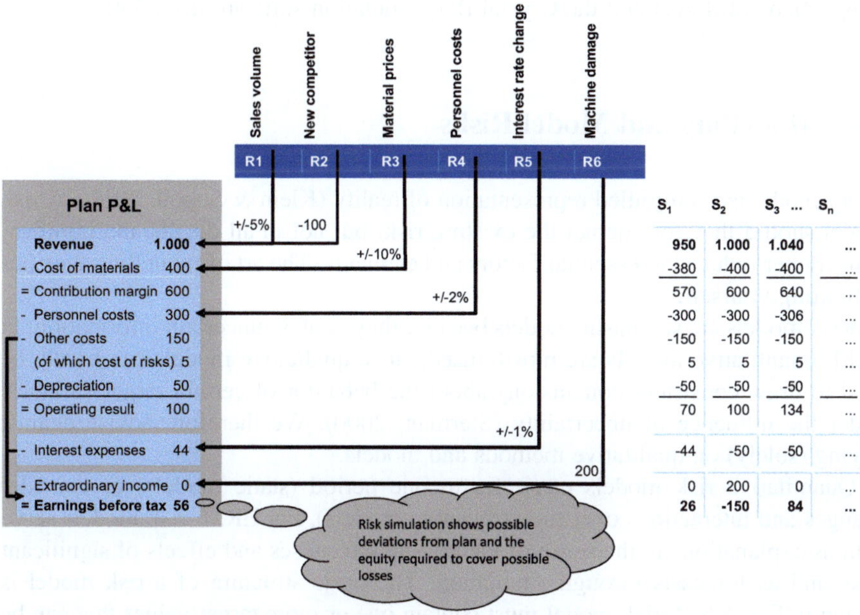

Fig. 5.3 MCS method for risk aggregation. Source: Gleißner and Wolfrum (2019, S. 31)

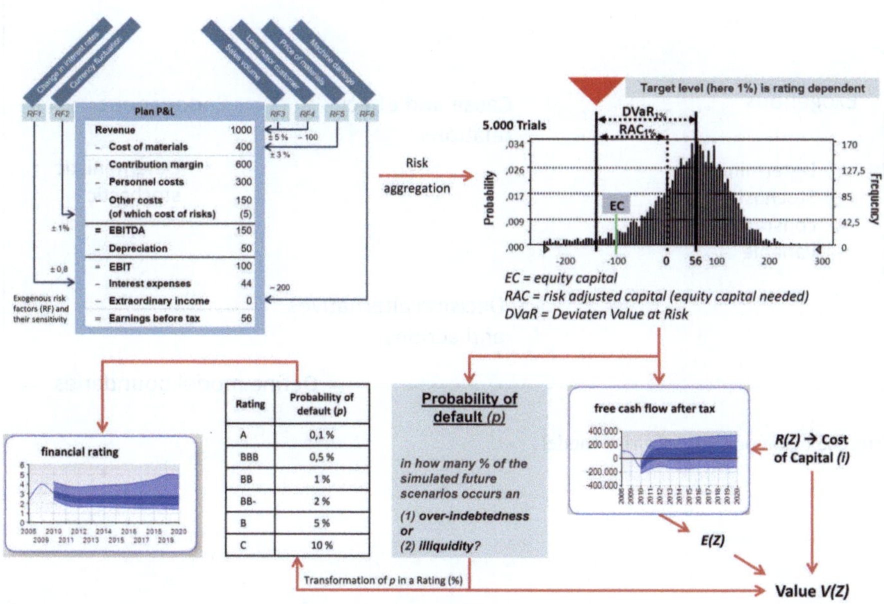

Fig. 5.4 Corporate planning, risk aggregation, and valuation with MCS. Source: Gleißner (2019, p. 1252)

Figure 5.3 summarizes the procedure and shows how risk aggregation with Monte Carlo simulation can be used to calculate equity needed and the probability of a serious crisis of the company.

An effective way of aggregating risks is presented below: Monte Carlo simulation using Microsoft Excel and the Crystal Ball simulation software (Fig. 5.4).

5.6 Modelling and Model Risks

Every model is a simplified representation of reality (Klein & Scholl, 2012). A risk model should therefore depict the existing risk, but not in all details and ramifications, rather reduced to essential factors and elements. The art of modelling thus lies in limiting yourself.

Risk models are stochastic models because they contain uncertain information. In ERM, quantitative models are mostly used, since qualitative models can hardly be used to draw consistent conclusions about the behavior of certain target variables under the influence of uncertainty (Sterman, 2000). We therefore advise against relying (solely) on qualitative methods and models.

Quantitative risk models can refer to one period (static models) or consider changes and interactions over time (dynamic models). For ERM, risk models serve both as explanations in the sense of identifying the causes and effects of significant risks and as forecasts through simulation. The basic structure of a risk model is shown in Fig. 5.5. A risk model must contain one or more target values that can be

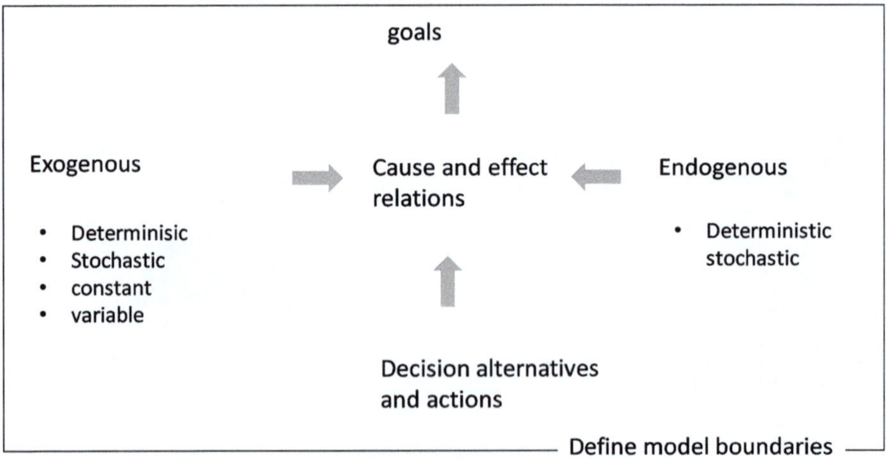

Fig. 5.5 Components of a risk model

used to estimate and evaluate the overall risks. The aggregation is influenced by the effects and interactions of various endogenous and exogenous variables, as well as the alternative courses of action chosen by the decision-makers. Some of these variables are stochastic, which means that the target variable(s) also behave stochastically.

Essential for the modelling is the definition of the model purpose and the model boundaries. Both also include the question of model detailing. The same steps can be followed for setting up a risk model as are proposed in economics for other models (Sterman, 2000; Rodrik, 2016). Model building is iterative; that means different steps are run through repeatedly to make the model clearer, more plausible, and more useful in relation to the model's purpose. The steps are as follows:

Step 1: Problem Definition

Begin by defining the problem scope and model boundaries. Identify the key risks and variables relevant to decision-making, and set the time horizon for the model. Document which aspects should be excluded, recognizing that no model can represent everything in terms of scope and detail.

Step 2: Information Gathering

Collect necessary information for model building and result interpretation. Understand factual correlations, compile historical data for estimating distributions, and conduct expert surveys on individual risks. Utilize external data sources such as studies and official statistics. Identify specific scenarios to be examined in the risk model, ensuring the formal simulation can accommodate them.

Step 3: Model Setup

Establish the formal model structure by determining variables, parameters, and their connections. Include both deterministic and stochastic relationships, allowing for changes over time. Consider various modeling methods and structural logics. Define the linkages between variables, number of time periods, and dependencies between variables and time points.

Step 4: Testing

Test the model for validity (internal consistency) and verification (alignment with intended purposes). While this isn't a mathematical proof of correctness, it ensures the model avoids contradictions and arbitrariness. Evaluate the model against specific criteria to confirm its usefulness for the intended application.

Step 5: Evaluation and Recommendations

Use the risk model to aggregate and evaluate risks, first assessing the extent of risk before management measures (gross risk) and then integrating risk reduction measures (net risk). Analyze predefined scenarios and conduct "What If" analyses. This process helps balance opportunities and risks, ensuring that risks taken are outweighed by corresponding opportunities and remain acceptable for the company. Incorporate risk indicators into the model to facilitate this assessment.

Finally, model and parameter risks are inherent uncertainties in risk modeling. Parameter risks arise from uncertainties about the level or distribution assumptions of parameters. These can be categorized into three types: known distribution with uncertain parameters, known parameters with uncertain distribution, and uncertainties in both parameters and distributions. To mitigate parameter risks, employ statistical tests, perform distribution calibrations, and conduct sensitivity analyses.

Model risks, on the other hand, stem from deficits in model design. These may include incorrect distribution assumptions, misrepresented variable relationships, or neglected important interactions. Model risks can lead to amplified market fluctuations, underestimated risks, or risk transfer to less informed actors.

While it's tempting to abandon models due to these risks, this approach is counterproductive. Every model is a simplification of reality, and the goal is to create models that are comparatively better than alternatives, including human intuition or qualitative assessments.

To enhance model reliability, involve users in development, allow for adjustments to model projections, and thoroughly document and test model assumptions and structure. Remember the focus should be on improving models rather than seeking perfection, as even imperfect models often outperform non-quantitative approaches in assessing aggregated risks.

5.7 Summary

- Risk quantification is the quantitative description of a risk using one or more frequency or probability distributions. In addition to the selection of suitable distributions, this also includes the estimation of the associated parameters.
- Important probability distributions for describing the impact of a risk are the normal distribution, the triangular distribution, and the uniform distribution. It is often necessary to combine distributions. For example, the risk of damage from a legal dispute can be described by a probability of occurrence (p) and a probability distribution for the damage if the lawsuit is lost. The latter is, for example, a triangular distribution specified by three parameters (minimum value, most probable value, maximum value).
- Risk aggregation is required to determine the overall risk scope of a project or company. The MCS is used to aggregate risks described by different probability distributions. This involves calculating a large representative number of risk-related possible future scenarios. For example, the expected value of cash flows and profit and various key figures for the overall scope of risk (such as the equity requirement, see Chap. 6 for further information) can be derived.
- The aggregation of risks using MCS is based on planning. Risk aggregation thus leads to bandwidth planning and creates transparency regarding planning

reliability and the data required to derive, for example, the probability of insolvency or a risk-adjusted cost of capital (see Chap. 10).

5.8 Exercises and Questions

1. Which statements about risk aggregation are false?
   (a) Risk aggregation is used to determine the total scope of risk (capital requirement).
   (b) Risk aggregation is necessary to identify serious crises (development threatening the existence of the company) from the combined effects of individual risks.
   (c) Monte Carlo simulation is a particularly suitable method for risk aggregation.
   (d) Risk aggregation is a synonym for risk analysis.

2. Which of the following risk measures is particularly suitable for measuring planning uncertainty?
   (a) Value at risk.
   (b) Expected shortfall.
   (c) Coefficient of variation.
   (d) Probability of insolvency.

3. Which of the following methods is suitable for aggregating different risks with reference to corporate planning (e.g., for determining equity requirements and the probability of a development jeopardizing the company's existence)?
   (a) Creation of a risk matrix (risk map).
   (b) Calculation of the sum of the expected loss values.
   (c) Monte Carlo simulation.
   (d) Stress test.

4. A company has recognized a provision for a risk that is expected to occur with a 60% probability within the financial year. The uncertain amount of loss is described using a triangular distribution. The minimum value of the loss is 1 million, the most probable value is 3 million, and the maximum value is 8 million. The provision corresponds to the expected value. What is the opportunity for the company?
   (a) 0 (there is no chance)
   (b) 1.8 million
   (c) 2.4 million
   (d) 8 million

References

Blokdyk, G. (2021). *Quantitative risk analysis: A complete guide - 2020 edition*.
Box, G. E. P., Jenkins, G. M., Reinsel, G. C., & Ljung, G. M. (2015). *Time series analysis: Forecasting and control* (5th ed.). Wiley.
Embrechts, P., Klüppelberg, C., & Mikosch, T. (1997). *Modelling extremal events: For insurance and finance* (1st ed.). Springer.
Gleißner, W. (2019). Cost of capital and probability of default in value-based risk management. *Management Research Review, 42*, 1243–1258.
Gleißner, W. (2022). *Grundlagen des Risikomanagements: Handbuch für ein Management unter Unsicherheit* (Management competence) (4th ed.). Verlag Franz Vahlen.
Gleißner, W., Füser, K. (2000). Innovative Prognoseverfahren für Unternehmensplanung auf Basis des Risikomanagements. *Der Betrieb*, 933–941.
Gleißner, W., & Wolfrum, M. (2019). *Risikoaggregation und Monte-Carlo-Simulation: Schlüsseltechnologie für Risikomanagement und Controlling. essentials*. Springer Fachmedien Wiesbaden. https://doi.org/10.1007/978-3-658-24274-9
Holton, G. A. (2004). Defining risk. *Financial Analysts Journal, 60*, 19–25.
Hunziker, S. (2021). *Enterprise risk management: Modern approaches to balancing risk and reward* (2nd ed.). Springer.
Kahneman, D., & Tversky, A. (1979). Intuitive prediction: Biases and corrective procedures. *TIMS Studies in Management Science, 12*, 313–327.
Kahneman, D., Sibony, O., & Sunstein, C. R. (2021). *Noise: A flaw in human judgment*. William Collins.
Klein, R., & Scholl, A. (2012). *Planung und Entscheidung: Konzepte, Modelle und Methoden einer modernen betriebswirtschaftlichen Entscheidungsanalyse* (Vahlens Handbücher der Wirtschafts- und Sozialwissenschaften) (2nd ed.). Franz Vahlen.
McNeil, A. J., Frey, R., & Embrechts, P. (2015). *Quantitative risk management: Concepts, techniques and tools*. Princeton series in finance. Princeton University Press.
Rieg, R., & Gleißner, W. (2022). Was ist ein erwartungstreuer Plan? *Die Wirtschaftsprüfung, 75*, 1407–1414.
Rodrik, D. (2016). *Economics rules: The rights and wrongs of the dismal science*. W. W. Norton.
Schosser, J. (2024). Beyond point forecasts: Uncertainty quantification in tensor extrapolation for relational time series data. *Communications in Statistics: Case Studies, Data Analysis and Applications*, 1–18.
Slovic, P. (2000). *The perception of risk: Risk*. Society and Policy Series.
Sterman, J. D. (2000). *Business dynamics: Systems thinking and modeling for a complex world*. Irwin/McGraw-Hill.
Vose, D. (2008). *Risk analysis: A quantitative guide* (3rd ed.). Wiley.
Wehrspohn, U., & Ernst, D. (2022). *Verteilungen als Grundlage des quantitativen Risikomanagements: Eine Übersicht verschiedener Anwendungsfälle. essentials*. Springer Gabler.

Chapter 6
Risk Metrics and Risk Measures

Abstract Risk metrics are used to measure and evaluate risk. Risk metrics include spread, volatility, the coefficient of variation, the Sharpe ratio, risk-adjusted performance indicators, sensitivity analysis, value drivers, and at-risk metrics like cash flow at risk and earnings at risk. These metrics help organizations identify potential risks and develop strategies to mitigate them.

Keywords Volatility · Coefficient of variation · Variance · At-risk metrics · Risk-adjusted return · Risk measures · Coefficient variation · Value at risk (VaR) · Conditional value at risk (CVaR) · Sharpe ratio · Risk-adjusted performance · Sensitivity analysis

Questions

- What are the key types of risk metrics used in enterprise risk management?
- How do risk-adjusted performance indicators, like the Sharpe ratio, aid in evaluating risk?
- How do at-risk metrics, such as cash flow at risk (CFaR) and earnings at risk (EaR), assist organizations in risk management?
- What strategies can organizations develop based on the evaluation of these risk metrics?
- How can risks described by different probability distributions be prioritized?
- What are typical risk measures?
- How are value-at-risk and expected shortfall to be interpreted economically?

Supplementary Information The online version contains supplementary material available at https://doi.org/10.1007/978-3-031-86425-4_6.

R. Rieg et al., *Enterprise Risk Management*, Springer Texts in Business and Economics, https://doi.org/10.1007/978-3-031-86425-4_6

Table 6.1 Overview of risk metrics

	One-sided	Two-sided
Dependent upon location	• Value at risk (VaR). • Conditional value at risk (CVaR)/expected shortfall (ES). • Range value at risk.	
Independent of location	• Deviation value at risk (DVaR).	• Spread/interquartile range. • Standard deviation. • Coefficient of variation (CV). • Variance (covariance).

6.1 Introduction to Risk Metrics and Risk Measures

Risk metrics or measures are key figures for assessing the extent of risk and form the basis of a quantitative risk assessment. They are relevant for risks that can be described by distributions and represent the risk inherent in the distribution of stochastic variables that can be easily interpreted. They enable a comparison of different risks and are important decision variables for risk control. The selection of the risk measure depends on the risk attitude of the decision-maker and the decision-making context (Kürsten & Straßberger, 2004, Gleißner, 2022).

Risk measures can be either location-dependent or location-independent and can include either one-sided or two-sided deviations from the target. Location-dependent risk measures depend on the expected value of a distribution and cannot be meaningfully interpreted without it. Location-independent risk measures represent relative deviations, for example, fluctuations of X around its expected values, E(X). One-sided risk measures focus only on one direction of deviation, positive or negative depending on the context, while two-sided risk measures include both positive and negative deviations (Table 6.1).

6.2 Spread

Risk-averse decision-makers prefer relatively safe outcomes, even if they have lower expected returns. Therefore, the spread between the best and the worst result can also be interpreted as risk.

The **interquartile range** contains the distance of the values between the second quartile (25%) and the third quartile (75%) of a risk distribution. The range or interquartile range takes opportunities into account but neglects the probability of occurrence of the various risk states. The span can be graphically represented by a tornado diagram (Fig. 6.1).

6.3 Volatility and Coefficient of Variation

Volatility is a more complex measure of risk. It describes the total fluctuation in the performance of a risk position. The greater the volatility, the greater the variation in performance, and the greater the risk. From a statistical point of view, volatility can

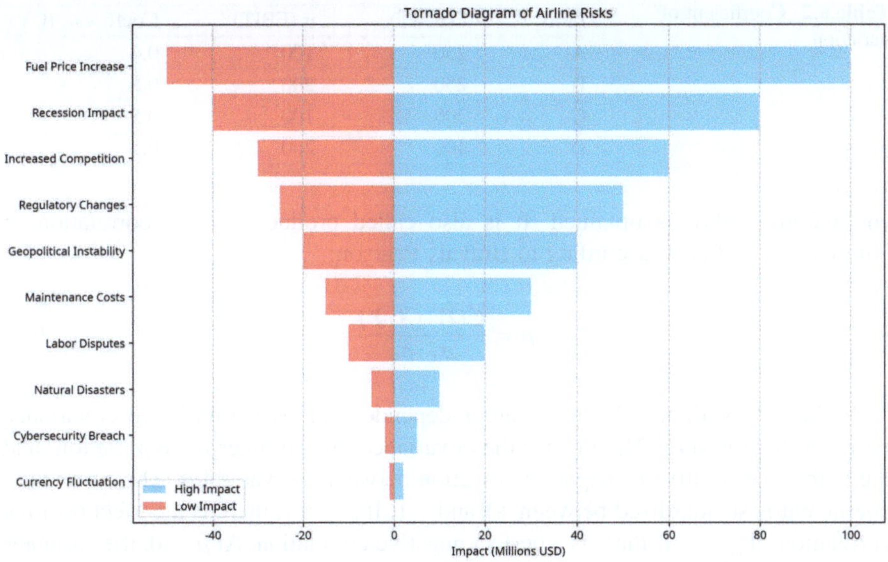

Fig. 6.1 Example tornado diagram for an airline company

be interpreted as the standard deviation from the expected value of a distribution. The standard deviation indicates the mean spread of individual values x_i of a distribution from their expected value $E(x)$. Since these deviations can be positive and negative, there is a danger that positive and negative deviations would partially or even completely cancel each other out when they are added up. Therefore, the individual deviations are first squared, summed up, and averaged to determine the variance of the distribution:

$$Variance = \sigma^2 = \frac{1}{n}\sum_{i=1}^{n}(X_i - E(X))2 \tag{6.1}$$

The root of the variance is the standard deviation.

$$\sigma = +\sqrt{\sigma^2} \tag{6.2}$$

The linear dependence of two random variables such as risks X and Y can be determined via the covariance COV (X, Y).

$$COV\ (x, y) = \frac{\sum\limits_{i=1}^{n}\left(X_i - \overline{X}\right)\cdot\left(Y_i - \overline{Y}\right)}{n} \tag{6.3}$$

COV is also needed for the aggregation of random variables and has already been mentioned in portfolio theory and the CAPM. If the covariance is normalized using the standard deviations of the random variables under consideration, the **correlation**

Table 6.2 Coefficient of variation

Firm	E(EBIT)	σ (EBIT)	Coeff. var. (CV)
A	250	100	0.4
B	250	200	0.8
C	200	100	0.5
D	400	200	0.5

coefficient ρ (rho) is obtained. It is also called product-moment correlation or correlation coefficient according to Bravais-Pearson:

$$\rho = \frac{COV\ (X, Y)}{\sigma_x \cdot \sigma_y} \tag{6.4}$$

If the two variables X and Y are independent of each other, the covariance between them is zero. The greater the covariance, the stronger the correlation, and the higher the positive or negative deviation between the variables. The correlation coefficient is standardized between +1 and -1. If $\rho = +1$, there is a perfect positive correlation; if $\rho = -1$, there is a perfect negative correlation. At $\rho = 0$, the variables are uncorrelated.

Since both variance and standard deviation depend on the expected value of a distribution and are thus location-dependent risk measures, they cannot be directly compared for different distributions. The **coefficient of variation** (CV) is more suitable as a risk measure. It is determined as the ratio of standard deviation and expected value:

$$CV(X) = \frac{\sigma\ (X)}{E(\mathrm{X})} \tag{6.5}$$

The coefficient of variation shows the risk of fluctuations around the expected value and can be used in several ways in ERM. For example, if the profit of a company is considered an uncertain variable, the coefficient of variation is a measure of the profit risk (see Table 6.2). The coefficient of variation makes it possible to compare the profit risk of different companies. The higher the coefficient of variation, the higher the probability of loss for the company. Likewise, different investment projects can be also compared with each other in terms of their earnings risk. Finally, the coefficient of variation can also be used as a risk measure in the calculation of the risk-adjusted cost of capital based on fluctuations in earnings fluctuations, or earnings risk (Gleißner, 2019); see Chap. 10.

6.4 At-Risk Metrics

At-risk metrics refer to a whole group of statistical risk measures that look at very different business targets, such as asset value, cash flow, or profit. The starting point of all at-risk metrics is the **value at risk**, which was originally developed to assess the market price risk of securities, especially shares. Therefore, the concept of value at risk is presented first. Subsequently, the methodology is applied to calculate profit risks (earnings at risk), liquidity, and corporate value risks (cash flow at risk).

The term **value at risk** (VaR) originates from the risk management of financial institutions and denotes:

- The maximum negative change in the value of a risk position (e.g., a security or a portfolio of securities, in monetary units).
- Within a certain period of time (holding period), which.
- Under normal market conditions.
- With a certain probability p (confidence level).
- Is not undercut (Vose, 2008).

The VaR is a monetary risk measure and always quoted positively. It always indicates a potential loss or downside risk. It is therefore based on an understanding of risk in the narrow sense. The **holding period** is also referred to as the liquidity period and is the period necessary to sell the risk position on the market. The holding period may be 1 trading day in the case of exchange-traded shares or several days, months, or even years in the case of medium-term investment projects. The **confidence level** is determined by the decision-maker and is significantly influenced by his risk attitude. The more risk-averse a decision-maker is, the higher the required confidence level is. Typical values for the confidence level are 95% or 99%, leaving a 5% or 1% probability of a loss exceeding the VaR.

Since the estimation of the VaR depends on the underlying assumptions regarding the distribution of a target value or a risk factor and the historical data on its parameterization as well as the at-risk method used, actual risks can also be greater in corporate practice than estimated by the risk metric. This was demonstrated by the global price collapses on the stock markets due to extreme events in 2001, 2008, and 2020. Even under normal market conditions, the VaR can exceed 1% or 5%, depending on the confidence level selected.

Another metric, the **deviation VaR** (DVaR) can be calculated in relation to the expected value. It refers to the deviations of the individual realized values Y from the expected value of a target variable *E*(*X*):

$$Y = E(X) - X \tag{6.6}$$

Y is a random variable and represents the distribution of possible deviations from the expected value. DVaR is calculated as follows:

$$DVaR\ (X) = E(X) - VaR\ (X) \tag{6.7}$$

DVaR is, therefore, a one-sided, location-independent risk measure. As in the other calculations, the confidence level is set to 95% or 99% depending on the risk attitude of the decision-maker and the available risk coverage potential (equity capital). The DVaR is also referred to as “relative VaR” (Gleißner, 2022, p. 269).

The **conditional value at risk** (CVaR, also called expected shortfall) shows the extent to which the VaR is exceeded. It sums up the possible values of the target variable beyond the probability p weighted by its probability of occurrence and thus corresponds to the expected value of the realizations of the target variable that lie below the $1 - \alpha$ confidence level. It is always larger than the VaR and thus, unlike the VaR, also takes extreme values into account (Gleißner, 2022, p. 271 f.).

$$CVaR_{\propto}(X) = -E(X|X < -VaR_{\propto}(X)) \tag{6.8}$$

For a normally distributed variable, the CVaR for the confidence level α and the quantile $q_{1-\alpha}$ of the standard deviation is calculated as follows:

$$CVaR_{\propto}(X) = -\left(E(X) + \frac{q_{1-\alpha}}{\alpha} \cdot \sigma(X)\right) \tag{6.9}$$

Figure 6.2 depicts a binomial distribution of a simulated cash flow. The VaR95% is US$-4, with an expected value of US$4.06; the DVaR, calculated as difference of both numbers, is US$8.06. The CVaR95% as weighted sum of all simulated values up to 5% gives US$-5.56.

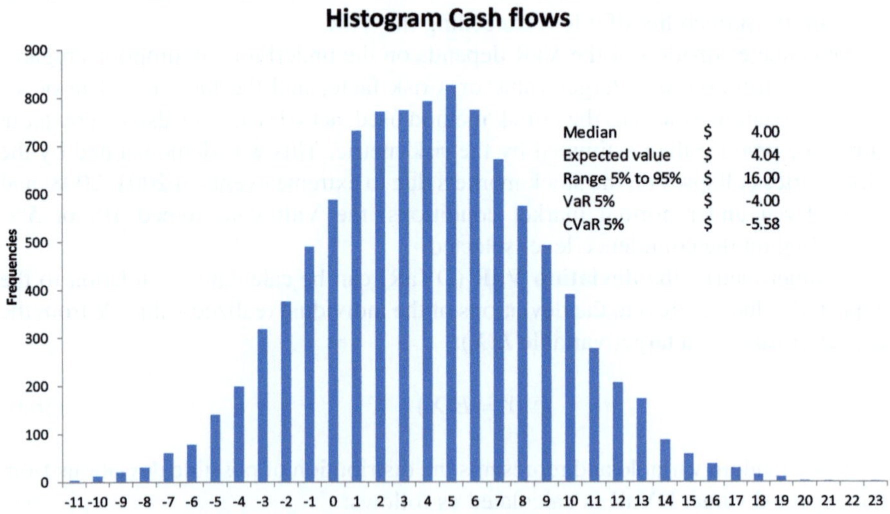

Fig. 6.2 Simulated cash flows for VaR, DVaR, and CVaR

6.5 Cash Flow at Risk and Earnings at Risk

For non-financial industries, the value at risk is calculated for an earnings figure such as cash flow, earnings, or profit. The observation horizon goes well beyond the usual holding periods of securities. The planning period in industrial companies is usually one quarter or 1 year or even longer.

For this reason, the literature recommends using the quarterly or annual **earnings at risk** (EaR) or **cash flow at risk** (CFaR) as target figures. The earnings at risk is the amount of profit earned during the period (quarter or year) that will occur with a given probability in a defined period of observation. Similarly, the cash flow at risk is the financial surplus that occurs with a certain probability in a defined period. The decision-making unit is the entire company or a division or other business unit (Hoitsch & Winter, 2004).

Theoretically, all methods for determining the value at risk can also be used to determine the EaR or the CFaR. However, due to lack of data history and the non-fulfillment of the normal distribution assumption of the risk factors, only the Monte Carlo simulation can be usefully applied.

6.6 Sharpe Ratio

The Sharpe ratio (SR) is a risk-adjusted measure (Sharpe, 1994). It is defined as the ratio of the excess return of an investment, a portfolio, or a company in relation to the standard deviation σ of this return, whereby the excess return is calculated as the difference between an expected value $E(r)$ and the risk-free interest rate r_f:

$$SR \equiv \frac{E(r) - r_f}{\sigma} \tag{6.10}$$

The alternative projects B and C have the same value for the Sharpe ratio (Table 6.3). However, their risk and thus the equity required as risk capital to cover the risk are very different. This means that the Sharpe ratio should not be used as the single criterion of advantageousness for investment projects.

In practice, Sharpe ratios are usually calculated based on **historical data**. Here, the Sharpe ratio is sensitive to the time periods and data considered (Sharpe, 1994; Lo, 2002). Furthermore, the future is not the past, and, for example, investment

Table 6.3 Example Sharpe ratio

	Alternative investments			
	A	B	C	D
Expected return	10%	8%	17%	23%
Risk (σ)	8%	10%	25%	30%
Sharpe ratio	1.00	0.60	0.60	0.70
	Risk-free interest rate (r_f) 2%			

funds show the typical **regression to the mean** (Malkiel, 2003), which means that high Sharpe ratios in the past will probably be significantly lower in the future and vice versa.

6.7 Risk-Adjusted Performance Indicators

To determine the risk-adjusted performance management of companies or business areas, specific risk-adjusted performance measures are needed to assess opportunities and risks (closely following Rieg, 2020). They expand the classic performance and profitability indicators to include risk aspects.

The return on risk-adjusted capital (**RORAC)** puts the expected profit in relation to the risk position induced by it, that is, the capital at risk. The latter can be determined, for example, via VaR or CVaR.

$$RORAC = \frac{E(earnings)}{risk\ adjusted\ capital} \cdot 100\% \tag{6.11}$$

To take risk into account in the numerator instead of in the denominator, a risk discount is deducted from the expected result. This results in the **RAROC** (risk-adjusted return on capital). The amount referred to here as the risk discount is the risk premium, but we use the word "risk discount" for linguistic reasons.

$$\begin{aligned} RAROC &= \frac{E(earnings) - risk\ premium}{capital\ employed} \cdot 100\% \\ &= \frac{E(earnings) - risk\ adjusted\ capital}{capital\ employed} \end{aligned} \tag{6.12}$$

The risk premium can be determined with a Monte Carlo simulation (MCS) using other assumptions. The procedure is identical to the derivation of the required cost of capital from internal planning. Finally, the risk can be considered in both the numerator and the denominator, which results in the risk metric **RARORAC** (risk-adjusted return on risk-adjusted capital). This ratio is the difference between the actual or planned RORAC and the target RORAC.

$$RARORAC = \frac{E(earnings) - cost\ of\ capital * risk\ adjusted\ capital}{risk\ adjusted\ capital} \cdot 100\%$$

$$RARORAC = \frac{E(earnings)}{risk\ adjusted\ capital} - cost\ of\ capital$$

$$RARORAC = RORAC - RORAC_{target} \tag{6.13}$$

6.8 Sensitivity Analysis and Value Drivers

The sensitivity indicates how sensitively the value of a target variable reacts to a change in one or more influencing variables. For this, there must be a functional correlation between the value of the target variable and the influencing variables under consideration. Sensitivity can then be calculated using the first derivation of this function according to the influencing variable (Burger & Buchhart, 2014; Wolke, 2016). Sensitivities thus show the effect sizes of risk factors. If sufficient historical data series are available, multi-variate regression analyses can be used to determine the sensitivities between risk factors and corporate goals.

In ERM, sensitivities are also referred to as exposures. **Exposures** are defined as the ratio of the relative change in value of the target variable divided by the relative change in the value of a risk factor. Typical risk factors are changes in exchange rates, commodity prices, or interest rates. Sensitivities allow an initial assessment of the strength of the effect of a risk factor on a company's target. However, a correlation model between the risk factor and the business objective is required. In addition, no probabilities of occurrence for the different manifestations of a risk factor and no interdependencies with other risk factors are considered.

Sensitivity analyses systematically examine the influence of individual risk factors on corporate objectives under ceteris paribus conditions. They form the basis for deriving value-driver models for risk assessment and management. Value driver models go back to Rappaport's concept of value generators. A **value driver** is an essential factor influencing the economic result of a company, for example, the profit or the company value. A distinction is made between financial and operational value drivers. Operational value drivers are upstream of financial value drivers, maybe return on sales, and are based on management decisions. In ERM, value drivers can be interpreted as risk factors.

Value drivers can be linked together in **value driver trees**. The term value driver hierarchy is sometimes used. Here, the overall objective of a company is successively broken down into its financial and operational value drivers. As the breakdown progresses, there is a transition from mathematically to empirically linked value drivers. In the case of empirical links, the effect strength between the value driver and the superordinate goal can be represented by sensitivities. In addition to the determination of sensitivities, a prerequisite for the successful use of value driver models is the restriction to essential value drivers to keep the model manageable. An example of a value driver tree for supply chain planning is shown in Fig. 6.3.

Value driver models can be used for risk assessment by defining scenarios for the best, worst, and most likely performance of the operational and financial value drivers and then determining the expected value of the company's target. Alternatively, the value drivers can also be represented by suitable distribution functions, and the distribution of the output variable of the value driver tree can be determined through Monte Carlo simulation. Possible deviations between the expected and planned value of the company's target can be interpreted as opportunities or risks. In addition, based on the sensitivities determined, bandwidths can be defined for the

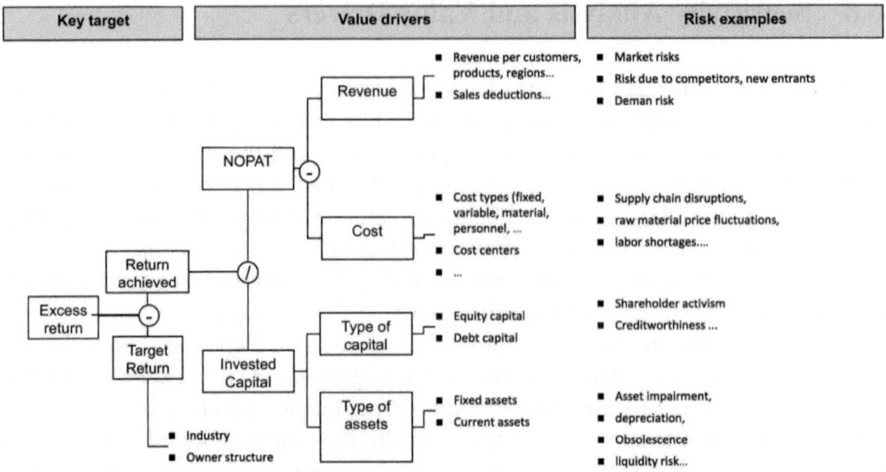

Fig. 6.3 Value drivers for risk analysis

value drivers that are still acceptable for achieving the corporate goals. Compliance with the ranges can be monitored using early warning systems.

The weighted average cost of capital (WACC) depends on the earnings risk. As this results from risk analysis and simulation-based risk aggregation, this value driver is precisely the "bridge" between value-oriented performance measures, such as economic value added, and ERM (Gleißner, 2019 and Chap. 11 on the derivation of capital costs from the overall scope of risk).

It is worth mentioning that although insolvency risk (the probability of insolvency) is also a value driver, it has so far been neglected in many traditional value driver analyses (see also Chap. 10).

6.9 Summary

- Risk measures express risks as numerical values, providing a clear basis for comparisons and prioritization of various risks. Common examples include the standard deviation and value at risk (VaR), which quantifies the potential loss that will not be exceeded with a given confidence level. These measures help assess equity requirements, providing a crucial connection to corporate financial decisions.
- Performance measures, such as the enterprise value, are critical indicators of the risk-return profile of an organization. Risk-adjusted performance measures integrate risk with profitability to support decision-making. Understanding these metrics is key for assessing how risks impact long-term financial sustainability and guiding future business strategies.

- Metrics like VaR, deviation VaR (DVaR), and conditional value at risk (CVaR) allow companies to quantify the downside risks associated with their operations. VaR provides a probability-based estimate of potential losses, while DVaR and CVaR extend this analysis by accounting for possible extreme losses. These metrics support risk aggregation and provide decision-makers with a better understanding of the company's risk exposure.
- Value at risk (VaR) is widely used for quantifying potential financial losses in various contexts, such as cash flows, earnings, and investments. Its application extends beyond the traditional finance sector to industrial firms, where it helps estimate the financial risks tied to operational factors such as production or logistics.
- Sensitivity analysis helps businesses understand how changes in key variables (e.g., sales, costs, or capital) affect their overall risk exposure. This tool allows management to identify critical risk drivers, guiding strategic decisions on how to optimize operations while managing risk.
- The weighted average cost of capital (WACC) plays a key role in assessing a firm's cost of capital in relation to its risks. Risk analysis and simulation-based risk aggregation inform WACC, making it a central value driver that connects enterprise risk management (ERM) and value-based management, particularly in assessing economic value added (EVA).

6.10 Exercises and Questions

1. Company A has an expected cash flow of US$200 million with a standard deviation of 50%. Company B has a cash flow of US$100 million with a standard deviation of US$30 million.

Calculate the coefficient of variation for both companies and interpret the planning reliability.

2. What significance do risk measures have for corporate management?
3. In the last 10 years, company C shows the following profits:

Year	2015	2016	2017	2018	2019	2020	2021	2022	2023	2024
Profit	10	12	6	9	13	13	11	15	18	16
σ										
CV										
VaR										

Determine the standard deviation (σ), coefficient of variation (CV), and value at risk of the profit (at probability level $p = 10\%$, i.e., $\text{VaR}_{10\%}$).

4. Exploring risk metrics:

   Company A and company B have different financial structures. Company A has a standard deviation of 20% on its projected cash flows of $10 million, while company B has a standard deviation of 15% on projected cash flows of $7 million.

Calculate the coefficient of variation for both companies and compare their risk profiles. Discuss which company has more financial planning reliability and why.

5. Monte Carlo simulation and risk aggregation:

   Assume company C is using Monte Carlo simulation to model its cash flow risk over the next year. The projected cash flow has an expected value of $50 million with a standard deviation of $15 million.

Simulate how a 10% increase in market volatility could affect the projected cash flow. How would the risk-adjusted value of the company change if the cost of capital is raised due to this volatility increase?

6. Value at risk (VaR) calculation:

   Company D expects a profit of $5 million, with a variance of $1 million. Using a confidence level of 95%, calculate the value at risk (VaR) for the company.

Interpret the VaR result in terms of potential financial risk.

Discuss how this VaR metric could influence the company's financial decision-making.

7. Impact of WACC on EVA:

   Company E is considering increasing its leverage, which would lower its weighted average cost of capital (WACC)

How would a lower WACC impact the economic value added (EVA) of the company?

Discuss the associated risks and potential downsides of increased leverage in the context of risk management.

8. Risk-adjusted performance measures:

   Company F reports a return on investment (ROI) of 12%, but its risk-adjusted return on capital (RAROC) is only 9%.

Explain the reasons for the difference between ROI and RAROC.

What strategies could company F implement to improve its RAROC, while maintaining or improving its overall risk profile?

9. Sensitivity analysis:

   Company G is highly sensitive to changes in raw material prices, which are expected to fluctuate between a 5% increase and a 10% decrease over the next quarter.

Perform a sensitivity analysis of how these price changes might affect the company's operational cash flow.

What risk mitigation strategies could the company adopt to reduce the impact of raw material price fluctuations?

References

Burger, A., & Buchhart, A. (2014). *Risiko-controlling*. Walter de Gruyter GmbH & Co KG.

Gleißner, W. (2019). Cost of capital and probability of default in value-based risk management. *Management Research Review, 42*, 1243–1258.

Gleißner, W. (2022). *Grundlagen des Risikomanagements: Handbuch für ein Management unter Unsicherheit* (Management competence) (4th ed.). Verlag Franz Vahlen.

Hoitsch, H.-J., & Winter, P. (2004). Die Cash Flow at Risk-Methode als Instrument eines integriertholistischen Risikomanagements. *Controlling und Management, 48*, 235–246. https://doi.org/10.1007/BF03251419

Kürsten, W., & Straßberger, M. (2004). Risikomessung, Risikomaße und Value-atRisk. *WISU - Das Wirtschaftsstudium, 33*, 202–207.

Lo, A. W. (2002). The statistics of Sharpe ratios. *Financial Analysts Journal, 58*, 36–52.

Malkiel, B. G. (2003). The efficient market hypothesis and its critics. *Journal of Economic Perspectives, 17*, 59–82.

Rieg, R. (2020). *Internationales controlling* (Lernbücher für Wirtschaft und Recht) (1st ed.). Vahlen.

Sharpe, W. F. (1994). The sharpe ratio. *The Journal of Portfolio Management, 21*, 49–58. https://doi.org/10.3905/jpm.1994.409501

Vose, D. (2008). *Risk analysis: A quantitative guide* (3rd ed.). Wiley.

Wolke, T. (2016). *Risikomanagement*, 3., überarb. u. akt. Aufl. de Gruyter/Oldenbourg.

Chapter 7
Strategic Perspective on Enterprise Risk Management

Abstract The implementation of the operational ERM process requires a strategic framework that links ERM with the corporate strategy and goals, the company's risk-bearing capacity, and its performance and incentive systems. The risk-bearing capacity depends on a company's financial reserves, liquidity, and creditworthiness, which can be measured by its financial rating. The risk-bearing capacity is related to the firm's overall risk exposure under different scenarios or for different probabilities of occurrence. The targeted risk-return profile, on the other hand, is an expression of the company's risk culture and the risk appetite of its shareholders and top management.

Keywords Insolvency · Rating · Risk appetite · Risk-bearing capacity · Risk culture · Risk tolerance · Risk strategy

Questions

- What are the objectives and tasks of strategic enterprise risk management (ERM)?
- What are the differences between strategic and operational ERM?
- Discuss the relevance of corporate risk culture for strategic ERM.
- How can risk strategy and risk objectives contribute to the integration of strategic management and ERM?
- How can a firm's risk appetite and risk tolerance be determined? How can its risk-bearing capacity be controlled?
- Discuss the relevance of a company's financial rating for the management of its financial risk-bearing capacity.

Supplementary Information The online version contains supplementary material available at https://doi.org/10.1007/978-3-031-86425-4_7.

R. Rieg et al., *Enterprise Risk Management*, Springer Texts in Business and Economics, https://doi.org/10.1007/978-3-031-86425-4_7

7.1 Fundamentals of Strategic Enterprise Risk Management

Strategic ERM is at the interface between strategic management (see Chap. 9) and the operational ERM and provides the framework for implementing the operational ERM process (see Chap. 8). Therefore, this chapter discusses the concept, objectives, and tasks of strategic ERM in detail.

There is **no common understanding** of the term "strategic ERM" in the literature. Some authors define strategic ERM as the management of strategic risks that affect the realization of corporate strategy and thus long-term firm performance and sustainability (Frigo & Anderson, 2011; Gleißner, 2023). According to this definition, strategic ERM and, thus, the management of strategic risks are considered to be the tasks of top management, whereas non-strategic risks are managed by decentralized managers as part of the operational ERM process. However, in corporate practice, it is often not possible to make a clear distinction between strategic and non-strategic risks, since many risks jeopardize both the short-term success of the company and the long-term implementation of its strategy. Strategic and non-strategic risks must be assessed using the same methods, and potential interdependencies have to be identified and assessed to calculate a firm's total risk exposure. It is therefore necessary to integrate the identification, quantification, and mitigation of strategic risks into the operational ERM process. Therefore, we follow an alternative approach defining strategic ERM as a framework for implementing and controlling the operational ERM process.

Definition Strategic ERM is a framework for the operational ERM process. This framework consists of an adequate risk culture integrated into the overall corporate culture, a risk strategy and risk objectives related to the overall corporate strategy and objectives, and a definition of risk appetite based on the risk-bearing capacity of the company. Strategic ERM aligns the risk culture, risk strategy, objectives, and risk appetite with the company's culture, strategy, objectives, and incentive and remuneration system to support the implementation of the strategy, facilitate the achievement of its objectives, and avoid its insolvency (see Fig. 7.1).

In the literature, the term **risk policy** is also used in the context of strategic ERM. The risk policy defines how ERM can support the achievement of strategic corporate goals and facilitate the development of corporate strategies that have an appropriate risk-return profile and do not jeopardize the risk-bearing capacity of the company (Hunziker, 2021). Whereas risk policy focuses on the derivation of risk strategies and targets and is more formalized, the concept of strategic ERM is broader and takes into account soft factors such as risk culture and risk attitude. The following figure shows the different elements of the strategic ERM framework.

Overall, strategic ERM has the following tasks (Vanini & Rieg, 2021):

- **Developing a risk culture** including a common understanding of risk and a joint risk awareness among a firm's managers and employees. The risk culture is an

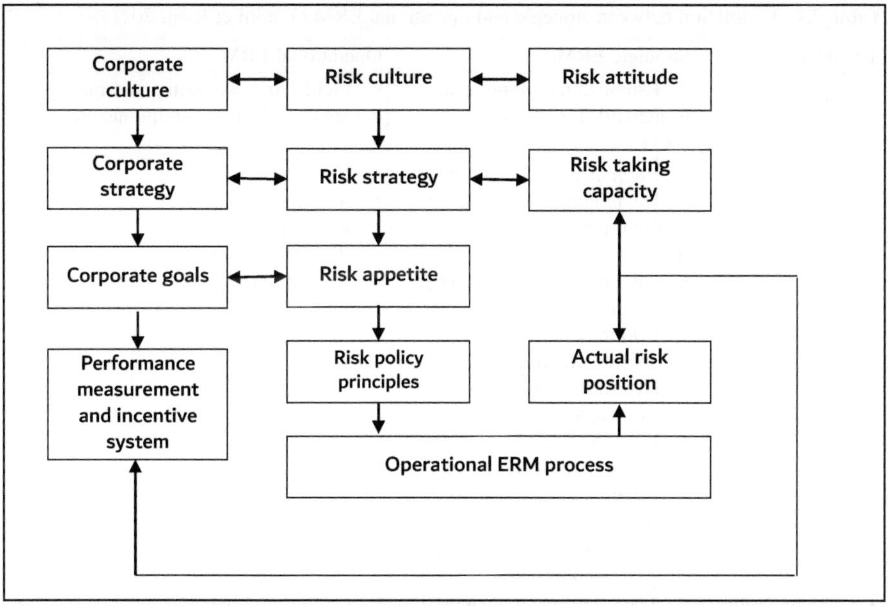

Fig. 7.1 Strategic ERM framework. Source: Vanini and Rieg (2021)

element of the overall corporate culture and is significantly influenced by the risk attitude of its stakeholders, especially of the owners and the top management.

- **Deriving a risk strategy** in alignment with the overall corporate strategy. The risk strategy should fix the core risks the company wants to take and its risk appetite. As a consequence, the risk strategy is closely related to the company's risk-bearing capacity.
- **Operationalizing the risk strategy through risk objectives** such as the target rating. Risk objectives are integrated into the company's control systems such as its goal system, its performance measurement system, and its incentive respective remuneration system.
- **Determining the risk-bearing capacity** depends on the equity and liquidity buffers of the firm and its financial rating. The ratio of overall risk exposure and the risk-bearing capacity significantly influences the probability of over-indebtedness and insolvency and thus the risk costs of the company.
- **Defining adequate risk-adjusted performance measures** as decision criteria for corporate management: For corporate management, suitable performance measures must be defined that allow the expected or achieved return to be weighed against the risk taken (e.g., the return on risk-adjusted capital [RORAC]).
- **Communicating the firm's risk policy,** including its risk culture, risk strategy, and risk objectives to managers and employees.
- **Establishing a long-term organizational framework** for the structural and procedural organization of operational ERM (see Chap. 12).

Table 7.1 Distinction between strategic and operational ERM (Vanini & Rieg, 2021)

Features	Strategic ERM	Operational ERM
• Approach	• Establishing a long-term framework for operational ERM	• Identifying, assessing, and managing corporate risks in a continuous process
• Tasks	• Implementing risk culture • Developing a risk strategy in alignment with the corporate strategy • Operationalization through risk targets • Communication through risk policy principles • Determining the risk-bearing capacity concept • Defining risk-adjusted performance measures • Fixing the organizational framework • Integration with incentive and remuneration systems	• Risk identification • Risk quantification • Risk reporting • Risk mitigation • Risk monitoring
• Responsibility	• Top managers and supervisory board supported by ERM function	• Operational risk managers or risk controllers, decentralized managers, and internal auditors

- **Integrating risk-adjusted performance measures** in the performance measurement, incentive, or remuneration systems as these systems significantly influence the risk attitude and thus the risk-taking of corporate managers (Gleißner, 2019).

Overall, strategic and operational ERM can be differentiated as follows (Table 7.1):

Subsequently, the different tasks of strategic ERM are discussed in more detail.

7.2 Implementing Risk Culture

Risk-aware behavior of managers and employees cannot be achieved only by setting up a formal ERM system, as this is often perceived as complex and bureaucratic by the managers and employees. The success of ERM therefore depends on the attitude of management and employees concerning the benefits and limitations of the ERM in general and their adequate risk behavior in particular. Thus, a "good" risk culture should improve the understanding of risks and the risk awareness of managers and employees and thus the acceptance of and trust in ERM throughout an organization (Gleißner, 2022).

Risk culture is part of the overall company culture. Corporate cultures have specific characteristics (Behrends, 2003):

- **Culture is a social phenomenon.** It is decisively shaped by the beliefs, values, motivations, and skills of the managers and employees and their interactions. The institutions, rules, and role expectations that are applied within an organization regulate managerial decision-making and behavior.
- **Culture has a shape.** The cultural characteristics must always be considered in their overall configuration, as single cultural aspects reinforce or neutralize each other and only unfold their effect in a specific corporate environment.
- **Culture has a generative character**, as it does not fix employees' behavior for all potential situations in a company but rather provides principles and recommendations for appropriate behavior in different situations.

Risk culture can be understood as norms, values, assumptions, and traditions of the behavior of individuals and groups within an organization that determine how they identify, understand, discuss, and manage risks in business (The Institute of Risk Management, 2012; Fraser & Simkins, 2016). According to Schein (2010), three elements of risk culture can be distinguished:

- **Fundamental assumptions and beliefs of managers and employees:** Fundamental risk-related assumptions concern, for example, the understanding of risk or the acceptance of the ERM framework. These basic assumptions are accepted by nearly all organizational members. For example, Mikes (2009) distinguishes between two basic attitudes of managers toward ERM:
  - **Calculative idealism**: Managers are convinced that risks can be managed quantitatively mainly using key figures and indicators. They emphasize risk modelling and quantification for risk identification and assessment.
  - **Calculative pragmatism**: Managers use risk measures less for decision support but consider them as indicators and try to supplement their statements with their experience and judgment.
- **Values, norms, and standards:** Whereas values represent abstract perceptions of a person about more or less desirable states, standards are behavioral maxims and expectations (e.g., the maximum risk acceptance of a company). Values and norms serve as a standard of judgment and orientation for employees. While values tend to be unconscious and can therefore hardly be directly influenced, norms are subject to conscious perception by employees and can therefore be shaped.
- **Artifacts**: Artifacts are the visible and conscious elements of the risk culture (cultural manifestations) and include, for example, symbols such as the representation of risks as traffic lights. They can be directly influenced by the ERM but are sometimes ambiguous and difficult to decipher.

There is a mutual relationship between the elements of risk culture. Thus, artifacts should clarify values and norms and make them tangible for the employees. Overall, the implementation of an adequate risk culture is the duty of the top management (COSO, 2017).

A **poor risk culture** arises when managers and employees are unaware of risks, ERM is viewed as an annoying constraint on profitability, or ERM procedures are treated as a mere compliance exercise. A company has a **strong risk culture** when the values and norms are clearly understood and accepted by managers and employees considering ERM as integral for firm performance. Managers and employees are motivated to identify risks and opportunities continuously and report them through the organization's hierarchy. In addition, it reduces managerial and employee misconduct (Grieser & Pedell, 2022; Hardy & Saunders, 2022).

Overall, there are several benefits of a strong risk culture (COSO, 2017; Jankensgård & Kapstad, 2021):

- **Scoping of strategy and business objective-setting:** Risk culture influences the strategic alternatives under consideration. Strategic alternatives that are not compatible with the risk culture should be eliminated from the decision-making process.
- **Early risk identification and better risk assessment:** An improved risk awareness and a common understanding of risk among managers and employees make it easier for them to identify and assess risks, as risk is a social construct and receives its meaning through the individual interpretation of employees, which in turn is influenced by social interaction with other employees (Collier et al., 2007).
- **Higher willingness to share and report risk-related information** (open lines of communication): A shared understanding of risk also leads to improved risk identification and communication.
- **Higher willingness of managers to incorporate risk into (proactive) decision-making**: As managers accept ERM, they increasingly integrate ERM measures into their decision-making processes. This leads to a reduction in decision-making complexity and better decision-making quality.

Risk culture is influenced by numerous internal and external factors (Fig. 7.2). **Internal factors** include the extent of decentralized decision-making autonomy, the nature of interaction and communication between management and employees, the incentive system, and the standards and rules for leadership and decision-making. For example, a pronounced risk culture usually requires a strong commitment of the top management, the setting of risk limits, a fault-tolerant communication culture, long-term incentive and remuneration systems, and the establishment of an ERM function with appropriate resources. **External factors** include regulatory requirements and expectations of stakeholders such as investors and banks (COSO, 2017).

There is some consensus in the literature that a firm's risk culture cannot be prescribed top-down but must be developed with the participation of the decentralized corporate units and as a component of corporate culture. The top management acts as a role model and can significantly influence risk culture through its leadership style and symbolic actions. Thus, the implementation of risk culture could not be delegated to risk managers. There are various approaches to foster the development of a strong risk culture (COSO, 2017; Jankensgård & Kapstad, 2021) which can be summarized to three groups (Grieser & Pedell, 2022):

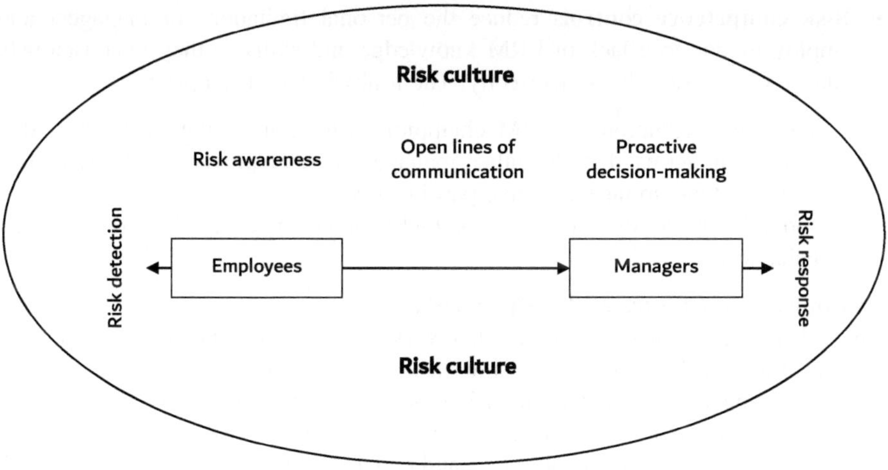

Fig. 7.2 Risk culture (Jankensgård & Kapstad, 2021)

- **Leadership controls** are mainly ensured by the top management and the supervisory board providing sense-making, orientation, and structure to the middle and lower management and the employees and thus reducing the control problem of lack of orientation. Examples are as follows:
  - Implementing adequate codes of conduct to inform about and legitimate correct behavior and visible symbolic and visible code-compliant actions by all managers, especially the top management.
  - The tone from the top demonstrates that the top management believes in the necessity of ERM and its contribution to value creation and considers it not only to serve external compliance requirements.
  - A participative management style to foster open and honest discussions about risks facing the entity.
- **Motivational controls** reduce the probability that managers and employees will take risks for opportunistic reasons although these risks are not beneficial to the company. They include the following:
  - The integration of risk targets into recruiting and promotion processes, performance measurement, and compensation systems to align risk-aware behavior and decision-making with performance.
  - Consistently embedding risk criteria in managerial decision-making when preparing key business decisions, which includes discussing and reviewing risk scenarios.
  - Enforcing accountability for all actions. Management documents policies of accountability and adheres to them demonstrating that a lack of accountability is not tolerated and practicing accountability is appropriately rewarded.

- **Risk competence controls** reduce the personal limitations of managers and employees due to a lack of ERM knowledge and skills so they unconsciously take risks or assess them incorrectly. The following are examples:
  - The implementation of ERM champions who can communicate the ERM process in terms that the other managers and employees understand and motivate them to take an active part in ERM.
  - Job training and rotation to develop ERM competencies and deepen risk-aware behavior.

Example: Risk Culture at the SAP Group
The risk management governance framework at SAP represents a comprehensive system of approaches and processes to ensure control through a clearly structured risk management system and a supporting risk culture. The risk culture is considered the basis of SAP's risk management system. Risk culture at SAP comprises a system of values, beliefs, knowledge, attitudes, and understanding concerning risks and risk management as part of our corporate culture. To support and continuously foster SAP's risk culture, we conduct risk activities for the entire SAP organization such as mandatory training in ethical behavior, code of conduct, and risk management (SAP Group, 2023, *Annual Report 2022*, p. 130).

7.3 Risk Attitude as a Component of Risk Culture

Risk culture is determined, among other aspects, by the risk attitudes of the managers and employees of an organization (Hunziker, 2021). The utility-theoretical definition and measurement of risk attitude were explained in Sect. 2.3. The concept of individual risk attitude is also discussed in psychology and management theory (Weber & Johnson, 2009). The number of terms and definitions is correspondingly diverse, some of which are used synonymously and some complementary (e.g., risk preference or risk aversion; (Vanini, 2024).

Individual risk attitude is not a stable personal characteristic but is influenced by numerous factors of the decision-making context. For example, short-term oriented incentives and compensation systems can lead to an increase in the risk-taking of managers. In addition, individual risk attitudes and thus risk-taking are influenced by peer groups. Company size and risk attitude of decision-makers are also positively correlated (i.e., managers in large companies tend to be more risk-averse than managers in smaller companies). In addition, risk attitude also seems to be influenced by the position in the company and the industry (for an intensive discussion, see (Vanini, 2024). In summary, individual risk attitude depends on the following **factors**:

1. **Context of a decision**. According to prospect theory, people tend to be risk-averse in a winning situation, while they are more risk-seeking in a loss situation. This phenomenon is named reference point dependency of risk attitude (Kahneman & Tversky, 1979).
2. **Controllability of risk.** If decision-makers believe they can control or influence risks, they are often more willing to take risks (Nosic & Weber, 2007).

3. **Personal characteristics of a decision-maker**, such as age, gender, or education. For example, women seem to be more risk-averse than men, and educated people are more risk-averse than uneducated people (Byrnes et al., 1999; Nicholson et al., 2005).
4. **Cultural background of a decision-maker.** An important cultural dimension is uncertainty avoidance describing the extent to which individuals feel threatened by uncertainty and ambiguity. Decision-makers from cultures with strong uncertainty avoidance tend to be more risk-averse (Hofstede, 2001).

Risk attitude has a strong impact on corporate ERM (Vanini, 2024):

- On the one hand, transparency about the risk attitude of owners and management is necessary. The risk attitude of the company owners determines the organizational **risk appetite** and the **targeted risk-return profile**. Agency problems arise when the risk attitude of the owners differs significantly from that of the management, as this increases the potential for opportunism of the management and agency conflicts between owners and management.
- The reference point dependency on risk attitude can lead to **excessive risk-taking** in crises. For example, in profit situations, there is the problem that managers act too risk-averse and thus tend to underinvest which endangers the long-term corporate performance. On the other hand, strong risk-seeking behavior in loss situations can result in excessive risk-taking.
- There are many interaction effects between risk perception and risk attitude. **Risk perception** arises as a result of cognitive processes and is influenced by numerous heuristics such as representativeness, availability, and anchor heuristics. It affects aspects such as the perceived extent of personal concern (Hunziker, 2021). Here, comprehensive management decision training is necessary to limit possible dysfunctional effects and to support an objective risk perception.
- Most **incentive and remuneration systems** are based on the assumption from agency theory that risk-averse managers must be financially motivated to take additional risks on behalf of risk-neutral owners (Jensen & Meckling, 1976). Expected corporate success can be understood as distributions of possible future goal realization. Managers' decisions change the distributions of the targets and thus the risk for the owners. This raises the question of how incentive and remuneration systems must be designed to align the risk attitude and risk-taking of investors and managers. Therefore, critical discussions concerning the appropriateness and risk of variable salary payments are increasing. For example, it was discussed if short-term-oriented remuneration systems increase the risk attitude of managers and promote excessive risk-taking, thus at least exacerbating the financial and economic crisis of 2008/2009 (Larcker et al., 2014).

7.4 Risk Strategy, Risk Objectives, and Risk Policy Principles

To implement their vision and strategic goals, top management defines a corporate strategy. Since risks can affect strategy implementation, the corporate strategy must also include statements concerning key business risks and how to manage them. In general, a **risk strategy** outlines how ERM can support the development and implementation of the strategy, fixes a firm's risk objectives, and describes the measures used to achieve them. A risk strategy is thus intended to increase the probability of implementing a corporate strategy successfully. It must be communicated in the company in an appropriate form (e.g., through a **risk policy**). A risk strategy contains the following information (Hunziker, 2021; Gleißner, 2022):

- The relationship between corporate and risk strategy
- The definition of core risks that result from the business model and should be taken by the company and non-core risks such as threats to physical safety that can be transferred to third parties (Jankensgård & Kapstad, 2021)
- Decision criteria for assessing the expected return and risk of decision alternatives
- The company's total risk-bearing capacity
- An upper limit for the total risk exposure for a non-violation of the risk-bearing capacity as well as the risk tolerance and risk appetite of the company
- The target ratio of expected return and risk of the different business units and the company as a whole
- Thresholds for triggering ad hoc risk communication
- Risk tolerances or risk and loss limits for transactions, organizational units, and the entire company

Specific risk targets are derived from the risk strategy. Risk targets are key figures measured by risk-adjusted performance indicators that can be used to evaluate and weigh the return and risk of decision alternatives. Risk objectives are, for example, the realization of a risk-opportunity ratio or an accepted tolerance around a specific objective. For the risk objectives, target values must be derived during the annual strategic and operational planning, responsible managers must be named, and measures for achieving the objectives must be developed (COSO, 2017) (Table 7.2).

Table 7.2 Examples of tolerance statements

Business objective	Target	Tolerance
Return on investment (ROI)	5% annual return on its portfolio	3% to 7% annual return
Online home delivery orders for a restaurant	Delivery within 40 minutes	30- to 50-minute delivery time
Minimize missed calls from a call center	2% of overall calls	1% to 5% of overall calls

Source: COSO (2017)

The risk strategy and risk objectives are communicated through risk policy principles. **Risk policy principles** are documented rules of conduct and instructions for action for managers and employees for a common understanding of risk and a uniform handling of risks. They are drawn up by top management, define a rough framework for action, and are to be integrated into all important managerial decisions (Diederichs, 2018; Gleißner, 2022). Key contents of the risk policy principles are fundamental statements on the concept of risk as well as on the goals and tasks of ERM, on risk objectives, in particular on target types and sizes, target relationships, and desired target characteristics, as well as on fundamental risk-related behaviors and potentials (Burger & Buchhart, 2014; Diederichs, 2018).

Nevertheless, risk strategy and risk policy have limitations (Hunziker, 2021):

- The risk strategy only represents formal regulations. To put the risk strategy into practice, it must be communicated to relevant stakeholders.
- It does not provide sufficient protection against fraud, corruption, or other illegal behavior.
- Due to national differences in risk perception and assessment, there is no intercultural translation of important risk components through the risk strategy and principles.
- Strategy and principles are only valid over a limited time period. Therefore, the description of the essential contents is often rather abstract and not very concrete.
- Strategy and principles should not degenerate into a mere marketing tool within the framework of external communication.

Example: Risk Management Policy at the SAP Group

The risk management policy issued by our Executive Board governs how we manage risk in line with the company's risk appetite and defines a methodology that is applied uniformly across all parts of the group [...]. Our risk management system is based on the framework published by the Committee of Sponsoring Organizations of the Treadway Commission (COSO) entitled "Enterprise Risk Management – Integrating with Strategy and Performance." Updated in 2017, this framework is built on four pillars, namely, a global risk management governance framework, a dedicated risk management policy, a global risk management organization, and a standardized risk management methodology [...]. The risk management policy is reviewed annually and stipulates responsibilities for conducting risk management activities and defines reporting and monitoring structures. Our global SAP risk management policy clearly states that each employee is responsible for active engagement in the risk management process as well as for the continuous identification of risks, based upon clear rules of engagement in adherence to the policy. The risk management system primarily analyzes risks. Opportunities are assessed or analyzed where it is deemed appropriate (source: SAP, 2023, *Annual Report, 2022*, p. 130).

7.5 Risk Appetite, Risk Coverage Potential, and Risk-Bearing Capacity

The risk appetite concept of an organization is the operationalization of its risk strategy and its risk policy. Often, a company's risk strategy and risk appetite are developed simultaneously, redefining each other during the strategy development process (COSO, 2017). Unfortunately, there is no consensus in the literature concerning the concept of risk appetite. In general, **risk appetite** covers "a firm's willingness and ability to bear risk in pursuit of upside potential" (Jankensgård & Kapstad, 2021). It describes the type and extent of risks that the management is willing to take to achieve corporate targets in a normal scenario. It is determined by the risk appetite of the shareholders and the firm's (financial) reserves and derived from corporate strategy and objectives. Besides, it acts as a benchmark for the allocation of risk capital to the business activities or units of a company (The Institute of Risk Management, 2011). In this regard, risk appetite answers the question of how much risk an organization is willing to accept and imposes a limit on managerial risk-taking.

In addition to "risk appetite," additional terms such as "risk tolerance" and "risk-bearing capacity" are used in the literature and must be distinguished from each other (Fig. 7.3).

The **risk-bearing capacity (RBC)** is the maximum amount of risk that a company can take without filing for insolvency. It is determined by the financial reserves and financial rating of a company (Hunziker, 2021). Exceeding the risk-bearing capacity might breach regulatory requirements or jeopardize the organization's ability to meet its contractual obligations. To avoid excessive managerial risk-taking, it is reasonable to fix a lower limit for organizational **risk tolerance**. Typically, risk tolerance statements are quantitative, defining bounds that can be

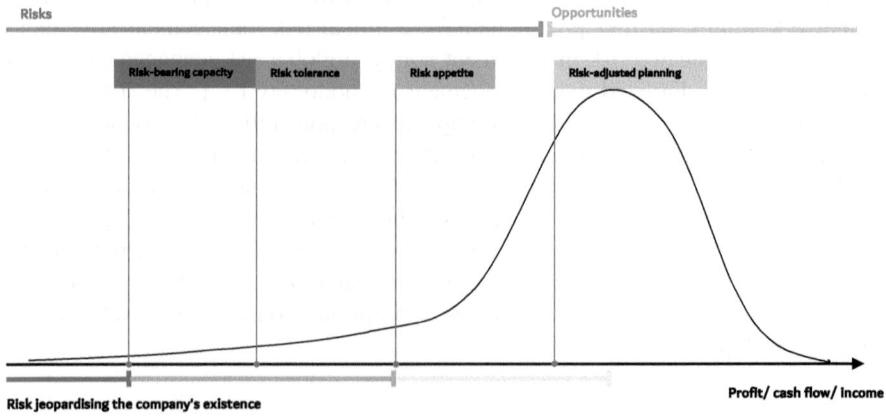

Fig. 7.3 Relationship between risk-bearing capacity, risk tolerance, and risk appetite. Source: Gleißner and Wolfrum (2017)

embedded in the operations of different business units. Thus, it fixes the maximum tolerated deviation from the planned corporate targets (e.g., in terms of profit or cash flow). Therefore, the risk tolerance sets the upper and lower limit of the accepted risk exposure, whereas risk appetite describes the target level of risk within the corridor under normal circumstances (Hardy & Saunders, 2022). Thus, the **risk buffer** is the difference between risk appetite and risk tolerance.

Example: Description of Risk-Bearing Capacity at the Lufthansa Group
The Lufthansa Group's risk management system includes a concept for calculating its risk-bearing capacity. It entails comparing an indicator of risk-bearing capacity based on liquidity with the aggregated top risks in order to ensure that sufficient funds are available to cover the risk. The top quantitative risks are weighted and aggregated on the basis of the risk value; the top qualitative risks are also incorporated into the model and assessed on an aggregate basis. This presentation is part of the quarterly reporting to the Executive Board (source: Lufthansa Group 2023, *Annual Report 2022*, p. 77).

As the concept of risk appetite is quite vague, it is difficult to implement in corporate practice, in particular when there are aspirational performance targets. In addition, there is no standard for a risk appetite statement for firms. Therefore, there are concerns that formal and written risk appetite statements in policy documents made firms more bureaucratic, over-governed, and slower to respond to opportunities (Jankensgård & Kapstad, 2021).

Setting the overall organizational risk appetite is an important task of the supervisory board, as it is highly associated with the other board functions, including the determination of the firm's strategic plan or compensation packages for the top managers. Therefore, the risk appetite statement should be integrated into the strategic and financial plans of the firm. Qualitative measures may include a statement of the significant risk exposures that the firm is willing to pursue and the significant risks the firm is aiming to avoid. Quantitative measures can include probabilistic statements such as the acceptable probability of a downgrade in the firm's credit rating classification or of a specified loss of firm value or earnings (Hardy & Saunders, 2022).

The risk-bearing capacity and thus risk tolerance and risk appetite depend on a firm's **risk capital**. Risk capital consists of a firm's buffer of financial resources that absorb potential losses and cover cash flow shortfalls to avoid insolvency. It increases with the portion of equity financing and highly liquid assets such as cash and cash equivalents, spare borrowing capacity, and cash payoffs from risk transfers (Jankensgård & Kapstad, 2021).

7.6 Operationalizing of Risk Tolerance and Risk Appetite

A firm must file for **insolvency** if its equity is depleted (over-indebtedness) or it is unable to meet its financial payment obligations. The maximum risk-bearing capacity, risk tolerance, and risk appetite can therefore be determined based on the financial reserves noted on the balance sheet and income statement since these reserves can prevent over-indebtedness. Besides, a company needs cash flow reserves to be able to meet its payment obligations even if risks arise (Gleißner & Wolfrum, 2017).

In general, a firm's **risk capital** consists of the available financial reserves of a company that can absorb the financial effects of risks. The cash flow-based risk capital covers the impact of risks on a firm's liquidity and thus its solvency. It depends on the company's future free cash flows and available credit facilities and assets which can easily be liquidated. The risk capital resulting from reserves in the income statement and the balance sheet absorbs the effects of risks leading to over-indebtedness. It depends on the earning potential of a company, its open and hidden buffers, and its equity capital (Gleißner, 2022). Different classes of risk capital can be distinguished according to their availability (Hölscher, 2002; Giebel, 2011). The following figure shows a potential classification (Table 7.3).

According to the going concern principle, assets that are indispensable for the company's existence should not be used as risk capital. Furthermore, in the event of a crisis, credit facilities may be reduced, and the planned surplus cash flow may not be realized due to unfavorable market conditions. The first-class risk capital can be used immediately and without additional effort, whereas the use of the second-class risk capital requires a certain amount of time. For example, taking out a new loan requires negotiations with the bank. The use of third-class risk capital also causes a negative reputational effect.

Table 7.3 Classes of risk capital (adapted from Hölscher, 2002)

Risk capital	Cash flow-related risk capital	Income statement- and balance sheet-related risk capital
• First class	• Cash inflow from risk premiums included in sales prices • Excess cash flows (after interest on borrowings, dividends, planned investments, and other expenses)	• Risk premiums calculated into sales prices • Excess profit • Provisions made for expected losses
• Second class	• Unused credit facilities • Additional credit facilities • Easy to liquidate financial assets • Easy to liquidate receivables	• Minimum profit • Hidden buffers in properties and plants.
• Third class	• Reduction in working capital • Other realizable assets • Other liquidity inflows	• Open reserves • Share capital/common stock

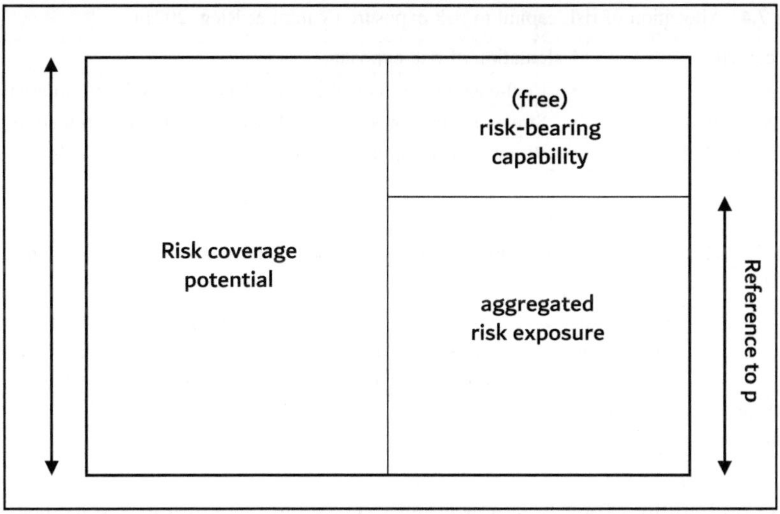

Fig. 7.4 Risk capital and risk-bearing capacity. Source: Gleißner and Wolfrum (2017)

In the next step, the risk capital is compared to the aggregated risk exposure of the company (see Chap. 8), and the free risk-bearing capacity is determined. The free RBC can be interpreted as the difference between the risk capital and the aggregated risk exposure of the company. The aggregate risk scope measures the scope of possible (liquidity-effective) losses of a period that will not be exceeded with a given probability (Gleißner & Wolfrum, 2015, 2017, 2021; Gleißner, 2022) (Fig. 7.4).

The RBC of a company is not violated if the aggregated risk exposure does not exceed the total risk capital (= risk coverage potential). However, the aggregated total risk exposure can be determined for different scenarios or confidence levels according to the risk attitude of the top management respective to the supervisory board (Table 7.4). The higher the risk aversion, the higher the confidence level applied in the value-at-risk simulation (Hölscher, 2002; Giebel, 2011).

According to the ongoing concern principle, the first-class capital should be sufficient to cover risks occurring in normal business conditions. The stress scenario depicts constellations with lower probability in which several risk factors occur simultaneously. Accordingly, a higher confidence level can be selected in the at-risk analysis. The worst-case scenario (crash scenario or maximum stress case) reflects an extremely negative development for the company and occurs very rarely. The global COVID-19 crisis from 2020 may serve as an example. In this scenario, the third-class risk capital must also be used to compensate for risks that have occurred.

Alternatively, the risk-bearing capacity (or the risk tolerance) can be assessed by the following two key figures (Gleißner, 2022):

- The maximum loss that can be absorbed until a development jeopardizing the company's existence occurs (risk-bearing capacity) or a fixed risk tolerance

Table 7.4 Allocation of risk capital to risk exposure (Vanini & Rieg, 2021)

Risk capital	Calculation of risk exposure
• First class	• Real-case scenario or 95% confidence level of VaR simulation
• Plus second class	• Stress scenario or 99% confidence level of VaR simulation
• Plus third class	• Worst-case scenario or 99.9% confidence level of VaR simulation

Table 7.5 Exemplary evaluation of risk-bearing capacity and risk tolerance (Gleißner, 2022, p. 345)

	Status quo		Status quo plus planned measure	
	Risk-bearing capacity value	Probability of exceeding RBC	Risk-bearing capacity value	Probability of exceeding RBC
Risk-bearing capacity	US$500 million	1%	US$350 million	2.5%

- The probability of a risk jeopardizing the company's continued existence (probability of a crisis or default)

The example in Table 7.5 shows that the company can afford a risk exposure of up to US$80 million without exceeding its risk tolerance. The probability of exceeding it is 8%. Insolvency and thus exceeding the risk-bearing capacity would only occur if the risk were to exceed US$500 million. The probability of this occurring is 1% (Table 7.5).

With respect to its targeted risk-return profile, a firm's **risk appetite** can be defined as the required additional return for one unit of additional risk exposure and thus can be regarded as the desired risk-return profile of a decision alternative (risk appetite B). The risk appetite B is measured by the parameter λ (Gleißner & Wolfrum, 2017; Gleißner, 2019):

$$\lambda = \frac{r_m^e - r_f}{\sigma_{r_m}} \tag{7.1}$$

with r_m^e is expected market return, r_f is risk-free interest rate, and σ_{r_m} is standard deviation of the market return.

The ratio λ corresponds to the Sharpe ratio. Historical analyses show that a value of 0.25 can be assumed for λ (i.e., for a 1% additional volatility of an investment on the capital market, an additional return of 0.25% is usually required). Alternatively, if the VaR rather than the standard deviation is used as a measure of risk, lambda becomes a variable dependent on p, which can be interpreted as a risk-adjusted requirement for return on equity. The following table shows an example of the assessment of different alternatives against the background of risk appetite B (Table 7.6).

Alternative B has the best risk-return profile. However, its risk exposure is not covered by the available risk capital. Therefore, this alternative is not a relevant option. The other two alternatives are both covered by the available risk capital; the

Table 7.6 Risk exposure, risk capital, and value contribution of alternatives

	Risk exposure	Risk capital	Yield	Value = yield − $\lambda\cdot$ risk exposure
• Status quo		• 100		
• Alternative A	• 40	• 60	• 20	• 20–0.25·40 = 10
• Alternative B	• 160	• −60	• 80	• 80–0.25·160 = 40
• Alternative C	• 60	• 40	• 22	• 22–0.25·60 = 7

Source Gleißner and Wolfrum (2017)

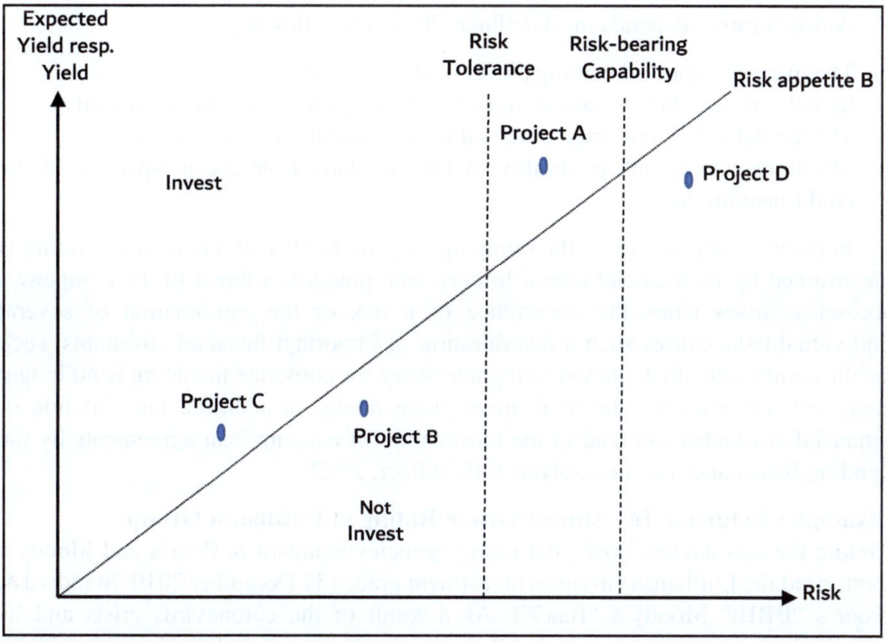

Fig. 7.5 Relationship between risk-bearing capacity, risk tolerance, and risk appetite B (based on Gleißner & Wolfrum, 2017)

largest risk-adjusted value contribution is accounted for by alternative A, which is thus the most beneficial. Figure 7.5 illustrates the relationships between RBC measured by the available risk capital, risk tolerance, and risk appetite B.

Project D should not be pursued as it jeopardizes the company's risk-bearing capacity. Project A should also not be undertaken despite a risk-return profile above risk appetite B, as it exceeds risk tolerance. Project B should also not be implemented as it does not meet the company's risk appetite. Therefore, only Project C should be implemented.

7.7 Financial Ratings as Alternative Approach to Determine Risk Appetite

A firm's **rating** is an estimate of its probability of default (PD) which can be interpreted as its probability of insolvency. A rating is a risk-oriented assessment of the future creditworthiness of a company. The insolvency risk can thus be expressed by the probability of default respective to the rating. For example, a BBB- rating in Standard and Poor's corresponds to an insolvency probability of up to 0.7% p.a.

A firm's rating depends on (Gleißner, 2022) the following:

- The average expected earnings level of the company
- Its risks as possible deviations from this earnings level (earnings volatility)
- The available risk coverage potential (equity and liquidity reserves)
- The transparency and credibility of the company from the perspective of the credit institutions

In practice, depending on the rating agency, 60 to 80% of a company's rating is determined by its financial ratios. In corporate practice, a threat to the company's existence arises when the occurrence of a risk or the combination of several individual risks causes such a deterioration of important financial covenants, such as the equity ratio, that a target rating necessary for corporate financing is no longer achieved, for example, the investment grade rating. In addition, the violation of financial covenants can lead to the termination of existing loan agreements by the lending banks and thus to insolvency (Gleißner, 2022).

Example: Return to Investment Grade Rating at Lufthansa Group
Before the coronavirus crisis, the rating agencies Standard & Poor's and Moody's both rated the Lufthansa Group as investment grade (31 December 2019: Standard & Poor's "BBB," Moody's "Baa3"). As a result of the coronavirus crisis and its impact, both agencies downgraded their ratings. However, in late November 2022, Standard & Poor's raised its rating to BB with a positive outlook. Moody's has given the Lufthansa Group a "Ba2" rating and raised its outlook to "stable" in early December 2022. Scope Ratings graded the Lufthansa Group at "BBB–" and therefore still in the investment grade range. Moreover, in July 2022 Scope Ratings raised its outlook to "stable."

Development of ratings

Rating/outlook	2022	2021	2020	2019	2018
Standard & Poor's	BB/positive	BB–/stable	BB–/negative	BBB/ stable	BBB–/ positive
Moody's	Ba2/stable	Ba2/negative	Ba2/negative	Baa3/ stable	Baa3/stable
Scope rating	BBB–/ stable	BBB–/ negative	BBB–/ negative	BBB/ stable	BBB–/ positive

Table 7.7 Rating and probability of insolvency

Rating	Rating note	Probability of insolvency (per year)
AAA/AA	1 bis 1.12	< 0.02%
AA–	< 1.25	< 0.03%
A+	< 1.42	< 0.06%
A	< 1.58	< 0.10%
A-	< 1.75	< 0.15%
BBB+	< 2.00	< 0.28%
BBB	< 2.25	< 0.48%
BBB–	< 2.50	< 0.78%
BB+	< 2.83	< 1.37%
BB	< 3.17	< 2.30%
BB–	< 3.50	< 3.61%
B+	< 3.75	< 4.95%
B	< 4.00	< 6.64%
B–	< 4.50	< 11.35%
CCC	4.50 bis 5	> 11.35%

Source: Gleißner (2022, p. 430)

The group aims to restore its investment grade ratings from all of the significant rating agencies. Investment grade ratings for the company's debt ensure good access to the capital markets and low funding costs and thus provide financial flexibility. The conditions for an investment grade rating include further improvement in the operating result and reduction of debt.

Source: Lufthansa Group 2023, *Annual Report 2022*, p. 25

Consequently, a **rating forecast** is used to analyze the effects of management decisions on a firm's financial covenants, rating, and thus risk of insolvency. It makes sense to determine the rating forecast for a risk-dependent stress scenario. For this purpose, the characteristics of the rating-specific financial ratios are determined under the stress scenario, and the future rating is derived from this. The RBC is then measured as the gap between the actual value of a corporate target (e.g., the equity ratio in %) and the value at which the company fails to meet a minimum required target for its financial covenants or rating (Gleißner & Wolfrum, 2017; Gleißner, 2022).

The following table shows an example of a firm's current rating of BB (status quo), which indicates with a probability of default of 1.05% p.a. This means that the firm must file for insolvency roughly once in 100 years. The absolute risk-bearing capacity is associated with a B rating. To determine this minimum rating, the investors can be asked about the largest PD they are willing to accept. In addition, the rating can be derived from the loan agreements and might reflect the minimum rating required from the bank for granting credit facilities. The risk tolerance limit fixes the accepted minimum rating and PD under normal business conditions (Table 7.7).

Table 7.8 Evaluation of a decision alternative (case study)

Target figure	Status quo	Alternative: foreign expansion	
Earnings (EBIT, plan 2017)	US$16 million	US$18.5 million	Significant increase in earnings
Risk (coefficient of variation)	19%	21%	Moderately increased risk
Cost of capital (WACC)	5.5%	5.7%	Moderately increased cost of capital
Rating forecast (plan)	BB+	BB+	No change
Enterprise value	US$153 million	US$168 million	Clear increase in value
Strategic fitting			Competences available

Source: Gleißner (2022, p. 448)

The risk-bearing capacity, risk tolerance, and risk appetite A and B, including the target and the minimum rating, are to be integrated into the strategic and capital planning as well as the performance measurement and remuneration systems, defined in a risk strategy and reviewed annually (Grieser, 2020). In addition, within the framework of integrated performance and risk-oriented corporate management, all decision alternatives must be analyzed based on their contribution to the performance and risk objectives, as the following example shows (Table 7.8).

7.8 Summary

- Strategic ERM is a long-term framework for the operational ERM process consisting of the development of an adequate risk culture and risk strategy, including risk objectives as a foundation for the risk appetite.
- Adequate risk culture is necessary for the development of a joint risk understanding and risk awareness within the company.
- The individual risk attitudes of the stakeholders, the managers, and the employees determine their risk behavior. The risk attitude of the shareholders should be the foundation for the targeted risk-return profile of the company.
- The risk-bearing capacity checks if the risk capital covers a firm's risk exposure measured during the operational ERM process.
- Additional concepts are a firm's risk tolerance and its risk appetite.
- The risk capital consists of a firm's financial and liquidity buffers. In addition, a minimum financial rating must be achieved to prevent a firm from insolvency.
- To ensure a targeted risk-return profile, adequate risk-adjusted performance measures must be defined and integrated in the performance measurement and incentive respective remuneration systems.

7.9 Exercises and Questions

1. What are the goals and tasks of strategic ERM?
2. Explain the elements of the strategic ERM framework for the operational ERM process.
3. What is risk culture? Why is it relevant for a successful implementation of ERM?
4. How can a risk culture be implemented in a company?
5. Discuss the relevance of individual risk attitude for ERM and risk culture.
6. Differentiate between the concepts of risk-bearing capacity, risk tolerance, and risk appetite.
7. What is the relevance of a firm's financial rating for its risk-bearing capacity, risk tolerance, and risk appetite?
8. Vanini Ltd. can implement three different strategic alternatives. Which alternative should the company choose?

	Δ Risk in million US$	RBC in million US$	Δ Income in million US$
Status quo		150	
Alternative A	100		40
Alternative B	150		60
Alternative C	200		100

9. Why are different classes of risk coverage potential calculated?
10. Calculate the risk coverage potential of Vanini Ltd. using the values from the profit and liquidity planning for the following year and the balance sheet:
    - Planned profit US$1 million, of which:
    - Planned allocation to revenue reserves and distributions—US$0.5 million.
    - Existing and planned provisions—US$0.3 million.
    - Book value of company real estate—US$0.3 million.
    - Market value: US$3 million—US$.
    - Existing open revenue reserves—US$1.5 million.
    - Share capital—US$0.2 million.
    - Long-term liabilities to credit institutions—US$5 million.
    - Undrawn credit lines—US$2 million.

References

Behrends, T. (2003). Organisationskultur. In A. Martin (Ed.), *Organizational behaviour - Verhalten in organisationen* (pp. 241–261). Kohlhammer.

Burger, A., & Buchhart, A. (2014). *Risiko-controlling*. Walter de Gruyter GmbH & Co KG.

Byrnes, J. P., Miller, D. C., & Schafer, W. D. (1999). Gender differences in risk taking: A meta-analysis. *Psychological Bulletin, 125*, 367–383.

Collier, P. M. M., Berry, A., & Burke, G. T. T. (2007). *Risk and management accounting: Best practice guidelines for enterprise-wide internal control procedures*. Elsevier.

COSO. (2017). Enterprise risk management - integrating with strategy and performance.

Diederichs, M. (2018). *Risikomanagement und Risikocontrolling* (4th ed.). Vahlen.

Fraser, J. R. S., & Simkins, B. J. (2016). The challenges of and solutions for implementing enterprise risk management. *Business Horizons, 59*, 689–698.

Frigo, M. L., & Anderson, R. J. (2011). Strategic risk management: A foundation for improving enterprise risk management and governance. *Journal of Corporate Accounting and Finance, 22*, 81–88.

Giebel, S. (2011). *Optimierung der passiven Risikobewältigung: Integration von Selbsttragen und Risikotransfer im Rahmen des industriellen Risikomanagements*. Schriftenreihe Finanz- und Risikomanagement, Bd. 16. Shaker, Aachen.

Gleißner, W. (2019). Cost of capital and probability of default in value-based risk management. *Management Research Review, 42*, 1243–1258.

Gleißner, W. (2022). *Grundlagen des Risikomanagements: Handbuch für ein Management unter Unsicherheit* (Management competence) (4th ed.). Verlag Franz Vahlen.

Gleißner, W. (2023). Uncertainty and resilience in strategic management: Profile of a robust company. *The International Journal of Risk Assessment and Management (IJRAM), 26*, 75–94.

Gleißner, W., & Wolfrum, M. (2015). Problemfelder der Risikoquantifizierung, Datenprobleme und Lösungs-strategien. In W. Gleißner & F. Romeike (Eds.), *Praxishandbuch Risikomanagement: Konzepte - Methoden - Umsetzung* (1st ed., pp. 274–263). Erich Schmidt Verlag.

Gleißner, W., & Wolfrum, M. (2017). Risikotragfähigkeit, Risikotoleranz, Risikoappetit und Risikodeckungspotential. *Controller Magazin, 42*, 77–84.

Gleißner, W., & Wolfrum, M. (2021). Probleme der Risikoquantifizierung und Lösungsstrategien. In S. Bier, A. Burgermeister, O. Disch, P. Gann, W. Gleißner, J.-S. Golz, C. Maron, C. Mayer, J. Offerhaus, E. Roßmeißl, F. Thom, S. Weichelt, G. Wieczorek, S. Wilke, & M. Wolfrum (Eds.), *Risikoquantifizierung: Grundlagen - Werkzeuge - Praxisbeispiele* (pp. 123–144). Schmidt.

Grieser, F. (2020). Risk appetite. *Controlling, 32*, 38–42.

Grieser, F., & Pedell, B. (2022). Exploring risk culture controls: To what extent can the development of organizational risk culture be controlled and how? *Journal of Accounting and Organizational Change, 18*, 752–788.

Hardy, M. R., & Saunders, D. (2022). Quantitative enterprise risk management. *International series on actuarial science*, 2022: 1. Cambridge University Press.

Hofstede, G. (2001). *Culture's consequences: Comparing values, behaviors, institutions and organizations across nations*. Sage.

Hölscher, R. (2002). Von der Versicherung zur integrativen Risikobewältigung: Die Konzeption eines modernen Risikomanagements. In R. Elfen & R. Hölscher (Eds.), *Herausforderung Risikomanagement: Identifikation, Bewertung und Steuerung industrieller Risiken* (1st ed., pp. 3–32). Gabler Verlag.

Hunziker, S. (2021). *Enterprise risk management: Modern approaches to balancing risk and reward* (2nd ed.). Springer.

Jankensgård, H., & Kapstad, P. (2021). *Empowered enterprise risk management: Theory and practice*. Wiley.

Jensen, M. C., & Meckling, W. H. (1976). Theory of the firm: Managerial behavior, agency costs and ownership structure. *Journal of Financial Economics, 3*, 305–360.

Kahneman, D., & Tversky, A. (1979). Intuitive prediction: Biases and corrective procedures. *TIMS Studies in Management Science, 12*, 313–327.

Larcker, D. F., Ormazabal, G., Tayan, B., & Taylor, D. J. (2014). *Follow the money: Compensation, risk, and the financial crisis*. Rock Center for corporate governance at Stanford University closer look series: Topics, issues and controversies in corporate governance No. CGRP-43. Stanford University Graduate School of Business Research Paper.

Mikes, A. (2009). Risk management and calculative cultures. *Management Accounting Research, 20*, 18–40. https://doi.org/10.1016/j.mar.2008.10.005
Nicholson, N., Soane, E., Fenton-O'Creevy, M., & Willman, P. (2005). Personality and domain-specific risk taking. *Journal of Risk Research, 8*, 157–176.
Nosic, A., & Weber, M. (2007). *Determinants of risk taking behavior: The role of risk attitudes, risk perceptions and beliefs*. Universität Mannheim.
Schein, E. H. (2010). *Organizational culture and leadership (2010)* (4th ed.). The Jossey-Bass business and management series.
The Institute of Risk Management. (2011). *Risk appetite & tolerance: Guidance Paper*, London.
The Institute of Risk Management. (2012). *Risk culture: Under the microscope - guidance for boards*. https://www.theirm.org/media/8447/risk_culture_a5_web15_oct_2012-executive-summary.pdf
Vanini, U. (2024). Risikoneigung und Risikoverhalten. In J. Basel & P. Henrizi (Eds.), *Psychologie von Risiko und Vertrauen: Wahrnehmung, Verhalten und Kommunikation* (pp. 107–126). Springer.
Vanini, U., & Rieg, R. (2021). *Risikomanagement: Grundlagen -- Instrumente -- Unternehmenspraxis* (Lehrbuch) (2nd ed.). Schäffer-Poeschel Verlag Stuttgart.
Weber, E. U., & Johnson, E. J. (2009). Decisions under uncertainty: Psychological, economic, and neuroeconomic explanations of risk preference. In P. Glimcher, C. Cramerer, E. Fehr, & P. Poldrack (Eds.), *Neuroeconomics: Decision making and the brain* (pp. 127–144). Elsevier.

Chapter 8
Operational Perspective on the ERM Process

Abstract Risks must be identified and assessed on an ongoing basis as part of the operational ERM process. Companies have various methods and tools at their disposal for this purpose, including early warning systems, scenario analyses, statistical risk modelling, and aggregation methods. Monte Carlo simulation (MCS) is particularly suitable for determining the overall risk exposure and thus for monitoring the risk-bearing capacity. In addition, a firm's risk status and risk-bearing capacity must be reported as part of internal risk reporting and external risk disclosure so that mitigation measures can be taken if necessary.

Keywords At risk · Monte Carlo simulation (MCS) · Risk aggregation · Risk disclosure · Risk identification · Risk quantification · Risk reporting

Questions

- Which are the objectives of risk identification?
- Which requirements must be fulfilled by risk identification?
- Which information sources, methods, and instruments can be used for risk identification? Differentiate between preventable, strategic, external, and novel risks.
- Discuss typical problems of risk identification.
- Describe the concept and the objectives of risk quantification.
- Justify the primacy of risk quantification.
- Which requirements must be fulfilled by risk quantification?
- Which methods and instruments can be used for risk quantification?
- How can risks be described by probability distributions? Differentiate between event risk and distribution risks.
- Discuss different approaches to risk aggregation.
- Which problems occur during risk quantification and aggregation?
- Describe the concept and objectives of risk reporting.

Supplementary Information The online version contains supplementary material available at https://doi.org/10.1007/978-3-031-86425-4_8.

R. Rieg et al., *Enterprise Risk Management*, Springer Texts in Business and Economics, https://doi.org/10.1007/978-3-031-86425-4_8

- What are the differences between internal risk reporting and external risk disclosure?
- Which requirements must be fulfilled by risk reporting and disclosure?
- What are the key design criteria for risk reporting?
- Discuss problems of risk reporting and disclosure.

8.1 Risk Identification

In practice, ERM is often structured as an **operational process** consisting of several stages: risk identification, risk quantification, risk aggregation, risk reporting and disclosure, and risk monitoring. The operational ERM process has the following **objectives** (COSO, 2017):

- Timely identification and intake of new emerging risks and confirmation of the relevance of already identified risks.
- Prioritization of identified risks for risk quantification.
- Quantification of the probability of occurrence and impact of material risks.
- Aggregation of risk and determination of the overall risk exposure.
- Risk mitigation in accordance with the risk-bearing capacity.
- Continuous monitoring of the ERM system and process.

This chapter focuses on the first four stages of the operational ERM process. The ERM system and the operational ERM process are monitored by supervisory bodies such as the supervisory board, internal audit, and external auditors. We therefore refer to Section 12, in which these functions and their tasks in the ERM system are explained.

During **risk identification,** all uncertain events and developments that have the potential to lead to deviations from the planned target must be identified. The purpose of risk identification is the creation of a **risk inventory,** which is the current, systematic, complete, and economic recording of all material sources of danger, causes of damage, disturbance potentials, and opportunities as well as their mutual dependencies. The risk inventory is sometimes also called the risk register (Jankensgård & Kapstad, 2021). While risk identification is continuous throughout the operational ERM process, the risk inventory comprises the complete survey of all risks of a company at a certain point in time (e.g., at the end of the year). The frequency of risk identification depends on the environmental dynamics and uncertainty and the complexity of the organization. It is carried out by top management and the risk owners in the decentralized units of an organization. The effectiveness of risk identification determines the effectiveness and efficiency of the further stages of the operational ERM process (COSO, 2017; Vanini & Rieg, 2021).

The foundation for risk identification is a comprehensive and specific risk definition and a non-overlapping **risk categorization** such as a risk catalogue (see Sect. 1.3). During risk identification, new and emerging risks must be identified, and the relevance of previously identified risks is checked. An initial assessment of identified risks is carried out, using the following assessment criteria (Jankensgård & Kapstad, 2021):

- Risk impact or extent of damage.
- Frequency or probability of occurrence.
- Interdependencies with other risks.
- Impact horizon (short, medium, or long term) or response period.
- Local significance (local, regional, national, or international).

8.1.1 Overview of Sources and Methods for Risk Identification

A company can use different methods to identify risks. Risk identification can be done systematically (e.g., by controlling early warning indicators) or unsystematically (e.g., by brainstorming). Some approaches are more suitable for identifying single risks such as checklists, while others are optimal for identifying aggregated risks such as system analyses). Overall, risk identification requires a large amount of internal and external information, which must be continuously collected, filtered, and processed. The following **sources** of information for risk identification are distinguished (COSO, 2017; Hunziker, 2021):

- Cognitive computing and artificial intelligence for the identification of new and emerging risks from large external volumes of data
- Data tracking from past events of risk occurrence
- Visits and inspections for internal or technical risks for visual risk identification
- Document analysis to identify process or organizational risks
- Analysis of planning assumptions and strategic and operative planning tools
- Surveys, interviews, and workshops with staff and experts
- Process and system analyses
- Early warning indicators and key risk scores

Due to digitalization, extensive structured and unstructured digital data (big data) are increasingly being used as sources of information for risk identification. Special analytical methods such as text mining are available for the evaluation of big data. These procedures are also referred to as **big data analytics**.

Example: Risk Identification in the Lufthansa Group

The closed and continuous risk management process, which is supported by IT, begins with the identification of current and future, existing and potential opportunities and risks from all material internal and external areas. The Lufthansa Group defines opportunities and risks as the possible positive or negative deviations from a forecast figure or a defined objective. The risks identified are checked for plausibility by the companies' risk coordinators and gathered together in the Group's risk portfolio. The risk portfolio documents the systematic entirety of all individual risks and constitutes the quality-assured result of the identification phase. As the risk landscape is dynamic and subject to change, the identification of risks is a continuous task for the risk owners. Risk owners are obliged at least once a quarter to verify that the risks for which they are responsible are complete and up to date. They also evaluate the extent to which circumstances involving risk have already been included in the forecast results and to what extent there are additional opportunities or risks of achieving a better or worse result than the one forecast. They actively manage opportunities and risks by means of risk mitigation instruments and measures. (source: *Annual Report 2022,* Lufthansa Group 2023, p. 76)

There are various methods for risk identification, all of which start either with recording the causes of a risk or analyzing the effects of a risk. The following sections present suitable methods grouped according to Kaplan and Mikes' (2012) categorization of risks into preventable, strategy, and external risks (for an overview, see also COSO, 2017; Vanini & Rieg, 2021). In addition, we add a section on the identification of novel risks. This is not an exhaustive list of methods. Moreover, most methods are suitable for identifying several types of risk.

8.1.2 Methods for the Identification of Preventable Risks

Preventable risks such as unauthorized manager or employee behavior or breakdowns of routine operational processes mainly have their causes inside the organization. Preventable risks are best identified by local managers and employees in decentralized business units. They are therefore controllable and should be avoided or eliminated when they have the potential to cause severe damage to the firm (Kaplan & Mikes, 2012). Nevertheless, preventable risks are often confounded with **business and decision problems**. Business and decision problems such as inefficient processes or underperforming business units indicate existing weaknesses or unfavorable conditions in a company that must be managed but that do not represent risks since their effects on targets are well known (Hunziker, 2021).

There are numerous **collection and search methods** used to identify preventable organizational and process risks (for a more detailed presentation, see Vanini & Rieg, 2021):

- **Site inspections** are among the collection methods. They identify visually detectable risks by inspecting risk-prone objects such as production facilities. Site inspections can be combined with checklists to obtain a general overview, uncover specific risks, or obtain additional information.
- **Risk checklists** also fall under collection methods. They are standardized questionnaires that enable the systematic and cost-efficient collection of well-known individual risks, risk-triggering factors, and vulnerable objects. They consist of open or closed questions. Questionnaires with closed questions are best suited for the identification of hazard potentials, as evaluation is easier and leads to concrete results more quickly compared to questionnaires with open questions. Frequently, risk checklists include an initial quantitative or qualitative assessment of identified risks. Nevertheless, risk checklists might prevent managers and employees from engaging in independent thought and thus may reduce risk identification to a mere ticking of boxes. In addition, the collected risks might be incomplete if newly emerging risks are not integrated or if there is a focus on more marginal

risks. Finally, they do not always establish a clear link to business objectives (Hunziker, 2021).

- **Risk workshops** try to combine the risk-relevant knowledge of managers and employees from different functions and hierarchical levels. Since these people are confronted with many risks during their daily work, they normally have a strong motivation to avoid or at least to reduce these risks and can provide expert information. The composition, number, and duration of risk workshops depend on the size of the company and the scope of the risks analyzed. The corporate risk manager should act as a facilitator and moderator. To ensure that dependencies and correlations between individual risks are taken into account, risk identification should take place along the value chain or within the organizational structure (Hunziker, 2021; Gleißner, 2022).
- **Process and system analysis methods** are primarily used to identify the risks of complex technical systems. These methods include failure mode and effects analysis (FMEA), fault tree analysis (FTA), and incident analysis. The aim of **FMEA** is to identify the sensitive components of a technical system. It was developed to analyze potential hazards in aircraft, but it is also suitable for other technical systems. During an FMEA, the potential effects of the failure of single (sub-)components on a complex technical system are analyzed (bottom-up approach). Possible causes of faults, their effects, and the threatened objects are documented in detail using worksheets, and an initial risk assessment is made with regard to probability of occurrence and the extent of possible damage. The starting point of an **FTA** is a failure of a technical system. The aim is to determine all possible causes and combinations of causes for this failure through a deductive top-down approach. In the first step, secondary causes of the disruption of the overall system are presented; these are then further broken down into the primary causes of disruption. A fault tree graphically represents all fault events that can lead to system damage. Complex fault events are further divided into simpler events by means of logical operators. With this method, even improbable event combinations with considerable error potential can be identified. However, detailed knowledge of the system is an essential prerequisite for the application of this method. **Incident analyses** attempt to systematize all target deviations that can be traced back to a common cause. The starting point is an undesired event (incident) that leads to subsequent events, which in turn can lead to deviations from the target. Incident analysis and FTA can be combined with FMEA (Romeike, 2018; Hunziker, 2021; Gleißner, 2022).

8.1.3 Methods for the Identification of Strategic Risks

Strategic risks result from the business model and strategy of a company. As they are often also the basis for considerable chances, they should not be totally avoided. To identity strategic risks, the ERM function can initiate **risk workshops** with the top management and the supervisory board. In addition, strategic environmental and

Table 8.1 SWOT matrix (source: Baum et al., 2013)

		Results of the company analysis	
		Strengths	Weaknesses
Results of the environmental analysis	Opportunities	Using the strengths of the company to exploit opportunities (growth strategy).	Overcoming the weaknesses of the company by exploiting the opportunities.
	Risks (threats)	Using the strengths of the company to minimize risks.	Minimizing the company's weaknesses and risks (defensive strategy).

business analysis methods, such as a SWOT analysis, can be applied (Kaplan & Mikes, 2012). A business model or a strategy often relies on implicit or explicit assumptions concerning the internal strength and weaknesses of a company and the future development of uncertain external factors, such as the behavior of competitors or changes in the prices of important raw materials. From the perspective of a company, these uncertain assumptions indicate strategic risks that must be identified, and their impact on the business strategy and performance must be assessed (Hunziker, 2021).

Environmental and business analyses are instruments of strategic management accounting. They are the basis for strategy development and can be used to identify possible threats and opportunities for strategy implementation (strategic risks). Company and environmental analyses include the analysis of success factors, SWOT analyses, product life cycle analyses, the experience curve concept, and competition analyses such as Porter's five forces or portfolio analyses. Due to the large number of approaches and instruments and the overlaps with strategic management accounting, we refrain from a detailed discussion of all instruments and refer the reader to the relevant literature. As an example, the SWOT analysis is presented and discussed below (Hunziker, 2021; Gleißner, 2022).

In **SWOT analyses**, the strengths, weaknesses, opportunities, and threats of a company are analyzed, compared to those of the main competitors, and classified in a matrix. The strengths and weaknesses of a company are examined using internal company analyses in which the strategic potentials of the company are evaluated by comparing its value chain with the value chain of its main competitors. To interpret the opportunities and threats, various environmental analyses are employed. One such environmental analysis method is Porter's industry structure analysis, which examines the threats to the company posed by new competitors, the bargaining power of buyers and suppliers, the threat from substitute products, and the intensity of competition in the industry. The company's risks and opportunities are derived from this examination. A SWOT analysis provides more detailed insights into the current state of an organization (core competencies), the target groups (target group focus and needs), the competitive environment (positioning, scope of services, unique selling propositions), and the positioning in the market (market presence). The results of the environmental and corporate analyses are evaluated by an internal analysis team and entered into a SWOT matrix (Romeike, 2018) (Table 8.1).

Another approach for the identification of strategic risks is the **analysis of uncertain management assumptions** underlying the business model, the strategic planning, and the operational planning and budgeting. Unfortunately, the management assumptions underlying business models and strategies are not always well documented, so risk managers have to interview the responsible managers to reveal their explicit and implicit assumptions and expectations concerning the future development of uncertain factors such as expected behavior of competitors. Afterward, the impact of these uncertain assumptions and expectations on the business model and the strategic objectives must be analyzed to identify the crucial risk factors for corporate success (Hunziker, 2021).

The planned profit for the following year is the result of an operational planning and budgeting process based on numerous assumptions regarding the short-term development of risk factors. However, these planning assumptions are often uncertain, so deviations from the planned profit development are likely to occur. For example, the future development of turnover depends on the planned sales volumes and the company's product pricing, and it is thus strongly affected by the forecasted market development and the behavior of competitors. By systematically varying the planning assumptions and conducting a detailed deviation analysis, the main risk factors for future firm performance can be identified. If necessary, early warning indicators for these risk factors can be defined and monitored. In addition, the variance analysis offers an initial approach to risk quantification by valuing the variances in monetary terms and estimating their probabilities of occurrence (Gleißner, 2022).

8.1.4 Methods for the Identification of External Risks

External risks arise from outside a company. These risks are beyond the control of the firm, and thus firms cannot prevent their occurrence but should reduce their impact. Examples are natural, economic, and geopolitical disasters with a mostly immediate impact; geopolitical and environmental changes with medium- and long-term effects; and competitive and technology risks with a medium-term impact. The typical methods for identifying external risks include early warning systems, stress testing, scenario analysis, and tools such as business war-gaming (Kaplan & Mikes, 2012). As stress testing and scenario analysis are also approaches for risk quantification, we discuss them in the following section and focus on early warning systems and business war-gaming here.

Early warning systems are based on specific **early warning indicators** that depict relevant environmental, political, social, or economic changes and have a cause-and-effect relationship with the corporate objectives. For example, a decline in the number of orders received by a plant manufacturer is an early warning indicator of a future drop in turnover. The quality of these early warning systems depends largely on the comprehensiveness and the validity of the selected indicators.

Table 8.2 Observation areas and examples of early warning indicators (source: Diederichs, 2018)

External area	Indicators		
Macroeconomic	• Interest • Exchange rates • Inflation rates • Net industrial production	• Collective wage level • Foreign trade • Money supply • Economic indices	• Business climate • Investment trends • Market growth
Society/culture	• Population growth • Population structure • Unemployment figures • Number of vacancies	• Trade union demands • Propensity to consume • Income development Educational level	• Lifestyle • Values • Migration movements
Technology	• Innovations • Material developments • Disruption of technological trend lines	• Change trends in production and process technology among competitors and research institutes	
Politics/law	• System stability • Political crises • Party relations • Change of government	• Legislative preparations/bills • Legal certainty • Political organizations	• Foreign and domestic political events or trends
Ecology	• Environmental compatibility of products and input materials		

Table 8.2 gives some examples of early warning indicators for different observation areas.

Business war-gaming is a strategic tool used by companies to simulate competitive scenarios, identify potential risks, and evaluate opportunities (Kaplan & Mikes, 2012). When external risks and opportunities are identified, the following process can be applied:

- **Scenario development:** The process starts with identifying relevant external factors such as market trends, competitor behavior, regulatory changes, and technological advancements. Based on these factors, several scenarios that could potentially impact the business are developed.
- **Simulation setup:** Teams within the company are assigned roles representing different stakeholders such as competitors, customers, suppliers, and regulatory bodies. The scenarios are then simulated in a controlled environment, often facilitated by a moderator or a team of moderators.
- **Gameplay:** Participants engage in a series of structured discussions, decision-making exercises, and role-playing activities to respond to the simulated scenarios. They make strategic choices based on the information available, their understanding of the market dynamics, and their assumptions about how competitors and other stakeholders might behave.

- **Analysis and learning:** Throughout gameplay, data is collected on the decisions made by participants and the outcomes of those decisions. After the simulation, this data is analyzed to identify patterns, trends, strengths, weaknesses, opportunities, and threats. Insights gained from the simulation help the company better understand the potential impact of external factors on its business.
- **Strategy refinement:** The insights gained from the war-gaming exercise are used to refine the company's strategic plans. This could involve adjusting existing strategies, developing contingency plans, reallocating resources, or identifying new opportunities for growth.
- **Iterative process:** Business war-gaming is an iterative process, meaning that companies may conduct multiple rounds of simulations to test different strategies, assumptions, and scenarios. Each iteration helps to deepen the understanding of the external environment and fine-tune its strategic responses.

Overall, business war-gaming provides companies with a structured approach to explore and prepare for potential external risks and opportunities. By simulating different scenarios in a controlled environment, companies can gain valuable insights that inform their strategic decision-making and enhance their ability to navigate an uncertain business landscape.

8.1.5 Methods for the Identification of Novel Risks

The above discussed preventable, strategic, and routine risks can be characterized as routine because the company is familiar with the management of these risks. However, there are also novel risks that result from unforeseen events, complex combinations of routine risks, and routine risks occurring at unprecedented scales and speeds (Kaplan et al., 2020). Kaplan et al. (2020) differentiate between **black swan risks** resulting from rare and unprecedented events (see also Chap. 1 and Taleb (2012)), **perfect storms** resulting from unforeseen combinations of routine risks, and **mega-risks** resulting from routine risks developing at very high speeds or on large scales. Other novel risks are dragon kings, gray swans, and gray elephants (Glette-Iversen & Aven, 2021). Novel risks often cannot be managed by routine risk management methods because their probabilities and impacts cannot be quantified. Even worse, due to multiple biases and a lack of risk consciousness and knowledge, they are often not even identified as risks (Kaplan et al., 2020; Hunziker, 2021).

Creativity techniques, Delphi studies, and the analysis of weak signals can be used to identify novel risks. **Creativity techniques** are unsystematic risk identification instruments. They are based on intuition and association, but the process of generating ideas is methodically supported. Novel risks are identified through associations with similar risks or confrontations with conceivable risks. **Brainstorming** involves moderated group discussions conducted in a workshop context to promote creativity. During the workshop, the participants spontaneously and unrestrictedly list potentially novel risks from their point of view. The suggestions

Table 8.3 Examples of weak signals (source: Baum et al., 2013)

Weak signal	Consequence
Advances in solid-state physics in the 1940s	Replacement of the tube by the transistor and processor
Increasing performance and standardization of microprocessors	Replacement of large computer systems by personal computers
Glasnost and perestroika in the former Soviet Union	Collapse of the Eastern Bloc and opening of markets in Eastern Europe
Experiments with laser propulsion for space rockets	Still unknown, but current rocket propulsion technology is 1000 times more expensive
Spread of the Internet	Change in private and corporate communication; discontinuation of traditional business models and emergence of new ones
Development of the blue diode by Shuji Nakamura	Replacement of traditional lighting technology with LEDs that can display the complete light spectrum

are not evaluated, since brainstorming focuses on quantity. Afterward, the suggestions are discussed, sorted, and structured by the participants. **Brainwriting** is a written creativity technique. **Delphi studies** are also helpful in identifying novel external risks. Expert knowledge can be gained either through surveys or review of the relevant technical literature. A Delphi survey is used to forecast complex, unstructured, long-term issues and novel developments with a long-term horizon. It combines expert opinions and condenses them to arrive at a consensus.

Another group of more strategically oriented early warning systems identify and evaluate qualitative **weak signals** that indicate long-term discontinuities in the economic, social, political, and technological environment of a company. These systems are based on the assumption that discontinuities do not occur suddenly but are announced by certain signals, including statements and opinions of key persons and organizations. Methodologically, they are based on Ansoff's concept of weak signals and diffusion theory, which argues that exogenous structural breaks do not occur suddenly and surprisingly but rather announce themselves through fuzzy information (i.e., weak signals; Ansoff, 1975). Weak signals represent relatively unstructured and qualitative information (e.g., the emergence of new needs, changes in basic attitudes, or even radical technological innovations; Holopainen & Toivonen, 2012; Baum et al., 2013; Diederichs, 2018). Examples of weak signals and their consequences can be found in Table 8.3.

Possible sources for weak signals include the Internet, social media communities, discussion or expert forums, publications in trade journals, trends in case law, announcements of changes in legislation, patents, and conference papers. In addition, machine learning approaches (e.g., artificial neural networks) have also proven their worth for pattern recognition in mass data (Holopainen & Toivonen, 2012).

Weak signals are **initially** very **vague** and **ambiguous** in terms of their impact on the company, but they become stronger and less fuzzy over time. The earlier the relevance of a weak signal is recognized, the more options a company has for action.

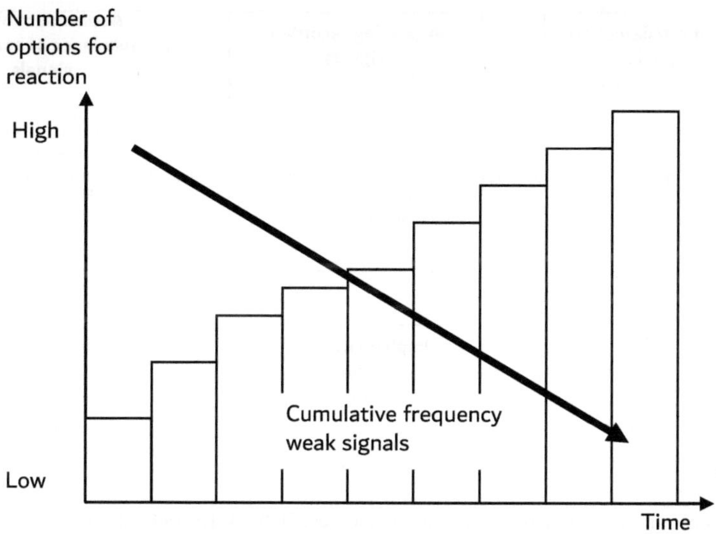

Fig. 8.1 Relationship between the cumulative frequency of weak signals and the number of opportunities for action (source: Ansoff, 1975; Hahn & Krystek, 2000)

However, the interpretation is also very uncertain, and the possible implications for an industry, market, or product are very difficult to derive (Ansoff, 1975) (Fig. 8.1).

Weak signals should be picked up by a 360° radar (strategic radar). The aim is to identify potential discontinuities in environmental development and to assess their impact on the company. **Scanning** refers to the process of searching the corporate environment for weak signals in an undirected manner. If the source of a potential discontinuity is identified and its nature is increasingly understood, the weak signal becomes a trend and must be continuously **monitored** (Ansoff, 1975; Burger & Buchhart, 2014; Diederichs, 2018) (Fig. 8.2).

Strategic early warning is very difficult to implement in corporate practice, as weak signals usually have to be recognized in their early phases and their relevance must be correctly interpreted in order to enable the company to gain a competitive advantage. Especially in the early phases, these signals are very diffuse and carry the risk of considerable misinvestment. In addition, this places heavy demands on companies' information processing capacity, but it can gain in importance through the use of business analytics approaches such as data mining or text mining.

8.1.6 Documentation of Identified Risks

Risk identification templates, bow tie analysis templates, and risk inventories can be used to document identified risks. **Risk identification templates** are used by many companies to systematically document risks identified throughout the company and

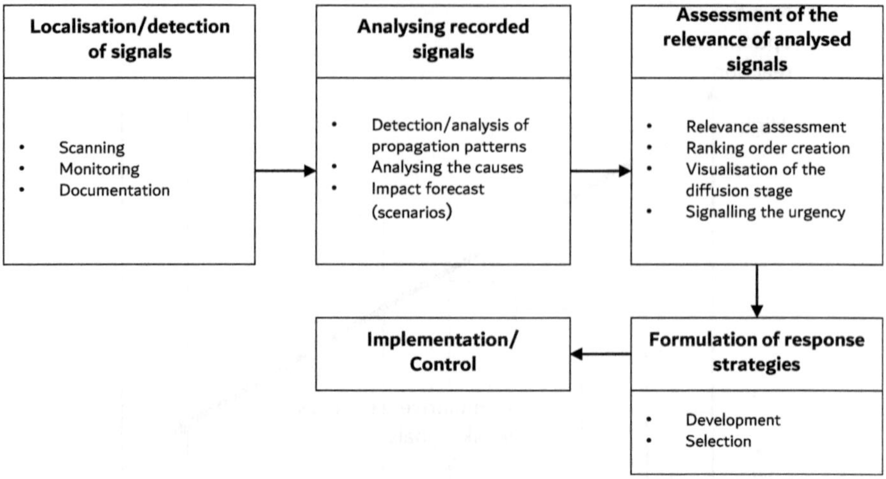

Fig. 8.2 Procedure of strategic early-warning (source: Hahn & Krystek, 2000)

derive initial assessment approaches, such as a first estimation of the probabilities of occurrence for various scenarios. Table 8.4, an example of such a template is presented.

However, the use of risk identification templates often leads to a large number of more or less material risks. In addition, identical risks are often named differently by employees and therefore recorded twice. For this reason, the risks identified locally must be cleared of redundancies and overlaps by the central risk manager before they are included in the risk inventory or risk register.

The **bow tie analysis** serves to visualize the different causes and effects of an identified risk and is quite useful for identifying interdependencies between the various risks of a company and developing a first approach for risk control (Romeike, 2018) (Fig. 8.3).

Following risk identification, the identified risks must be adjusted, aggregated, documented, and assigned to individual business units. A **risk inventory** or **risk register** can be used as a suitable instrument for this purpose. In a risk inventory, material risks and their initial assessments are presented in a condensed and comprehensive manner (Jankensgård & Kapstad, 2021). Management problems and non-material risks should not be included in the risk inventory to ensure that management attention is focused on the key risks (Hunziker, 2021). After a plausibility and consistency check, the risks recorded at the operational level are processed and adjusted for overlaps and redundancies. It is also important to clearly assign the identified and documented risks to specific risk categories and business units. An overview of losses actually incurred in the past period can be added to the risk inventory, providing information on the amount of losses, their causes, and the measures used to control them. A complete risk inventory is usually prepared once a year (COSO, 2017; Jankensgård & Kapstad, 2021).

Table 8.4 Risk identification sheet (source: Vanini & Weinstock, 2006)

Risk identification template					
• Company: • Division: • Business unit:					
• Risk owner:					
• Risk: • Risk category:					
• Detailed risk description, including causes:					
• Early-warning indicators:	• 1 • 2 • 3				
• Probabilities of occurrence p.a.:	• Very unlikely • $p < 1\%$	• Unlikely • $1\% < p < 10\%$	• Likely • $10\% < p < 20\%$	• Very likely • $20\% < p < 40\%$	• Acute • $p > 40\%$
• Effects	• Worst case • EBIT • Cash flow • Others		• Real case • EBIT • Cash flow • Others		• Best case • EBIT • Cash flow • Others
• Trend	• Increasing		• Stable		• Decreasing
• Description of risk scenario including interdependencies					

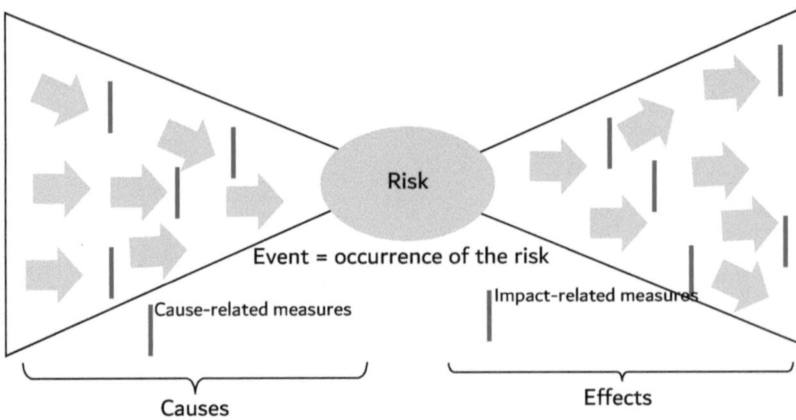

Fig. 8.3 Framework for a bow tie analysis (source: Romeike, 2018)

8.1.7 Problems of Risk Identification

All methods of risk identification have strengths and weaknesses. A standardized risk checklist supports a consistent risk identification and, if structured appropriately, ensures a systematic approach. SWOT analyses, early warning systems, and system analyses also reveal a high degree of systematicity. A bow tie analysis is particularly useful for risk communication due to its structured visualization (Burger & Buchhart, 2014; Romeike, 2018). The main problem is that the methods discussed above only allow for the identification of certain types of risks. An employee survey, for example, is usually limited to internal risks. Site visits and processes or system analyses concentrate on visually recognizable or technical risks. **Completeness** is of central importance in risk identification, as unidentified risks cannot be assessed and controlled in the ERM process. To capture as many risks as possible, different instruments should be combined so that the advantages of individual instruments are capitalized upon and their weaknesses are compensated for. For example, the initial risk identification could be based on brainstorming, and risks that have been identified are regularly reviewed using checklists. Moreover, identifying the same risks through different instruments provides certainty that the risks have been correctly identified. Since it is not possible to identify all relevant opportunities and risks, buffers should always be planned in the risk-bearing capacity concept to cover the impacts of unexpected risks.

Overall, risk identification faces many problems (Diederichs, 2018; Hunziker, 2021):

- Risks are **often recorded twice** because both the cause and effect of a risk are noted (e.g., Risk 1 might be power failure in production, and Risk 2 could be loss of sales due to business interruption because of fire or power failure).

- Often, there is **no standardized risk categorization** upon which to base risk identification, so risks are not identified and documented in a uniform manner. As a result, there is a danger of risk overlaps that must be cleared up before risk quantification. In addition, the **variety of identified risks** makes the identification of risk interdependencies and risk quantification very difficult.
- There is a **goal conflict** between a complete risk identification and an economic one because a complete identification of all risks is very time-consuming and expensive.
- In addition, risk identification captures not only true risks but **also business and decision problems** such as organizational and process deficiencies. These business and decision problems must be dealt with, but they are not managed by ERM as they are not uncertain and are entirely under the control of management.
- Overall, there is a danger of **focusing too much on internal and operational risks** (operational blindness) and less on strategic and external risks. In addition, relevant (external) stakeholders are not involved in risk identification, leading to an incomplete risk inventory.
- Furthermore, firms are often reluctant to conduct a thorough risk identification and analysis in very profitable business units.
- To limit the variety of risks, **only material risks** should be identified. However, assessing the economic materiality of risks requires their prior identification, so this demand cannot be met.
- Additionally, there is a danger in risk identification that significant risks are not recognized (**meta-risk**). In particular, the identification of strategy and novel risks causes great problems due to a lack of empirical values.
- Successful risk identification depends to a large extent on the technical and methodological competence and confidence of the employees involved, since risks can rarely be determined objectively and require subjective interpretation. The **employees' understanding of risk** and their willingness to communicate risk are shaped by the company's risk culture. An insufficient risk culture and overly formal risk recording procedures can cause employees not to report risks because they fear negative consequences.
- In many companies, there is a pronounced bottom-up approach to risk identification, so **cross-divisional risks** are often not identified.
- Furthermore, risk identification cannot be completely separated from risk quantification, meaning that there is an overlap of tools and responsibilities.

8.2 Risk Quantification

8.2.1 Concept and Objectives of Risk Quantification

During the second stage of the operational ERM process, all identified risks must be quantified. There is no consensus concerning the definition of risk quantification in the literature. In some cases, the terms risk measurement, risk quantification, risk analysis, and risk assessment are even used synonymously. During **risk quantification**, a financial value is assigned to opportunities and risks as an expression of their materiality. For this purpose, different scenarios must be created for event risks and should include the probability of occurrence and extent of damage or respective gain. Distribution risks must be described by adequate distribution functions to be able to quantify the risk. A **risk analysis** examines the extent to which risk factors influence the value of risks. However, not all risks are valued in financial terms. For example, ESG risks relate to non-monetary corporate objectives or important stakeholders' objectives (e.g., the reduction of carbon emissions). In such cases, non-financial risk quantification becomes necessary. In the case of an insufficient or missing data basis, qualitative risk assessment (e.g., through subjective risk classification) is often suggested. Despite its widespread use in corporate practice, qualitative risk assessment must be considered as inadequate since it offers great scope for subjectivity (Hunziker, 2021; Gleißner, 2022). Overall, the term used in this textbook is "risk quantification," which is defined as follows:

Definition: Risk quantification includes the analysis of the causes of risks (risk factors), the quantification of the probability of occurrence, and the determination of the impact of risks on the financial and non-financial corporate objectives. Thus, risk quantification includes the description of risk using one or more probability functions for the probability of occurrence and the impact of a risk.

A distinction is made between the gross quantification of risks without consideration for the effects of risk mitigation measures and the net quantification used to evaluate the residual risk after mitigation (Diederichs, 2018). The **objectives** of risk quantification are (Burger & Buchhart, 2014; Gleißner, 2022):

- The quantification of single risks.
- The prioritization of risks based on an adequate risk measure.
- The quantification of risk interdependencies.

Risk quantification can be described as a **process** involving the following steps (Vanini & Rieg, 2021):

- First, a rough materiality assessment of the identified risks is recommended before an elaborate risk quantification is carried out. Subsequently, only material risks need to be quantified. Nevertheless, risks that are not (yet) classified as material are recorded in the risk inventory and regularly checked for their relevance (Hunziker, 2021).
- Then, the single risks are analyzed in detail. That means that the probability of occurrence of the risk and its impact on corporate goals must be quantified (COSO, 2017). Overall, material risks should be described with adequate probability distributions (Gleißner, 2022; Hardy & Saunders, 2022). If there are no objective probabilities of occurrence, subjective probabilities can be used (e.g., based on expert estimates). If the experts are very uncertain in their estimates, these can be described as confidence intervals or probability distributions.
- A **correlation analysis** must be conducted to check whether there are risk interdependencies (Gleißner, 2022):

- Independent risks do not influence each other in their respective impacts on the company's objectives (e.g., the fire risk in production and the interest rate risk in capital procurement). Thus, their correlation coefficient is zero.
- Positive dependent risks each reinforce the other's impact on the company's objectives (e.g., fire risk in production and image risk). The correlation coefficient of two positive dependent risks is between 0 and 1.
- Negative dependent risks each weaken the other's effect on the company's goals. For example, the price development of two shares in a share portfolio can run in opposite directions; if the price of one share falls, the price of the other shares rises. This effect is also called **risk diversification**. Their correlation coefficient is between 0 and − 1.

Methods for risk quantification must fulfill these **requirements** (Kremers, 2002; Burger & Buchhart, 2014; COSO, 2017):

- Broad applicability to different types of risks to enable a uniform risk quantification throughout the company and thus support risk aggregation.
- Objective measurement by incorporating external market data to limit manipulation and discretion in risk quantification.
- Monetary quantifiability of the risk impact, as this makes risks comparable.
- A specified time horizon that is used for the related strategy and business objectives.
- Consideration of risk interdependencies in the risk quantification to facilitate identification of diversification and accumulation effects.
- Aggregability of risks to the overall risk status to enable determination of the company's overall risk position and thus verification of the company's risk-bearing capacity.
- Easy comprehensibility and interpretability of the risk measure to facilitate acceptance by decision-makers and ensure its use to derive control measures.

8.2.2 *Overview of Methods for Risk Quantification*

In the literature, there is a large variety of methods for qualitative risk assessment and risk quantification (Kremers, 2002; COSO, 2017; Gleißner, 2022). **Quantitative methods** attempt to assess risks based on probability distributions (for the various probability distributions and their characteristics, see Chap. 5). For this, quantitatively measurable corporate objectives and a distribution to quantify the occurrence of a risk and its (financial) impact must be available. In the case of qualitative instruments, only a verbal assessment of the relevance of the risks is made. Special data requirements are not imposed here.

A **qualitative assessment and thus non-quantification of risk** are criticized, as this means that the risk is implicitly set at "zero" in the aggregation to the overall risk status and thus as non-existent. Another argument in favor of quantifying risks is that it contributes to a more objective discussion in management and supports the

Table 8.5 Data requirements of risk assessment instruments (source: Vanini & Rieg, 2021)

Instrument	Identification of risk factors	Corporate objectives as measures of damage potential	Description of occurrence and impact with a probability distribution
Risk classification	Not necessary	Qualitative and quantitative	Not necessary
Risk portfolio	Not necessary	Qualitative and quantitative	Not necessary
Scenario analysis	Necessary	Quantitative	Necessary
Statistical quantification	Necessary	Quantitative such as EBIT Cash flow, firm value	Necessary

derivation of risk control measures. In addition, the development of a risk measurement model requires an intensive discussion of possible risk factors and thus contributes to risk transparency in the company. It enables risk aggregation and thus a review of risk-bearing capacity as well as an integration of the assessed risks into strategic and operational planning and budgeting (Hunziker, 2021; Gleißner, 2022).

The selection of a quantification method depends on the available data to describe a risk. Some methods require the identification of risk factors, the estimation of probabilities of occurrence, and the probability distributions to describe the impact of a risk. Other methods have lower data requirements, as can be seen in Table 8.5.

Example: Risk Quantification in the Lufthansa Group

Once the risks have been identified, all the individual risks are measured according to uniform measurement principles. Risks are generally evaluated on a net basis (i.e. taking implemented and effective management and monitoring instruments into account). A methodological distinction is made between qualitative and quantitative risks. Regardless of the risk type, objective criteria or figures derived from past experience are used for the evaluation wherever possible. Risk measurement thus forms the basis for consolidating similar individual risks into an aggregate risk [...]. Qualitative risks are mostly long-term developments with potentially adverse consequences for the Lufthansa Group. As concrete information is often not available, these risks cannot or cannot yet be quantified. In the context of qualitative risks, the risk management process involves a strategic approach to uncertainty. In order to evaluate such risks as systematically as possible in spite of this, estimates are made about their significance and their magnitude. Significance describes the potential impact of the individual risk—for example, on the Group's reputation, business model or earnings. The estimate of magnitude assesses how pronounced or intense the (weak) signals are that indicate a potential risk to the Lufthansa Group or a specific company. [...] Quantitative risks are those whose potential effect on earnings can be estimated. A distinction is made between different probabilities of occurrence. The extent of loss is given as the potential monetary impact on the planned Adjusted EBIT. Depending on the type of risk, this may relate either to relatively infrequent event risks, such as an IT failure following a cyberattack, or to risks from deviations from planned business developments, due to fuel price volatility, for instance. Quantitative risks therefore form the basis for the overarching verification of potential deviations from plans and forecasts. The thresholds for classifying the monetary Adjusted EBIT effect are defined centrally for the Lufthansa Group and for the

Group companies according to standardized criteria. (source: Lufthansa Group 2023, *Annual Report 2022,* p. 77 f.)

8.2.3 Necessary Information for Risk Quantification

For the quantification of risks, their description as **probability distributions** is required. For example, a probability distribution can be used to describe the frequency with which a risk occurs in an observation period. In addition, a probability distribution is required for the possible impacts of the risk (i.e., the range of losses or gains). Alternatively, a simplified description using only one probability distribution may be possible under certain circumstances. In such a case, the range of effects of the risk in a period is indicated by a probability distribution. Binomial distributions are often used to depict simple event risks, which describe a risk using a probability of occurrence and an extent of damage (e.g., the loss of a key customer). For the description of distribution risks, on the other hand, a triangular distribution, which can be derived from a scenario analysis with worst, best, and real case, a normal distribution or a PERT distribution are often applied. If the risks are also to be mapped over several periods, their linkage by stochastic processes is necessary (Gleißner, 2022; Hardy & Saunders, 2022).

In principle, there are various ways of collecting **data for the selection or estimation of distribution functions** (Hunziker, 2021; Gleißner, 2022):

- Historical data from publicly available databases (e.g., for financial risks or internal company loss databases).
- Industry benchmark data (e.g., turnover volatilities of competitors).
- Expert estimates and forecasts (Jankensgård & Kapstad, 2021)

The collection of data and the quantification of risk are always associated with strong uncertainties, which is why the creation of the greatest possible transparency is the main requirement for data collection. The main requirements for a high degree of transparency in data collection and risk quantification are (Gleißner, 2022):

- Transparency about the sources of information and the calculation and simulation methods.
- Transparency about the integration of extreme events.
- Validation of subjective expert estimates by other experts and benchmark data.
- Consideration of parameter uncertainties (e.g., in expert estimates of probabilities of occurrence and extent of damage).
- Use of a uniform forecast period and consideration of stochastic dependencies between individual risks.

For risk quantification, the impact such as the extent of damage is more important than the probability of occurrence, since the company's continued existence must be secured even if rare risks such as natural disasters or pandemics occur (e.g., through preventive measures, emergency plans, or insurance). In addition, estimating the probability of occurrence of very rare risks is difficult, and it cannot be ruled out that precisely these risks will occur in the next year (Hunziker, 2021).

Example: Estimating Probabilities of Occurrence for Rare Event Risks
Vanini GmbH has identified $N = 25$ independent event risks, each with a probability of occurrence $p = 1\%$ p.a. Calculate the probability that one of the risks will occur the next year.

The calculation is based on the following formula:

$$\boldsymbol{p_{ges}} = \mathbf{1} - (\mathbf{1} - \boldsymbol{p})^{N.}$$

P amounts to 22.2% for the following year (source: Hunziker, 2021, p. 102).

8.2.4 *Qualitative Risk Assessment*

If risk quantification is not possible, a qualitative risk assessment with risk classifications might be the first step to evaluate the materiality of identified risks. In addition, quantified risks can be visualized in risk portfolios and their respective risk maps.

Risk Classifications
If no or only little quantitative information on risks and their underlying risk factors is available, **risk classifications** are used to verbally assess the materiality of a risk. Materiality is an expression of the overall relevance of a risk to the objective of a company. In addition, risk classes can be formed according to various criteria (e.g., the threat to the company's success or liquidity). In risk classifications, no measurement models are applied; instead, a subjective assessment is made by managers, employees, or external experts (Burger & Buchhart, 2014; Gleißner, 2022). Table 8.6 shows a one-dimensional risk classification according to the materiality for the annual net profit and enterprise value.

An initial risk classification enables the definition of a filter that identifies the risks that are to be subjected to further analysis and quantification. Risk classifications are applicable to almost all types of risks due to their low data requirements. However, qualitatively classified risks cannot be aggregated, and the risk-bearing capacity cannot be controlled (Hunziker, 2021).

Risk Portfolios or Risk Maps
A risk portfolio visualizes and documents the risks of a business unit or company in a two-dimensional matrix. The terms "risk portfolio," "risk matrix," and "risk map" are often used synonymously (see also Burger & Buchhart, 2014; Duijm, 2015; Olson & Wu, 2020a; Hunziker, 2021; Gleißner, 2022). **Qualitative or quantitative criteria** can be used as dimensions of a risk portfolio. An example is presented in

Table 8.6 Relevance scale (source: Gleißner, 2022, p. 152)

Relevance class	Degree of influence	Estimated impact in % of EBIT	Explanation
1	Insignificant risk	<3%	Insignificant risks do not have a noticeable impact on either the annual surplus or the value of the company
2	Medium risk	<20%	Medium risks cause a noticeable impairment of the net profit for the year
3	Significant risk	<100%	Significant risks reduce the annual net profit considerably or the enterprise value noticeably
4	Serious risk	≥100%	Serious risks lead to a net loss for the year and significantly reduce the value of the company
5	Risk threatening the existence of the company	>50%	Risks that jeopardize the continued existence of the company as a going concern have a significant probability of occurring

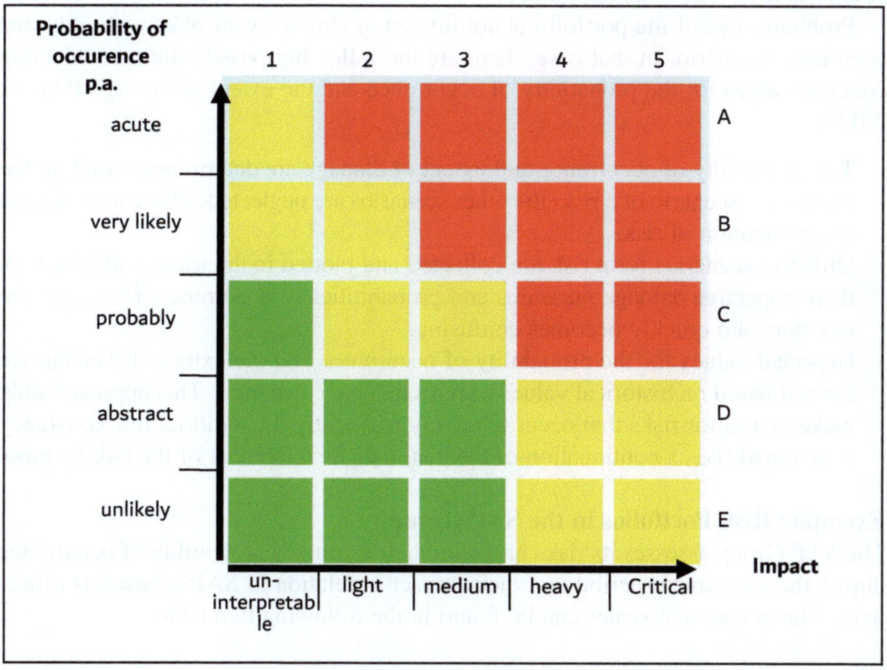

Fig. 8.4 Example of a qualitative risk portfolio (Vanini & Rieg, 2021)

Fig. 8.4. Here, the probability of occurrence and the extent of damage of a risk are either described verbally or ranked ordinally. Then, the assessed risks are entered into the map.

Appropriate **norm strategies** for risk mitigation are derived depending on the position within the map. In Fig. 8.4, all risks in the dark-colored upper right area of the matrix are classified as highly threatening. Mitigation measures are required to reduce the probability of occurrence or the impact of these risks. The light-colored diagonal line, representing the medium risks for which mitigation measures may have to be taken, is the risk threshold. The risk threshold can be interpreted as the limit of the risk-bearing capacity of a business unit or a company. Risks that lie above the risk threshold must be reduced through mitigation measures (Diederichs, 2018). Medium-ranked risks at the threshold must be monitored intensively for changes in the probability of occurrence or the extent of damage. Risks assigned to the lower left of the portfolio tend to have a low relevance. There is no acute need for action.

The dimensions of a risk portfolio can also include **quantitative criteria**. For example, in the above example, concrete quantitative values can also be specified for the probability of occurrence and the extent of damage; that is, the percentage of the damage amount in relation to the planned annual net profit of a company is conceivable as an evaluation value.

Problems arise if the portfolio is not limited to simple event risks with only one occurrence scenario. In that case, there are the following possibilities for selecting concrete values for the probability of occurrence and the extent of damage (Duijm, 2015):

- The probability of occurrence and extent of damage are determined based on the worst-case scenario of a risk; the other scenarios are neglected. This can lead to an overestimation of risk.
- Different scenarios for a risk are collected and plotted in the same portfolio with their respective damage measures and probabilities of occurrence. However, the risk portfolio quickly becomes confusing.
- Expected values for the probability of occurrence and the extent of damage are formed based on historical values of risks that have occurred. This approach only makes sense for risks that occur relatively frequently. In addition, risk constancy is assumed (i.e., a continuation of the historical development of the risk factors).

Example: Risk Portfolios in the SAP Group

The SAP Group assesses its risks based on their estimated probability of occurrence during the assessment period and their impact in relation to SAP's business objectives. The assessment scales can be found in the following two tables.

The scales for measuring these indicators are given in the following tables.

Probability/Likelihood of Occurrence	Description
1% to 19%	Remote
20% to 39%	Unlikely
40% to 59%	Likely
60% to 79%	Highly Likely
80% to 99%	Near Certainty

Impact Level	Impact Definition	Impact
Insignificant	Negligible negative impact on business, financial position, profit, and/or cash flows	From €0 to €25 million
Minor	Limited negative impact on business, financial position, profit, and/or cash flows	From €25 million to €50 million
Moderate	Some potential negative impact on business, financial position, profit, and/or cash flows	From €50 million to €100 million
Major	Considerable negative impact on business, financial position, profit, and/or cash flows	From €100 million to €500 million
Business-Critical	Detrimental negative impact on business, financial position, profit, and/or cash flows	From €500 million

The risks are then classified into a risk portfolio and classified as high (H), medium (M), or low (L).

Probability	Insignificant (€0 to €25 million)	Minor (€25 million to €50 million)	Moderate (€50 million to €100 million)	Major (€100 million to €500 million)	Business-Critical (from €500 million)
80% to 99%	L	M	H	H	H
60% to 79%	L	M	M	H	H
40% to 59%	L	L	M	M	H
20% to 39%	L	L	L	M	M
1% to 19%	L	L	L	L	M

Impact

L = Low Risk M = Medium Risk H = High Risk

(source: SAP Group 2023, *Annual Report 2022,* p. 133)

Due to their low data requirements, risk portfolios are applicable for almost all risks. However, risk portfolios have numerous **methodological problems** (Duijm, 2015; Hubbard, 2020; Hunziker, 2021; Gleißner, 2022):

- Risk portfolios are particularly suitable for the representation of event risks represented by a single scenario and thus a single probability of occurrence and extent of damage. Distribution risks lead to various deviations from targeted objectives and thus cannot be represented in a risk matrix. Event risks which might occur more than once in an observation period cannot be described by a risk portfolio.

- Correlations, and thus combination effects between individual risks, are neglected in the portfolio presentation. This prevents risk aggregation and makes risk management more difficult. In particular, it is not possible to derive the degree of threat of the existence of a company.
- Risks in the non-acceptable range will rarely occur in corporate practice, as they would call the company's entire business model into question. Rare event risks with a high extent of damage, such as the risk of a pandemic, do not fall into the non-acceptable range of the risk portfolio and are thus not a priority for risk management.
- With qualitative risk portfolios, the verbal scales are interpreted subjectively and are subject to numerous cognitive biases. They are interpreted in different ways for different individuals, making the risk assessments of different managers incomparable. For example, Berger (2018, p. 46 ff.) concludes from the results of his survey that individuals assign very different quantitative values to certain qualitative assessments of the probabilities of occurrence (excluded, rare, occasional, medium, possible, frequent, probable, highly probable, or certain). Even the extreme points of the scale were not clearly assigned 0% (excluded) and 100% (certain).
- In quantitative risk portfolios, the formation of classes for the probability of occurrence and the extent of damage leads to an inadmissible reduction of information. In the SAP example, risks with a probability of occurrence between 1% and 19% are assigned to the same class. In addition, the threshold values for the delimitation of the different portfolio fields are difficult to determine practically.
- In addition, the risk threshold can hardly be justified methodically, since not all points along the risk threshold have the same value for their expected damage. The expected loss value of a risk results from the multiplication of the loss amount and the probability of occurrence of a risk. Therefore, the relationship between the amount of damage and the probability of occurrence has the form of a hyperbola, not a straight line as is assumed by the risk threshold. This is a particular problem when the risk portfolio is used to prioritize risks.

Overall, risk portfolios are not suitable as a basis for ERM, despite their widespread use in corporate practice. The frequently mentioned argument that many risks are not quantifiable and therefore such methods must be used does not solve the abovementioned methodological problems with the instrument (vgl. Weiterführend Hubbard, 2020). The main point is that a risk portfolio does not allow the aggregation of all risks, so calculation of the overall risk exposure is not possible. Therefore, risk portfolios should only be used in ERM for risk visualization and not for risk assessment.

8.2.5 Scenario Analysis

"Single-value" corporate planning, which specifies exactly one target value for each corporate objective, is still widespread and implemented in most companies. However, due to increasing environmental uncertainty, exact target values are difficult to determine. Rather, it is a question of which range a company can expect a target value to fall into in the future. The range of potential deviations from target values can be interpreted as risks (negative deviations) and respective opportunities (positive deviations). Therefore, scenarios for describing the effects of the uncertainty of risk factors on corporate objectives can be defined for the main risks and opportunities. Realizations of corporate objectives must be calculated if the scenario is actualized, and deviations from the planned values must be quantified.

A **scenario** describes a possible future constellation of relevant environmental and corporate factors and their interdependencies. Theoretically, an unlimited number of scenarios can be set up by combining environmental and corporate developments. In practice, three scenarios are often used (Hunziker, 2021; Gleißner, 2022):

- In the **best-case scenario**, the most favorable of all possible environmental developments is presented. The best-case scenario can be used to determine opportunities with respect to the main corporate targets.
- The **base, real case, or trend scenario** describes the most probable development. This is the target value which should be used in the corporate budget.
- The **worst-case scenario** describes the worst of all possible developments and can be used to determine the risk included in the corporate budget.

The range of possible developments between the best-case and worst-case scenarios is referred to as a **scenario funnel** (Fig. 8.5). Furthermore**, crash scenarios or stress scenarios** are sometimes set up for extreme risk constellations. It is important that scenarios do not overlap and can therefore be assigned their own probability of occurrence. They should be comprehensive, include extreme developments, and nevertheless be plausible (Hardy & Saunders, 2022). The literature suggests that scenarios should be defined for all significant risks of a company and stored in a database. If the company has suitable software, the scenarios can be linked using Monte Carlo simulation (MCS), and their aggregated effects on the business target can be simulated (Hunziker, 2021).

Finally, the effects of the various scenarios on the company's goals are analyzed. Depending on the type and extent of the impact, measures must be developed for the individual scenarios, and their impacts on the company's goals must be analyzed (Fig. 8.6).

Tornado diagrams are used in corporate practice to visualize the results of a scenario analysis. A tornado diagram shows the impacts of risks and opportunities for the worst- and best-case scenarios without any consideration of probabilities and is only based on single-risk scenarios (Hunziker, 2021).

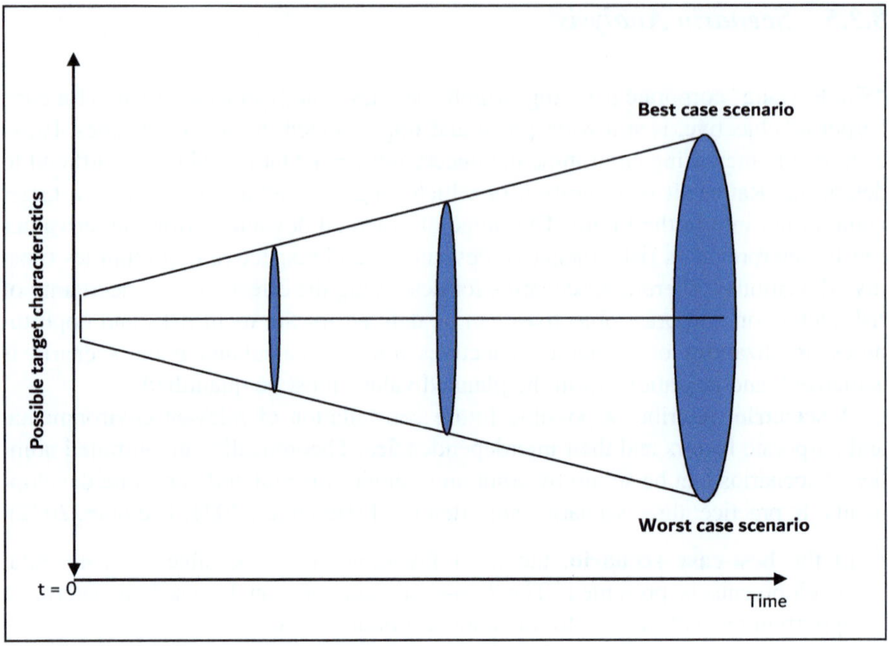

Fig. 8.5 Derivation of a scenario funnel (Vanini & Rieg, 2021)

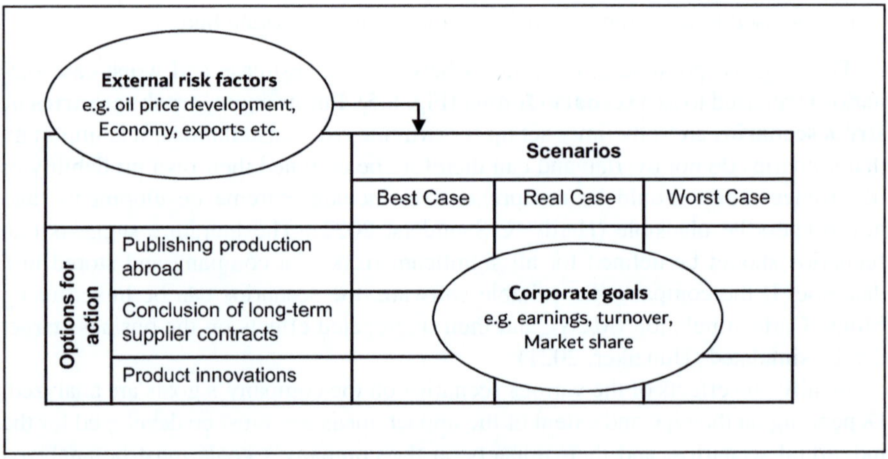

Fig. 8.6 Scenario-measure matrix (Burger & Buchhart, 2002)

Example: Tornado Diagram in the BASF Group
In its 2022 Risk Report, the BASF Group classifies its main opportunity and risk factors according to their impacts on EBIT:

Potential short-term effects on EBIT of key opportunity and risk factors subsequent to measures taken[a]

Possible variations related to:	Outlook 2023 –	Outlook 2023 +
Business environment and sector		
Market growth	■■■■■■	■■■□□□
Margins	■■■■■■	■■■■■□
Competition	□□□□■■	■□□□□□
Regulation/policy	□□□□■■	□□□□□□
Company-specific opportunities and risks		
Procurement	□□□□■■	■□□□□□
Supply chain	□□□□■■	■■□□□□
Investments/production	□□□■■■	□□□□□□
Acquisitions/divestitures/cooperations	□□□□■■	□□□□□□
Personnel	□□□□□■	□□□□□□
Information technology	□□□□□■	□□□□□□
Compliance/legal	□□□□□■	■□□□□□
Tax	□□□□■■	■□□□□□
Financial		
Exchange rate volatility	□□□□■■	■■□□□□
Other financial opportunities and risks	□□□■■■	■■□□□□

□□□□□■	< €100 million
□□□□■■	≥ €100 million < €500 million
□□□■■■	≥ €500 million < €1,000 million
□□■■■■	≥ €1,000 million < €1,500 million
□■■■■■	≥ €1,500 million < €2,000 million
■■■■■■	≥ €2,000 million < €2,500 million

a Using a 95% confidence interval per risk factor based on planned values; summation is not permissible. Excludes European gas price volatility.

(source: BASF Group 2023, *Annual Report 2022*, p. 158)

Scenario analyses are very common in business practice and are used in strategic and operational planning, crisis management, business continuity management, and ERM. They are suitable for the evaluation of rather short-term risks (e.g., when different scenarios are set up and deviations from the plan are analyzed within the framework of annual budgeting) but can also be used for the analysis of strategic risks when long-term scenarios are set up. By using the worst-case, real case, and best-case scenarios, it is also possible to quantify a risk with a **triangular distribution**.

8.2.6 Risk Quantification by Probability Distributions

Risks can be interpreted as random events that occur with a certain probability and have a quantifiable impact on a relevant target value of a company (opportunity or loss potential). The **probability of occurrence** describes the degree of uncertainty of the realization of an event. According to the axiomatic concept of probability, a probability is a real number in the interval [0,1]; an impossible event has a probability of zero, and a certain event has a probability of one. Laplace's classical concept of probability derives the probability p(A) from the frequency of event A within a certain time interval in relation to a total number of events (e.g., throws of the dice). This was the basis for the development of the statistical or frequentist concept of probability, which uses the law of large numbers to deduce the probability of an event from its observed frequency during a fixed period. There is also the subjective concept of probability, which is based on the experience-based, subjective assessment of probability by one or more people and therefore does not represent an objectively measurable variable (Lindley, 2014). Both frequentist and subjectively determined probabilities are often used in ERM.

For risk quantification, the previously identified risks must be described with suitable **probability distributions** (Romeike & Stallinger, 2021; Gleißner, 2022; Hardy & Saunders, 2022). To select the appropriate probability distribution, the characteristics of the risks, in terms of their frequencies and their effects, are examined based on an analysis of historical data or expert considerations. For example, if the risk results from a single event (**event risk**), such as the default of a major customer, a binomial or Bernoulli distribution can be used to model the probability of occurrence. A Poisson distribution is used in the event of potential multiple risk occurrences during a period. The impact of such an event risk can be modelled by a constant if only one impact is possible. Alternatively, the effect of an event risk can be described by a normal distribution for different but symmetrical effects, a uniform distribution for different but equally probable effects, or a triangular or PERT distribution for asymmetrically distributed risk effects. The latter distributions can also be used for modelling **distribution risks** such as currency or

Table 8.7 Overview of risks for a car manufacturing company (source: Vanini & Heise, 2017)

Risks	Impacted corporate objective	Effect	Risk type
• Market risks (e.g., development of customer demand in automotive markets)	• Sales	• Volatility in sales due to demand and price fluctuations	• Distribution risk
• Supply chain risks (e.g., development of material costs)	• Production costs	• Production and price-related cost fluctuations	• Distribution risk
• Political risks (e.g., introduction of tariffs in the USA)	• Production costs	• Increase in production costs	• Event risk
• Legal risks (e.g., due to the diesel exhaust scandal)	• Other operating result	• Compensation and penalty payments	• Event risk

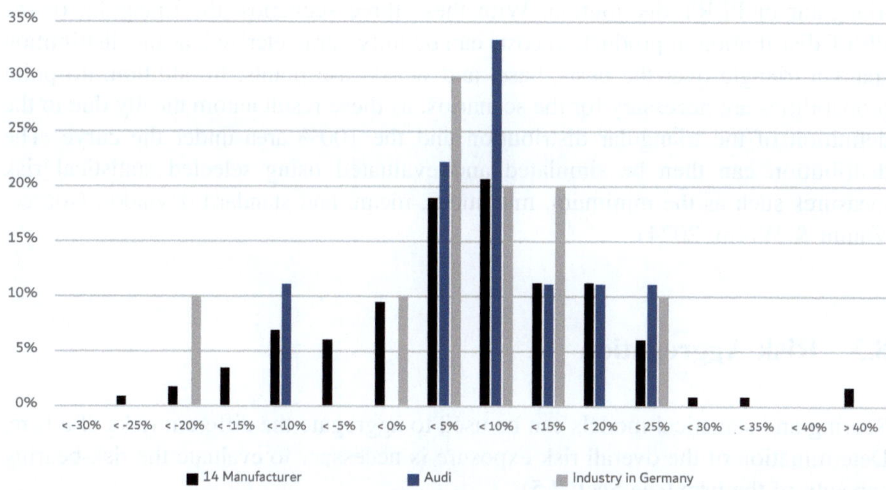

Fig. 8.7 Relative frequencies of annual sales changes of the Audi Group and its peer groups (source: Vanini & Heise, 2017)

interest rate risks. In this case, the risk results from the volatility of the uncertain risk factors.

As an example, Table 8.7 shows an extract of potential risks for a German car manufacturer and their characteristics.

Historical data can be analyzed to determine the distribution function for risk modelling. Figure 8.7 shows the sales fluctuations of Audi, a German car manufacturer, compared with 14 other car manufacturers and the industry as a whole.

Histograms are used to determine the distributions for risk modelling. The histogram in Fig. 8.7 shows that the risk of sales fluctuation could be approximated by a triangular or normal distribution. If there is sufficient historical data, the distribution assumptions can also be checked using statistical fitting tests such as the Kolmogorov-Smirnov test for the normal distribution.

Example: Quantification of the Production Risk

In a company, the risk of production cost deviations must be analyzed and quantified. Interviews are conducted with experts responsible for production to map the range of fluctuation in production cost per unit. The experts consider it almost impossible for production costs to fall below US$1.50 per unit (best-case scenario) and rate even this value as almost impossible. After some discussion, the worst-case scenario is set at a maximum of US$2.00/unit, although this value is also considered almost impossible. The production experts estimate the realistic value at US$1.84/unit; this is also included as a target value in the annual planning. The potential for the production costs per unit to fluctuate within the interval between US$1.50/unit and US$2.00/unit presents a distribution risk. The unit costs can assume any value within the defined range, which is why continuous probability distributions are suitable for risk modelling. However, as the values can occur with different probabilities and their distribution is also not symmetrical, the risk is best modelled using a triangular or PERT distribution. With these three scenarios, the triangular or the PERT distribution of production costs can be fully parameterized, as the distribution spans a triangle over the best-, base, and worst-case points. In addition, no point probabilities are necessary for the scenarios, as these result automatically due to the definition of the triangular distribution and the 100% area under the curve. The distribution can then be simulated and evaluated using selected statistical risk measures such as the minimum, maximum, mean, and standard deviation (source: Vanini & Worm, 2024).

8.3 Risk Aggregation

Scoring and statistical models can be used to aggregate the different risks of a firm. Determination of the overall risk exposure is necessary to evaluate the risk-bearing capacity of the firm (see Sect. 7.5).

8.3.1 Scoring Models

If differently scaled risks have been identified, but neither the probability of occurrence nor a functional relationship to the company's objectives can be determined, **scoring models** can be applied for risk aggregation (Burger & Buchhart, 2014):

- First, the identified individual risks must be assigned to specific risk categories.
- Then, non-overlapping criteria for risk assessment are defined for each risk category (e.g., urgency and damage effect) and weighted. All weights must add up to 100%. An evaluation scale must be determined for evaluating criteria.
- Finally, all risks must be evaluated and weighted for different decision alternatives. The single-weighted evaluations have to be added to an overall risk score.

Due to their low data requirements, scoring models can be applied to almost all types of risk. They support the comparability and aggregation of differently scaled risks. However, they are **highly subjective**, as the determination of scoring criteria, their weighting, and the assignment of point values are at the discretion of the individual decision-maker. In addition, there are often numerous risk interdependencies in corporate practice which are neglected in scoring models (Hubbard, 2020). Nevertheless, banks use scoring models for rating procedures to determine the creditworthiness of their loan customers and in procedures assessing country risks (Diederichs, 2018). Overall, scoring models cannot be used to determine an overall financial risk exposure nor, therefore, to evaluate the risk-bearing capacity of a firm.

8.3.2 Statistical Models

There are different statistical methods for the aggregation of risks described with probability distributions (Olson & Wu, 2020b). **Analytical methods** such as the variance-covariance approach assume that all single risks are normally distributed. Then, the total risk exposure is also assumed to follow a normal distribution that can be completely described by its expected value and standard deviation. In addition, correlations between different risks can be integrated into the calculation. **Non-parametric simulation methods** simulate the impact of various risks on corporate objectives, such as the EBIT based on a risk model. The result is a simulated distribution of the value of the corporate objective. The risk model can be based on historical data (historical simulation) or different statistical distributions (Monte Carlo simulation).

Due to its simple method, the **variance-covariance approach** is used in practice, but it has numerous methodological problems. In particular, the assumption of a normal distribution of risks can lead to a systematic underestimation of extreme risks. Additionally, non-linear correlations cannot be integrated, and the model complexity increases with the number of risks. In addition, covariances and correlations must be determined for all single risks. **Historical simulation** is also a relatively simple approach because it is not based on any assumptions concerning the distribution of risks. However, its quality depends significantly on the representativeness of the historical data for the future development of the risks. In total, both approaches rely on assumptions that are rarely fulfilled in corporate practice.

Monte Carlo simulation (MCS) breaks away from these rigid assumptions and allows the aggregation of risks described with different distribution functions. Therefore, we concentrate on MCS for risk aggregation.

Implementing an MCS requires four steps to be completed (Olson & Wu, 2020b; Gleißner, 2022):

- First, a risk simulation model must be set up to model the features of the various risks, their interdependencies, and their impact on the selected target figure (e.g.,

EBIT) or firm value. All single risks must be modelled. This includes the selection of adequate probability distributions and their parametrization based on historical data or expert estimates.

- The simulation model must be verified and validated to ensure that it is free from logical errors and is a valid representation of the simulated corporate targets.
- Then, the simulation is carried out and distributions of the target variables are generated. The number of simulations runs, the simulation horizon, and the confidence level for the risk analysis have to be determined. Simulation means that possible realizations of the single risks are randomly drawn from their underlying distributions, and their impact on the value of the target variable is determined. Distributions of the values of target variables, such as the EBIT or cash flow, are generated through a large number of simulation runs.
- Finally, the simulated distribution of the target variable must be analyzed using adequate risk and performance measures such as expected values or VaR (for a discussion of the different risk measures, see Chap. 6).

The steps of an MCS will be illustrated using as an example the determination of the total risk exposure for the planned EBIT of the Audi Group, a German car manufacturer (for a detailed presentation, see Vanini & Heise, 2017; another example can be found in Andrén et al., 2005). To determine the risk exposure for the targeted EBIT, **integrated profit and loss (P&L) planning** is required in the form of a **simulation model**. Significant relationships between individual planning variables (e.g., the planned fixed assets and depreciation), as well as between planning variables and both the uncertain environmental assumptions and the decision variables (e.g., turnover, forecast market development, and sales prices), must be modelled mathematically. A simplified P&L account can be used as a starting point for the simulation of the potential realizations of the EBIT (Gleißner, 2022). During the simulation runs, realizations of the distributions of the single risks are randomly generated, and their impacts on the EBIT are calculated to simulate the distribution of the future EBIT (Figs. 8.8 and 8.9).

There are different kinds of **simulation software** available. In business practice, Microsoft Excel, with or without corresponding add-ins such as Crystal Ball or Risk Kit, statistical software such as R, and specific planning software can be applied (Grisar & Meyer, 2015). The number of simulation runs should be sufficiently large to capture the effects of rare event risks. The result of the simulation is a representative distribution of the target value such as EBIT that can be further analyzed. Key risk and performance measures can then be calculated (Hunziker, 2021).

Figure 8.10 reveals the expected EBIT of Audi Group compared to the planned EBIT, the maximum and the minimum simulated EBIT, the probability of a negative EBIT, and the EBIT-at-Risk (EaR) specified for a fixed confidence level. Table 8.8 shows the values for performance and risk measures for the simulated EBIT of the Audi Group for 1000, 5000, and 10,000 simulation runs.

The table reveals that with an increasing number of simulation runs, the range of results becomes wider as the probability of realizing extreme event risks increases. The expected EBIT can be compared with the planned EBIT and the previous year's

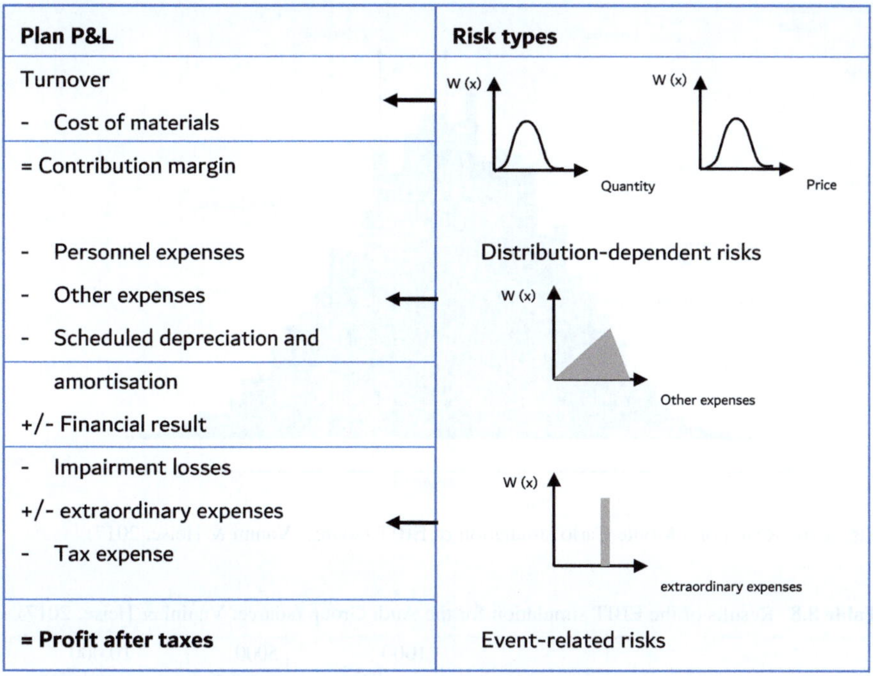

Fig. 8.8 P&L planning model (source: Burger & Buchhart, 2002, p. 246)

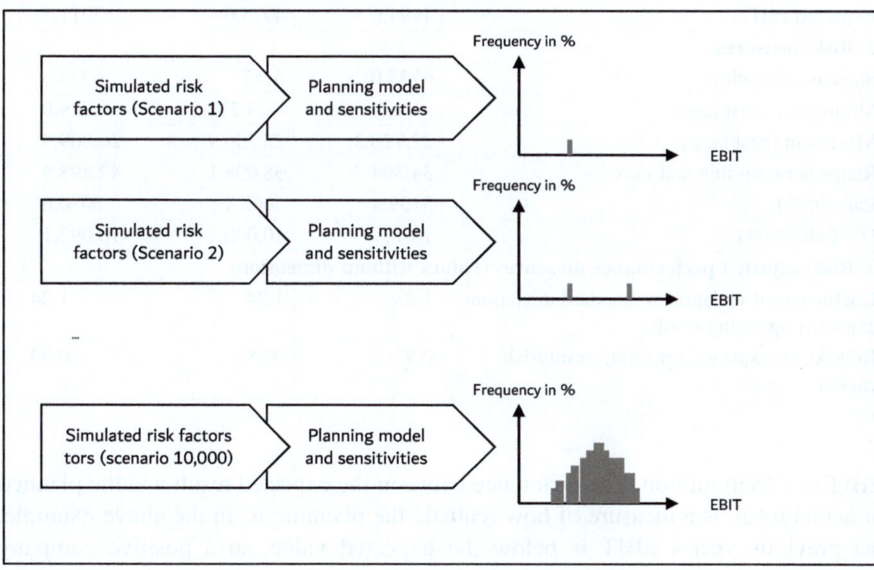

Fig. 8.9 Procedure for EaR determination (based on Diederichs, 2018)

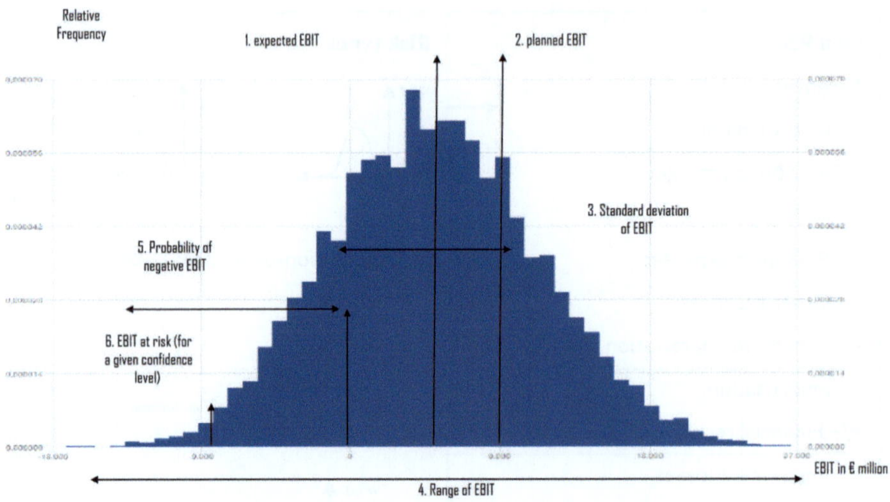

Fig. 8.10 Result of a Monte Carlo simulation of EBIT (source: Vanini & Heise, 2017)

Table 8.8 Results of the EBIT simulation for the Audi Group (source: Vanini & Heise, 2017)

All values in € million unless otherwise stated	1000 simulation runs	5000 simulation runs	10,000 simulation runs
1. **Performance measure**			
Expected EBIT	4994.6	4975.0	5011.5
2. Risk measures			
Standard deviation	6125.0	6187	6233.3
Minimum (worst case)	−11,668.33	−14,271.2	−16,089.0
Maximum (best case)	22,726.3	23,736.9	26,809.9
Range between min and max	34,394.7	38,008.1	42,898.9
EaR (95%)	5139.4	5065.4	5080.6
DV EaR (95%)	10,134	10,040.4	10,092.1
3. **Risk-adjusted performance measures (values without dimension)**			
Coefficient of variation = standard deviation/ expected operating result	1.23	1.24	1.24
RORAC = expected operating result/risk capital	0.97	0.98	0.99

EBIT of €4836 million. The difference between the expected result and the planned or actual result is a measure of how realistic the planning is. In the above example, the previous year's EBIT is below the expected value, so a positive company development is expected. However, Table 8.8 also shows that the risk of missing the planned EBIT is relatively high since the spread around the mean value and the coefficient of variation are relatively large. Significant upward and downward deviations are possible (range). A negative EBIT may even occur with a certain probability. The company should reduce the dispersion of EBIT realizations through targeted measures.

The **earnings-at-risk (EaR)** is a very important risk measure. It is defined as the profit that will not be undercut in a specified planning period with a given probability (Diederichs, 2018). The confidence level should be determined with respect to risk attitudes of the owner and top management. The more risk-averse a decision-maker is, the higher the confidence level should be. The deviation earnings-at-risk (DVEaR) is calculated as the difference between the target value of the EBIT and the EaR.

The MCS determines the total risk exposure and thus the necessary equity capital requirement of the company for a large number of possible scenarios. Of particular relevance is the proportion of simulated scenarios in which equity becomes negative, meaning that the company is bankrupt. By determining the probability of default, it is possible to assign the company to a rating class. The determined equity capital requirement and the rating assessment can in turn be used to determine the company's capital costs (Gleißner, 2022).

The quality of an MCS is influenced by the following factors (Bleuel, 2006; Burger & Buchhart, 2014):

- The validity of the simulation model (i.e., how well the single risks are described with distribution functions and aggregated in the model).
- Parametrization.
- The number of simulations runs (a compromise must be made between the accuracy of the results and the associated computational effort).

8.3.3 Problems During Risk Quantification and Aggregation

During risk quantification and aggregation, the following problems arise (Vanini & Rieg, 2021):

- The quantification of **extreme risk events** such as the COVID-19 pandemic often causes severe problems due to the lack of historical data and valid expert estimations. Extreme risks are erroneously represented by damage expectation values, which often entail the risk of misjudgments when the probability of occurrence is very low. Alternatively, extreme risks can be represented by scenarios or extreme value distributions, as addressed in Chap. 4.
- Estimates of the extent of damage and probability of occurrence are based on subjective assessments, benchmark values, or historical data. All approaches have problems. For example, people arrive at different risk assessments simply because of their different risk attitudes. Moreover, probability distributions for future events cannot always be derived from historical time series. No historical values exist for very rare extreme events, such as those arising from black swan risks (Taleb et al., 2009).

- Many risk quantification tools and risk models are very complex and require extensive statistical understanding. This can lead to issues with understanding and acceptance among managers and employees. Hunziker (2021, p. 105) speaks of **black box models** that are not completely understood by decision-makers. In corporate practice, the lack of methodological know-how is often cited as the main obstacle to the use of simulation models in ERM (Grisar & Meyer, 2015). If managers do not understand the results of complex risk models, they will likely not integrate them into their decisions; if they do integrate them, they will draw the wrong conclusions from the models.
- Using complex assessment methods can also lead to **model risks** and "blind faith" in the model. For example, the relationships between specific risk factors and corporate goals are sometimes unstable over time, which should lead to ongoing adjustments of the measurement model. If the risk model is faulty or not updated, there is a chance that risks will be fundamentally misjudged by an unsuitable model and that wrong decisions will be made by management (see Sect. 5.6).
- Due to multiple risk interdependencies and the different time horizons of risk factors, risk aggregation is especially apt to lead to problems. However, risk aggregation is necessary for determining the total risk exposure as it controls the risk-bearing capacity and risk mitigation.

8.4 Risk Reporting

8.4.1 Concept, Objectives, and Types of Risk Reporting

Risk reporting follows risk identification, quantification, and aggregation and is the foundation for risk mitigation and monitoring. It is necessary because essential risk-relevant information usually accumulates in decentralized corporate units and centralized ERM departments and must be communicated from there to managerial decision-makers, especially top management (Burnaby & Hass, 2009; Hunziker, 2021). In the literature, the term "risk reporting" is not defined uniformly. This textbook uses the following definition of risk reporting (Vanini & Rieg, 2021):

Definition: Risk reporting comprises the generation, processing, transmission to internal and external addressees, and storage of information regarding opportunities and risks. The main objectives are to create transparency about the company's main risks, opportunities, total risk exposure, and risk-bearing capacity; to prepare decisions about necessary mitigation measures; and to support risk monitoring. In addition, risk reporting has a documentation function.

Through **internal risk reporting**, internal decision-makers are comprehensively and continuously provided with risk-relevant information. The internal addressees include managers responsible of effective risk governance and the risk-bearing capacity, risk owners accountable for the effective management of risks, and the supervisory board (COSO, 2017). Internal risk reporting has to meet the following requirements (Burger & Buchhart, 2014; Hunziker, 2021):

- Integration—Risk reporting must be fit into existing management and board reporting structures concerning company performance and strategy achievement so that risk information can be fully incorporated into decision-making.
- Timeliness—The reporting frequency must be adapted to the company-specific risk situation and the regularity of important managerial meetings. In general, it is useless to provide an isolated risk report once a year as it would not be possible to include it in managerial decision-making.
- Materiality—The scope and level of detail of risk reporting are determined by the addressees' respective information needs.
- Accuracy—Quantified risks should be reported without any faults in risk reporting.
- Completeness—The comprehensiveness of the reported risks and opportunities depends on their materiality and the informational needs of the addressee. The report should include information about the company's total risk exposure and its risk-bearing capacity.
- Uniformity—This ensures uniform risk communication and the comparability of different risks.
- Flexibility—Risk reporting must be adaptable to changing risk situations.
- Economic efficiency—The economic benefit of the risk reports must be greater than the expense of their preparation and use.

External risk reporting builds on the internal reporting. It usually includes an evaluation of the firm's total risk exposure, the most material individual risks, and the ERM system implemented by the company. It can be divided into formal reporting within the framework of external accounting (risk disclosure) and informal reporting with additional risk-relevant information for important stakeholders of the company. Potential addressees of external risk reporting are (COSO, 2017):

- Investors or shareholders who do not have access to internal risk information and wish to identify opportunities and threats to the company's development and (financial) performance.
- Banks that want to assess the firm's creditworthiness through a rating.
- Suppliers that need to verify the company's solvency at all times.
- Media that are especially interested in corporate success, scandals, or failure.
- Public and supervisory authorities interested in long-term firm development.

In some countries, there are legal requirements concerning risk disclosure in a section of the annual financial reporting; in the USA, it is included in the SEC filings (for an overview, see Ibrahim et al., 2022). In Germany, all medium-sized or large companies must prepare a (group) management report that communicates opportunities and risks. The main goal of external risk disclosure is improved transparency about the opportunities and risks of a company and the maturity of its ERM system. Usually, external risk reporting is based on internal risk reporting. Figure 8.11 shows the connection between internal and external risk reporting and disclosure.

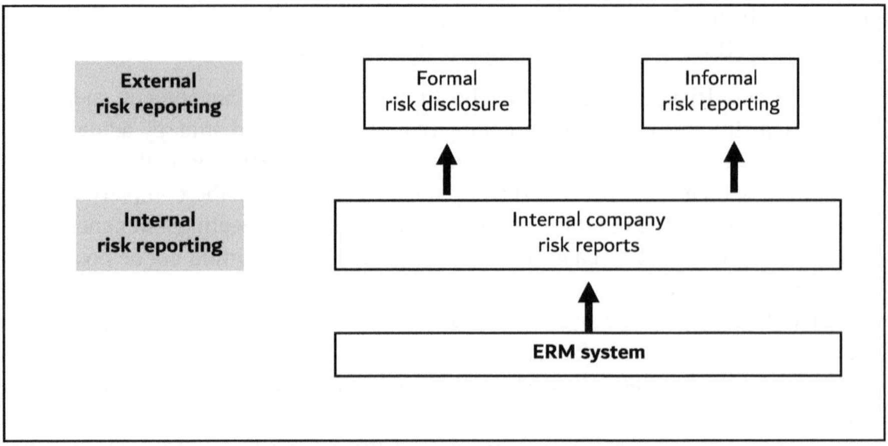

Fig. 8.11 Interaction of internal and external risk reporting (source: Diederichs, 2018)

Internal risk reporting and external risk disclosure differ primarily in terms of **scope** and **frequency**. External risk disclosure provides highly aggregated risk information, whereas internal risk reporting communicates more detailed and addressee-related information to support the respective decision-maker directly in deriving adequate risk mitigation measures. While external risk disclosure is usually linked to the company's annual or quarterly financial reporting, internal risk reporting is carried out more frequently. Suddenly emerging material risks or a material increase or decrease in already identified risks must be communicated immediately within the company (ad hoc reporting; Hunziker, 2021).

8.4.2 Design of Internal Risk Reporting

The design of internal risk reporting can be structured according to different parameters (Diederichs, 2018; Vanini & Rieg, 2021; Gleißner, 2022) (Fig. 8.12).

- **"What for?"** This determines the purposes of the risk report. Risk reports can be prepared to document risks, prepare steering decisions, or support mitigation decisions.
- **"What?"** The purpose of the report determines the report content. Significant factors influencing the report contents include the information needs and competencies of the addressees. Relevant contents include single risks and opportunities, their causes, the total risk exposure, the risk-bearing capacity, material risk interdependencies, and mitigation measures. In addition, key risk indicators and measures may be reported; the report may also contain an analysis of new, emerging, or changing risks (COSO, 2017). To avoid causing information overload in the report addressees, the report contents must be limited to the

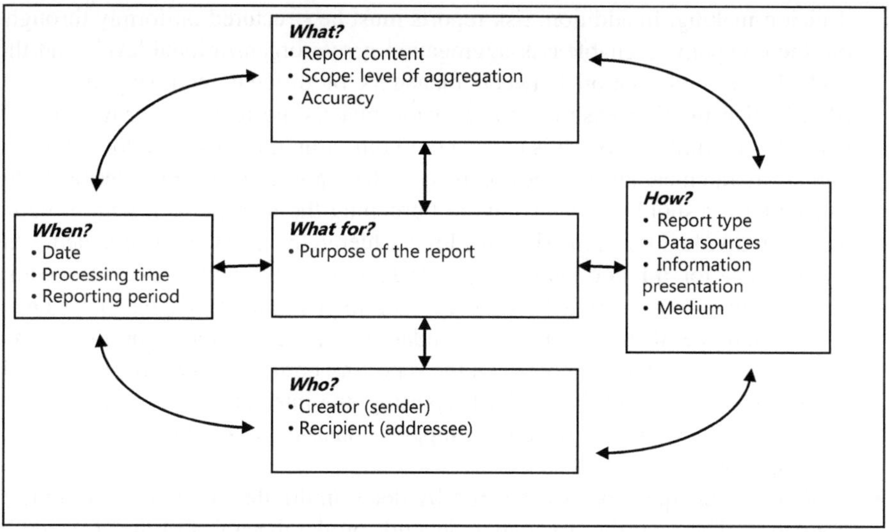

Fig. 8.12 Basic design parameters of risk reporting (source: Diederichs, 2018)

information relevant for decision-making. Thus, the subjective information needs of the addressees must be analyzed. In general, detailed qualitative information about possible causes of risk is needed for recipients at lower hierarchical levels so that they can derive appropriate mitigation measures. However, recipients with a higher hierarchical position require more aggregated information about the financial consequences of risks and mitigation measures. Another way to avoid information overload is to set **materiality thresholds** for each level of the hierarchy. Materiality thresholds have an important filtering function in risk reporting. They determine the level at which risks must be reported to higher authorities and are determined by the management with the support of risk controlling along the corporate hierarchy.

- "**Who?**" This question is answered by determining the report senders and recipients as well as their communication channels. Internal risk reports are prepared by risk owners in operational units since this is where risks are identified and initial assessments are made. In the operative units, risks are often recorded in risk identification templates and then summarized in risk inventories. The addressees of these de-centrally prepared risk reports are the managers of the decentralized units, who must decide on measures for risk mitigation. These risk reports are also communicated to a central risk management unit that aggregates the reports for the executive board. Other addressees are the supervisory or advisory board (the company's control body), internal and external auditors, and (risk) consultants (COSO, 2017).
- "**How?**" This is determined by the design of the internal risk report. Risk reports should generally be integrated into the company's reporting system so that management uses risk information as well as performance information for

decision-making. In addition, risk reports must be structured uniformly throughout the company to enable risk aggregation across organizational levels and the exchange of information between managers of different company divisions. **Standard reporting** ensures that decision-makers are regularly provided with risk-relevant information. It is carried out bottom-up (i.e., from the lowest to the highest hierarchical level in the company). The report contents are determined by exceeding threshold values. To avoid burdening the management with a multitude of individual risks, the risks for higher hierarchy levels are aggregated. The requirement for **ad hoc reporting** is triggered by the occurrence of specific circumstances (e.g., new material risks) and the exceeding of threshold values, which are higher than those used in standard reporting. Ad hoc reporting ensures immediate communication between the reporting entities, management, and risk control units. For monthly standard reporting, the integration of risk and performance reporting is recommended to support consistent risk-return-oriented decision-making.

- **"When?"** This question is answered by determining the internal risk reporting frequency. The reporting frequency depends on the dynamics of the company's risk situation, among other factors (COSO, 2017). A distinction is made between regular **standard reports**, which are prepared on specific reporting dates (e.g., at the end of the month or quarter), and **ad hoc reports** that are prepared on specific occasions (e.g., when risk budgets are exceeded).

8.4.3 Design of the External Risk Disclosures

The primary functions of external risk disclosure are information, transparency, and documentation. Disclosure should **reduce information asymmetries** between management and external stakeholders such as analysts, investors, or other interest groups regarding the company's overall risk exposure, risk-bearing capacity, and ability to manage its risks and opportunities. In addition, the company can signal that it complies with legal requirements and adapts to the reporting standards of its industry. Therefore, disclosure can contribute to establishing a positive relationship of **trust and transparency** with a firm's stakeholders. In particular, voluntary risk disclosure can be seen as a means of business communication (Hunziker, 2021).

The content and frequency of external risk disclosure are mainly determined by regulatory and capital market requirements. Studies have found a large impact of nationality and the influence of (institutional) investors on risk disclosure practices. Other studies have revealed that the disclosed risk information is mostly qualitative, and analysts and investors have difficulties extracting relevant risk-related information (for a thorough discussion, see Ibrahim et al., 2022).

The **economic effects** of risk disclosure on **firm value** and its **cost of capital** are contradictory. On the one hand, improved reporting to investors and analysts can lead to better estimates of the firm's future cash flows and thus to a reduction of variance uncertainty and smaller risk premiums being included in the cost of capital.

One the other hand, however, if risk information indicates more or even excessive risk-taking, the investors suffer from greater uncertainty concerning the variance of future cash flows. This can lead to an increase in risk premiums and thus a higher cost of capital (for a model-theoretical derivation, see Heinle & Smith, 2017). However, empirical studies suggest a negative correlation between the scope and quality of external risk reporting and the cost of capital (Khlif & Hussainey, 2016).

8.4.4 Problems of Risk Reporting and Risk Disclosure

In the context of risk reporting and disclosure, a variety of problems can arise (Diederichs, 2018; Hunziker, 2021):

- Internal risk reporting often focuses heavily on the standardized presentation of single risks to fulfill the **regulatory requirements** for external risk disclosure. Such reporting does not support managerial decision-making as it fails to link a firm's risk exposure with its business performance. In addition, standardized, quarterly, or even annual reporting cannot support daily managerial decision-making as it does not offer current information. Therefore, more frequent, integrated reporting of risk and performance is recommended.
- In some cases, too much detailed information is provided, which can lead to **information overload** or inconsistencies that impair the acceptance of risk reporting. The risk report must give an overview of the total corporate risk exposure, risk-taking capacity, main risks and opportunities impacting the risk exposure, and risk mitigation measures. The report must contain this information, but it must not add extraneous additional details.
- There is a **goal conflict** in the design of internal and external risk reporting. While all risks must be reported comprehensively and transparently in internal risk reporting, companies want to present a more positive picture concerning their risk exposure in external risk disclosure. The disclosure of negative risk-relevant information can lead to negative assessments by analysts and thus to decreased firm value and increased cost of capital.
- Particularly in external risk disclosure, there is often insufficient communication of basic assumptions, ERM methods, and the parameters for risk quantification. Firms often seem to **underestimate** their **downside risk** in annual reports, and consequently, external risk disclosures are often of limited value for external addressees.

8.5 Summary

- Risk identification is the initial step of the operational ERM process and involves the timely identification of all material risks (and opportunities).

- There are many methods for the identification of risks, including risk checklists, risk workshops, system analyses, SWOT analyses, early warning systems, business war-gaming, and creativity techniques.
- The success of risk identification depends on a common understanding of risk, an "identification-friendly" risk culture, a systematic and complete risk catalogue, the use of suitable instruments, and the methodological competencies of the risk owners.
- Risk quantification includes the analysis of underlying risk factors and the assessment of their probability of occurrence and impact on a firm's objectives.
- The prerequisite for risk quantification is an inventory of identified risks and a description of their main characteristics.
- The success of risk quantification depends primarily on the appropriateness of the quantification model, the availability of sufficient data for the parametrization of the model, and the methodological competence of the responsible risk manager.
- The key risk factors, their interdependencies, and their functional relationships with the relevant corporate goals must be integrated into a risk model. In addition, the model must be updated regularly to limit model risks.
- There are numerous instruments for risk quantification. The instruments for qualitative risk assessment are risk classifications and risk portfolios. Risk quantification requires that the probability and impact of risks are described using probability distributions. Alternatively, scenario analyses can be applied to determine the range of potential risks and opportunities.
- The aggregation of single risks to determine the overall risk exposure of a company requires quantification. If necessary, uncertain information for risk assessment can be represented by suitable distribution functions. When aggregating risks, risk interdependencies must be considered.
- Risk-relevant information is generated and transmitted to internal and external addressees as risk reports.
- The objectives of risk reporting are to provide information, document the company's risk situation, prepare risk migration, and support risk monitoring.
- Risk reporting must be consistent, up-to-date, complete, accurate, flexible, economical, and integrated into the corporate reporting system.
- Internal risk reporting is the basis for external risk disclosure.
- Internal risk reports are provided by decentralized risk owners and the central ERM unit. The recipients of internal risk reports are the central ERM unit, managers, and risk control bodies such as the supervisory board.
- A distinction is made between standard reporting of regular information about the company's risk situation for internal decision-makers and ad hoc reporting on emerging material risks.
- External risk disclosure is primarily aimed at current and potential investors and lenders. It is controlled by numerous regulatory requirements and is intended to inform the external addressees about the material risks of the company and the implementation of the ERM and internal control system.

8.6 Exercises and Questions

1. Why is risk identification crucial for the effectiveness of the operational ERM process?
2. What is the result of risk identification?
3. Discuss the necessity of risk quantification.
4. What are the objectives of risk quantification within the operational RM process?
5. Explain the basic procedure for risk assessment.
6. Explain the procedure for determining the earnings-at-risk for an industrial company using Monte Carlo simulation.
7. Vanini SE carries out a Monte Carlo simulation to determine the distribution of its EBIT for the following year. The minimum EBIT in the worst-case scenario is US$ − 750,000; the maximum EBIT is US$5,770,000; the average EBIT is US$3,000,000; the standard deviation of the EBIT is US$1,300,000; and the EaR has a confidence level of 95%, a holding period of 1 year, and a loss probability of 15%. Vanini SE plans for an EBIT of US$3,500,000. Discuss the risk and performance situation of the company for the following year.
8. Which problems are encountered during risk quantification and aggregation? Develop a solution for each problem you have named.
9. What are the tasks of risk reporting?
10. Which conflicts of interest exist between the design of internal risk reporting and external risk disclosure?
11. What is the content of an internal risk report? Differentiate the contents according to the informational needs of the report addressees.
12. What is the difference between standard and ad hoc risk reporting? Create a tabular comparison based on selected criteria.
13. Explain the key functions and requirements of external risk disclosure.
14. Which problems are encountered in risk reporting and disclosure?

References

Andrén, N., Jankensgård, H., & Oxelheim, L. (2005). Exposure-based cash-flow-at-risk under macroeconomic uncertainty. *Journal of Applied Corporate Finance, 17*, 76–86.

Ansoff, H. I. (1975). Managing strategic surprise by response to weak signals. *California Management Review, 18*, 21–33.

Baum, H.-G., Coenenberg, A. G., & Günther, T. (2013). *Strategisches controlling*. Schäffer-Poeschel.

Berger, T. (2018). Interpretation von begriffen zur umschreibung von wahrscheinlichkeiten. *Controller Magazin, 33*(4), 46–48.

Bleuel, H.-H. (2006). Monte-Carlo-Analysen im Risikomanagement. *Controlling, 18*, 371–378. https://doi.org/10.15358/0935-0381-2006-7-371

Burger, A., & Buchhart, A. (2002). *Risiko-Controlling*. Oldenbourg.

Burger, A., & Buchhart, A. (2014). *Risiko-controlling*. Walter de Gruyter GmbH & Co KG.

Burnaby, P., & Hass, S. (2009). Ten steps to enterprise-wide risk management. *Corporate Governance: The international journal of business in society, 9*, 539–550.
COSO (2017). Enterprise risk management - integrating with strategy and performance.
Diederichs, M. (2018). *Risikomanagement und Risikocontrolling* (4th ed.). Vahlen.
Duijm, N. J. (2015). Recommendations on the use and design of risk matrices. *Safety Science, 76*, 21–31.
Gleißner, W. (2022). *Grundlagen des Risikomanagements: Handbuch für ein Management unter Unsicherheit* (Management competence) (4th ed.). Verlag Franz Vahlen.
Glette-Iversen, I., & Aven, T. (2021). On the meaning of and relationship between dragon-kings, black swans and related concepts. *Reliability Engineering and System Safety, 211*, 107625.
Grisar, C., & Meyer, M. (2015). Use of Monte Carlo simulation: An empirical study of German, Austrian and Swiss controlling departments. *Journal of Management Control, 26*, 249–273. https://doi.org/10.1007/s00187-015-0213-2
Hahn, D., & Krystek, U. (2000). Früherkennungssysteme und KonTraG. In D. Dömer, P. Horváth, & H. Kagermann (Eds.), *Praxis des Risikomanagements* (Vol. 2000, pp. 74–97). Stuttgart.
Hardy, M. R., & Saunders, D. (2022). Quantitative enterprise risk management. *International series on actuarial science*, 2022: 1. Cambridge University Press.
Heinle, M. S., & Smith, K. C. (2017). A theory of risk disclosure. *Review of Accounting Studies, 22*, 1459–1491.
Holopainen, M., & Toivonen, M. (2012). Weak signals: Ansoff today. *Futures, 44*, 198–205.
Hubbard, D. W. (2020). *The failure of risk management: Why it's broken and how to fix it* (2nd ed.). Wiley.
Hunziker, S. (2021). *Enterprise risk management: Modern approaches to balancing risk and reward* (2nd ed.). Springer.
Ibrahim, A. E. A., Hussainey, K., Nawaz, T., Ntim, C., & Elamer, A. (2022). A systematic literature review on risk disclosure research: State-of-the-art and future research agenda. *International Review of Financial Analysis, 82*, 102217.
Jankensgård, H., & Kapstad, P. (2021). *Empowered enterprise risk management: Theory and practice*. Wiley.
Kaplan, R. S., & Mikes, A. (2012). Managing risks: A new framework. *Harvard Business Review, 90*, 48–60.
Kaplan, R. S., Leonard, H. B., & Mikes, A. (2020). *Novel risks*. Harvard Business School.
Khlif, H., & Hussainey, K. (2016). The association between risk disclosure and firm characteristics: A meta-analysis. *Journal of Risk Research, 19*, 181–211.
Kremers, M. (2002). *Risikoübernahme in Industrieunternehmen*. Sternenfels Verlag.
Lindley, D. V. (2014). *Understanding uncertainty. Wiley series in probability and statistics*. Wiley.
Olson, D. L., & Wu, D. (2020a). Risk matrices. In D. L. Olson & D. Wu (Eds.), *Enterprise risk management models* (pp. 17–31). Springer. https://doi.org/10.1007/978-3-662-60608-7_2
Olson, D. L., & Wu, D. (2020b). Value at risk models. In D. L. Olson & D. Wu (Eds.), *Enterprise risk management models* (pp. 79–91). Springer Nature. https://doi.org/10.1007/978-3-662-60608-7_6
Romeike, F. (2018). *Risikomanagement. Studienwissen kompakt*. Wiesbaden. https://doi.org/10.1007/978-3-658-13952-0
Romeike, F., & Stallinger, M. (2021). *Stochastische Szenariosimulation in der Unternehmenspraxis: Risikomodellierung, Fallstudien, Umsetzung in R*. Springer.
Taleb, N. N. (2012). *The black swan: The impact of the highly improbable* (2nd ed.). Random House.
Taleb, N. N., Goldstein, D. G., & Spitznagel, M. W. (2009). The six mistakes executives make in risk management. *Harvard Business Review, 87*, 78–81.
Vanini, U., & Heise, L. (2017). Monte-Carlo-Simulation in der GuV-Planung des Audi-Konzerns-Eine Fallstudie. In L. Nadig & U. Egle (Eds.), *CARF Luzern 2017: Controlling. Accounting. Risiko. Finanzen* (pp. 547–562). Verlag IFZ-Hochschule Luzern.

Vanini, U., & Rieg, R. (2021). *Risikomanagement: Grundlagen -- Instrumente -- Unternehmenspraxis* (Lehrbuch) (2nd ed.). Schäffer-Poeschel Verlag Stuttgart.

Vanini, U., & Weinstock, M. (2006). Risikoinventur bei der HSH N Real Estate AG. *CON, 18*, 379–386.

Vanini, U., & Worm, F. (2024). *Risikoorientierte Unternehmenssteuerung: Fallstudien für die Risikomodellierung und ein Management unter Unsicherheit*. Schäffer-Poeschel.

Chapter 9
Strategy, Resilience, Robustness, Sustainability, and ERM

Abstract The task of strategic risk management, which constitutes an important part of ERM, is to identify and strategically manage uncertainties, opportunities, and risks such as threats to success factors.

This chapter explains the importance of risk management in ensuring the sustainable success of an organization. Building on the model of a robust company, it shows how financial sustainability (strength), a robust strategy, organizational resilience, and the ability to deal with risks improve the future viability of a company. A robust company is one that is highly likely to withstand the effects of risks due to its characteristics—even if the risks were not recognized or managed as part of a risk analysis. The most important characteristics of such a company are summarized at the end of the chapter, expressed as 20 core criteria. In this context, the importance of sustainability is also discussed.

Keywords ESG · Financial sustainability · Future viability · QScore · Resilience · Robustness · Robust company · Robust strategy · Sustainability

Questions
1. What are the key elements of a corporate strategy?
2. What characterizes "robust" strategies?
3. Which factors are of central importance for the sustainable success of a company?
4. What significance does ERM have for the sustainable success of a company?
5. Which specific questions and criteria can be used to systematically assess the robustness, survivability, and future viability of a company?
6. Which key figures are needed to assess financial sustainability?
7. What are the special features of assessing "sustainability risks"?

Supplementary Information The online version contains supplementary material available at https://doi.org/10.1007/978-3-031-86425-4_9.

R. Rieg et al., *Enterprise Risk Management*, Springer Texts in Business and Economics, https://doi.org/10.1007/978-3-031-86425-4_9

9.1 Overview

This chapter discusses the many interfaces of enterprise risk management (ERM) and corporate strategy. Corporate strategy describes the guidelines for the future development of a company, which should build and secure the "success potentials" essential for sustainable success. Corporate strategies, and thus strategic corporate planning, are long-term oriented, necessitating forecasts about the future developments of factors such as market conditions and technologies. However, such forecasts are particularly uncertain due to the long forecast period. The effects of corporate strategy measures are also uncertain. When developing a corporate strategy and deciding on strategic options for action (strategy variants), the associated opportunities and dangers (risks) must be considered (see risk-adequate valuation of strategic alternatives in Chap. 10). In particular, the search for strategic risks, such as the threat to business models and success factors, must be systematically analyzed. Strategic management should, therefore, always be understood as strategic risk management (Gleißner, 2022 and Gleißner/Berger, 2024). Formally, an optimal strategy maximizes enterprise value—given certain constraints accepted by the owners with regard to the scope of risk (e.g., the probability of insolvency). The enterprise value can be understood as a key figure for the earning-risk profile (see Chap. 10). The further development of a corporate strategy should be supported by guidelines that link the findings from strategic management and ERM approaches. The goal is to secure the company's success in the long term through a corporate strategy that is as resilient or robust as possible. This chapter explores the model of a "robust company" and the characteristics companies must have to ensure a high probability of surviving the risks associated with any business activity. For example, it is shown that such companies have pricing power due to their core competences, avoid critical dependencies, and take care to consider the associated risks in all business decisions.

9.2 Resilience, Robustness, and Risk in Strategic Management

The ability of a system, especially a company, to withstand risk and thus ensure its continued existence is referred to as "resilience" or "robustness."

Following Hillmann and Günther (2021), p. 31, organizational resilience can be defined as follows: organization resilience is the ability of an organization to maintain functions and recover fast from adversity by mobilizing and excessing the resources needed.

Resilience means that, following a negative shock, a system such as a company can return to the level that existed before the shock. This could refer, for example, to the level of cash flow. Another and important special case of organizational resilience is supply chain resilience. Supply chain resilience is the ability to persist,

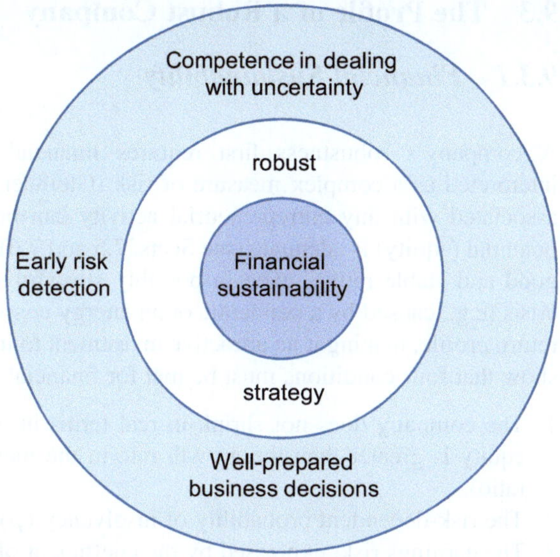

Fig. 9.1 Characteristics of a robust company

adapt, or transform in the face of change (Wieland & Durach, 2021, p. 2; Novak et al., 2021; Iyengar et al., 2021).

Brunnermeier (2021) sees resilience as a necessary but not sufficient condition for sustainability and assumes a narrower understanding of the term "robustness" (pp. 19–20). "Robustness, unlike resilience, is about the ability to resist shocks without adapting" (Brunnermeier, 2021), p. 18.

According to Brunnermeier (2021), robustness and resilience have many similarities (e.g., the safety buffer and redundancies in the system), whereas company risk resilience emphasizes the functionality of the organization and supply chain. Gleißner (2023) broadly defines the term "robustness" as the ability of a system to survive (negative) shocks while maintaining a defined minimum level of success (performance) in the long term. Such shocks are the result of risks with severe impacts at a random point in time and uncertainty impact.

Robustness, which encompasses the ability to survive, can also be described as "future viability." A robust company pursues a strategy that is highly likely to ensure at least a sufficient minimum level of performance, even given the impossibility of predicting the specifics of the future.

Consequently, it can be stated that under conditions of uncertainty, a strategic management model must consider **(1) financial sustainability** (see Sect. 9.3.1), **(2) robustness of the strategy**, and **(3) strong skills in dealing with opportunities and threats (risks)**. From these conceptual building blocks, the model of a "robust company" with these exact characteristics can be specified (see Fig. 9.1 and Gleißner, 2023).

The following description of the robust company is the result of integration and further development of earlier writings on the robust company and sketches of the overall model presented here (see Gleißner, 2023).

9.3 The Profile of a Robust Company

9.3.1 *Financial Sustainability*

A company's robustness first requires financial sustainability, which can be interpreted as a complex measure of risk (Gleißner, 2022). It means that the risks associated with any entrepreneurial activity can be managed if its risk coverage potential (equity) is adequate (see Sects. 7.5 and 7.6). The company, therefore, has a good and stable rating, even in possibly stressful scenarios such as an economic crisis (e.g., caused by a pandemic or an energy crisis). It has an above-average risk-return profile, making it an attractive investment to its owners. Gleißner et al. (2022) show that four conditions must be met for financial sustainability:

1. The company does not shrink in real terms in the long run (and the return on equity is greater than the growth rate in the medium term to secure the equity ratio).
2. The risk-dependent probability of insolvency (p) is low ($p < 1\%$ p.a.).
3. The earnings risk, expressed by the coefficient of variation CV of profits, is low (CV $< 40\%$).
4. The return on capital is higher than the cost of capital c (derived from C) (cf. (Gleißner, 2019); see Chap. 10 for the calculation).

Ensuring high financial sustainability is a secondary condition of owners who want to limit their entrepreneurial risk ("safety-first concept"; (Telser, 1955) see Fig. 9.2). Empirical evidence shows that companies with high financial sustainability

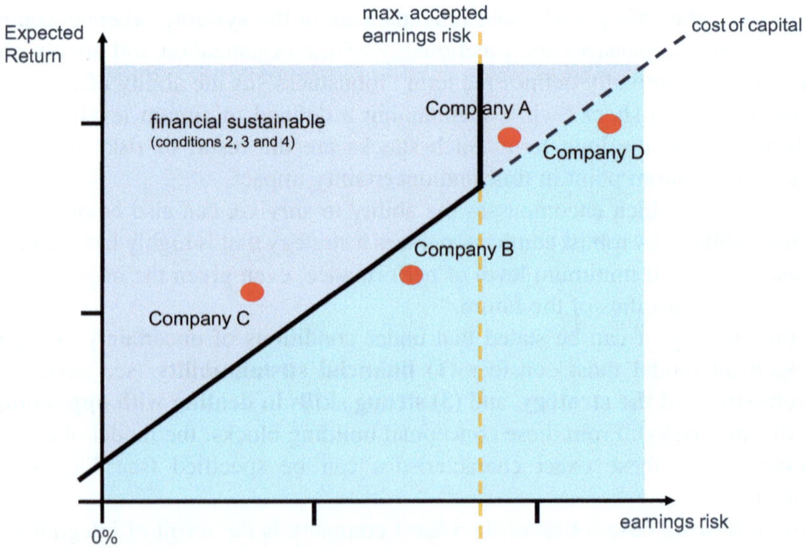

Fig. 9.2 Risk-return profiles

also generate high risk-adjusted excess returns on stock markets (Gleißner et al., 2022).

Financial sustainability, measured by financial ratios, is primarily a reflection of the impact of a company's strategy to safeguard its economic situation in the long term. Robust companies, therefore, have a robust corporate strategy.

9.3.2 *Robust Strategy and Organizational Resilience*

In the long run, only a robust strategy can ensure success and financial sustainability and increase the value of the company. The corporate strategy defines the basic long-term orientation and success of the company, which serve as a guideline for the company's future development (Hill & Schilling, 2023; Whittington et al., 2023).

One of the first decisions made as part of the portfolio strategy is the selection of strategic business units (SBU) that a company operates. This is assessed based on market attractiveness, which also determines risk, and the potential for success that can be achieved by the company, relative to its competitors.

A business strategy is then created for each strategic business unit in which the company is active or intends to become active. The strategy reflects their core competencies, their competitive advantages, and the design of the value chain (see Fig. 9.3).

A robust strategy focuses on core competencies that are valuable in the long term, difficult to copy, and usable in a variety of ways (Prahalad & Hamel, 1990; Gleißner, 2023). According to the capability-based view, "dynamic skills" such as adaptability are essential competencies (Teece et al., 1997). Such core competencies allow the

Description of a business area strategy (business model)

Core competences	**Strategic thrust**
• What competence and resources do we have? • What expertise and resources do we need? • What makes our core competence scalable? • What safeguards our core competence?	• What are our primary goals? • Which secondary conditions (e.g. credit rating) should be considered? • Which value drivers - growth, return, risk - should be changed and how? • What are our growth drivers? • What are our return drivers? • What are our risk drivers?
Business areas (BA) and competitive advantages	**Value chain**
• Which BAs (product-target-region) exist that are (a) attractive and (b) fit our core competence? • What are the needs and buying criteria of customers in BA? • What benefit/problem solution do we offer (value proposition)? • With regard to which purchasing criteria do we have verifiable competitive advantages? • What should the customer pay for and how (revenue model)?	• Which value creation activities are covered in the enterprise? • What investments and variable and fixed costs does it generate? • How do we reach the customers of the target group? • Which key suppliers (and partners) cover the other value creation activities?

Fig. 9.3 Description of a business area strategy (business model) as a basis for assessing robustness

realization of new business models to defend against or exploit disruptive innovations. The company builds its competitive advantage on this basis, geared to customer requirements, which helps to differentiate the company from its competitors and to retain customers in the long term. This leads to "pricing power" and the ability to pass on cost fluctuations to business partners. Risky and unattractive fields of activities or customer groups are avoided, as are critical dependencies (Pinkwart et al., 2022, pp. 773–778). Adequate diversification is therefore ensured. The value chain is designed in such a way that only activities that are not better outsourced to others are performed within the company, as long as this does not lead to critical dependencies. The company designs its work processes to be as uncomplicated as possible. In addition, redundancies and reserves ensure organizational resilience [for an explanation of the basic concept, see Hillmann and Günther (2021) and Ayyub (2014)] and meet basic requirements with regard to corporate sustainability (Korinth & Lueg, 2022). The company is attractive to competent employees (e.g., because of its purpose). Conditions are created for self-organizing: agile structures give employees the freedom and incentive to act flexibly and on their own initiative as much as possible. Sufficiently broad diversification, as well as loss and liability limitations, should ensure that even unexpected extreme negative events like an economic crisis do not endanger the company's survival.

Robust strategies increasingly consider more requirements from the context of "sustainability," especially concerning economy, social, and governance (ESG) matters. The importance of financial sustainability has already been pointed out (see Sect. 9.3.1). "Sustainability risks" will be dealt with in Sect. 9.4. Regarding the corporate strategy itself, it is increasingly important to note that a suitable business purpose with a clearly recognizable contribution to satisfying the needs of stakeholders today and in the future is becoming more and more important for the attractiveness of firms. Specifically, in many industries, the (perceived) sustainability of a company's business model and service delivery processes are important as a purchase criterion by customers, and thus "perceived sustainability" becomes a purchase criterion and differentiation potential (and potential competitive advantage). As stated above, sustainability risks must also be taken into account in this risk analysis, such as our costs from the future emission of CO_2 or reputational damage as a result of possible environmental pollution or when human rights are violated in the supply chain.

The possibilities of making strategic decisions to reduce risk and improve robustness are exemplified by currency risks or foreign exchange risks ("FX-Risks"). Whereas transaction-related exchange rate risks (transaction exposure) are mainly managed using financial risk management instruments, economic exchange rate risks are mainly managed by adjusting strategy (see, e.g., Gleißner, 2022, pp. 363–366):

1. Regional diversification, to reduce geopolitical risks and dependence on changes in individual currencies
2. Synchronization of the currency structure of sales and costs (natural hedge)
3. Pronounced product differentiation to create pricing power

9.3.3 The Ability to Deal with Risk

To ensure the protection of the company, ERM must systematically address existing risks (opportunities and threats), to be able to adapt and react as early as possible (Teece et al., 1997; Gleißner, 2023). Risks lead to negative deviations from the plan, which endanger the company's financial stability, especially its rating, and can trigger crises. A robust company needs strong skills in dealing with opportunities and threats. In particular, it must be able to:

1. Systematically identify, quantify, and aggregate risk (see Chap. 8)
2. Initiate adequate risk mitigation measures at an early stage
3. Take appropriate account of the risks associated with every top-management decision (see Chaps. 2, 7, and 10)

Therefore, ERM is an important element in a strategic management approach that safeguards the robustness of a company. A company requires both an efficient risk management system and procedures for risk analysis. Such strategic risks arise from the following:

1. Threats to success potentials
2. Changes in competitive forces in the industry environment (e.g., increasing dependence on suppliers or threats caused by substitute products)
3. Severe economic crises triggered by economic risks (e.g., financial crises, geopolitical crises, or supply crises), including pandemics, energy crises, and wars

These main areas of strategic risk should be analyzed in turn in a structured manner, with particular attention being paid to economic risks that can lead to an economic crisis (such as geopolitical crises, a pandemic, or raw material supply crises).

In addition to the uncertain premises for operational planning, which always represent risks, a specific analysis of strategic risk is required (Gleißner, 2022; Kaplan & Mikes, 2016; Nocco & Stulz, 2022; see also Chap. 8).

To this end, the main risks are first quantified (i.e., described by a suitable probability distribution). Then, risks are prioritized, the usefulness of risk management measures is assessed, and the equity and liquidity requirements needed to cover the risks are calculated.

Robust companies need adequate procedures for risk aggregation. Only with the results of risk aggregation is it possible to make well-founded assessments of financial sustainability, the need for equity and liquidity, and thus the threat situation of the company overall. The aggregation of risk requires the use of stochastic simulation methods (e.g., Monte Carlo simulation; see Chap. 5). This involves analyzing a large representative sample of possible risk-related future scenarios. In this way, a realistic range of future earnings and liquidity developments can be shown. The probability that covenants will be breached or that a target credit rating can no longer be achieved can be derived directly ("probability of insolvency"; see

Sect. 8.2 and Chap. 10 for the link to the value of a company as a performance measure).

Based on this information, the strategy aims to improve the risk-return profile and make the company robust (e.g., by risk mitigation). An important starting point for reducing strategic risks is, for example, to reduce dependencies (e.g., on individual suppliers or customers).

A company crisis can arise when major risks are taken as a result of a top-management decision. It is therefore necessary for a robust company to ensure organizationally that the risks associated with every top-management decision are analyzed and taken into account in the decision calculation (see Chap. 10). The strategic decisions required for further development of the corporate strategy are fundamentally entrepreneurial and therefore require decision templates with which changes in the risk-return profile can be assessed. An increase in corporate risk leads to higher negative deviations from the plan, higher potential losses, and thus a need for more equity. This, in turn, leads to rising costs of capital, and thus the company value becomes a measure of success (Gleißner, 2019, see Chap. 10).

9.4 Sustainability and ESG

In recent years, the importance of sustainability for corporate strategy and risk management has been increasingly discussed. Sometimes the sustainability of corporate management is understood as a good ESG score (E, environmental; S, social; G, governance). The topic of sustainability is important for risk management and a sustainably successful corporate strategy. However, the correlations are somewhat more complex than they appear at first glance.

Firstly, it should be noted that ESG does not mean sustainability. In general, "sustainable development" is understood to mean development that meets the needs of people living today and those living in the future (Brundtland Commission, 1987). The evaluation of entrepreneurial activity on the environment and society (i.e., E and S) is certainly relevant here but must be considered in context. In addition to the effects of entrepreneurial activity on the environment and society, the primary benefit of entrepreneurial activity for customers, as particularly important stakeholders, must first be considered. From this perspective, a distinction can be made between three aspects of sustainable (strategic) corporate management (see Fig. 9.4).

1. First, a company needs to be able to survive, as only an existing company can contribute to satisfying people's needs. The first requirement is therefore "financial sustainability" (see Sect. 9.3.1), which is a key factor for survival and future viability (see Sect. 9.3).
2. The company's contribution to satisfying the needs of other people, especially customers, must then be assessed. The decisive factor here is the time of business (purpose), and satisfied customers who buy a company's products are proof that the company provides a benefit and thus contributes to satisfying needs.

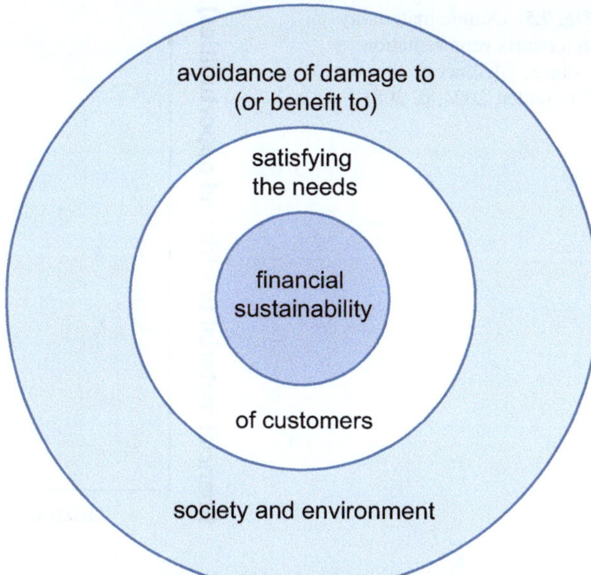

Fig. 9.4 Characteristics of sustainable companies (source: Gleißner & Weissman, 2024, p. 41)

3. Furthermore, the additional effects of the business activity on the environment and society must also be taken into account, although these in turn often have repercussions for the company itself (e.g., because customers with a preference for environmental protection regard a company's environmentally friendly production as a purchase criterion; see 2).

When assessing the robustness and future viability of a company, all of the abovementioned aspects of sustainability must potentially be considered. In some sectors in particular, environmental orientation and social commitment are purchasing criteria that are important for generating sales and offer opportunities for differentiating the company. Success in the sales market is then dependent on the perceived sustainability of the company (e.g., specifically environmental and social orientation).

Sustainability risks or ESG risks must also be considered both for the assessment and improvement of a company's robustness and for the task of risk management. **Sustainability risks** are those that have a financial and at the same time relevant non-financial impact on the environment and society (e.g., CO_2 emissions). Like all other risks, sustainability risks must be properly quantified and taken into account in risk aggregation. Typical sustainability risks include the following:

- The uncertain costs of CO_2 emissions
- Possible compensation payments due to environmental damage caused or other breaches of the law

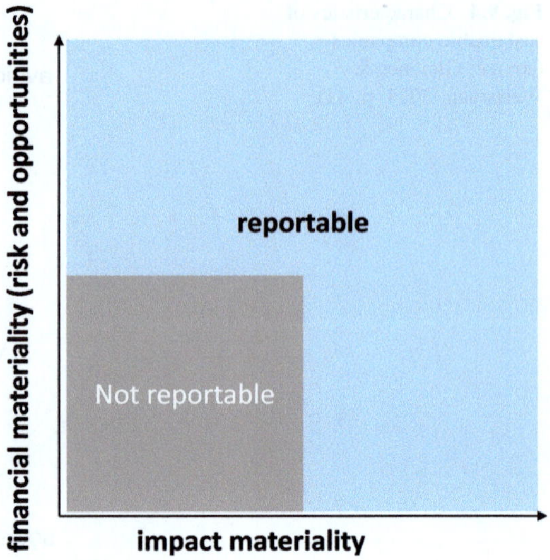

Fig. 9.5 Double materiality in a matrix representation (source: Gleißner & Baumüller, 2024, p. 208)

- Reputational damage and thus loss of sales as a result of breaches of sustainability requirements that important customers expect (e.g., human rights violations in the value chain)

The greater the proportion of such sustainability risks in the overall scope of risk, the more intensive the risk management must be to deal with them. The adequate management of such risks is therefore essential for ensuring the robustness and future viability of the company.

From a regulatory perspective, it should be noted that in the European Union financial and non-financial impact of sustainability risks must be disclosed in the annual report in accordance with the Corporate Social Responsibility Directive (CSRD) and the associated European Sustainability Reporting Standards (ESRS). The first step is to assess which "sustainability aspects" are material (materiality analysis). An issue is considered material if it has either a significant impact on the environment and society or a financial impact. The assessment of the financial impact in the materiality analysis (see Fig. 9.5) must be carried out consistently and in accordance with the specifications of risk management and the methods used here for risk quantification. Risk management and the risk quantification methods it uses also play a major role in sustainability reporting and the prioritization of sustainability aspects.

9.5 Examples of Robust Companies

Examples of very robust companies that have both a particularly robust strategy and financial sustainability can easily be found among large, listed companies (Gleißner, 2023). The robustness of Nvidia's strategy, for example, is based on its almost monopoly-like technological core competences. LVMH's robustness is based on the brand portfolio that is virtually unique in its market and its competence in brand management. The robustness of some software companies, such as SAP or Oracle, is based not only on technological skills and patents but also on the high transaction costs that their customers would incur in the event of a software change, which create pricing power. The robustness of strategy and business models (e.g., from Amazon, Apple, ASML, Microsoft, Nestlé, or the rating agencies Standard & Poor's and Moody's) can be easily seen based on the criteria outlined above.

9.6 Summary

- Effective risk management is an essential prerequisite for a robust company that has a high degree of future viability and is therefore highly likely to be successful in the long term.
- Robust companies are characterized by financial sustainability (financial stability) and a robust strategy in addition to strong skills in dealing with uncertainty (i.e., good risk management). They are therefore able to withstand the effects of many risks, possibly not even recognized in detail, without a serious crisis.
- Information from risk management is required to assess the future viability and thus the survivability of a company. To assess financial sustainability, key figures are needed to record the insolvency risk (credit rating) and the earnings risk, such as the profit or cash flow volatility (coefficient of variation of profit) calculated by means of risk aggregation.
- Two complementary approaches make it possible to secure the company's long-term success: It is the task of risk management to identify all risks that, individually or in combination, could jeopardize the continued existence of the company and, if possible, to manage them adequately. In addition, it is the task of strategic management to make the company and its strategy so robust that it can withstand the (negative) effects of many risks that may not even be recognized individually.
- Sustainability is becoming increasingly important to corporate strategy and risk management. Sustainability as perceived by the customer often becomes an important purchasing criterion, and sustainability risks, which have financial and non-financial impacts (on society and the environment), are playing an increasingly important role in risk management.
- A prerequisite for improving the robustness of the corporate strategy is its adequate and complete description. In particular, the (core) competences of the

company, the business areas and associated competitive advantages, and the basic design of the value chain should be explained.

9.7 Exercises and Questions

1. In addition to financial sustainability and a robust strategy, what is the other requirement of a "robust company"?
   a) High equity ratio
   b) Strong ability to deal with opportunities and threats (risks)
   c) Focus on fast-growing markets
   d) Highly efficient work processes
2. What characterizes "sustainability risks"?
3. What are typical strategic risks and how can they be identified?
4. Why are the findings of a sound risk analysis important for the development of corporate strategy?
5. As an exercise, you can also assess the robustness of your company—or another one—using the following criteria.

The aim of this exercise is to assess the robustness of a company using checklists.

The following checklist summarizes the most important characteristics of a robust company and makes it possible for managers to assess the robustness of their companies through a simple self-check. The 20 orientation questions explained below provide a rough indication of the future viability of a company and highlight areas with particular potential for improvement.

The following overview explains the assignment of the valuation symbols – –, –, 0, +, and ++ to the items of the "QScore" (for the QScore model that measures robustness and future viability, see Gleißner & Weissman 2024). In compact analysis, the context-dependent weighting and plausibility check of individual questions in the QScore model are not possible. In an indicative assessment, users are recommended to determine a percentage for each individual question and then calculate the average. To be sustainable, businesses should achieve at least 50% (zero) in all 10 dimensions.

A rating of "0" reflects the fact that:

- the business achieves at least an average score on the criterion relative to other businesses (better than the 50% quantile),
- economic and legal minimum requirements are fulfilled, regardless of whether other companies also achieve this.

A score of "+", which indicates above-average strength, is achieved by only a few companies on average across all criteria, even among those with capital market capability, which is why they receive a bronze medal as a special seal of quality. The best companies in the world achieve an average degree of fulfillment of all criteria of

Table 9.1 Orientation questions on the future viability of a company (based on Gleißner & Weissman, 2024)

		––	–	0	+	++
Q1	Has the company had a positive real sales growth rate in recent years, and is it expected to grow at a positive rate over the next 3 years?					
Q2	Is either the probability of insolvency derived from financial ratios or the credit rating low (i.e., <1% p.a.)?					
Q3	Is the earnings risk (planning uncertainty), low, and will it remain low over the next 3 years?					
Q4a	Is the return on equity clearly above the cost of equity (which depends on the level of earning risk; see Chap. 10)?					
Q4b	Is the (adjusted) EBIT margin high?					
Q5a	Does the company have highly competent and motivated employees?					
Q5b	Is the company attractive for competent employees (e.g., through positive purpose(s) and corporate culture)?					
Q5c	Do owners and employees see a business purpose or vision because of which intergenerational livelihood security is sought?					
Q6a	Is the company active in attractive and growing markets that offer opportunities for differentiation?					
Q6b	Does the company have solid core competencies that lead to clear competitive advantages in terms of purchasing criteria important to customers?					
Q6c	Does the company succeed in avoiding critical dependencies on just a few customers, suppliers, or business partners?					
Q7	Are the value creation processes and support processes resilient (e.g., through redundancies, inventories, and flexibility?					
Q8a	Does the company have a good management accounting control system?					
Q8b	Is there an effective corporate governance and compliance system?					
Q9a	Based on its robust strategy, can the company rule out the existence of individual risks that could jeopardize its existence (e.g., threats to the key success factors) with a high degree of probability?					
Q9b	Does the risk management system meet all requirements? Specifically, are the material risks systematically identified, appropriately quantified, and carefully monitored?					
Q9c	Is risk aggregation (Monte Carlo simulation) undertaken as part of integrated corporate planning, enabling assessment of equity capital requirements and the probability of a crisis?					
Q9d	Is the company's risk coverage potential (equity capital and liquidity resources) significantly greater than the aggregated total risk volume (equity requirement, value at risk 99%)?					

(continued)

over 85% (i.e., a ++ across the board), which deserves a "gold medal" due to their outstanding future viability.

Table 9.1 (continued)

		– –	–	0	+	+ +
Q10a	Are there binding rules and regulations for the preparation of top-management decisions (e.g., on investments)?					
Q10b	Are documented decision papers available for all important top-management decisions? Do they contain all essential contents (e.g., on options for action, assumptions, forecasts, risks, and the effects on the overall scope of risk)?					

Based on the basic considerations, the following Table 9.1 shows an overview of 20 questions that help to assess the robustness of a company and to make a first prioritization of improvement potentials.

References

Ayyub, B. M. (2014). Systems resilience for multihazard environments: Definition, metrics, and valuation for decision making. *Risk Analysis, 34*, 340–355.

Brundtland Commission. (1987). *Report of the world commission on environment and development: Our common future, United Nations*. https://sustainabledevelopment.un.org/content/documents/5987our-common-future.pdf. Accessed 30 April 2024.

Brunnermeier, M. K. (2021). *The resilient society*. Harper Business.

Gleißner, W. (2019). Cost of capital and probability of default in value-based risk management. *Management Research Review, 42*, 1243–1258.

Gleißner, W. (2022). *Grundlagen des Risikomanagements: Handbuch für ein Management unter Unsicherheit* (Management competence) (4th ed.). Verlag Franz Vahlen.

Gleißner, W. (2023). Uncertainty and resilience in strategic management: Profile of a robust company. *The International Journal of Risk Assessment and Management (IJRAM), 26*, 75–94.

Gleißner, W. & Berger, Th. (2024). Enterprise Risk Management: Improving Embedded Risk Management and Risk Governance. Risks, 12, 05.12.2024, https://www.mdpi.com/3074192

Gleißner, W., & Baumüller, J. (2024). Doppelte Wesentlichkeit gem. CSRD und Nachhaltigkeitsrisiken: Ein Vorschlag für eine Operationalisierung samt Integration in das Risikomanagement. *KoR - Zeitschrift für kapitalmarktorientierte Rechnungslegung, 24*, 202–209.

Gleißner, W., & Weissman, A. (2024). *Das zukunftsfähige Familienunternehmen: Mit dem QScore zu Unabhängigkeit, Resilienz und Robustheit*. Springer Gabler.

Gleißner, W., Günther, T., & Walkshäusl, C. (2022). Financial sustainability: Measurement and empirical evidence. *Journal of Business Economics, 92*, 467–516.

Hill, C. W. L., & Schilling, M. A. (2023). *Strategic management: An integrated approach* (14th ed.). Cengage Learning.

Hillmann, J., & Günther, E. (2021). Organizational resilience: A valuable construct for management research? *International Journal of Management Reviews (IRMR), 23*, 7–44.

Iyengar, D., Nilakantan, R., & Rao, S. (2021). On entrepreneurial resilience among micro-entrepreneurs in the face of economic disruptions - A little help from friends. *Journal of Business Logistics, 42*, 360–380.

Kaplan, R. S., & Mikes, A. (2016). Risk management – The revealing hand. *Journal of Applied Corporate Finance, 28*, 8–18.

Korinth, F., & Lueg, R. (2022). Corporate sustainability and risk management: The U-shaped relationships of disaggregated ESG rating scores and risk in the German capital market. *Sustainability, 14*, 1–15.

Nocco, B. W., & Stulz, R. M. (2022). Enterprise risk management: Theory and practice. *Journal of Applied Corporate Finance, 34*, 81–94.

Novak, D., Wu, Z. Z., & Dooley, K. J. (2021). Whose resilience matters? Addressing issues of scale in supply chain resilience. *Journal of Business Logistics, 42*, 323–335.

Pinkwart, A., Schingen, G., Pannes, A.-T., & Schlotböller, D. (2022). Improving resilience in times of multiple crisis: Commentary from a German economic policy point of view. *Schmalenbach Journal of Business Research, 74*, 763–786.

Prahalad, C. K., & Hamel, G. (1990). The core competence of the corporation. *Harvard Business Review, 68*, 3–15.

Teece, D., Pisano, G., & Shuen, A. (1997). Dynamic capabilities and strategic management. *Strategic Management Journal, 18*, 509–533.

Telser, L. G. (1955). Safety first and hedging. *The Review of Economic Studies, 23*, 1–16.

Whittington, R., Regnér, P., Angwin, D., Johnson, G., & Scholes, K. (2023). *Exploring strategy.* Pearson.

Wieland, A., & Durach, C. F. (2021). Two perspectives on supply chain resilience. *Journal of Business Logistics, 42*, 315–322.

Chapter 10
Value-Based Management and Enterprise Risk Management

Abstract This chapter outlines the relationship between value-based management and enterprise risk management (ERM). In particular, it is made clear that information from risk analysis and risk aggregation is especially relevant for modern value-based management. ERM provides the risk information that is required to provide unbiased projected values of cash flows or earnings and derive a risk-adequate cost of capital from the fluctuation around this planned value (planning uncertainty). By linking ERM and value-based management, one obtains **value-based ERM**. This uses insider information about existing risks as the basis for assessing the risk-return profile of options for action. In contrast to traditional concepts such as the capital asset pricing model for deriving the cost of capital, the approach can be used on apparently imperfect capital markets and in consideration of rating and financing restrictions. The application is shown in this chapter with a case study (strategy valuation).

Keywords Coefficient of variation · Cost of capital · Credit rating · Capital Asset Pricing Model (CAPM) · Distress risk · Earnings risk · Economic value added (EVA) · Incomplete replication · Insolvency · Probability of insolvency · Rating; Risk-adjusted capital (RAC) · Simulation-based valuation · Valuation · Value · Value-based management

Questions

- How can ERM and value-based management be combined?
- How can risk measures determined through risk aggregation be used to derive risk-appropriate cost of capital?
- How can the value driver "probability of insolvency" (distress risk), which depends on the scope of risk, be taken into account in value-based management?

With the methods shown in this chapter, you will be able to evaluate companies and their projects and investments taking risks into account. The effects of risk on (1) the

---

Supplementary Information The online version contains supplementary material available at https://doi.org/10.1007/978-3-031-86425-4_10.

R. Rieg et al., *Enterprise Risk Management*, Springer Texts in Business and Economics, https://doi.org/10.1007/978-3-031-86425-4_10

expected value of cash flows and (2) the risk-adjusted discount rate (cost of capital) are considered. For example, the following problem can be solved: is an investment in Project A preferable to an investment in Project B if Project A is expected to yield higher earnings, but has higher risks?

10.1 Introduction: Risk and Value

Every management activity is associated with opportunities and threats, which manifest in particular in the uncertain consequences of the decisions. The value contribution of ERM results from rating and financing restrictions as well as capital market imperfections such as taxes, transaction costs, and insolvency costs. Due to capital market imperfections and lack of investor diversification, reducing idiosyncratic risks can also generate value (Nocco & Stulz, 2022). Low cash flow volatility reduces the likelihood of having to rely on expensive external sources of financing or of violating contract covenants. Empirical capital market research confirms that companies with low fundamental risk generate high risk-adjusted excess returns and exhibit significantly higher resilience in the face of economic crises (Joyce & Mayer, 2012; Walkshäusl, 2013; Gleißner et al., 2022; Traut, 2023). Risk thus influences the value of a company. The enterprise value is the certain amount of money that is equivalent for the owner to the uncertain cash flow from the company. It depends on (1) the expected amount, (2) the timing, and (3) the risk of the cash flows the owner accrues. The enterprise value is thus a measure of the risk-return profile of all future payments (income, cash flow, or net operating profit after taxes [NOPAT]). Calculating the enterprise value as a function of various strategic options for action—strategy valuation—is a necessary task within the framework of value-oriented corporate management.

To achieve the kind of integrative and decision-oriented risk management that is to be strived for, close cooperation with management accounting makes sense (Berger & Gleissner, 2018; Gleißner, 2020). While traditional risk management concepts monitor existing risks, COSO enterprise risk management (version 2017) is a suitable platform for decision-oriented risk management (Hunziker, 2021; see also Chaps. 2 and 11). As a result, this is a central component of value-based management (Gleißner, 2019).

10.2 Value-Based Management

Value-based management is a corporate management approach that aims to make top-management decisions in such a way that a sustainable improvement in the risk-return profile results in an increase in wealth for the owners (see Jensen & Meckling, 1976 for a discussion of principal-agent relationships between corporate management and owners and Jensen, 2001 for more on the significance of corporate value). Rappaport (1999) provided an important impetus for value-based management by establishing enterprise value and shareholder value as measures of success and control variables for companies. In the shareholder value approaches suggested by Rappaport (1999) and Company et al. (2020), variants of the discounted cash flow (DCF) method are applied to obtain a suitable metric to evaluate or compare management activities, especially investments.

However, this first generation of methods was primarily capital market-oriented control methods because the cost of capital rate for discounting the (free) cash flows is derived from historical stock return fluctuations (beta factor of the CAPM) and not from the future earnings risks of the company.

The enterprise value can be explained as a function of the following primary value drivers:

- Capital employed, which is essentially dependent on the turnover and its growth rate
- Expected return on capital
- Cost of capital c, which is derivable from earnings risks
- The probability of insolvency *p*, which is expressed by the credit rating and largely acts like a negative growth rate *g* in the long term and strongly influences financing costs (Gleißner, 2010; Saha & Malkiel, 2012)

The product of return on capital and capital employed in each period (year) is the expected result (earnings or free cash flow).

The central idea of value-based management is the orientation toward the interests of the owners (shareholders), who, unlike other stakeholders such as customers or employees, do not receive contractually secured payments from the company. A basic principle of value-based management is that corporate value and thus asset growth for the owners can only be created if the return on capital is higher than the risk-adequate cost of capital. Growth of invested capital only makes sense if this condition is met. Empirical capital market research has proven the importance of growth and profitability for explaining stock returns (Fama & French, 2015; Kyosev et al., 2020).

Value-based performance measure ratios are necessary to achieve the advantages of value-based management, such as the orientation toward the interests of the owners and the consideration of future cash flows and their risks. Value-oriented metrics are particularly suitable as performance measures that form the basis for top-management decisions. They should also be able to be used for the ex-post assessment of the performance of the company management and individual business units. Important indicators for value-based management are economic value added (EVA™; see Chew & Stern, 2008), cash flow return on investment (CFROI), cash value added (CVA), and Tobin's q (Kaldor, 1966). Many value-based management systems were developed based on a value contribution or residual profit concept such as EVA™, which uses NOPAT instead of cash flow as a basis (Young & O'Byrne, 2001):

$$\mathrm{EVA}_t^{\mathrm{TM}} = \mathrm{NOPA}_t\text{–}\mathrm{WACC}_t \times \mathrm{Investment}_t. \tag{10.1}$$

Value-based management is based on the net present value calculation and thus on the concept of discount cash flow (DCF). The first generation of value-based management approaches and threats (risks) captured it rather rudimentarily because, following the hypothesis of perfect markets, the cost of capital rates was derived from historical stock return fluctuations (mostly with the help of capital asset pricing models, CAPM; see critique in Sect. 10.3 and Gleißner, 2019).

The central task of value-based corporate management is to prepare top-management decisions under uncertainty, using the enterprise value or "decision value" as a standard of assessment (Matschke & Brösel, 2021; Gleißner, 2019). This key figure expresses the risk-return profile of the options for action to be assessed. It is necessary to weigh up the return and risk of options for action, taking into account existing restrictions, especially with regard to the maximum accepted scope of risk ("safety first"; see Kataoka, 1963). Figure 10.1 illustrates two alternative strategies, A and B, for which the return (expected return) and risk (risk-adjusted cost of capital) are compared.

Preparing top-management decisions on projects (options for action) requires a sound strategy, operational planning based on this strategy, and an analysis of opportunities and threats (risks). In addition to the expected profitability, which is also dependent on the extent of existing opportunities and threats (risks), risk indicators are required to determine the aggregate total risk level (on the *x*-axis in Fig. 10.1) and the probability of a serious crisis using suitable key figures.

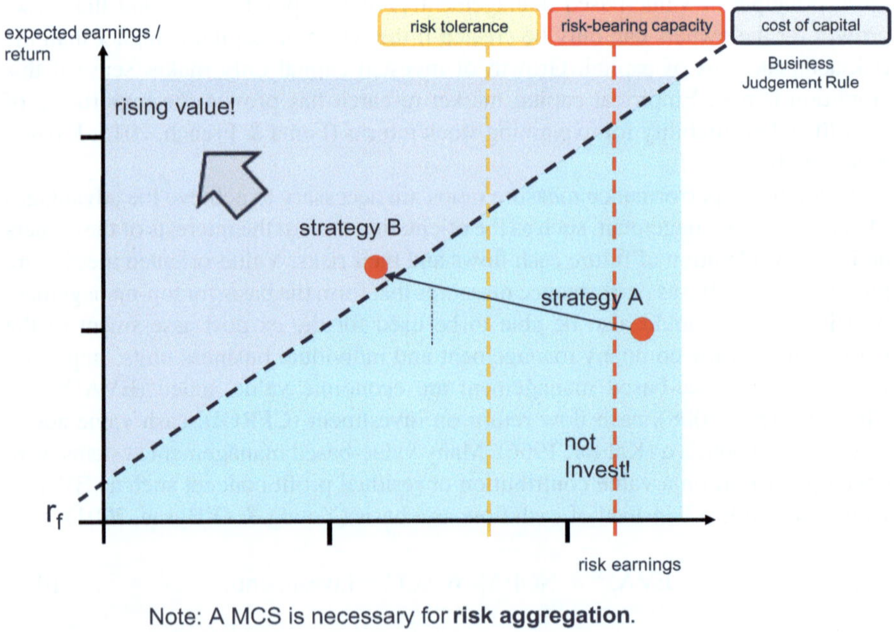

Fig. 10.1 Risk-return profile with limits for risk tolerance, risk-bearing capacity, and risk appetite

10.3 Problems with Value-Based Management Based on CAPM

Currently, the determination of a company's value is mostly based on the discounted cash flow method (DCF method). The planned values of the cash flow, profit, or flow to equity provided by the company are usually discounted to the present with a calculated discount rate based on the Capital Asset Pricing Model (CAPM). The CAPM cost of capital (Damodaran, 2012; Matschke & Brösel, 2021) is based on the beta factor, which is derived from historical volatility of stock returns, whether of the company itself or companies in a peer group. The CAPM world assumes a perfect capital market and thus refrains from rating and financing restrictions and the resulting insolvency risks (Shleifer & Vishny, 1997).

Since the 1980s, empirical capital market research has uncovered various influences on equity returns—anomalies that cannot be explained by the CAPM. Fama and French (1993) established an empirically based three-factor model that constitutes an effective alternative to the CAPM. This model focuses on the price-to-book ratio (the HML factor) and the size of the enterprise (SMB, "small minus big") as factors that can explain equity returns. Using this model, Carhart (1997) developed a four-factor model that included the momentum factor, which numerous empirical studies have confirmed to be an additional factor for explaining equity returns (Jegadeesh & Titman, 1993). Fama and French (2015) presented a five-factor model.

For risk-management purposes, the volatility anomaly is particularly interesting because it demonstrates the importance of risk and questions a basic assumption of the theory of perfect capital markets, namely, that higher risk (volatility) leads to higher return (Ang et al., 2009; Zhang, 2009). Joyce and Mayer (2012) and Gleißner et al. (2022) indicate that low fundamental risk (cash flow volatility of the company) causes higher stock returns. The empirically confirmed relevance of enterprise-specific (idiosyncratic) risks, such as those expected to be in imperfectly diversified capital market operators, is taken to be additional justification for business risk management (for corresponding valuation models, see Merton (1987)). The volatility anomaly corresponds to the risk-return paradox, which is well-known in the field of strategic management research (Budd, 1993; Bowman, 1980). Even very profitable and low-risk companies achieve above-average stock market returns (quality companies per (Piotroski, 2000); see also Asness et al. (2019)). This can be explained by their systematic undervaluation.

Empirical studies of capital markets also describe the distress risk anomaly. (Campbell et al., 2008) show that not even the stock market adequately accounts for ratings and the probability of default (p). Companies with heightened p produce below-average stock market returns that cannot be explained by the CAPM or Carhart's model (1997), and consequently, p is a relevant value driver (see Sect. 10.6). In his work on model assumptions and the empirical results of recent years, Dempsey (2013) concludes that the CAPM has completely failed (Shleifer & Vishny, 1997; Lamont & Thaler, 2003; Rossi, 2016; Fernandez, 2019).

The methods used by many valuation analysts should be viewed with extreme skepticisms. Many valuation errors can be identified (for methodical classification see Gleißner & Follert (2022) and Gleißner & Kamarás (2023)). The following list highlights the most common problems in the valuation practice and shows why one should not trust 'simple' valuations (for a classification of this method and alternatives, see Gleißner & Meckl (2023)).

1. Applying the discounted cash flow method requires forecast values for earnings and cash flows that are unbiased in a statistical sense (mean values). These must be calculated considering both existing opportunities and threats (risks) (Behringer & Gleißner, 2021; Rieg & Gleißner, 2022). Due to a lack of risk analysis and risk aggregation (see Chap. 6), unbiased plan values are not typically used in practice; instead, values that have been created with targets other than company valuation are employed. These are often ambitious plan values, leading to the reported company value being too high. However, other variants, such as conservative values (results in a company value that is too low) or most probable values, are wrong. Even if creating an unbiased plan was the goal, the method for achieving the planned values must be critically examined. The possible combinations of asymmetric risks (especially those with a low probability of occurrence), which can significantly influence the expected value, are often either not considered at all or not considered appropriately. The development of unbiased planning is—under realistic assumptions—only possible with the help of a planning-related risk aggregation (MCS, Monte Carlo simulation).
2. Due to the known to be unrealistic assumptions (e.g., perfect capital market) and the lack of suitability of the CAPM to explain stock returns, as shown by many studies, CAPM cost of capital rates is problematic (Matschke et al., 2010; Matschke & Brösel, 2021). They look at historical fluctuations in stock returns, which are not relevant for a long-term investor in an imperfect capital market, instead of the risks of future cash flows, which are actually relevant to the valuation. Since the assumptions indicate a perfectly diversified investor who only bears cross-company, systematic risks, the company-specific (idiosyncratic) risks are ignored in the valuation calculation. However, it is precisely these risks that are of particular importance for a medium-sized entrepreneur who is not well diversified (Ernst & Gleißner, 2019 and 2023; Kerins et al., 2004). This, too, generally leads to a considerable overestimation of company values.
3. Insolvency risks are also often ignored, although these largely determine the expected amount and the timing of cash flows (Saha & Malkiel, 2012; Franken et al., 2020; Friedrich, 2016). In the long term, in the continuation phase, they have the effect of a negative growth rate. However, neglecting the risk of insolvency is synonymous with a valuation in which the probability of insolvency is set to zero, which leads to a significant overestimation of the company value, especially for companies with a medium or low rating (see Sect. 10.6).

Conclusion: Simple DCF analysis based on the CAPM produces heavily distorted, often significantly inflated company values. Therefore, it should not be the basis of value-based management and top-management decisions (e.g., assessment of strategies). A proper valuation requires more than applying the usual simple "recipes." For example, systematic identification, quantification, and aggregation of risks are necessary to map the effects of existing opportunities and threats on the expected value of cash flows and earnings. The discount rates should reflect the riskiness of the cash flows relevant to the valuation. The insolvency risks, which underlie the finite life expectancy of a company, must also be considered in the valuation. All these aspects are considered in a **simulation-based valuation** (Gleißner, 2019; Ernst, 2022; Gleißner & Ernst, 2023). This method should be used in value-based management, especially for the valuation of strategic options for action ("strategy valuation").

This simulation-based valuation is also based on the DCF calculation. However, the above mistakes are avoided by explicitly considering the risks of a company in the valuation. Moreover, it is not necessary to assume a perfect capital market or the availability of capital market data (stock returns) from companies (Gleißner & Follert, 2022; Dorfleitner & Gleißner, 2018).

10.4 How Risks Influence a Company's Value

Traditional value-based management concepts often only link risk to the cost of capital. However, the information about a company's risks provided by enterprise risk management creates the basis for considering the various effects of risks on the value of the company.

A company's value can be influenced by its risks in several distinct ways:

- Risks affect the expected value of cash flows.
- Risks affect the probability of insolvency (probability of default), which itself exerts an implicit influence on expected cash flow values and the way they change over time.
- Risks influence the cost of debt (Baule, 2019) and may affect the cost of equity (Gleißner, 2019).

Consequently, companies must attend to the reality that risks can potentially influence (1) the expected value of cash flows $E(\text{CF})$ and, simultaneously, (2) the risk discount (in the counter) or risk premium (in the nominator, r_z). This effect on risk R, with a risk amount expressed by the risk measure $R(\text{CF})$, is illustrated in Fig. 10.2.

Earnings and insolvency risks become a challenge for corporate valuation when the cash flows (earnings or profits) described by corporate planning don't correspond to the expected cash flow. Especially problematic are cases where the probability of insolvency is left entirely unaccounted for.

A major part of corporate planning and value-based management is based on target values that result from corporate control. This is important when it comes to

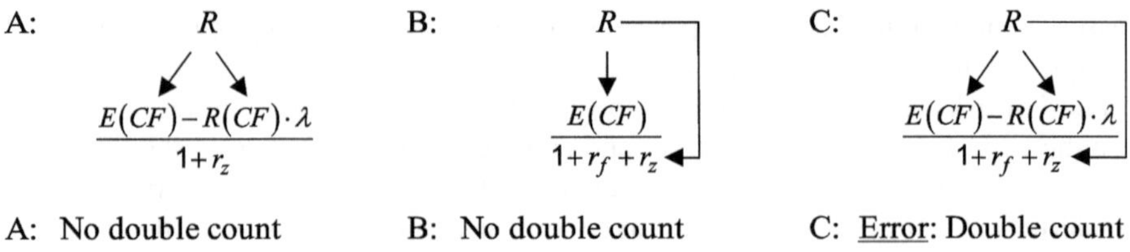

Fig. 10.2 Effects of an asymmetric risk (*R*)

controlling a company: evaluating a company and making business decisions in the sense of the business judgment rule require expected values that can be achieved *on average*, taking into account existing opportunities and threats (Gleißner, 2021).

10.5 Risk Analysis, Earnings Risk, and Valuation

In corporate valuation, risk analyses are the chief source of useful information for considering earnings risk and insolvency risk. It is crucial to take such analyses into account alongside corporate planning. In practice, despite being aware of the existence of opportunities and threats, many companies do not consider them in their valuation. This leads to serious errors.

Systematic analysis and aggregation of a company's risks are required for a risk-adequate (more precisely, simulation-based) rating. This task should fall to the company itself, its valuator, or both. Strategic risks (see Chaps. 7 and 9) and uncertain assumptions regarding corporate planning should always be incorporated into risk analysis. The presence of an uncertain planning assumption indicates that opportunities and threats exist in the relevant area and that plan deviations may therefore occur.

All risks, especially those based on uncertain assumptions during corporate planning, must be characterized using an appropriate probability distribution (e.g., by specifying minimum value, most likely value, and maximum value or by using a normal distribution; see Chap. 5). To derive the total risk exposure on all risks and their interrelations, a risk aggregation is necessary.

An aggregation of the various risks related to corporate planning can only be made using a Monte Carlo simulation (see Chap. 5). In such a simulation, numerous representative possible scenarios resulting from risk are calculated and evaluated. This immediately yields the probability of insolvency due to excessive debt or illiquidity (insolvency risk).

The unbiased expected value of cash flows can be derived from this "bandwidth planning," which results from risk aggregation. This value often differs from the planned value (e.g., due to an excess of risks). The extent of divergence from the expected value determines a risk-adequate cost of capital (Gleißner, 2019); (Gleißner & Ernst, 2023). This value is directly dependent on the variation coefficient of cash flows (flow to equity)—more precisely, the relationship between standard deviation and expected value. The value similarly depends on the risk-return profile of available investment alternatives (e.g., risk-free government bonds or broad stock market).

The underlying principle is simple: higher cash flow volatility (earnings risk) results in a greater deviation from the plan and, consequently, higher demands for returns (increased discount rates/cost of capital).

The derivation of equations for a risk-adequate valuation technique is based on the so-called "incomplete replication" method (with risk-value models; see Dorfleitner & Gleißner, 2018). Unlike the CAPM, for example, this method of valuation does not require the assumptions of perfect or complete capital markets. Since historical fluctuations in stock returns are also not required, this method can also be used without issue to value unlisted companies or strategic action options (strategy valuation).

The derivation of the valuation equations is based on an unrestrictive assumption: two risky cash flows at the same time have the same value if their expected value and the selected risk measure (e.g., the standard deviation) match (Dorfleitner & Gleißner, 2018). A valuator must therefore decide on the risk measure and determine which alternative investment options should be considered.

The discount rate and the certainty equivalent are factors which bridge the gap between corporate value and the aggregated earnings risk. Unlike traditional "capital market orientated" valuation (e.g., using the CAPM), costs of capital from bandwidth planning can be directly derived from the earnings risk because of risk analysis and risk aggregation. Consequently, consideration of a peer group or historical stock return fluctuations, both of which are typical beta factors in the CAPM, is obviated.

Simulation-based business valuation thus uses the data of an analysis of risks aggregated by means of Monte Carlo simulation and is based on semi-investment-theoretical valuation, risk-value models, and the method of incomplete replication (Dorfleitner & Gleißner, 2018; Dorfleitner, 2022; Gleißner & Follert, 2022).

The starting point for deriving the valuation equation is, as mentioned, the following assumption: two cash flows CF_1 and CF_2 that occur at the same time have the same value if they match in the expected value $E(\text{CF})$ and the selected risk measure $R(\text{CF})$. To derive the valuation equation for the value $V(\text{CF})$ of a cash flow CF, a replication portfolio is constructed. This is composed of a share x of the risk-free investment (e.g., AAA-rated bonds) with the interest rate r_{f} and y of the risky investment opportunity (e.g., a global stock index with an uncertain market return r_m). One chooses x and y in such a way that the expected value and risk of this replication portfolio correspond exactly to those of the cash flow to be valued. Therefore, the value $V(\text{CF}) = X + Y$.

To calculate the value $V(\text{CF})$, the covariance $\text{COV}(\text{CF}, r_m)$ can be used as a risk measure in analogy to the CAPM. In this way, only non-diversifiable risks are included in the valuation (Dorfleitner & Gleißner, 2018). Then applies:

$$V(\mathrm{CF}) = X + Y = \frac{E(\mathrm{CF}) - \frac{E(r_m) - r_f}{\sigma^2(r_m)} \cdot \mathrm{COV}(\mathrm{CF}, \mathrm{r}_m)}{1 + r_f}$$

$$= \frac{E(\mathrm{CF}) - \lambda^\sigma \cdot \sigma(\mathrm{CF}) \cdot \rho}{1 + r_f} \tag{10.2}$$

with

$$\lambda^\sigma = \frac{\text{market risk premium}}{\sigma(r_m)} = \frac{E(r_m) - r_f}{\sigma(r_m)}$$

λ is the Sharpe ratio, the market price of the risk. $E(r_m)$ and $\sigma(r_m)$ are the expected value and standard deviation of the market return, and ρ is the correlation of CF to r_m. This correlation shows the share of valuation-relevant (systematic) risks and is thus a risk diversification factor (d).

Equation (10.2) corresponds to the safety equivalent variant of the CAPM, whose valuation result can thus be derived as a special case (Robichek & Myers, 1967). From Eq. (10.2), risk-adequate discount rates or cost of capital rates (c) can be derived for use in a DCF valuation common in valuation practice, provided that $E(\mathrm{CF}) - \lambda \cdot R(\mathrm{CF}) \cdot d > 0$.

$$V(\mathrm{CF}) = \frac{E(\mathrm{CF})}{1 + c} = \frac{E(\mathrm{CF}) - \lambda \cdot R(\mathrm{CF}) \cdot d}{1 + r_f} \tag{10.3}$$

Using the standard deviation as a measure of risk, that is, ($R(\mathrm{CF}) = \sigma(\mathrm{CF})$), Eq. (10.3)) is solved according to the cost of capital rate (c) (Gleißner, 2019).

$$c = \frac{1 + r_f}{1 - \lambda^\sigma \cdot \frac{\sigma(\mathrm{CF})}{E(\mathrm{CF})} \cdot d} - 1 = \frac{1 + r_f}{1 - \lambda^\sigma \cdot \mathrm{VC}(\mathrm{CF}) \cdot d} - 1 \tag{10.4}$$

$$\approx r_f + \lambda \cdot \mathrm{VC}\left(\widetilde{\mathrm{CF}}\right) \cdot d$$

with

$$\lambda^\sigma = \frac{r^e_{m - r_f}}{\sigma_{r^m}}$$

where λ is the Sharpe ratio.

VC represents the variation coefficient of cash flow. Specifically, it is the relation of earnings risk $\sigma(\mathrm{CF})$ to expected earnings $E(\mathrm{CF})$, where both are influenced by risks. This coefficient expresses the *usual range of variation*—the planning uncertainty—as a percentage.

If the ratio VC represents the coefficient of variation for the flow to equity (FTE), the cost of equity is calculated. Correspondingly, the coefficient of variation for the free cash flow (FCF) results in the weighted average cost of capital (WACC). One advantage of the method presented here is that it allows direct conclusions to be drawn regarding the total cost of capital. That is, it is not necessary to determine the costs of equity or debt and their weights at respective market values.

Excess return per unit of risk is demonstrated by λ, which expresses the risk-return profile of investment alternatives. For illustration, suppose λ amounts to a market-typical 0.25. This means that a 0.25% increase in return is expected per added unit of risk.

Since stakeholders diversify their investments and therefore do not necessarily bear the total effects of a company's risk $\sigma(\text{CF})$, a risk diversification factor (d) must be considered (Gleißner & Ernst, 2019 and 2023). This factor, which corresponds to the correlation to the market portfolio in the CAPM, expresses the proportion of an enterprise's risks that a stakeholder must carry (see Eq. (10.2)).

The model can be generalized for any period t (for the continuation phase in particular, see Dorfleitner, 2022). Then, instead of Eq. (10.3))):

$$V_0\left(\widetilde{\text{CF}_\text{t}}\right) = \frac{E\left(\widetilde{\text{CF}_\text{t}}\right)}{(1+c)^t} = \frac{E\left(\widetilde{\text{CF}_\text{t}}\right) - \lambda_t^\sigma \cdot \sigma\left(\widetilde{\text{CF}_\text{t}}\right) \cdot d}{(1+r_\text{f})^t} \tag{10.5}$$

from which c can be derived again.

For the valuation equation to be complete, the return of the stock market index can be assumed to be lognormally distributed and modelled via a Brownian motion (Dorfleitner, 2022). This results in λ_t^σ as

$$\lambda_t^\sigma = \frac{e^{t\cdot\mu'_m + t\cdot\frac{\sigma'_m}{2}} - \left(1+r_f\right)^t}{e^{t\cdot\mu'_m + t\cdot\frac{\sigma'_m}{2}} \cdot \sqrt{e^{t\cdot\sigma'^2_m} - 1}} \tag{10.6}$$

λ_t^σ shows the excess profit of an investment in the risky alternative investment (stock market index) compared to a risk-free investment (with interest r_f) per unit of risk. μ'_m and σ'_m denote the expected value and the standard deviation of the 1-year lognormally distributed returns of the market portfolio (e.g., S&P 500). Furthermore, $r'_f = \ln\left(1+r_f\right)$ and $r'_m = \ln(1+r_m)$.

Therefore, risk management and value-based management are linked.

10.6 Risk of Insolvency (Distress Risk) as Value Driver

The existence of a company is finite, as is the expected value of its limited lifetime of existence. The effects of the insolvency are the interruption of the cash flow (flow to equity) in the event of insolvency being dealt with first. Other aspects, such as insolvency costs and the impact of the probability of insolvency on the cost of debt, will be considered later.

An obvious effect of insolvency risk is first the possibility that the owners' cash flow will stop (i.e., it has a finite expected value). However, the probability of insolvency and an unlimited life are not contradictory. Even with an insolvency probability of $p > 0$, companies can basically exist forever since there is no certain point in time when their existence ends. In each year of the infinite future, the probability of existence is greater than zero. The insolvency probability thus leads to a finite expected value of the lifetime of companies, but not to a limitation of the lifetime.

Table 10.1 shows the corresponding expected values for the expected lifetime (L) of a company for various characteristics of the insolvency probability per year (p).

In the event of insolvency, as mentioned above, the cash flow to the owners generally stops, even if ownership of the company is transferred to the previous creditors and it is continued. The probability p with which the payment stream breaks off within 1 year is relevant for the valuation (the cash flows to the owners in the event of insolvency are usually zero anyway). The insolvency risk can be measured using the expected level of insolvency costs and the probability of insolvency (p). Various methods, some of which can be used in combination, exist for recording insolvency risk in company valuations:

Method A

One method is the deterministic "surcharge rate method": the recording of the probability of insolvency p, estimated (for example) by a credit rating as a "surcharge rate" on the cost of capital in the continuation phase (an "infinite annuity"—see Franken et al., 2020 and Saha & Malkiel, 2012) with either (a) supplementary consideration of survival and insolvency scenarios in the detailed planning phase or (b) simulation of the detailed planning (cf. method C).

Method B

Insolvency risk can be expressed as the probability of insolvency, which assumes an uncertain development of cash flows or earnings before interest and taxes (EBIT), as described by a binomial model (Friedrich, 2016) or a stochastic EBIT process. The disadvantages of this method are that it lacks reference to corporate planning and risk analysis and that it fails to record scenarios with negative free cash flows.

Method C

Table 10.1 Assignment of the probability of insolvency (p) and lifetime (L)

Rating	per annum probability of insolvency (p)	Expected lifetime (L)
A	0.1%	1000
BBB	0.5%	200
BB	1.0%	100
BB-	2.0%	50
B	5.0%	20

Note: In the case of insolvency risk, at each point in time, there is a probability ($1 - p$) that the company will continue to exist, and $L = 1/p$ applies

Finally, one can employ a stochastic simulation of free cash flows and earnings based on a quantitative risk analysis and risk aggregation in an integrated planning model (i.e., a P&L and balance sheet planning using a Monte Carlo simulation to derive expected values; see also Chap. 5).

In the detailed planning phase of a company's first years ($t = 1$ to T), the probability of insolvency must be considered when determining the unbiased expected values of earnings. A scenario with often-zero returns to the owners is a typical result of insolvency. Since companies with low credit ratings encounter problems in acquiring employees and customers, indirect insolvency costs are directly and often implicitly included in corporate planning.

With simulation-based planning, the insolvency risk can automatically be recorded in expected values in the detailed planning phase (method C). When risks are aggregated with reference to corporate planning, a Monte Carlo simulation for risk aggregation is used to calculate a large number of representative risk-related potential scenarios. The expected value (mean value of the scenarios) and the frequency of insolvency scenarios can be derived directly from these scenarios.

In the continuation phase (terminal value phase), following detailed planning ($t > T$), the initially expected cash flows are usually updated with a growth rate g. Insolvency can also occur in any year of the continuation phase, which can be recorded using method A. If the probability of insolvency remains constant, this leads to continuously decreasing expected values of cash flows, as shown in Fig. 10.3 (Saha & Malkiel, 2012; Franken et al., 2020).

With a constant probability of insolvency p, a discount rate c, and a growth rate g of the expected values of the cash flow (flow to equity) $CF^e = E(CF)$ (without insolvency, the "conditional expected value"), the following terminal value, value V of cash flows during continuation phase (here already starting at $t = 1$), results:

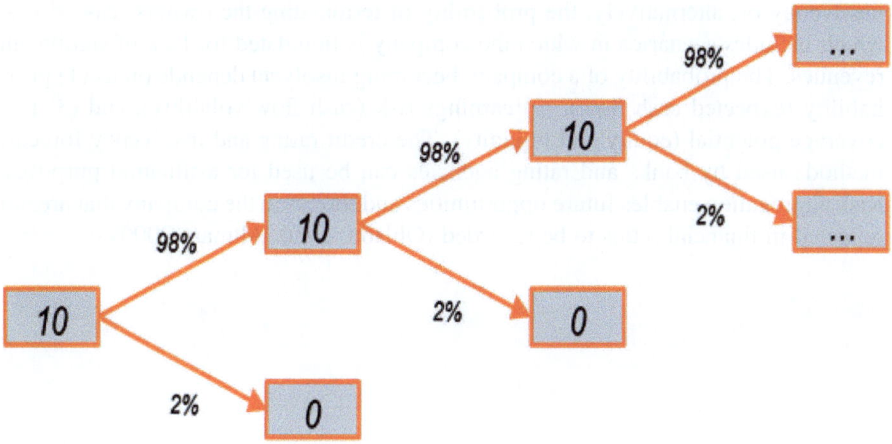

Fig. 10.3 Effect of the probability of insolvency ($p = 2\%$) on expected cash flow

$$V(\mathrm{CF}) = \sum_{t=1} \frac{\mathrm{CF}^e(1-p)^t \cdot (1+g)^t}{(1+c)^t} = \frac{\mathrm{CF}^e \cdot (1-p) \cdot (1+g)}{c-g+p \cdot (1+g)} \approx \frac{\mathrm{CF}^e}{c-g+p} \quad (10.7)$$

When determining an infinite series, the probability of insolvency as well as the growth rate appears in the numerator in each period. However, dissolving the series leads to the appearance of the probability of insolvency (like the growth rate) as a "surcharge" in the denominator (but this is not a risk premium). In the continuation phase, the probability of insolvency p thus has the effect of a "negative growth rate" (Gleißner, 2019).

Smaller companies typically have a higher coefficient of variation and, consequently, higher probability of insolvency and higher costs of capital. The connections described here contribute to explaining the size effect (Grabowski, 2018).

The probability of insolvency also impacts interest rates and cost of debt (Baule, 2019). A higher probability of insolvency leads c.p. to higher contractual interest rates or higher credit spreads of bonds. However, borrowing costs (i.e., the expected return on debt) do not rise as sharply. When calculating the cost of capital, it is not the contractual interest on borrowed capital that is decisive, but rather the cost of borrowed capital (debt) (i.e., the expected return of the borrower). Contractual interest rates on debt (c_D) will be higher than the cost of debt (c_D) because the possibility that a company will not pay in the event of insolvency must be considered. For example:

$$c_D = \left(c_D^0 + 1\right) \cdot (1-p) - 1 \approx c_D^0 - p \quad (10.8)$$

In addition to the effect of insolvency risk on the expected value and development over time of cash flows, insolvency risk can also influence tax shields and the cost of equity (c_{EQ}).

The best measure for determining the level of insolvency risk is the probability of insolvency or, alternatively, the probability of terminating the owners' cash flows, which includes scenarios in which the company is liquidated for lack of significant revenues. The probability of a company becoming insolvent depends on its (1) profitability (expected cash flow), (2) earnings risk (cash flow volatility), and (3) risk coverage potential (equity and liquidity). The credit rating and insolvency forecast methods used by banks and rating agencies can be used for estimation purposes. Risk aggregation enables future opportunities and threats to the company that are not reflected in financial ratios to be recorded (Ohlson, 1980; Altman, 2000).

10.7 The Rating Related Model

The alternative calculation of c depending on risk-adjusted capital (RAC) is a very simple one (Ernst & Gleißner, 2023) and (Dorfleitner & Gleißner, 2018). Risk-adjusted capital (RAC) is the equity needs to cover losses caused by risk and is a result of the risk aggregation. It applies when the amount of debt is limited by a percentage of the total investment in shares. If EQ is the equity invested, D is the debt, and b is the debt limit as a percentage of the total investment in the market portfolio (D-RAC), the rule is:

$$D = b \cdot (\mathrm{EQ} + D) \Leftrightarrow D = \frac{b}{1-b} \cdot \mathrm{EQ} \tag{10.9}$$

For this leverage, the expected rate of return is $1/(1-b)$ times the market risk premium ($= r_\mathrm{m} - r_\mathrm{f}$) higher than the rate of return for a risk-free asset, e.g., for 50%, you must add two times the market risk premium to the return of the risk-free asset to get the discount rate (c). Thus, all that is required to apply the heuristic are the values for r_m and r_f.

Currently, the general procedure for limiting the amount of debt follows the rules of rating. Here, the loan amount is determined on the basis of the accepted probability of default ($p^{\max}$).

For the estimation procedure concerning the leveraged investment in the market portfolio, the mean and the standard deviation of its rate of return (σ_{r_m}) are required. If c_D is the contracted rate of return for the share Lombard credit, q_p is p-% quantile of the standardized normal distribution, and we make some simplifying assumptions, the discount rate is calculated as follows:

$$c_\mathrm{EQ} = \frac{r_m \cdot (1 + c_D) - r_f \cdot \left(1 + r_m^e + q_p \cdot \sigma_{r_m}\right)}{c_D - \left(r_m^e + q_p \cdot \sigma_{r_m}\right)} \tag{10.10}$$

For $c_D = r_\mathrm{f}$, the formula can be further simplified as follows:

$$c_\mathrm{EQ} = r_f + \frac{r_m^e - r_f}{-\left(r_m^e + q_p \cdot \sigma_{r_m}\right)} \tag{10.11}$$

Obviously, the discount rate depends on the accepted probability of insolvency (p) and the corresponding value for q_p. The denominator expresses the equity portion of the leveraged portfolio (equity requirement as a percentage of the investment) that is necessary for a normal distribution of returns, so that the probability of insolvency just reaches p. It is important to note that by using the method of “incomplete replication” and risk-value models, it is possible to derive these results as specific case of a general approach for the valuation of risky cash flows (Dorfleitner & Gleißner, 2018).

Table 10.2 Average cumulative probability of insolvency/default from 1981 to 2020 (in percent)

Rating	Time horizon							
	1	**2**	**3**	**4**	**5**	**6**	**7**	**8**
AAA	0.00	0.03	0.13	0.24	0.34	0.45	0.51	0.59
AA	0.02	0.06	0.11	0.21	0.30	0.41	0.49	0.56
A	0.05	0.13	0.22	0.33	0.46	0.60	0.76	0.90
BBB	0.16	0.43	0.75	1.14	1.54	1.94	2.27	2.61
BB	0.63	1.93	3.46	4.99	6.43	7.75	8.89	9.90
B	3.34	7.80	11.75	14.89	17.35	19.36	20.99	22.31
CCC/C	28.30	38.33	43.42	46.36	48.58	49.61	50.75	51.49
	9	**10**	**11**	**12**	**13**	**14**	**15**	
AAA	0.64	0.70	0.72	0.75	0.78	0.84	0.90	
AA	0.63	0.70	0.76	0.82	0.88	0.93	0.99	
A	1.05	1.20	1.34	1.46	1.59	1.71	1.84	
BBB	2.93	3.24	3.55	3.80	4.03	4.28	4.54	
BB	10.82	11.64	12.33	12.99	13.59	14.09	14.65	
B	23.50	24.62	25.58	26.31	26.99	27.63	28.24	
CCC/C	52.16	52.76	53.21	53.68	54.23	54.69	54.76	

The simplest way to assess the probability of insolvency (default) is to use the exogenous credit ratings (e.g., from a rating agency). An estimate of the probability of default can be directly derived from a published rating, as shown in Table 10.2.

We can now calculate the discount rate in addition to the rating or the probability of insolvency (p). This depends on the profitability, the leverage ratio, and the total volume of risk of the firm.

If we assume the following:

- Rating = BBB-
- $p = 0.5\%$ and, therefore, $q_p = -2.576$
- $c_D = 5\%$ and $r_{\mathrm{f}} = 4\%$
- $\sigma_{r_m} = 20\%$ and $r_m^e = 8\%$

then

$$c_{\mathrm{EQ}} = \frac{r_m \cdot (1 + c_D) - r_f \cdot \left(1 + r_m^e + q_p \cdot \sigma_{r_m}\right)}{c_D - \left(r_m^e + q_p \cdot \sigma_{r_m}\right)} = \frac{8\% \cdot (1 + 5\%) - 4\% \cdot (1 + 8\% - 2.576 \cdot 20\%)}{5\% - (8\% - 2.576 \cdot 20\%)} = 12.7\% \qquad (10.12)$$

It is easy to calculate the cost of capital for different credit ratings if we assume that

$c_d = r_f + p + r_Z$ with a simplifying assumption of a constant premium $r_Z = 0.5\%$ charged by the creditor (Table 10.3):

Table 10.3 Rating levels

Rating	p	q_p	c_{EQ}
AAA	0.00001%	−5.20	8.2%
BBB	0.25%	−2.81	11.9%
BB	0.95%	−2.35	13.5%
B	4.7%	−1.67	16.6%

For normal rating levels, the result does not differ much from the rule of thumb, and, again, there is no need for capital market data or cash flow parameters of single firms.

10.8 Simulation-Based Valuation and Top-Management Decisions

The defining characteristic of a simulation-based assessment is the explicit consideration of business-related risks (opportunities and threats) and the application of Monte Carlo simulation for calculating risk-related future scenarios. The resulting "multi-value" planning (bandwidth planning) structure allows expected values of cash flows or earnings to be derived directly. It also determines and captures insolvency risk and allows discount rates to be derived directly from the uncertainty of cash flows (i.e., without evaluating stock return fluctuations). Simulation-based valuation also meets regulatory requirements for risk management (e.g., in Germany § 1 StaRUG, Corporate Stabilization and Restructuring Act).

The main characteristics and advantages of a simulation-based business valuation based on the analysis of business risks can thus be summarized as follows (Ernst, 2022; Ernst & Gleißner, 2023):

1. Only with simulation-based planning can the expected values of cash flows or earnings be derived in a comprehensible manner.
2. A plausibility check of the planning and planning logic is carried out.
3. A simulation-based valuation can be used to consider the impact of insolvency risk on the value of the company.
4. A simulation-based business valuation allows the derivation of a risk-adjusted discount rate (cost of capital) directly from the simulation results.
5. A simulation-based valuation can represent a basis for preparing top-management decisions.
6. The probability of insolvency can be derived by evaluating key financial figures and considering the combination effects of risks via risk aggregation and Monte Carlo simulation (Füser et al., 2010).
7. Finally, there is an additional benefit for companies, namely, compliance with legal requirements for risk management (Gleißner, 2022, pp. 490–493 and pp. 513–523).

Risk analysis and risk aggregation accomplish transparency in planning certainty, and aggregated earnings risk (cash flow volatility) allows for the deviation of risk-adequate cost of capital. This way expected values of profits or cash flows (*numerator*) and the discount interest rate (*denominator*) are consistently defined, and problems associated with the CAPM, such as biased cost of capital, are avoided (due to market flaws; Dempsey, 2013; Gromb & Vayanos, 2010; Shleifer & Vishny, 1997; Fernandez, 2019).

The methods outlined so far are not only applicable when determining the value of a company based on the current strategy and operational business planning while taking risks into account. As explained in the introduction, they are particularly important for comparing different options for action (such as projects or investments) concerning their risk-return profile. A what-if analysis is carried out, and alternative courses of action are assessed in terms of the impact on expected cash flows and the level of risk. The risk-return profile is then mapped to the enterprise value (decision value). This procedure is explained in Chap. 13 using a case study.

10.9 Summary

- Proper valuation of a company is impossible without analyzing its risks. The value of a company is dependent on its earnings risks or cash flow volatility, which influence the expected volume of cash flow and affect the risk-adequate cost of capital (discount rate). Negative fluctuations in earnings can lead to insolvency. Insolvency leads to the interruption of cash flow to the owners and thus influences the expected earnings value and its development over time (in the terminal value phase).
- As a result, the following recommendations can be derived for the practice of company valuation:
  - A proper valuation of a company requires an analysis of the risks to which it is exposed. Such risk analysis complements the plausibility check in corporate planning and creates a prerequisite for deriving expectation-loyal plan values (for free cash flows and earnings).
  - In risk analysis, risks are first systematically identified, then quantitatively described using probability distributions, and finally aggregated with reference to corporate planning using a Monte Carlo simulation. This results in multi-value bandwidth planning.
  - The expected values of cash flows and earnings can be directly derived using risk analysis and risk aggregation. Thereby, there is a transition from a target plan, which is often prepared for corporate management, to the expected values that are required for the application of the DCF method (or capitalized earnings value).

 - In addition, risk analysis and risk simulation enable the direct derivation of risk-adjusted discount rates (cost of capital) and the recording of insolvency risk.
 - In a company valuation, at minimum, those risks that the company to be valued identifies itself (e.g., in the risk reporting of risk management) and those that can be derived directly from corporate planning (essentially including all uncertain planning assumptions) must be considered.

- The analysis of a company's risks is clearly necessary for a proper valuation. The consideration of the risks of a company's stocks (e.g., expressed by the beta factor) is not sufficient. Only under the unrealistic assumption of a perfect capital market do cash flow and share yield fluctuations coincide. It is the company's risks that determine the uncertainty of future earnings and cash flows, the probability of insolvency, and the discount rate (Gleißner & Ernst, 2023).
- The valuation procedures outlined here, especially the method of simulation-based company valuation, should be seen as the basis of a modern and further developed value-based management concept (linking of value-based management and value-based risk management). In such value-based risk management, the enterprise value is used as a measure of success (performance measure) and decision criterion in accordance with the original ideas of value-based management. It is then an expression of the risk-return profile. In contrast to the derivation of costs of capital via the beta factor of the CAPM, this method requires the perfection of the capital market and the representativeness of past stock return fluctuations for future cash flow fluctuations of the company. To assess the success of business units and the valuation of strategic options for action with investments, the "insider information" of enterprise risk management, especially from risk analysis and risk aggregation, is used. Based on corporate strategy and operational corporate planning, expected plan values of cash flows and flow to equity or free cash flow can be derived, which can also be realized on average, while taking risks into account. From the volatility of the cash flows, expressed by a suitable risk measure (such as the coefficient of variation), a cost of capital rate can be derived as a risk-appropriate requirement for the return without recourse to capital market information. Furthermore, this approach also considers the value driver probability of insolvency, which has often been ignored in value-based management.
- Overall, ERM thus becomes a central pillar of a more thoroughly developed value-based management.

10.10 Exercises and Questions

1. What are the primary determinants of the probability of insolvency?

   a) Financing structure.
   b) Expected earnings, risk coverage potential (equity), earnings risk.

c) Reputation and working capital management.
d) Corporate growth and capital turnover.

2. Calculate the risk-adequate cost of capital under the following assumptions: risk-free interest rate $r_f = 3\%$, coefficient of variation of profit CV = 0.4, risk-return profile of alternative investment options (Sharpe ratio) $\lambda = 0.25$, and risk diversification factor $d = 0.5$.

   a) 3.0%
   b) 8.4%
   c) 9.2%
   d) 10.5%

3. Which of the following statements about a simulation-based business valuation is *not* true?

   a) The valuation is based on the results of a risk aggregation (Monte Carlo simulation).
   b) The valuation assumes perfect capital markets.
   c) Cost of capital can be derived from the amount of risk in earnings and cash flows expressed by a risk measure (such as the coefficient of variation).
   d) The data basis for the valuation is corporate planning and risk analysis.

4. What is the approximate insolvency probability p (per year) of a company with a rating of "BB"?

   a) 0.1%
   b) 1%
   c) 5%
   d) 10%

5. Which statement about value-based management is *not* appropriate?

   a) The value driver "cost of capital" must be calculated based on stock return fluctuations using the beta factor (CAPM).
   b) The probability of insolvency is a value driver.
   c) Higher earnings risks (coefficient of variation of earnings) reduce the enterprise value.
   d) The shareholder value is always equal to the stock market value.

6. How do risks influence the enterprise value?
7. What effect does the probability of insolvency have on the enterprise value?
8. Why is an enterprise value calculated based on the CAPM and beta factor not suitable for evaluating a company's potential strategies?
9. Consider the following three projects (A, B, C) in which a company can invest in TUS$. I_0 is the necessary investment amount.

Project	I_0	E(CF)	σ(CF)
A	100	110	33
B	200	210	21
C	300	340	68

In all projects, the investment is made at $t = 0$ and the uncertain return is expected after 1 year ($t = 1$). The following parameters apply for the valuation: the risk-free interest rate is $r_f = 3\%$, and the market price of the risk is $\lambda = 0.25$. Risk diversification options in the company and at the level of the owner are not taken into account, so the risk diversification factor is $d = 1$.

a) Calculate the risk-adjusted cost of capital (c) for the projects.
b) Determine the net present value (NPV) of the projects, and decide which ones should be carried out in the absence of investments or other restrictions.
c) Explain how the standard deviation of the repayment (σ(CF), i.e., the amount of risk of the projects), can be determined.
d) Now assume that the company's investment opportunities are limited. Which key figures could be used to assess the attractiveness of projects? Which of the projects appears to be the most attractive for the company?

References

Altman, E. I. (2000). *Predicting financial distress of companies: Revisiting the Z-score and ZETA models*. New York University.

Ang, A., Hodrick, R. J., Xing, Y., & Zhang, X. (2009). High idiosyncratic volatility and low returns: International and further U.S. evidence. *Journal of Financial Economics, 91*, 1–23.

Asness, C. S., Frazzini, A., & Pedersen, L. H. (2019). Quality minus junk. *Review of Accounting Studies, 24*, 34–112.

Baule, R. (2019). The cost of debt capital revisited. *Business Research, 12*, 721–753.

Behringer, S., & Gleißner, W. (2021). Unternehmensplanung als Grundlage für die Unternehmensbewertung: Die Perspektive der Wirtschaftsprüfer. *Die Wirtschaftsprüfung (WPg), 74*, 857–864.

Berger, T., & Gleissner, W. (2018). Integrated management systems: Linking risk management and management control systems. *International Journal of Risk Assessment and Management, 21*, 215–231. https://doi.org/10.1504/IJRAM.2018.093751

Bowman, E. H. (1980). A-risk-return-paradoxon for strategic management. *Sloan-Management Review, 21*, 17–33.

Budd, J. L. (1993). *Characterizing risk from the strategic management perspective*. Dissertation, Kent State University.

Campbell, J. Y., Hilscher, J., & Szilagyi, J. (2008). In search of distress risk. *The Journal of Finance, 63*, 2899–2939.

Carhart, M. M. (1997). On persistence in mutual fund performance. *The Journal of Finance, 52*, 57–82.

Chew, D. H., & Stern, J. M. (Eds.). (2008). *The revolution in corporate finance* (4th ed.). Blackwell.

Company, M., Koller, T., Goedhart, M. H., & Wessels, D. (2020). *Valuation: Measuring and managing the value of companies. Wiley finance*. Wiley.

Damodaran, A. (2012). *Investment valuation: Tools and techniques for determining the value of any asset* (Wiley finance series) (3rd ed.). Wiley.

Dempsey, M. (2013). The CAPM: A case of elegance is for tailors? *Abacus, 49*, 82–87.

Dorfleitner, G. (2022). On the use of the terminal-value approach in risk-value models. *Annals of Operations Research, 313*, 877–897.

Dorfleitner, G., & Gleißner, W. (2018). Valuing streams of risky cashflows with risk-value models. *Journal of Risk, 20*, 1–27.

Ernst, D. (2022). Simulation-based business valuation: Methodical implementation in the valuation practice. *Journal of Risk and Financial Management, 15*, 200 ff.

Ernst, D., & Gleißner, W. (2023). Total beta: A view from outside. *The Value Examiner*, 5–14.

Fama, E. F., & French, K. R. (1993). Common risk factors in the returns on stocks and bonds. *Journal of Financial Economics, 33*, 3–56.

Fama, E. F., & French, K. R. (2015). A five-factor asset pricing model. *Journal of Financial Economics, 116*, 1–22.

Fernandez, P. (2019). *Is it ethical to teach that beta and CAPM explain something?* IESE Business School.

Franken, L., Gleißner, W., & Schulte, J. (2020). Insolvenzrisiko und Berücksichtigung des Verschuldungsgrads bei der Bewertung von Unternehmen: Stand der Diskussion nach Veröffentlichung des IDW Praxishinweises 2/2018. *Corporate Finance, 11*, 84–96.

Friedrich, T. (2016). Corporate valuation and risk of insolvency: Binomial models as a means to capture the effects of insolvency. *Die Betriebswirtschaft (DBW), 76*, 521–543.

Füser, K., Gleißner, W., & Leibbrand, F. (2010). Theoretical principles and methods for rating softwares. In Y. Zhang (Ed.), *Domestic and foreign credit theory studies an standardization practices: = Guo nei wai xin yong li lun yan jiu yu biao zhun hua shi jian* (pp. 304–322). China Metrology Publ.

Gleißner, W. (2010). Unternehmenswert, Rating und Risiko. *Die Wirtschaftsprüfung, 63*, 735–743.

Gleißner, W. (2019). Cost of capital and probability of default in value-based risk management. *Management Research Review, 42*, 1243–1258.

Gleißner, W., & Ernst, D. (2019). Company valuation as result of risk analysis: Replication approach as an alternative to the CAPM. *Business Valuation OIV Journal, 1*, 3–18.

Gleißner, W. (2020). Integratives Risikomanagement: Schnittstellen zu Controlling, Compliance und Interner Revision. *Controlling, 32*, 23–29. https://doi.org/10.15358/0935-0381-2020-4-23

Gleißner, W. (2021). *Entrepreneurial decisions*. https://www.researchgate.net/publication/352994314_Entrepreneurial_Decisions_Business_Judgement_Rule. Accessed 16 May 2025.

Gleißner, W. (2022). *Grundlagen des Risikomanagements: Handbuch für ein Management unter Unsicherheit* (Management competence) (4th ed.). Verlag Franz Vahlen.

Gleißner, W., & Kamarás, E. (2023). *Company valuation using the DCF method and CAPM: You shouldn't trust the result*. https://papers.ssrn.com/sol3/papers.cfm?abstract_id=4396512. Accessed 16 May 2025.

Gleißner, W., & Follert, F. (2022). Unternehmensbewertung im Spannungsfeld zwischen Zweckadäquanz und Praktikabilität: Ein Lösungsansatz für die gerichtliche Abfindungsbemessung. *Betriebswirtschaftliche Forschung und Praxis, 74*, 395–419.

Gleißner, W., & Kamaras, E. (2023). *Company valuation using the DCF method and CAPM: You shouldn't trust the result*. https://papers.ssrn.com/sol3/papers.cfm?abstract_id=4396512. Accessed 24 April 2024.

Gleißner, W., & Meckl, R. (2023). Methoden der Unternehmensbewertung und ihre Anwendung bei M&A. *Wirtschaftswissenschaftliches Studium, 52*, 17–21.

Gleißner, W., Günther, T., & Walkshäusl, C. (2022). Financial sustainability: Measurement and empirical evidence. *Journal of Business Economics, 92*, 467–516.

Grabowski, R. J. (2018). The size effect continues to be relevant when estimating the cost of capital. *Business Valuation Reviev, 37*, 93–109.

Gromb, D., & Vayanos, D. (2010). Limits of arbitrage. *Annual Review of Financial Economics, 2*, 251–275.

Hunziker, S. (2021). *Enterprise risk management: Modern approaches to balancing risk and reward* (2nd ed.). Springer.

Jegadeesh, N., & Titman, S. (1993). Returns to buying winners and selling losers: Implications for stock market efficiency. *The Journal of Finance, 48*, 65–91.

Jensen, M. C. (2001). Corporate budgeting is broken – Let's fix it. *Harvard Business Review, 70*, 94–101.

Jensen, M. C., & Meckling, W. H. (1976). Theory of the firm: Managerial behavior, agency costs and ownership structure. *Journal of Financial Economics, 3*, 305–360.

Joyce, C., & Mayer, K. (2012). *Profits for the long run: Affirming the case for quality.* http://csinvesting.org/wp-content/uploads/2012/06/gmo_wp_-_2012_06_-_profits_for_the_long_run_-_affirming_quality.pdf. Accessed 16 May 2025.

Kaldor, N. (1966). Marginal productivity and the macro-economic theories of distribution. *The Review of Economic Studies, 33*, 309–319.

Kataoka, S. (1963). A Stochastic Programming Model. *Econometrica, 31*, 181–196.

Kerins, F., Smith, J. K., & Smith, R. (2004). Opportunity cost of capital for venture capital investors and entrepreneurs. *The Journal of Financial and Quantitative Analysis, 39*, 385–405.

Kyosev, G., Hanauer, M. X., Huij, J., & Lansdorp, S. (2020). *Does earnings growth drive the quality premium?* https://papers.ssrn.com/sol3/Delivery.cfm/SSRN_ID3190046_code2061164.pdf?abstractid=2794807&mirid=1. Accessed 16 May 2025.

Lamont, O. A., & Thaler, R. H. (2003). Anomalies: The law of one price in financial markets. *Journal of Economic Perspectives, 17*, 191–202.

Matschke, M. J., & Brösel, G. (2021). *Business valuation: Functions, methods, principles. Finance.* UVK Verlag; Narr Francke Attempto Verlag GmbH + Co. KG.

Matschke, M. J., Brösel, G., & Matschke, X. (2010). Fundamentals of functional business valuation. *Journal of Business Valuation and Economic Loss Analysis, 5.*

Merton, R. C. (1987). A simple model of capital market equilibrium with incomplete information. *The Journal of Finance, 42*, 483–510.

Nocco, B. W., & Stulz, R. M. (2022). Enterprise risk management: Theory and practice. *Journal of Applied Corporate Finance, 34*, 81–94.

Ohlson, J. A. (1980). Financial ratios and the probabilistic prediction of bankruptcy. *Journal of Accounting Research, 18*, 109–131.

Piotroski, J. D. (2000). Value investing: the use of historical financial statement information to separate winners from losers. *Journal of Accounting Research, 38*, 1–41.

Rappaport, A. (1999). *Shareholder-Value: Ein Handbuch für Manager und Investoren* (2nd ed.). Schäffer-Poeschel.

Rieg, R., & Gleißner, W. (2022). Was ist ein erwartungstreuer Plan? *Die Wirtschaftsprüfung, 75*, 1407–1414.

Robichek, A. A., & Myers, S. C. (1967). Valuation of the firm: Effects of uncertainty in a market context. *The Journal of Finance, 21*, 215–227.

Rossi, M. (2016). The capital asset pricing model: A critical literature review. *Global Business and Economics Review, 18*, 604–617.

Saha, A., & Malkiel, B. G. (2012). DCF valuation with cash flow cessation risk. *The Journal of Applied Finance, 22*, 175–185.

Shleifer, A., & Vishny, R. W. (1997). The limits of arbitrage. *The Journal of Finance, 52*, 35–55.

Traut, J. (2023). What we know about the low-risk anomaly: A literature review. *Financial Markets and Portfolio Management, 37*, 297–324.

Walkshäusl, C. (2013). The high returns to low volatility stocks are actually a premium on high quality firms. *Review of Financial Economics, 22*, 180–186.

Young, S. D., & O'Byrne, S. F. (2001). *EVA and value-based management: A practical guide to implementation*. McGraw Hill.

Zhang, C. (2009). On the explanatory power of firm-specific variables in cross-sections of expected returns. *Journal of Empirical Finance, 16*, 306–317.

Chapter 11
Enterprise Risk Management and Business Planning

Abstract Business planning and budgeting are important tools for many organizations. They are used to set goals, allocate resources, and evaluate performance. Plans and budgets relate to the future and are therefore uncertain. There is always the risk of not achieving a plan. Thus, rational managers should always consider risks as well as opportunities in planning and budgeting. The chapter first discusses the reasons and general ways to integrate risk before explaining several approaches to risk integration. It also highlights that an operational plan has many functions and are not necessarily identical to forecasts.

Keywords Budgeting · Corporate planning · Monte Carlo simulation · Planning

Questions

1. What are the main functions of operational planning and budgeting?
2. Which types of risks are prevalent in operational planning and budgeting?
3. How can organizations integrate risks in operational planning and budgeting?
4. Are there different plans for different purposes? Why or why not?
5. Why are forecasts not necessarily the same as plans?

11.1 Corporate Planning and Risk: An Overview

Corporate planning is the systematic process of preparing and prescribing future decisions and actions to achieve given goals of a company (see also de Smit & Rade, 1980). It is both a means and an end. While this is also true of strategic planning, in this chapter we focus on operational planning, which typically involves concrete, detailed steps for a time horizon of 1 year or less that take the strategy and other constraints as given.

Supplementary Information The online version contains supplementary material available at https://doi.org/10.1007/978-3-031-86425-4_11.

R. Rieg et al., *Enterprise Risk Management*, Springer Texts in Business and Economics, https://doi.org/10.1007/978-3-031-86425-4_11

Operational planning encompasses non-financial plans like prescribed actions or production volumes as well as financial planning, often called budgeting. Nonetheless, the terms budgeting and (operational) planning are often used interchangeably in the literature and in practice. The importance of planning and budgeting is readily apparent as they are the primary means of implementing strategy, coordinating and integrating activities within the organization, and directing employee behavior (Malmi & Brown, 2008; Hamann, 2017).

While many practitioners and some scholars complain about planning and budgeting because of time and resourced consumed that seem not to outweigh its benefits (Wallander, 1999; e.g. Jensen, 2001), there is no alternative for most firms. The reason is that organizations need an instrument to coordinate and control decisions and actions of employees and alternatives for planning and budgeting seem not to exist for many organizations. Also, empirical studies highlight the positive performance effects of planning and budgeting (Hamann et al., 2023), not least of which is that, as said before, planning coordinates actions and decisions in firms and helps them use limited resources more efficiently.

On a more sober note, the way planning and budgeting are used in corporate practice often lacks an adequate discussion of opportunities and risks. While managers are quick to emphasize the opportunities presented by their plans, the risks associated with them are underestimated or not mentioned at all. The usual quantitative plan or budget uses one number to capture all risks and opportunities (Collier & Berry, 2002; Behringer & Gleißner, 2018), but this is not adequate. Risks and opportunities arise from a myriad of future developments. A single number cannot capture the possible future of earnings, for example.

11.2 Risks and Opportunities in Plans and Budgets

Every plan or budget is based on assumptions about the future—about the state of the economy, commodity prices, exchange rates, and sales success, to name a few. As the future is unknown, these assumptions represent uncertainty. Uncertain planning assumptions are risky because they can lead to deviations from the plan and cause companies to miss their targets.

Any well-founded plan should therefore be transparent about the underlying assumptions and considerations. In sales planning, for example, it is important to be clear about the prices the company sets; the assumptions made about the competitors' pricing, the overall demand, and the state of the economy; and the way this affects sales. When foreign currencies are involved, assumptions must also be made about the relevant exchange rates. Some of these assumptions, like the company's prices, might be risk-free if they are fixed over the planning period. However, many other planning assumptions are uncertain and risky. Wherever a risky planning assumption appears in the planning process, there is a risk. Corporate planning covers an essential part of enterprise risk management simply by summarizing all risky planning assumptions in a structured way, namely, the risk inventory.

Example 11.1: How a Plan Might Be More Uncertain than It Looks at First Sight

Suppose a small company plans to sell 1000 units at US$10 per unit. The planned revenue is US$10,000. Is the actual revenue likely to be that high? No—because none of the planned values is realistically certain to occur, we must assign a probability to each value. Suppose that both the sales volume and the price will occur with a probability of 70%. Is the probability of the planned sales quantity also 70%? Again, no. The revenue is determined by the sales quantity and the price, so the individual probabilities must be multiplied together. In this case, the probability that the planned revenue of US$10,000 will occur is $0.7 \times 0.7 = 0.49$, or 49%; in other words, it will occur less than half the time (see also Savage, 2012).

Why is it important to consider these risks? Many plans are overly optimistic. For example, consider software development projects and their frequent cost and schedule overruns (Rahmandad & Repenning, 2016). This leads to a non-achievement of targets through excessive costs and late completion, undermining employees' motivation as they encounter more and more obstacles and difficulties as the project progresses. Formulating plans optimistically and underestimating the effort and duration is called the planning fallacy (Buehler et al., 1994).

First, it is important to understand that plans do not represent the entire reality of an organization, just as a map does not represent the actual landscape. Second, there is a high degree of uncertainty about the future—both the actions and decisions within your own company and those of suppliers, customers, and competitors. These two aspects mean that a) variances between the plan and the actual situation will be the rule rather than the exception and b) it is difficult to say whether a plan is "right." After all, no one can predict with certainty whether sales will increase by 1.3% or 1.4%. It follows that:

- Forecasts, plans, and (future) reality do not have to coincide, but they should not be too far apart. Since plans express intentions and forecasts are predictions, the two need not coincide. However, plans that deviate strongly from a forecast require convincing justification and may indicate implausible plans and questionable assumptions. If reality deviates significantly from the plan, it may be due to poor planning or unforeseen events. In the latter case, a company must decide for itself whether plans need to be adjusted.
- Even if plans and forecasts do not accurately predict the future, they are not useless. Rather, they serve to coordinate future decisions, actions, and resource allocations to achieve a goal. They also provide motivation by setting goals and actions for the relevant people in the organization.
- It will be difficult to say that a planned target or calculation is plausible but easier to say that it is implausible. If a company's sales have typically grown between 1% and 2% in recent years, a targeted increase of 20% would be implausible and require explanation.

Many different risks can affect an organization. We have already covered the area of strategic risks (Chaps. 7 and 8), but there are also important risks along a company's value chain. This chapter focuses on and explains some of these risks that are especially relevant for operational planning and budgeting (Gleißner, 2022). First, there are many risks stemming from markets.

- **Sales**: This is surely the biggest singular risk in a manager's mind. Future sales and revenues affect a firm's bottom line directly, but they are uncertain. The following are indicators of high risk in this function: low share of regular customers, low differentiation of own products from those of competitors, strong dependence on a few large customers, pronounced seasonal or cyclical fluctuations, stagnating demand, low barrier to market entry, high intensity of competition, and technological upheavals.
- **Procurement/supply chain**: To produce and sell products, firms must purchase materials and services from suppliers. Such risks are more relevant if firms face high purchasing costs related to overall costs, high dependence on specific materials or services delivered by only a few suppliers, and/or high price volatility. Strategic sourcing or supply chain risks concern companies' dependency on their suppliers and how they manage them. Operational risks often arise from purchasing prices and volumes, supplier selection, and quality problems with purchased materials.

Second, there is a broad array of **financial risks**, including financial solvency, capital market risks, default risks, interest rate risks, and currency risks. These risks are directly or indirectly related to operational planning and budgeting, as the following examples illustrate:

- **Lack of financial solvency** is the main reason for declaring bankruptcy. If a company's operating plan is too optimistic or an adverse event occurs and it incurs large losses, it must use cash. However, without profits and positive operating cash flow, a company will quickly run out of cash.
- A similar risk may arise from loan agreements, which often contain **covenants** that define rules for the financial and economic choices that a company must make. If such covenants are breached, the lending bank may terminate the loan. Examples of covenants are a maximum ratio of debt to earnings, a minimum amount of net worth, a rating above a threshold, and a maximum ratio of debt to equity. Business plans must take covenants into account so as not to violate them and jeopardize the company's future refinancing.

The next section discusses how to integrate these risks into an operational planning and budgeting process.

11.3 Considering Uncertainty and Risk in Planning and Budgeting

Organizations have several options for considering uncertainty and risks in operational planning and budgeting (Rieg, 2024). Perhaps surprisingly, the first approach is to **ignore uncertainty and risk**. This makes sense when the level of uncertainty is low or its impact on the business is likely to be negligible. For example, all cost types in profit planning are uncertain, but it is not necessary to deal with them in detail in the case of small items such as office supplies, consumables, or scheduled depreciation. They either have a small impact on profit or else generally change little or not at all.

Another way of dealing with risk is to prepare alternative plans, the proverbial **Plan B**. This means that a contingency plan for a specific development or situation is drawn up at the same time as the actual plan (Plan A). Uncertainty is considered when the plan is created. Every company must decide for itself what developments or situations require such contingency plans. They choose certain risks that could have a massive impact, such as a pandemic, a cyberattack, or the loss of key suppliers.

For less extreme events, **flexible planning** can be used. It allows for adjustments to certain events or developments already included in Plan A. An example is a predefined adjustment of the planned budget for consumables based on the actual production quantity.

A **rolling forecast and plan** is another option to deal with uncertainty in forecasting and planning. It produces projections and forecasts more frequently and regularly to better anticipate and adapt to changes. However, more frequent planning leads to more planning effort, and it is important to limit this by restricting the plan to a few parameters and automating it. It is helpful to distinguish between a rolling forecast and the subsequent rolling planning. A forecast or trend extrapolation is used to extrapolate past developments. Plans are characterized by decision-making and setting goals or targets for future actions.

The use of **scenarios** is familiar from strategic intelligence and planning. The idea is to identify and articulate possible future developments. Strategic planning focuses on identifying unusual and extreme events and understanding their impact. Operational planning is less extreme. Its goal is to identify events that affect operational business activities. We already discussed scenario analysis in Sect. 4.2 and Chap. 8. The transition from scenario planning to flexible planning is fluid. The terms are indeed vague. All that remains is to find your own definition of the terms for your own application.

Bandwidth planning is a form of stochastic planning, meaning that it assumes that individual planning variables are uncertain, so that the target figures of the plan, such as EBIT or profit after tax, are also uncertain. In practice, bandwidth planning is performed using an MCS. Based on the previous planning calculation, the key variables that are assumed to be uncertain must be identified. Parameters must be defined for each, including the type of distribution and characteristic values of the distribution. The frequency distribution of the target variable can then be derived from the risk measures through multiple planning runs with different characteristics of the distributions. An example is presented in Sect. 11.4.

Rather than using more planning and budgeting and producing ever more detailed plans, other approaches focus on less planning and budgeting. Instead of trying to plan for details that are uncertain and often impossible to predict, an organization might build **buffers** to increase resilience and flexibility. In this way, companies can protect themselves against fluctuations and have reserves that can be used in unforeseen circumstances. A typical example of a buffer is inventory. Evidence shows that companies with low inventories relative to sales are less profitable, likely because they are less able to respond to short-term fluctuations in demand or supply bottlenecks (Obermaier & Donhauser, 2012). Other buffers include liquidity, equity, credit lines, excess staff, and budget slack (Elmassri & Harris, 2011). However, while their benefits are less obvious and measurable, buffers have visible and measurable costs. It is also not clear that having more buffers produces better results. In this respect, it is more advisable to maintain a minimum level of buffers. The number of buffers needed must be determined on a case-by-case basis.

Another way to reduce planning detail is to **focus more on targets** than on specific actions. This gives front-line managers more freedom to act while still holding them accountable for achieving the goal (Möller & Marks, 2021).

The latest trend is for planning and budgeting to be more **agile**. Broadly speaking, this means that companies should be able to adapt quickly and flexibly to changes. This means that the planning system should adapt to changes in the company's business model. When the business model changes rapidly, the planning system should also change rapidly. Business activities are shifting to online relationships, creating new revenue and cost models that require new management indicators and plans. On the other hand, business analytics tools can be used to gain insights from large volumes of data (IGC and Möller, 2022).

Given that these ideas are rather new and sometimes underdeveloped or even contradictory, it is still unclear whether these approaches will actually support organizations to cope with uncertainty and risks.

11.4 Integrating Risk into Planning and Budgeting: An Example

This section describes the steps needed to integrate uncertainty and risk into an operational plan or budget. They are illustrated using a profit and loss statement as the planning framework (see also Alviniussen & Jankensgaard, 2009). The **first step** is to establish the planning model, which is the structure and logic of the plan. Since integrating risk does not necessitate starting from scratch but rather involves modifying and adapting plans where appropriate, organizations typically rely on an

Table 11.1 Plan of income statement

Step 1: Planning model and start data		Plan
Revenue		$1,000.00
Cost of Goods Sold (50% of revenue)		$500.00
Personnel costs		$325.00
Depreciation		$75.00
Earnings before Interest and Taxes (EBIT)		$100.00
Interest expense		$50.00
Extraordinary expenses	see Table 11.2	
Earnings before Taxes (EBT)		$50.00

Table 11.2 Choice of distribution and parameters

Step 2: Assumptions about uncertainty and relevant parameters		
Position	*Distributed as …*	*Parameter*
Revenue	Triangular	Min: 950, mean: 1000, max: 1050
Cost of Goods Sold	Normal	Mean: 50%, Standard dev. : 3%
Personnel costs	Normal	Mean: 325, standard dev. 30, min: 300
Extraordinary expenses = Customer payment defaults		No. of defaults p.a.: 5 (Poisson distribution) Size of default: 4 (PERT distribution)

existing planning structure. Table 11.1 presents an example of a plan for an income statement before taxes containing some startup data.

The **second step** is to consider which positions are most prone to uncertainty and risk. For each, it is necessary to define an appropriate distribution of possible values as well as the parameters required for a specific distribution. In this example, the extraordinary expenses are caused by customer payment defaults. The calculation of defaults requires two inputs: the frequency of defaults in a given time horizon and the average value of a given default. The frequency can be modelled as a Poisson distribution because it is count data. For the value of a default, a PERT distribution is chosen. Both data sources are combined in a compound distribution (see Sect. 5.7). Table 11.2 shows the selected distributions and parameters.

The **next step 3** is to use this information and simulate the result for different parameter values. This can be done using a spreadsheet or specialized software. Either way, the MCS typically generates several thousand random numbers to iterate the plan. The resulting distributions of EBIT and EBT targets are shown in Fig. 11.1, along with a sensitivity analysis of the relative influence of the input variables. The shift of the EBT distribution to the left compared to the EBIT distribution is due to the inclusion of extraordinary expenses. The sensitivity analysis highlights the negative impact of Cost of Goods Sold (COGS) and the costs of personnel. This is less surprising given the nature of these costs. Table 11.3 lists additional quantitative information useful for evaluating the plan.

A strong contrast between EBIT and EBT is evident throughout the results. The 95% value at risk (VaR) is very different for both targets and shows for EBT a clear negative value. The return on equity (RoE) is around 1.5% for EBT, but this hides

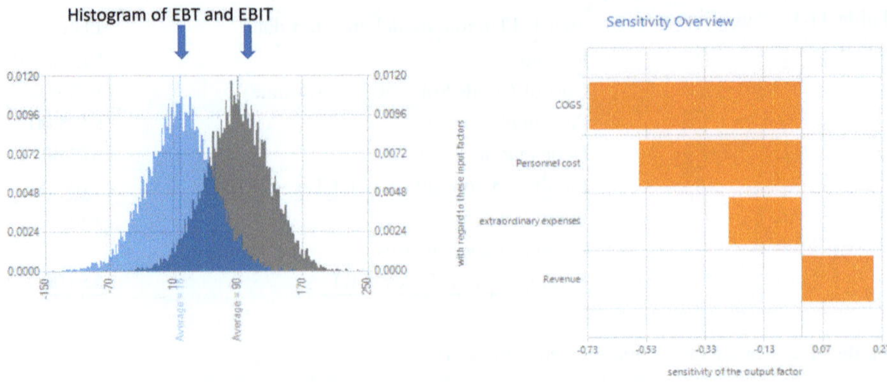

Fig. 11.1 Distribution of EBIT and EBT, sensitivity of input variables

Table 11.3 Key indicators of simulation results

Distribution of simulated results	**EBIT**	**EBT**
5% Percentile = 95% VaR	$24.01	−$49.57
25% Percentile	$63.30	−$9.19
50% = Median	$90.05	$18.48
75% Percentile	$116.04	$45.53
95% Percentile	$152.31	$83.52
Key indicators	**EBIT**	**EBT**
Expected value (a)	$89.47	$18.00
Standard deviation (b)	$38.91	$40.34
Coefficient of Variation (b)/(a)	0.43	2.24
prob(losses)	1.11%	32.71%
CVaR for prob(losses)	−$14.65	−$26.89
Return on equity ROE	7.46%	1.50%

the high probability of negative net earnings of nearly 33%. The cumulative weighted value of all the simulated earnings, the conditional value at risk (CVaR), is more than double for EBT than for EBIT, meaning that the firm might need to provide more risk-bearing financial capacity.

In light of these results, the company should consider mitigating some of the risks. This is **Step 4**. Several measures are available. For example, the company may sell some of its receivables to reduce losses from customer defaults. This is called factoring. However, there is a cost to selling receivables, so the cost of factoring must be balanced against the losses avoided. Suppose the company can sell receivables in such a way that the average count of defaults is reduced from 5 to 3 and the maximum loss is reduced from 10 to 8. Factoring costs US$5. The resulting simulation shows a reduction of risk that is visible within the key indicators (Table 11.4).

Before deducting the cost of factoring, the expected EBT increases from US$17 to around US$27, so more or less by US$10. While deducting the cost of factoring will reduce the additional expected EBT by US$5, the other risk metrics show that

Table 11.4 Effects of mitigating risk on key indicators

Key indicators	EBIT	EBT		
Expected value (a)	$89.62	$27.67	Cost of factoring	
Standard deviation (b)	$38.68	$39.39	$5.00	
Coefficient of Variation (b)/(a)	0.43	1.42	Not yet deducted	
prob(losses)	1.26%	23.93%		
CVaR for prob(losses)	−$15.24	−$24.11		
Return on equity ROE	7.47%	2.31%		
Comparing EBT before/after Factoring				
Key indicators	**EBT before**	**EBT after**	**Change**	**... in %**
Expected value (a)	$18.00	$27.67	$9.67	54%
Standard deviation (b)	$40.34	$39.39	−$0.95	−2%
Coefficient of Variation (b)/(a)	2.24	1.42	−0.82	−36%
prob(losses)	32.71%	23.93%	−8.78%	−27%
CVaR for prob(losses)	−$26.89	−$24.11	$2.78	10%
Return on equity ROE	1.50%	2.31%	0.81%	54%

(a) the variability of profits is reduced (the coefficient of variation is now only 1.49) and (b) the probability and value of simulated losses are also reduced to 25% and US $25, respectively. Consequently, the return on equity increases. Overall, this risk mitigation measure seems promising.

The resulting plan after risk mitigation includes net risks that are not covered or reduced by other measures. This means the company itself must bear the remaining risks. The **last step** is to present such a risk-adjusted plan to a firms' management. A more elaborated example with an integrated operational and financial plan including cash flows and balance sheet is provided in Chap. 13.

11.5 Overcoming Risk Blindness in Planning and Budgeting

Seizing opportunities while avoiding excessive risks is a prerequisite for the future economic success of companies—especially in an increasingly volatile business environment. Brexit, the COVID-19 crisis, and technological discontinuities such as the transition to electric mobility are just a few examples of sources of increasing uncertainty. Rational corporate management must deal with all opportunities and risks arising from external developments and internal decisions.

However, supervisory boards, managers, and management accountants often do not recognize risks appropriately; the same is true for planning and budgeting. Several **challenges** occur in practice (Gleißner et al., 2021):

1. Owners and management make decisions based primarily on profits rather than the risks the decision will create.

2. Management accountants and managers think in simple, single numbers rather than in bandwidths and probabilities.
3. Simulation techniques for evaluating the quality of plans and the volume of risk are seldom used (Grisar & Meyer, 2015).
4. Methods for risk- and reward-based comparison of different plan alternatives are lacking.
5. Firms often do not understand the need to comply with the business judgment rule, which states that corporate decisions must be based on a sufficient information base that includes opportunities as well as risks.
6. The weighted average cost of capital (WACC) in value-based management does not include the adequate cost and risk of insolvency.

There are several possible ways of mitigating these challenges. First, it should be made clear that managing means balancing opportunities and risks at the same time. Second, the adequate assessment of risks can be learned, and appropriate instruments are available (Hubbard, 2014). Adequate methods are needed to capture risks in decision-making due to the pronounced psychological errors people make when dealing with risks intuitively. In particular, risk targets should be integrated into performance measurement. Risk-adjusted performance measures assess the success of a decision in relation to the risk taken. In addition to the enterprise value, examples include the return on risk-adjusted capital (RORAC), risk-adjusted return on capital (RAROC), and risk-adjusted return on risk-adjusted capital (RARORAC). Chapter 6 discussed these in detail, and Chap. 10 showed how it is possible to convert risk in the cost of capital to link risk management and value-based management.

Risk is a stochastic concept. The adequate description of risk requires knowledge of probability distributions and stochastic processes. Quantifying a risk requires the use of statistical methods (e.g., to estimate parameters such as the probability of occurrence). Management accountants need to use MCS for risk aggregation (see Chap. 5). In addition, the results must be presented using appropriate risk measures, such as at-risk measures and coefficients of variation. Appropriate management of opportunities and risks also requires adequate knowledge of mathematical language, concepts, and procedures. More intensive teaching of the mathematics of uncertainty at universities is therefore recommended.

11.6 Summary

- Planning and budgeting are important management tools.
- The risk of missing a plan is the norm, not an exception.
- The sources of risks in operational planning and budgeting include markets, finance, and operations.
- There is a variety of existing approaches for integrating risks in budgeting and planning.

- Quantitative risk integration can use Monte Carlo simulation (MCS) for risk aggregation and derivation of risk-adjusted performance metrics.
- Plans have to fulfill several functions, often involving trade-offs, and do not have to be identical to forecasts.

11.7 Exercises and Questions

1. Explain the importance of planning and budgeting for an organization.
2. Discuss how plans and budgets reflect the risks and opportunities of a business.
3. Some managers think that the difference between the plan and the actual should be as small as possible. Comment on that opinion.
4. Identify possible risks in the operational plan of a manufacturing company.
5. Why is ignoring uncertainty and risk sometimes an option in planning and budgeting?
6. Which benefits does rolling budgeting offer?
7. Explain the concept of bandwidth planning.
8. Buffers to protect against uncertainty and risk are one option in dealing with risk in planning. Discuss the pros and cons of using buffers in inventories.
9. Name and explain the steps in using Monte Carlo simulation for operational planning.
10. Most firms use only one plan for multiple functions of planning. However, some people suggest using at least two plans: one for decision facilitation and one for management control. Discus pro and cons of both approaches.
11. Some companies have cost structures with high fixed costs and low variable costs, while others have cost structures with low fixed costs and high variable costs. This is exemplified by the difference between a company that produces and streams self-produced media content and one that licenses third-party content and streams it. Discuss the difference in cost structure related to risks and opportunities for the profitability of such firms.

Exercise 1: Risk Assessment for Cacao Café

You start as the new risk controller at the coffee house chain Cacao Café. The company buys coffee beans on the world market, roasts them, and delivers them to its own coffee houses. Discuss which risk measures you consider appropriate for the topics listed below and which measures would be useful for dealing with these risks.

a) Coffee bean purchase prices: The global market for coffee beans is characterized by volatile prices. Demand on the global market is not nearly as volatile but shows a more or less steady upward trend. In this context, you wonder why these price fluctuations occur and how their risks can be measured and possibly mitigated.

b) Meeting delivery dates: In addition to general price fluctuations, Cacao Café company is also affected by the fact that it purchases from multiple suppliers and cannot exercise market power. How can you identify and manage these risks?
c) Market: While coffee consumption is generally on the rise, the number of competitors operating coffee houses, bars, and cafés has increased disproportionately. The management of Cacao Café sees a way out of this competitive situation by focusing on specialty coffees. You are not convinced by this strategy. What opportunities and risks do you see, and how could the risk be measured?
d) Production: The company also roasts its own coffee. In addition to purchase prices, energy costs and quality criteria must be considered. What metrics can be used to measure production risks?

Exercise 2: Risk Metrics
Below are the following data for two firms:

in mUS$	Company A	Company B
E(EBIT)	$200	$180
Stddev (EBIT)	$50	$100
Capital employed	$750	$1000
Capital at risk	$350	$350
Required return	10%	12%

Calculate the following metrics for both companies and interpret them. Which company faces more risks?

a) Return on investment
b) Coefficient of variation
c) Risk-adjusted return on capital (RAROC)

References

Alviniussen, A., & Jankensgaard, H. (2009). Enterprise risk budgeting: Bringing risk management into the financial planning process. *Journal of Applied Finance, 19*, 178–192.

Behringer, S., & Gleißner, W. (2018). Die Unternehmensplanung als Grundlage für die Unternehmensbewertung: Eine empirische Studie. *Die Wirtschaftsprüfung, 71*, 312–319.

Buehler, R., Griffin, D., & Ross, M. (1994). Exploring the "planning fallacy": Why people underestimate their task completion times. *Journal of Personality and Social Psychology, 67*, 366–381. https://doi.org/10.1037/0022-3514.67.3.366

Collier, P. M., & Berry, A. J. (2002). Risk in the process of budgeting. *Management Accounting Research, 13*, 273–297. https://doi.org/10.1006/mare.2002.0190

de Smit, J., & Rade, N. L. (1980). Rational and non-rational planning. *Long Range Planning, 13*, 87–101. https://doi.org/10.1016/0024-6301(80)90036-9

Elmassri, M., & Harris, E. (2011). Rethinking budgetary slack as budget risk management. *J Applied Accounting Research, 12*, 278–293. https://doi.org/10.1108/09675421111187700

Gleißner, W. (2022). *Grundlagen des Risikomanagements: Handbuch für ein Management unter Unsicherheit* (Management competence) (4th ed.). Verlag Franz Vahlen.

Gleißner, W., Rieg, R., & Vanini, U. (2021). Risikoblindheit im Controlling und wie man sie überwindet. *Controlling, 33*, 66–72. https://doi.org/10.15358/0935-0381-2021-5-66

Grisar, C., & Meyer, M. (2015). Use of Monte Carlo simulation: An empirical study of German, Austrian and Swiss controlling departments. *Journal of Management Control, 26*, 249–273. https://doi.org/10.1007/s00187-015-0213-2

Hamann, P. M. (2017). Towards a contingency theory of corporate planning: A systematic literature review. *Management Review Quarterly, 67*, 227–289. https://doi.org/10.1007/s11301-017-0132-4

Hamann, P. M., Halw, O., & Günther, T. W. (2023). Meta-analysis of the corporate planning–organizational performance relationship: A research note. *Strategic Management Journal, 44*, 1803–1819. https://doi.org/10.1002/smj.3476

Hubbard, D. (2014). *How to measure anything: Finding the value of "intangibles" in business* (3rd ed.). Wiley.

IGC, Möller, K (Ed.). (2022). *Controlling & agility: Fundamentals, approaches, examples, and recommendations for the future finance function.* FH OÖ Forschungs & Entwicklungs GmbH.

Jensen, M. C. (2001). Corporate budgeting is broken – Let's fix it. *Harvard Business Review, 70*, 94–101.

Malmi, T., & Brown, D. A. (2008). Management control systems as a package—Opportunities, challenges and research directions. *Management Accounting Research, 19*, 287–300. https://doi.org/10.1016/j.mar.2008.09.003

Möller, K., & Marks, D. (2021). Flexible Fortschrittssteuerung als Target Operating Model der finanziellen Führung: Förderung unternehmerischen Verhaltens statt rigider Budgetorientierung. *Controlling, 33*, 14–21.

Obermaier, R., & Donhauser, A. (2012). Zero inventory and firm performance: A management paradigm revisited. *International Journal of Production Research, 50*, 4543–4555.

Rahmandad, H., & Repenning, N. (2016). Capability erosion dynamics. *The Strategic Management Journal, 37*, 649–672. https://doi.org/10.1002/smj.2354

Rieg, R. (2024). Unternehmensplanung: Umgang mit Unsicherheit und Risiko. *Controller Magazin, 43*, 10–14.

Savage, S. L. (2012). *The flaw of averages: Why we underestimate risk in the face of uncertainty.* Wiley.

Wallander, J. (1999). Budgeting — An unnecessary evil. *Art and Management, 15*, 405–421. https://doi.org/10.1016/S0956-5221(98)00032-3

Chapter 12
Organizational Aspects of Enterprise Risk Management

Abstract For successful implementation, enterprise risk management (ERM) must be well organized. That means that specific ERM tasks in the operational ERM process must be assigned to specific positions in a firm and organized into a specific process over time. The idea of ERM organization is closely related to the theoretical concept of risk governance, which aims to solve agency problems resulting from ERM. Depending on the regulatory requirements, size, and complexity of a firm, the relevant ERM actors (which include risk owners, risk managers, and management accountants) and approaches for implementing ERM vary. A firm's risk managers can take on different roles, such as compliance champions or business partners, depending on the main ERM relations of the firm. Especially in larger companies, many different functions are involved in ERM. The three lines (of defense) model can be used for an efficient and effective task sharing of these functions. Overall, ERM implementation can achieve different maturity levels in corporate practice.

Keywords ERM maturity · Risk governance · Risk manager · Three lines (of defense)

Questions
- Explain the basic concept of risk governance.
- What are the objectives and design principles of ERM organization?
- Who are the main actors in corporate ERM?
- What are the main impact factors on ERM in organizations?
- Distinguish between the different tasks and roles in ERM.
- Describe the three lines (of defense) concept.
- What are the benefits of and problems with different ERM maturity models?

Supplementary Information The online version contains supplementary material available at https://doi.org/10.1007/978-3-031-86425-4_12.

R. Rieg et al., *Enterprise Risk Management*, Springer Texts in Business and Economics, https://doi.org/10.1007/978-3-031-86425-4_12

12.1 The Concept of Risk Governance

So far, we have discussed various concepts and methods for strategic and operational ERM, including the firm's risk appetite for the determination of the maximum risk exposure, early warning systems for risk identification, or Monte Carlo simulation (MCS) for risk quantification. To successfully implement ERM in corporate practice, **responsibilities** for the specific tasks involved in strategic risk management and the operational RM process must also be defined and **assigned to business units and departments**. Overall, the supervisory board delegates the overall ERM responsibility to the top management, especially the CEO, who further delegates partial duties and responsibilities for practical reasons (Jankensgård & Kapstad, 2021). During this process, consideration must be given to possible agency problems as well as potential synergy and specialization effects of centralizing the ERM function, without foregoing the risk-specific knowledge of the decentralized units.

Approaches and problems with ERM implementation and organization are discussed within the concept of **risk governance**. The concept of risk governance can be regarded as a "set of mechanisms that counteract the agency problem of risk management" (Jankensgård & Kapstad, 2021). It has an external and an internal dimension. According to Renn (2008), risk governance is an activity "that requires consideration of legal, institutional, social and economic contexts in which a risk is evaluated, and involvement of actors and stakeholders who represent them." Risk governance analyzes the complex network of external and internal actors, rules, conventions, processes, and mechanisms of corporate risks and fixes regulations on how relevant risks are identified, analyzed, quantified, communicated, and controlled. Renn (2008) defines five elements of risk governance: pre-assessment, appraisal, characterization, evaluation, management, and communication of risks.

Risk governance is not a specific corporate function but rather an approach that supports the top management in effectively and efficiently implementing the ERM function in companies. Therefore, approaches, principles, and norms of **good corporate governance**, which serve to moderate agency conflicts and information asymmetries between the different stakeholders of a company, are integrated into ERM organization. Based on these approaches and principles, the firm-specific organizational options for the design of the ERM function, the potential level of decentralization within the organization, and the necessary steering activities of the top management and the supervisory board are developed (Stein & Wiedemann, 2016).

Overall, risk governance is about clarifying the roles and responsibilities of the strategic ERM and operational ERM processes. The top management and supervisory board have to fix an adequate level of risk governance institutionalization and determine the involved corporate institutions and functions, the degree of their independence from top management, the organizational structure, and the demarcation from already existing departments with similar functions, such as internal audit or management accounting. Overall, risk governance also stresses the decision-facilitating perspective of ERM (Stein & Wiedemann, 2016). These questions are discussed in the next sections of this chapter.

12.2 Objectives, Concepts, and Design Principles of ERM Organization

The organization of ERM is part of the strategic ERM framework and is therefore part of the responsibility of the top management. A distinction is made between the organizational structure and the process organization of ERM. In the organizational structure, ERM tasks are assigned to specific positions. Several positions with related tasks are often grouped into departments or organizational units, and the positions are equipped with the competencies necessary for the fulfillment of the tasks. ERM process organization regulates the factual, temporal, personnel-related, and spatial sequence of the fulfillment of ERM tasks. Thus, we arrive at the following definition:

Definition. ERM organization assigns the ERM tasks to specific positions within and outside of the company (organizational structure) and provides these positions with the necessary competencies. The process organization arranges the ERM tasks in a sequence that makes sense in terms of subject matter, personnel, and time (operational ERM process). The aim of the organizational structure and process organization is to improve the effectiveness and efficiency of ERM.

Only aspects of the formal organization are considered in the term "ERM organization." Informal structures belong to the concept of risk culture. The goal of improving the effectiveness and efficiency of ERM is further concretized by Diederichs (2018, p. 183 f.), who specifies the following **requirements**:

- The ERM organization should ensure the stability and flexibility of corporate risk management.
- The ERM organization should contribute to the development of an adequate risk culture and risk awareness in the company.
- The ERM organization should support the early identification of all relevant risks in all business units of the company.
- The ERM organization coordinates the operational ERM process.
- The ERM organization should ensure the implementation of control measures and thus contribute to securing the existence of the company.

Overall, ERM organization contributes to managing risk and thus achieving strategy and business objectives. The organizational structure of a firm is often aligned with its legal structure and management structure, as these both determine how a firm operates and define the reporting lines and decision authorities (COSO, 2017).

The following aspects must be taken into account when designing the ERM organization (Diederichs, 2018; Gleißner, 2022):

- **Institutionalization of ERM function**: The question here is whether ERM should be integrated into the existing organization or an independent unit should be created for ERM (integration versus separation). In addition, aspects of cooperation with other corporate functions and units such as management accounting, internal audit, or compliance must be defined.
- **Assignment of ERM tasks and decision authorities**: The tasks of the operational ERM process must be assigned to specific positions or units. In addition, the positions and units must be provided with the necessary decision authority and competencies to fulfill their tasks. This includes, for example, information and veto rights.
- **Integration in the company hierarchy**: The degree of centralization and the hierarchical integration of the ERM function must be determined. The ERM function can be assigned to the entire board, to a particular board member such as the Chief Financial Officer (CFO), or to a hierarchically lower executive such as the Head of Finance. In addition, ERM tasks can be assigned to a central ERM unit or distributed among several decentralized units.

These individual aspects are discussed in more detail below.

12.2.1 Institutionalization of the ERM Function

The first question that needs to be clarified is whether the ERM function should be fully or partially separated from the rest of the organization (separation) or whether it is the responsibility of each manager whose decisions create risks for the company (integration). The question of institutionalization or separation is closely related to the concept of **risk ownership**. Risk ownership is the idea that for each risk there should be a specific individual or unit that has the responsibility for managing it. Risk ownership creates accountability in the risk management process and avoids the situation that failures and losses simply happen for lack of attention. A risk owner is responsible for assessing and reporting risk, but importantly also has the decision-making authority, that is, controls the firm's risk response (Jankensgård & Kapstad, 2021).

As a starting point, the supervisory board delegates the overall risk ownership to the CEO, who, in large companies, further delegates the ownership of specific risks within the company.

In its pure form, **integration** means that no separate ERM positions are created, but the fields of activity of existing positions are expanded. The prerequisite is that the positions have the necessary expertise and time to take on ERM tasks. The integration approach is often applied in relatively small companies. Typically, decentral managers are named as risk owners for different risks and are responsible for the identification, assessment, reporting, and management of those risks. Integration often allows for earlier risk identification and more flexible risk response. In addition, it improves cooperation and information exchange throughout the

Table 12.1 Advantages and disadvantages of integrating and separating the ERM function (source: Vanini & Rieg, 2021)

	Integration approach	Separation approach
Advantages	• Linking factual and risk decisions • Less need for coordination • Better risk identification, as the operating units know their risks best • Cost-effective, as no parallel organizational structure is set up	• High prioritization of RM tasks • Relieving the operational units • Development of methodical knowledge and special knowledge possible • Ensure uniform implementation of the RM
Disadvantages	• Lack of an institutionalized and independent ERM function • Overloading the decentralized units • Danger of overlooking important risks because ERM is not given enough attention in day-to-day operations • Limited coordination of decentralized ERM activities	• Lack of insight into specific processes and risks of the operational units/existence of information asymmetries • No development of technical and methodological ERM knowledge in the operational units • Coordination needed between decentralized units and centralized ERM function

organization (COSO, 2017). In the case of **separation**, at least one independent ERM position is implemented. In smaller companies, ERM tasks can also be assigned to the management accounting unit. The ERM unit mostly supports managers in employing adequate ERM methods, coordinates all ERM activities throughout the company, and is responsible for aggregated risk reporting (Burger & Buchhart, 2014; Diederichs, 2018; Hunziker, 2021). These units know their specific risks best and are responsible for their identification and management. Table 12.1 summarizes the key advantages and disadvantages of integrating or separating the ERM function:

Both the integration and the separation approaches have numerous advantages and disadvantages. Furthermore, it is not possible to have a total separation approach with no participation of the operative units in the operational ERM process. Therefore, in practice, there are often mixed forms (i.e., ERM tasks are taken over by both primary organizational units and special ERM functions) (Hunziker, 2021).

12.2.2 *Assignment of ERM Tasks and Decision Authorities*

After deciding on the extent of institutionalization or separation of the ERM function, the question arises as to the possible assignment of different ERM tasks to specific positions and units. Risk governance begins with the **supervisory board,** which should challenge the strategy, the risks connected with this strategy, the strategic decisions of the top managers, and their impact on the risk-return profile and the risk-bearing capacity of the firm. The supervisory board has to make sure that ERM is effectively implemented, the risk appetite is appropriately defined, and the business portfolio is reviewed with regard to its risks and its performance. In addition, it must ensure that the managers fulfill the legal and fiduciary requirements. Thus, the supervisory board must be independent from the executives and regularly informed about the key risks of the firms (risk oversight). As a necessary precondition, an operational ERM process including risk reporting has to be established. The board must also have some basic ERM competencies (Hunziker, 2021; Jankensgård & Kapstad, 2021).

In larger companies, the ERM function is not normally the exclusive task of a single risk manager but is executed by various positions and units, such as ERM experts, risk managers, auditors, and management accountants, as they have special knowledge concerning single risks or ERM methodologies (Arena & Arnaboldi, 2014). Thus, the top management further delegates ERM tasks and responsibilities throughout the organization. The delegation of ERM tasks follows two principles. First, risks can be identified, evaluated, and mitigated in the business units in which they arise (**controllability principle**). For example, financial risks can be identified, assessed, and mitigated in the treasury unit, whereas performance risks can be identified, assessed, and mitigated in the operational business units that produce and distribute the related products or services. However, risks cannot always be clearly assigned to specific organizational units. For example, an increase in interest expenses on overdrafts is caused by the financing of working capital and thus ultimately by production, but control of this interest rate risk takes place in the treasury department. Since complex methods and instruments are used in ERM, the assignment of ERM tasks to positions with corresponding methodological competencies is also conceivable (**control principle**; Wolke, 2016). Ultimately, ERM tasks are often assigned to specific positions in accordance with both principles.

According to the controllability and control principles, there are different positions and organizational units that should be involved in ERM. First of all, ERM tasks are performed by the **top management**, which has total responsibility for ERM implementation, sets the strategic ERM framework for the operational ERM process, defines the risk strategy and the risk appetite, and appoints the risk manager (s) (Gleißner, 2022).

For the identification, assessment, and mitigation of single risks, a specific understanding of the business context is usually necessary. Therefore, these tasks are often assigned to **decentralized risk owners** in operative business units within the primary organization. The risk owners have information advantages and more expertise with respect to their specific risks and potential risk factors. Thus, they are responsible for the management of risks in their area of responsibility, identifying, managing and monitoring "their" risks in accordance with the corporate risk strategy and risk appetite as well as with risk mitigation decisions of the ERM committee. In addition, risk owners deliver risk-related information for central risk reporting (Hunziker, 2021; Gleißner, 2022).

However, risk assessment and quantification require specific methodological competencies, which is why the decentralized risk owners are supported by centralized and decentralized **risk managers** or **ERM units**. The centralized risk manager's respective ERM unit is also responsible for the definition of ERM standards, the coordination of the ERM activities of the decentralized units, risk aggregation, risk reporting, and ERM documentation (Gleißner, 2022). In addition, cross-functional risks must be identified, quantified, aggregated, and managed (Diederichs, 2018). It is important to notice that risk managers have a coordinator role but do not manage risk themselves. They provide tools and methodologies and support the operative managers in the management of their risks (Hunziker, 2021). The tasks and roles of risk managers are discussed in detail in Sect. 12.3.

A certain degree of centralization is also necessary, as synergies can be utilized in risk management where appropriate (e.g., correlation and diversification effects can be considered during risk aggregation). A portfolio view is taken and hedging transactions and other risk responses can be coordinated (Jankensgård & Kapstad, 2021). Depending on the company's size, structure, and environmental dynamics, decentralized ERM positions may also make sense as they provide technical and methodological support to the operational risk owners and coordinate ERM implementation. In addition, they assume an interface function with the central ERM unit and are members of the ERM committee. The tasks of the decentralized ERM units can also be taken over by the decentralized (risk) controlling or management accounting.

ERM takes on greater significance when a **Chief Risk Officer (CRO)** is employed (Lee & Shimpi, 2005; Mikes, 2010). The CRO has overall responsibility for the ERM implementation; appoints risk managers, risk controllers, and risk owners; determines the basic ERM methods; decides on risk measures; and represents ERM in the management body (Hunziker, 2021). The CRO is considered an essential building block of good corporate governance (Beasley et al., 2005) and a success factor for the implementation of a high-quality ERM strategy and an adequate ERM system (Liebenberg & Hoyt, 2003; Pagach & Warr, 2011). However, the establishment of a CRO must not call into question the overall responsibility of all top managers (Gleißner, 2022).

The **ERM committee** is an interdisciplinary, advisory body without any operating responsibilities, dedicated to establishing a holistic view of ERM and breaking up the silo perspective. The committee should consist of high-ranking members of the firm's main business units and corporate functions, such as compliance, strategic planning, management accounting, and security management (Jankensgård & Kapstad, 2021). The ERM committee has the following tasks (Hunziker & Meissner, 2017; Diederichs, 2018):

- Analyze the key risks from the perspective of the company
- Analyze the key strategic decisions from a risk perspective
- Support risk managers in the design, further development, and adaptation of all components of the ERM system
- Support the operational units in the implementation of the ERM process
- Develop, modify, improve, and coordinate risk management measures and regulations
- Development of risk mitigation measures

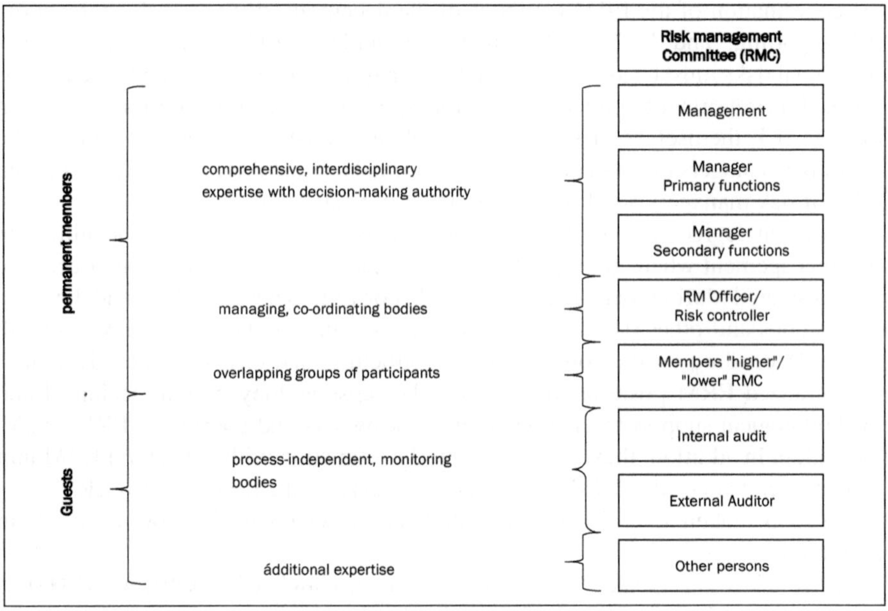

Fig. 12.1 Composition of the ERM committee (adapted from Diederichs, 2018)

- Coordinating and monitoring limit compliance and ensuring the risk-bearing capacity

A possible composition of the ERM committee is shown in Fig. 12.1.

ERM cannot be understood without reference to internal audit, compliance, and other related functions that also serve to establish risk oversight and limit risk exposure. **Internal audit** is a more generalist function that, on behalf of the supervisory board, provides assurance that the integrity of important processes is maintained and monitors a firm's compliance with regulatory requirements (Jankensgård & Kapstad, 2021). The activities of the operational ERM process and the ERM system must also be constantly monitored by **internal and external control bodies**. Internal control bodies also include process-independent units such as internal audit or the supervisory board; the external control bodies are the auditing companies. Internal audit reports go directly to the supervisory board and monitor the adequacy, effectiveness, and efficiency of the ERM system and processes. The supervisory board is a control body independent of internal company institutions and checks whether the executive management has implemented an ERM system in accordance with the relevant regulatory requirements. In doing so, the supervisory board draws on the reports of the internal and external auditors. The external auditors

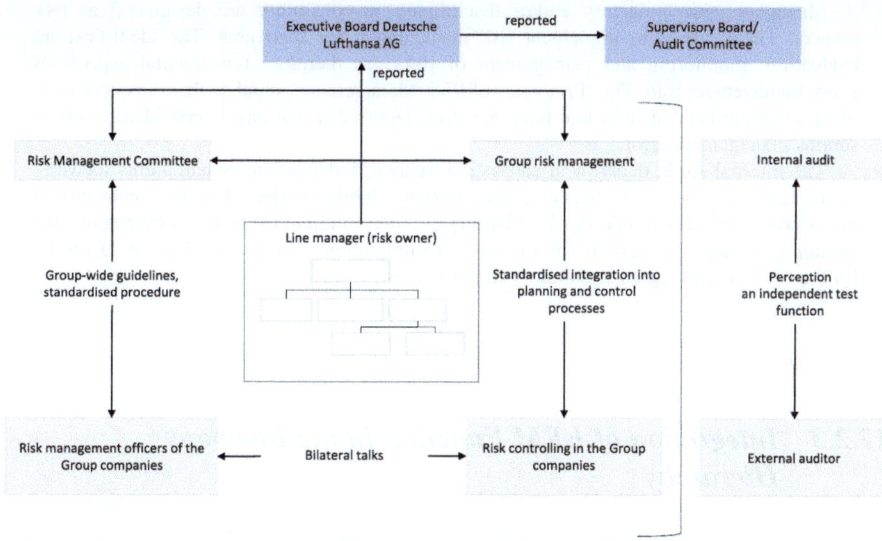

Fig. 12.2 ERM at the Lufthansa Group (source: Lufthansa Group 2024, *Annual Report 2023*, p. 125 f)

also form an independent control instance auditing both the ERM system and the various control mechanisms within a company.

As there are numerous overlaps between the tasks of process-dependent, process-independent, and company-external monitoring bodies, extensive cooperation between the different control bodies with a comprehensive exchange of information is necessary (Diederichs, 2018).

Example: ERM Actors and Organization in the Lufthansa Group

The risk report of the Lufthansa Group includes the following description of the ERM actors and their organizational cooperation (Fig. 12.2):

> The Supervisory Board's Audit Committee monitors the existence and effectiveness of the Lufthansa Group's risk management. The Risk Management Committee ensures, on behalf of the Executive Board, that processes, structures, and rules are established to identify, manage and assess business risks at an early stage across all functions and processes. It is also responsible for improving the effectiveness and efficiency of risk management. Appointments to and the responsibilities of the committee are defined in internal regulations. The Corporate Controlling department has functional responsibility for ensuring that the risk management system is standardised across the Group. [...] Group risk management is responsible for implementing uniform standards and methods, for coordinating and continuously refining the risk management process and for all risk management reporting in the Lufthansa Group. The managing directors or management boards of all the companies covered by the risk management system also appoint risk managers. They are responsible for implementing the Group guidelines within their own companies and are in close, regular dialogue with the Lufthansa Group's risk management function. In addition, they ensure that risk-relevant information is agreed with the planning and forecasting processes in their company (risk controlling).

Managers with budgetary and/or disciplinary responsibility are designated as risk owners. Their role is to implement risk management for their area. The identification, evaluation, monitoring and management of risks are therefore fundamental aspects of every management role. The 'Principles of Risk Management' stipulate that the occurrence of material predictable risks that have not been reported in the past is considered to be a serious management error.

The Internal Audit department carries out internal, independent system audits focusing on the appropriateness, effectiveness, and economic viability of the risk management system practised in the Lufthansa Group. [...] During its annual audit of the financial statements, the auditor examines the system for the early identification of risks in place at Deutsche Lufthansa AG with regard to statutory requirements.

12.2.3 Integration of ERM Function in the Company Hierarchy

If an ERM unit is to be institutionalized in order to support the risk owners located in the top management as well as in the decentralized business units, it must be determined whether centralized and decentralized ERM units are needed, where to locate them in the corporate hierarchy, and how to organize the division of labor between them. In the case of **complete centralization,** a centralized ERM unit determines the risk policy and all ERM standards; the business units only execute the standards and report their risks to the centralized ERM unit where they are managed. In the case of **complete decentralization**, all ERM tasks are carried out in the decentral business units and supported by decentralized ERM units. A central ERM unit is not implemented (Diederichs, 2018; Jankensgård & Kapstad, 2021).

Both approaches have advantages and disadvantages (Table 12.2).

In corporate practice, there are often **mixed implementations**. For example, a centralization of the ERM function that allows the realization of synergies as

Table 12.2 Advantages and disadvantages of centralizing or decentralizing the ERM function (source: Vanini & Rieg, 2021)

	Centralization of ERM function	Decentralization of ERM function
Advantages	• Avoidance of duplication of work • Assumption of the coordination function • Development of special knowledge is possible • Holistic, cross-company risk management using synergy effects	• Higher expertise for risk identification and management • Higher motivation of the employees • Promoting the risk culture • Faster and more flexible response possible
Disadvantages	• Extending the information, communication, and decision-making channels • Risk that the knowledge of the decentral units is not used	• Danger of duplication of work • No identification of cross-process or cross-divisional risks • Neglect of RM coordination

uniform risk quantification methods could be implemented. Correlations between the different risks of the decentralized business units can be considered during risk aggregation and only the net risk exposure must be hedged. A decentralization is reasonable when the risks of the business units are very different, and decentral units have better information access and expertise for risk identification, quantification, and management. Nevertheless, if the decentralized units manage their risk independently, there is always the danger of opportunistic exploitation of their information advantage and thus the delayed reporting of risks or the omission of control measures. From an agency theory point of view, appropriate incentives for risk identification and control must be taken into account. In addition, even in a decentralized approach, some coordination is necessary. That means that the central ERM units direct or influence decentral ERM activities by issuing things such as guidelines and policies.

12.2.4 *Types of ERM Organization*

In small companies, ERM tasks are usually taken over directly by the management. There is no separate ERM organization in the firms. There are different types of ERM organization for medium-sized and larger companies, as shown in Fig. 12.3.

ERM can be implemented as a staff unit of the management. In this way, specialization advantages can be used, and the management can be supported, but ERM then often suffers from acceptance problems and is not comprehensively integrated into decision-making processes. Alternatively, ERM can be organized as a line function (e.g., as a sub-unit of the finance department). The advantages to

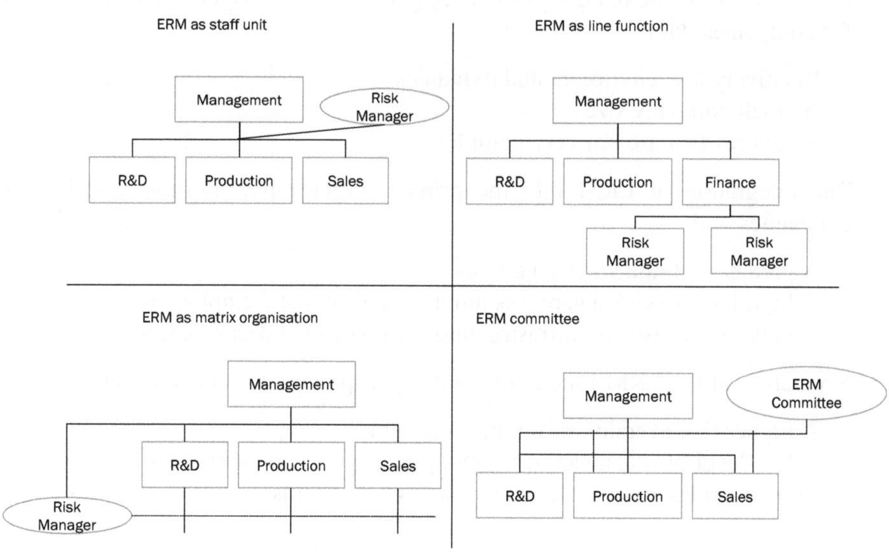

Fig. 12.3 Approaches of the ERM organization (source: Hunziker & Meissner, 2017)

this approach are the existence of defined responsibilities and competencies as well as the realization of specialization advantages. However, there is also the danger of ERM being "siloed." ERM can also be implemented as a matrix organization. This allows ERM aspects to be integrated into operational decision-making but involves a higher potential for conflict and a greater need for coordination, and it is therefore considered cumbersome. ERM can also be organized as a cross-functional and cross-hierarchical committee through which the advantages of centralization and decentralization are to be combined. However, this solution also harbors a certain potential for conflict and often suffers from a lack of decision-making powers (Hunziker, 2021).

12.2.5 Contextual Factors of ERM Organization

There is no one-size-fits-all approach to designing the RM function for all companies. Rather, numerous contextual factors influence the design of the ERM organization (Beasley et al., 2005; Burger & Buchhart, 2014; Mikes & Kaplan, 2015; Wolke, 2016):

- A decentralized ERM organization, which offers increased flexibility and speed of risk response, is more suitable for companies that:
  - Operate in a dynamic corporate environment
  - Are relatively large
  - Have complex structures
- A central ERM organization, which can then identify and manage all risks in a timely manner while realizing efficiency gains in risk management, is more likely for companies with
  - Relatively low environmental dynamics
  - A small company size
  - Structures that are not very complex
- The integration of ERM into the primary organization is more suitable for companies with
  - A greater willingness to take risks
  - A high level of risk awareness among managers and employees
  - A better expertise and infrastructure for ERM on a decentralized basis
- Separation of the ERM function is more appropriate for companies with
  - A higher risk aversion of the management
  - A low level of risk awareness among managers and employees
  - More complex risk management methods and tools

In addition, ERM organization is often related to the general assignment of decision authority, accountability, and responsibility to all levels of the entity and the type of reporting lines and communication channels. Smaller companies often cannot afford a separate ERM unit. For them, the integration concept is preferable for cost reasons. The separation of ERM is more feasible for larger companies (COSO, 2017).

12.3 Tasks, Roles, and Competencies of Risk Managers

There is no uniform definition of the **tasks** of a risk manager in the literature. Up to now, such definitions have mostly been based on extensive compilations of tasks that more or less cover all possible ERM activities. For example, the risk manager elaborates and implements organizational ERM standards, develops ERM tools for risk quantification, moderates risk workshops, defines thresholds for risk reporting, and collects and aggregates individual risk reports and other relevant documents (Gleißner, 2022). The possible job and function titles of risk managers are similarly heterogeneous—Chief Risk Officer (CRO), risk controller, risk manager, ERM officer, or ERM coordinator.

While there have been numerous studies on the task and competency profiles of management accountants (Rieg et al., 2023), only a few studies have been conducted for risk managers so far. Nevertheless, there is empirical evidence that the range of tasks of risk managers has become broader (Colquitt et al., 1999). Based on her analysis of 479 job advertisements from various industries in German-speaking countries, Vanini (2018) concludes that risk managers have a very broad spectrum of tasks, ranging from the development of ERM standards and coordination and training activities to taking on tasks of the operational ERM process. Other major tasks—especially in the finance and insurance sector—are risk quantification and risk reporting. In addition, compliance-related tasks such as the identification of relevant regulatory norms and standards and their implementation, monitoring, and control activities, as well as compliance management tasks, are also performed by risk managers (Rieg & Vanini, 2021). In addition, the task profiles and roles of risk managers may change due to changing environmental conditions. For example, Vanini et al. (2022) found that risk managers were at least partially involved in managing the impacts of measures and restrictions due to the COVID-19 crisis on their firms. Furthermore, the risk managers interviewed indicated that they would be more involved in business continuity management and crisis management in the future (see also Will, 2020).

Due to the broad task profile of risk managers, it could be asked whether these task profiles could be condensed to a list of specific **roles**. A role is defined as a consistent set of expected tasks and the way in which tasks are to be performed by a social position in the company (Wiswede, 1977). Roles can be described by formal elements such as task and competence profiles. The complexity of a role increases with the number of its tasks and requirements. Mikes (2010) attempts to further distil these bundles of tasks and how they are performed to condense them into role models. She identifies three basic roles for risk managers: The **compliance champion** focuses on implementing systems to ensure compliance with legal and internal regulations. Such a CRO also establishes the risk management framework, including risk governance (Stein & Wiedemann, 2016). The **modelling expert** focuses on the development of complex risk measurement methodologies and models. In addition, the risk manager may act as a **business partner**, with two variants of this role. The strategic advisor supports management in all risk-related issues, while the strategic controller provides an overview of all corporate risks (see also Mikes, 2008). Karanja and Rosso (2017) expand on the concept of roles, distinguishing between interpersonal, informational, and decision-making roles. In their study, the authors conclude that CROs primarily act as leaders, enablers, and strategists. Depending on the substantive and temporal alignment of the ERM function and strategic management, Slagmulder and Devoldere (2018) identify three roles of risk managers: (1) protector of the core business when there is no integration of ERM into the strategy process, (2) strategic challenger when risk managers challenge new strategies after their independent development by management, and (3) business partner when risk managers are fully integrated into the strategy development process.

According to the heterogeneity of their roles and tasks, risk managers have a very broad **competence profile**. In a survey of risk managers in Germany and Switzerland, Vanini and Gutacker (2019) show that risk managers are required to have methodological competencies concerning risk quantification, decision-making skills, and analytical and IT competencies. In addition, risk managers should understand their company's business model, have knowledge of the industry and the economy, and know the legal and statistical basis of risk management. They should also be persuasive and communicative team players (Lee & Shimpi, 2005). Due to the development and application of appropriate tools for risk modelling and assessment, communication skills are particularly relevant for the success of risk managers (Hall et al., 2015). Despite the stronger strategy and decision orientation of EM called for by, for example, COSO ERM (2017), corresponding competencies such as strategy skills and organizational knowledge are very rarely required of risk managers in corporate practice (Vanini & Hunziker, 2020).

12.4 Three Lines (of Defense) Model

To organize cooperation and to ensure the independence of the relevant ERM functions, the three lines of defense (TLD) model was developed and proposed by the Institute of Internal Auditors (IIA) in 2013 (The Institute of Internal Auditors, 2013; Jankensgård & Kapstad, 2021). In this model, three independent lines of risk defense are established, as Fig. 12.4 shows:

The **first line of defense** consists of managers of the business units, who are assigned as risk owners and are expected to identify, assess, and manage their material risks, for example, through effective internal control procedures. The

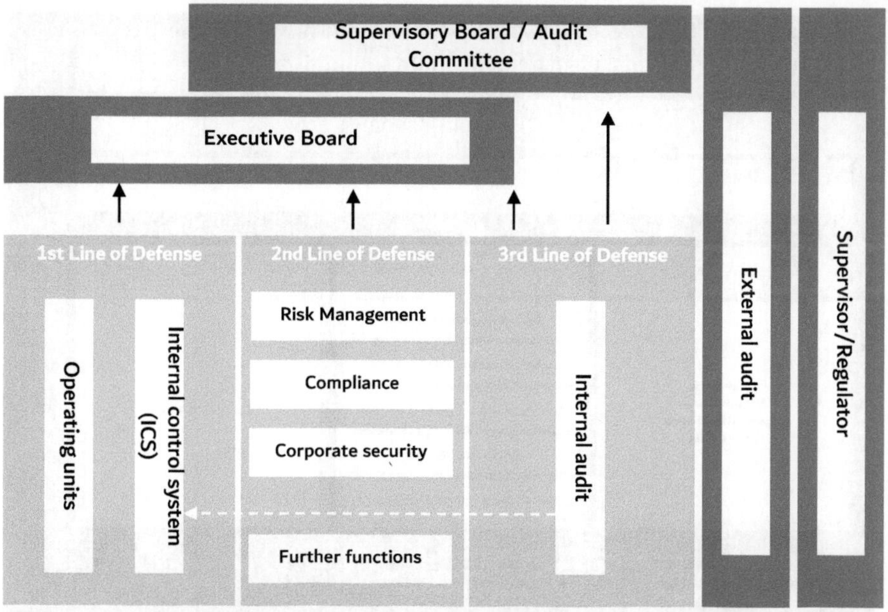

Fig. 12.4 Three lines of defense concept (source: Gleißner et al. (2022) with further references)

second line of defense consists of central corporate functions such as risk, compliance, or corporate security that are responsible for the functionality of the essential control systems and support the first line "by facilitating and monitoring the implementation and adherence to risk management standards and practices" (Turner, 2022). The **third line** of defense consists of the internal audit, which monitors the control procedures of the first, and the second line functions and preserves and improves the integrity of the main processes. Thus, the third line provides independent assurance. In addition, internal auditing directly reports to the top management and the supervisory board (Jankensgård & Kapstad, 2021; Gleißner, 2022).

The TLD model has been implemented in many companies. Nevertheless, the implementation has been criticized as bureaucratic and inconsistent. Although the model proposes a one-system-fits-all approach, firms have adapted it according to their size or the complexity of their business model and environment. In addition, the TLD model has been criticized as being too focused on risks and formal regulatory requirements and not accounting for chances or contributing to value creation. Moreover, the role of the supervisory board and its committees has not been defined within the TLD structure, and the multiplicity of responsibilities for ERM can lead to low effectiveness when no organizational unit really feels itself to be in charge of the overall ERM system (Davies & Zhivitskaya, 2018; Turner, 2022).

Therefore, the IIA revised the model and developed a principle-based approach referred to as the "Three Lines Model" (TL). The model avoids the term defense and thus takes into account that the aim is not only to protect but also to create shareholder value. Based on six governance principles, the model defines key

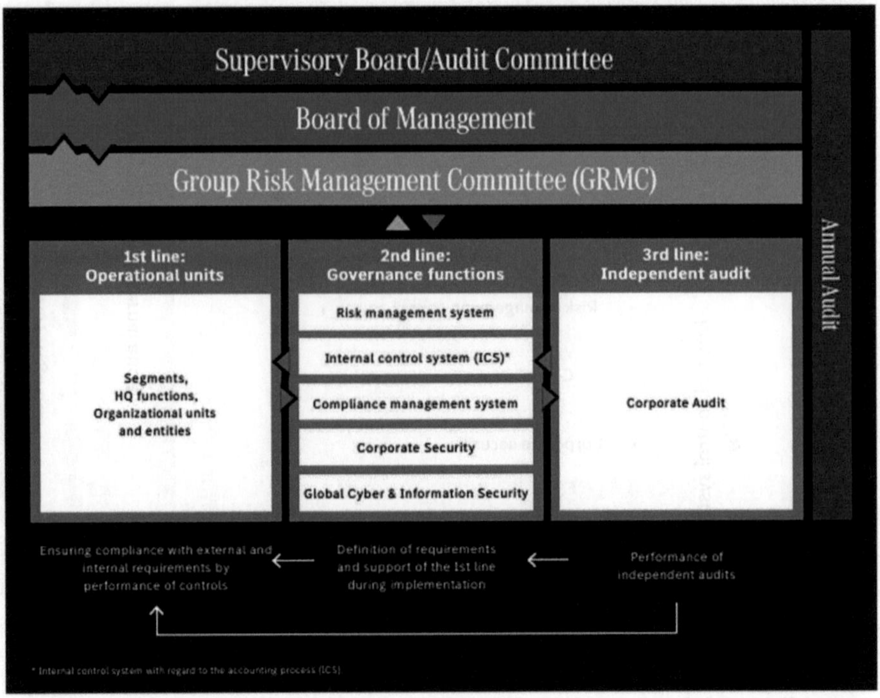

Fig. 12.5 Concept of the three lines (source: Mercedes Benz Group 2024, *Annual Report 2023*, p. 141 f)

roles and their relationship. Overall, it allows greater flexibility since it does not fix which departments take over which roles and sit within each of the three lines. In addition, it allows for interaction and communication between the three lines and a more company-specific implementation (The Institute of Internal Auditors, 2020).

Example: Overview of the Mercedes-Benz Group's Control and Monitoring System

The risk report of the Mercedes-Benz group includes the following description of the ERM organization according to the TL concept (Fig. 12.5):

> The operating units in the form of the individual segments, Group functions, organisational units and Group companies form the first line. Their task is to ensure the implementation of internal and external guidelines, and they are responsible for the implementation of controls, operational risk management and risk management processes in their respective units.
>
> In the second line, the risk management system, the accounting-related internal control system, the compliance management system, Group Security and Global Cyber & Information Security act as governance functions. They define the corresponding minimum requirements and standards for methods, processes, and systems for use in the first line and set the framework for cooperation. Their tasks also include regular reporting to the Board of Management and the Supervisory Board. They also support the first line in the corresponding implementation.

In the third line, Corporate Audit monitors the appropriateness and effectiveness of the implemented processes and the governance functions of the first and second lines through independent and risk-oriented audits. It monitors whether the statutory conditions and the Group's internal policies concerning the control and risk management system of the Group are adhered to and the associated processes are appropriately designed. If required, measures are initiated in cooperation with the respective management.

The Group Risk Management Committee (GRMC) is responsible for ensuring the continuous improvement of the risk management system and the internal control system (including the compliance management system) and for assessing their appropriateness and effectiveness with regard to the Group's risk situation and the scope of the business activities. It is chaired by the members of the Board of Management of Mercedes-Benz Group AG responsible for Finance & Controlling/Mercedes-Benz Mobility and Integrity, Governance & Sustainability. In addition, the GRMC was composed as of 31 December 2023 of representatives from Mercedes-Benz Group Finance, the Legal Affairs department, the Compliance unit, Corporate Security, Global Cyber & Information Security and the member responsible for the finances of the Board of Management at Mercedes-Benz Mobility AG. The Corporate Audit department contributes material findings on the internal control and risk management system.

The Board of Management, Audit Committee, and Supervisory Board are informed regularly and as needed about potential significant control weaknesses, the appropriateness and effectiveness of the implemented controls and the risk situation. The Audit Committee and the Supervisory Board of Mercedes-Benz Group AG and the Supervisory Boards of Mercedes Benz AG and Mercedes-Benz Mobility AG are responsible for monitoring the internal control and risk management system, including its appropriateness and effectiveness.

12.5 Integrative ERM and Risk-Orientated Management Accounting

As **management accounting** supports managerial decision-making, especially of top management decisions, the integration of ERM and management accounting can lead to improved integration of risk information in the preparation of decisions. The idea is based on the approach that risks are defined as potential deviations from targets. Therefore, the identification, quantification, and monitoring of risks should be anchored as far as possible in planning and management accounting and sometimes also in the company's quality management. In this approach, the first step is to look for every opportunity to integrate existing management systems (planning, controlling, budgeting, and quality management) to enable integrated decision-making based on performance and risk.

Corporate planning is usually based on uncertain assumptions about future developments. These uncertain assumptions represent precisely those risks that could trigger deviations from the plan and must therefore be recorded, evaluated, and, if necessary, managed through suitable risk measures as part of ERM. This integrative approach initially utilizes information about **uncertain planning assumptions** and deviations that actually occur later to identify and evaluate risks, thereby integrating the task of identifying and quantifying risks into the planning, controlling, and budgeting processes. Those responsible for planning and budgeting thus also become risk officers for those risks that affect their normal field of activity and can trigger deviations from the plan.

As can be seen from the examples above, key ERM tasks can be integrated directly into management accounting and also into quality and project management. At these points, a highly efficient takeover of original ERM tasks (e.g., risk identification and quantification) by management accounting is possible and hardly triggers any additional workload. It also ensures that the information on risks that is implicitly available in management accounting is utilized consistently. The central staff function of the risk controller is primarily responsible for coordinating and developing methods for ERM and very ERM-specific tasks, such as deriving the overall scope of risk and capital requirements with the help of risk aggregation, regardless of whether this is integrated into management accounting or assigned directly to management.

In addition to increasing the **efficiency of ERM**, operational and strategic management accounting also benefits from this closer connection with ERM. In planning and budgeting processes, new risks can be identified and communicated. On the contrary, ERM findings on risks that have been identified (e.g., as part of risk assessments or process analyses) should also be communicated to management accounting. Furthermore, the additional knowledge gained by ERM about the aggregated total risk exposure enables management accounting to realistically assess **planning reliability**, differentiate between random and statistically significant deviations (based on their scope), and weigh risks and returns against each other. Therefore, this additional available information on the aggregated scope of risk can then be utilized further (e.g., in the context of value-oriented management systems) by using the scope of risk to infer the equity required to cover possible losses and thus the cost of capital (discount rate) as the central value driver. Perhaps the most direct advantage for controlling is the possibility of using the results of the risk analysis to determine plan values that are true to expectations. Only plan values true to expectations provide a suitable data basis for the preparation of decisions by management accounting.

In total several benefits of integrating risk information into management accounting exist:

- Adequate risk-adjusted cost of capital for equity and debt
- Transparency of plans and budgets regarding opportunities and risks
- Planned values are more in line with expected values
- Variance analyses can build on risk-adjusted analyses

The interaction of ERM and management accounting leads to the assumption of essential basic ERM tasks by the company's existing management control systems, which enables a high level of efficiency. This also increases the acceptance of ERM. In this case, ERM is primarily considered as a task and less as an independent organizational unit.

12.6 ERM Maturity Models

Maturity models originate from quality management and software development. Probably the best-known maturity model is the capability maturity model integration (CMMI) model from Carnegie Mellon University, which has also served as the basis for the development of other maturity approaches in various disciplines and industries. A **maturity level** is used to assess the extent to which a particular object meets defined requirements in terms of its effectiveness and efficiency. The models have a fixed number of maturity levels for certain dimensions of the object under investigation (e.g., people, organizations, etc.). The maturity levels build on each other in their sequence and can be evaluated by corresponding criteria. A higher maturity level is reached when all criteria of the maturity level and the lower maturity levels are fulfilled.

There are different ERM maturity models that can be at least partially transferred into each other despite having different levels of maturity. Table 12.3 gives an overview of different ERM maturity models and their maturity levels:

Low ERM Maturity
At the first level in Hillson's (1997) model, there are no ERM approaches established in a company, and there is no risk awareness among managers and employees. At the second level (Novice ERM), there are initial RM approaches but no formalized and structured ERM process. Hillson's second stage corresponds to the first stages of the other two maturity models. In Gleißner and Mott's (2008) model, there are initial ERM approaches at the first level in the form of claims and insurance management,

Table 12.3 Overview of the different maturity models (source: expanded from Vanini & Rieg, 2021)

	Hillson (1997) RMM	Gleißner and Mott (2008) Gleißner, Stein, and Wiedemann (2021)	Mikes (2009)	Aven and Thekdi (2020)
Level 1	Naive risk organization	Damage management	Risk silo management	Beginner
Level 2	Novice risk organization	Regulatory risk management	Integrated risk management	Intermediate
Level 3	Normalized risk organization	Economic risk management	Risk-based management	Advanced
Level 4	Natural risk organization	Integrated value-based risk management	Holistic risk management	
Level 5		Value-based risk management		
Level 6		Risk governance Embedded risk management		

Table 12.4 Four ideal types of enterprise risk management (source: Mikes, 2009)

	Risk silo management	Integrated risk management	Risk-based management	Holistic risk management
Institutional background	International regulation of bank	Rating agency expectation of bank capital adequacy	Rise of shareholder value imperative	Rise of risk-based internal control (Anglo-Saxon and German corporate governance)
Related theme in the literature	Risk quantification	Risk aggregation	Risk-based performance measurement	Management of non-quantifiable risks
Focus on	Measurement and control of risk silos; calculation of minimum regulatory capital; tuning capital to the regulatory standard	Assigning a common denominator of risk to the risk silos (economic capital); fine-tuning capital to a given solvency standard, risk limit setting	Calculation of shareholder value created; linking risk management with performance measurement	Inclusion of non-quantifiable risks into the risk management framework; providing senior management with a "strategic view" of risks
Techniques	Loss distribution; value-at-risk; credit rating models; standardized and advanced measurement approaches set by regulators	Economic capital	Risk-adjusted return on capital (RAROC); shareholder value added; risk pricing; risk transfer; portfolio risk management	Scenario analysis; sensitivity analyses, control self- assessment; special risk reviews

while ERM also fulfills the legal requirements at the second level. However, ERM is implemented as an isolated solution. Mikes (2009) speaks of risk silos in this context. In her model, isolated quantification of the different types of risks takes place at the risk silo management level. In the process, more and more risks are made accessible to quantitative measurement. Value at risk is mentioned as an important method for risk quantification. At this level, the legal requirements for ERM are also fulfilled; the most important risks are monitored, evaluated, and summarized in a risk inventory. In addition, risk management strategies and a risk manual exist. The following figure provides an overview of Mikes' model (Table 12.4).

Aven and Thekdi (2020) state that there is no formalized ERM manager or function at the beginner level of their ERM maturity model. Instead, ERM is roughly based on a risk strategy, and some employees have at least some risk management-specific expertise. Concerning the risk culture, there is at least some agreement among the supervisory board and the top management about the organization's risk appetite and risk policy. At the very least, local and industry-specific regulations are met, and some form of risk prioritization is implemented. A basic ERM process is established and continuously monitored.

Medium-to-High ERM Maturity

Level 3 in Hillson's (1997) model is called normalized risk management. Here, basic RM approaches are integrated into the company's projects and processes. The next development level in Mikes' (2009) model is called integrated risk management. At this level, the previously quantified risks are aggregated, and their interdependencies are considered. The aggregation of differently quantified risks is a particular challenge for ERM. Also, the interrelationships between individual risks (e.g., in the form of correlations) are not always measurable in practice. Another feature of this development stage is the backing of the quantified risks with risk capital to cover the losses when the risk occurs.

Gleißner and Mott (2008) also refer to this stage as economic ERM and highlight that the effects on corporate goals and the rating are systematically analyzed. There is a pronounced risk awareness among all employees, and ERM is integrated into corporate processes and, especially, decision-making. The third stage of development is risk-based management in that all ERM processes are integrated into operational corporate management. Risk-return ratios are calculated for important managerial decisions. Stochastic planning, a risk-bearing capacity calculation, and systematic risk diversification are established. The term "integrated value-oriented ERM" is also used for this level. The fourth level is called "holistic risk management." The aim of a holistic ERM approach is to assess and manage non-quantifiable risks (e.g., strategic risks or image risks). Rather, a strategic view of corporate risks is taken. In addition, the individual risk preferences of the owners are incorporated into the decision-making process through risk-benefit calculations. This stage of development is also driven by corporate governance or ERM standards.

In the second (intermediate) and third (advanced) stages of the ERM maturity model developed by Aven and Thekdi (2020), dedicated risk managers are established, resources for regular risk management and reporting are provided, and formal ERM procedures are implemented. At the advanced level, high uncertainty and black swan risks are also identified, quantified, and integrated into formal ERM processes.

Measurement of ERM Maturity

There are **questionnaires and criteria** for the measurement of the different maturity levels for each ERM maturity model. As a rule, a higher maturity level can only be reached when all criteria of the lower maturity levels and the criteria of the targeted maturity level are completely fulfilled. The assessment of the criteria is mostly done by self-assessment of the companies, but an independent assessment by an external auditor is also often possible. Table 12.5 gives an overview of the ERM maturity criteria of Hillson's model.

It is not reasonable for all companies to always reach the highest level of maturity. Rather, the maturity level must be appropriate in relation to the risk profile of the company, its dynamics, and the risk factors in its environment.

Table 12.5 Attributes of RMM levels (source: Hillson, 1997)

Dimensions	Level 1—naïve	Level 2—novice	Level 3—normalized	Level 4—natural
Culture	• No risk awareness • Resistant/reluctant to change • Tendency to continue with existing processes	• Risk process may be viewed as additional overhead with variable benefits • RM only used on selected projects	• Accepted policy for RM • Benefits recognized and expected • Prepared to commit resources to reap gains	• Top-down commitment to RM, with leadership by example • Proactive RM encouraged and rewarded
Process	• No formal processes	• No generic formal process, although some formal methods may be in use • Process effectiveness depends heavily on the skills of the in-house RM team and availability of external support	• Generic processes applied to most projects • Formal processes, incorporated to quality system • Active allocation and management of risk budget at all levels • Limited need for external support	• Risk-based business processes • Regular refreshing and updating of processes • Routine risk metrics with consistent feedback for improvement
Experience	• No understanding of risk principles or language	• Limited to individuals with little formal training	• In-house core of expertise, formally trained in basic skills • Development of specific processes and tools	• All staff are risk-aware and use basic skills. Learning from experience as part of the process • Regular external training of skills
Application	• No structured application • No dedicated resources • No risk tools	• Inconsistent application • Variable availability of staff • Ad hoc collection of tools and methods	• Routine and consistent application to all projects • Committed resources • Integrated set of tools	• Second nature, applied to all activities • Risk-based reporting and decision-making • State-of-the-art tools and methods

12.7 Summary

- Risk governance consists of external and internal organizational mechanisms for the ERM process to reduce agency problems related to risk management.

- The organizational structure assigns the ERM tasks and the competences necessary for their completion to specific positions of organizational units. The process organization places the tasks in a meaningful relationship to each other in terms of subject matter, time, personnel, and space. The organizational structure and the process organization ensure the effective and efficient implementation of the operational ERM process.
- The degree of institutionalization and centralization of ERM is determined within the framework of the organizational structure.
- ERM takes place in the company based on a division of labor between managers, employees of the operative units, central (and decentralized) ERM units, and other internal and external control bodies such as management accounting, internal auditing, or the supervisory board.
- The cooperation between the different positions and organizational units with respect to ERM can be organized based on the TL(D) model.
- Risk managers take on different roles in the company, such as compliance champions or business partners, that determine their tasks and thus their competence profile.
- Due to the definition of risks as deviations from corporate targets, ERM tasks can also be integrated into the management accounting function, which is usually responsible for planning, budgeting, and performance evaluations in a company.
- There are different levels of ERM implementation, also known as ERM maturity levels. Not every company should aim for the highest maturity level.

12.8 Questions and Exercises

1. Define the term "risk governance" in the context of ERM.
2. Which criteria need to be considered when implementing an ERM organization?
3. Which positions and organizational units are involved in ERM? Which ERM tasks do they take on? Create a tabular overview.
4. Which roles can risk managers take on? Which task and competence profiles would you assign to the individual roles?
5. Describe the three lines of defense (TLD) model. What are the differences between the TLD and the TL model?
6. Discuss the benefits of an integrated approach to ERM and management accounting.
7. Distinguish between different levels of ERM maturity in companies.

References

Arena, M., & Arnaboldi, M. (2014). Risk and performance management: Are they easy partners? *Management Research Review, 37*, 152–166. https://doi.org/10.1108/MRR-08-2012-0180

Aven, T., & Thekdi, S. (2020). *Enterprise risk management: Advances on its foundation and practice*. Routledge, Taylor & Francis Group.

Beasley, M. S., Clune, R., & Hermanson, D. R. (2005). Enterprise risk management: An empirical analysis of factors associated with the extent of implementation. *Journal of Accounting and Public Policy, 24*, 521–531.

Burger, A., & Buchhart, A. (2014). *Risiko-controlling*. Walter de Gruyter GmbH & Co KG.

Colquitt, L. L., Hoyt, R. E., & Lee, R. B. (1999). Integrated risk management and the role of the risk manager. *Risk Management and Insurance Review, 2*, 43–61.

COSO. (2017). Enterprise risk management - integrating with strategy and performance.

Davies, H., & Zhivitskaya, M. (2018). Three lines of defence: A robust organising framework, or just lines in the sand? *Global Policy, 9*, 34–42.

Diederichs, M. (2018). *Risikomanagement und Risikocontrolling* (4th ed.). Vahlen.

Gleißner, W. (2022). *Grundlagen des Risikomanagements: Handbuch für ein Management unter Unsicherheit* (Management competence) (4th ed.). Verlag Franz Vahlen.

Gleißner, W., Mott. (2008). Risikomanagement auf dem Prüfstand - Nutzen, Qualität und Herausforderungen in der Zukunft. ZRFG Zeitschrift for Risk, *Fraud & Governance, 2*, 53–63.

Gleißner, W., Stein, V., Wiedemann, A. (2021). Die business judgement rule als treiberder evolution des risikomanagements. *Der Betrieb, 27*(28), 1485–1490.

Gleißner, W., Günther, T., & Walkshäusl, C. (2022). Financial sustainability: Measurement and empirical evidence. *Journal of Business Economics, 92*, 467–516.

Hall, M., Mikes, A., & Millo, Y. (2015). How do risk managers become influential? A field study of toolmaking in two financial institutions. *Management Accounting Research, 26*, 3–22.

Hillson, D. A. (1997). Towards a risk maturity model. *The international journal of project and Business risk management, 1*, 35–45.

Hunziker, S. (2021). *Enterprise risk management: Modern approaches to balancing risk and reward* (2nd ed.). Springer.

Hunziker, S., & Meissner, J. O. (2017). *Risikomanagement in 10 Schritten*. Springer.

Jankensgård, H., & Kapstad, P. (2021). *Empowered enterprise risk management: Theory and practice*. Wiley.

Karanja, E., & Rosso, M. A. (2017). The Chief Risk Officer: A study of roles and responsibilities. *Risk Management, 19*, 103–130.

Lee, C. R., & Shimpi, P. (2005). The chief risk officer: What does it look like and how do you get there? *Risk Management, 52*, 34–38.

Liebenberg, A. P., & Hoyt, R. E. (2003). The determinants of enterprise risk management: Evidence from the appointment of chief risk officers. *Risk Management and Insurance Review, 6*, 37–52.

Mikes, A. (2008). Chief risk officers at crunch time: Compliance champions or business partners? *Journal of Risk Management in Financial Institutions, 2*, 7–25.

Mikes, A. (2009). Risk management and calculative cultures. *Management Accounting Research, 20*, 18–40. https://doi.org/10.1016/j.mar.2008.10.005

Mikes, A. (2010). Becoming the lamp bearer. *Enterprise risk management. Today's leading research and best practices for tomorrow's executives*, 71–85.

Mikes, A., & Kaplan, R. S. (2015). When one size doesn't fit all: Evolving directions in the research and practice of enterprise risk management. *Journal of Applied Corporate Finance, 27*, 37–40.

Pagach, D., & Warr, R. (2011). The characteristics of firms that hire chief risk officers. *Journal of Risk and Insurance, 78*, 185–211.

Renn, O. (2008). *Risk governance: Coping with uncertainty in a complex world. Earthscan risk in society series*. Earthscan.

Rieg, R., & Vanini, U. (2021). Compliance als Aufgabe des Risikomanagements? Ein empirischer Vergleich von KMU und Großunternehmen anhand von Stellenanzeigen. *Zeitschr. für KMU und Entrepreneurship, 69*, 247–273.

Rieg, R., Meier, J.-H., & Finckh, C. (2023). Beware of the watchdog! Role communication in job advertisements for management accountants. *Journal of Applied Accounting Research, 24*, 889–909.

Slagmulder, R., & Devoldere, B. (2018). Transforming under deep uncertainty: A strategic perspective on risk management. *Business Horizons, 61*, 733–743. https://doi.org/10.1016/j.bushor.2018.05.001

Stein, V., & Wiedemann, A. (2016). Risk governance: conceptualization, tasks, and research agenda. *Journal of Business Economics, 86*, 813–836. https://doi.org/10.1007/s11573-016-0826-4

The Institute of Internal Auditors. (2013). *The three lines of defense in effective risk management and control*. https://theiia.fi/wp-content/uploads/2017/01/pp-the-three-lines-of-defense-in-effective-risk-management-and-control.pdf

The Institute of Internal Auditors. (2020). *The IIA's three lines model: An update on the three lines of defense*. https://www.theiia.org/globalassets/documents/resources/the-iias-three-lines-model-an-update-of-the-three-lines-of-defense-july-2020/three-lines-model-updated-english.pdf

Turner, D. (2022). Three lines of defence—is it the right model? *Journal of Financial Compliance, 5*, 237–247.

Vanini, U. (2018). Rollenmodelle von Risikomanagern–Ein empirischer Vergleich von Fremdbild und Selbstbild. Nadig, L. und Egle, U.(Hrsg.): *CARF Luzern*, 227–244.

Vanini, U., & Gutacker, H. (2019). Rollen und Zufriedenheit von Risikomanagern–Ergebnisse einer Befragung in Deutschland und der Schweiz. *Controller Magazin, 44*, 58–64.

Vanini, U., & Hunziker, S. (2020). Kompetenzprofile von Risikomanagern: Anforderungen nach COSO ERM und Umsetzungsstand. *Controlling, 32*, 30–37.

Vanini, U., & Rieg, R. (2021). *Risikomanagement: Grundlagen -- Instrumente -- Unternehmenspraxis* (Lehrbuch) (2nd ed.). Schäffer-Poeschel Verlag Stuttgart.

Vanini, U., Hunziker, S., & Unruh, A. (2022). Dynamische Fähigkeiten und Krisenbewältigung: Der Beitrag des Risikomanagements zur Bewältigung der COVID-19-Krise. *Betriebswirtschaftliche Forschung und Praxis, 74*, 649–677.

Will, M. (2020). The CoViD-19 pandemic and the end of corporate risk management as we know it. *CEREM, 4*, 89–115. https://doi.org/10.29015/cerem.888

Wiswede, G. (1977). *Rollentheorie*. Kohlhammer.

Wolke, T. (2016). *Risikomanagement*, 3., überarb. u. akt. Aufl. de Gruyter/Oldenbourg.

Chapter 13
Case Studies: Risk Analysis, Company Valuation, and Strategy Valuation

Abstract This chapter uses two case studies to illustrate how key methods and concepts of modern enterprise risk management explained in the book can be applied. The case study in Sect. 13.1 shows how a company's strategic option can be evaluated in a risk-appropriate manner. In particular, it illustrates the implementation of the valuation methods explained in Chap. 11, which combine risk analysis and aggregation with discount rate and shareholder value. The case study in Sect. 13.2 shows how an existing integrated business plan is linked to risks to generate a range planning using risk aggregation (Monte Carlo simulation). It shows how key metrics are derived to describe the overall risk exposure of the business.

Keywords Case study · Corporate planning · Corporate strategy · Risk analysis · Valuation

Questions
- How can a company evaluate a strategy by weighing risk and return?
- How can a traditional corporate planning expanded into range planning by linking it with identified and quantified risks?

13.1 Case Study: Strategy Valuation

13.1.1 Overview

Besides adequate risk valuation (simulation-based valuation), another important field of application of risk analysis is strategy valuation (for an alternative case study, see Gleißner & Ernst, 2019). This is used to prepare decisions to be made by the board of directors or management. In the following case study, a strategy valuation is carried out for a listed company. This valuation method is based on

Supplementary Information The online version contains supplementary material available at https://doi.org/10.1007/978-3-031-86425-4_13.

R. Rieg et al., *Enterprise Risk Management*, Springer Texts in Business and Economics, https://doi.org/10.1007/978-3-031-86425-4_13

the standard deviation or the coefficient of variation of cash flows, which captures the extent of possible deviations from the plan (see Chap. 10). As with CAPM, the shareholders' risk diversification options are also considered. The effect of an outsourcing strategy on shareholder value is examined. Doing this enables us to determine whether this strategy makes sense considering return and risk. The idea of outsourcing was derived from the consideration of the strategic positioning and the essential success potential. The relevant section of the value chain does not show any viable potential for success in the company. Thus, an outsourcing strategy was developed through cooperation between the departments established for controlling, production, and logistics to reduce costs and increase earnings by lowering purchasing prices and reduce risks by replacing part of the fixed costs with variable costs.

Whether the corresponding concept is promising and thus leads to an increase in value is examined in the case study. In preparation for the strategy valuation, the aggregated total risk volume (earnings risk), the rating (probability of insolvency), and the risk-adjusted shareholder value (as a measure of success) are first determined to establish the status quo. Subsequently, an evaluation is performed to determine how a planned measure set out to optimize the supply chain (outsourcing of a key section of the value chain) will affect these parameters. The aim is to use the risk-return profile (and the shareholder value as a performance measure) to make a well-founded assessment of the economic added value of this idea, which initially appears strategically plausible.

13.1.2 Company Valuation with CAPM

The initial situation of the this case company can be characterized by the following figures: With total assets representing the capital employed (CE) of CE = US$100 million, the company has an equity ratio of 30% (Gleißner & Ernst, 2023). The interest-bearing net financial liabilities (debt) amount to D = US$50 million, and the non-interest-bearing debt is US$20 million. In the fiscal year t(0), an operating profit (EBIT) of US$11.5 million and a profit (taxes are neglected for the sake of simplicity) of US$10 million were generated on sales of US$200 million. Without growth, all profit can be distributed. The valuation is carried out using the flow to equity method (capitalized earnings method), but the entity valuation variant based on FCF is shown for comparison (Matschke & Brösel, 2021). The difference between EBIT and profit is the interest expense. The return on capital employed (ROCE) is therefore as follows:

$$\text{ROCE} = \frac{\text{EBIT}}{\text{CE}} = \frac{\text{US\$11.5 million}}{\text{US\$100 million}} = 11.5\% \tag{13.1}$$

In corporate planning, for the financial year $t = 1$ and all subsequent years, US$10 million profit is assumed with the highest probability (as planned value Profit ^{plan}). This profit is to be distributed to the shareholders (earnings = flow to equity = profit). Due to the difficult market conditions, management does not expect any growth in the future (growth rate $g = 0$). The valuation-relevant free cash flow (FCF) also allows the full distribution of profits. Using the Gordon-Shapiro model for an infinite annuity, the shareholder value (**Value**) is calculated here—based on assumptions considered to be credible and plausible—as follows (growth rate g would reduce FCF by CE * g and earnings by CE * g * equity ratio):

$$\text{Value}_1 = \frac{\text{FCF}^{\text{plan}}}{\text{WACC} - g} - D \approx \frac{\text{Profit}^{\text{plan}}}{c} = \frac{\text{Earning}^{\text{plan}}}{c} \tag{13.2}$$

The discount rate (cost of equity, c) is traditionally first derived based on historical stock return fluctuations using CAPM. Assuming, for comparison purposes, an expected return on the market portfolio (r_m^e) of 8%, a risk-free rate (r_f) of 3%, and a standard deviation of the market return (σ_m) of 20%, the beta factor can first be determined if the following two pieces of information are also derived from the historical stock price fluctuations (capital market data):

- Correlation (ρ) of the stock return to the market return 0.5.
- Standard deviation of the stock return (σ_i) 25%.

The beta factor is calculated as follows:

$$\beta = \rho \cdot \frac{\sigma_i}{\sigma_m} = 0.5 \cdot \frac{0.25}{0.2} = 0.625 \tag{13.3}$$

In accordance with the well-known CAPM return equation, the discount rate, assuming that the CAPM assumptions are valid, is as follows:

$$c^{\text{CAPM}} = r_f + \left(r_m^e - r_f\right) \cdot \beta = 0.03 + (0.08 - 0.03) \cdot 0.625 = 6.1\% \tag{13.4}$$

and for the shareholder value,

$$\text{Value}_1 = \frac{\text{Earning}^{\text{plan}}}{c^{\text{CAPM}}} = \frac{10}{6.1\%} = 163.9 \tag{13.5}$$

Value_1 stands for the value of variant 1, which corresponds to the CAPM approach. In this "traditional" approach, information on the risks of future earnings is not considered, nor is the probability of insolvency (p) expressed by the credit rating. Furthermore, no consideration is given to the extent to which the planned value, in this case the most probable value (modal value), is actually unbiased.

13.1.3 Risk-Adequate Company Valuation in the Initial Situation

In the following, the valuation case is refined to determine the "risk-adequate value" in the initial situation. In doing so, it is assumed that quantitative risk analysis has been carried out as part of risk management and that the aggregated total risk volume has been calculated using Monte Carlo simulation, which is explained in more detail below. In our case study, the risk aggregation for the status quo of the company (i.e.,

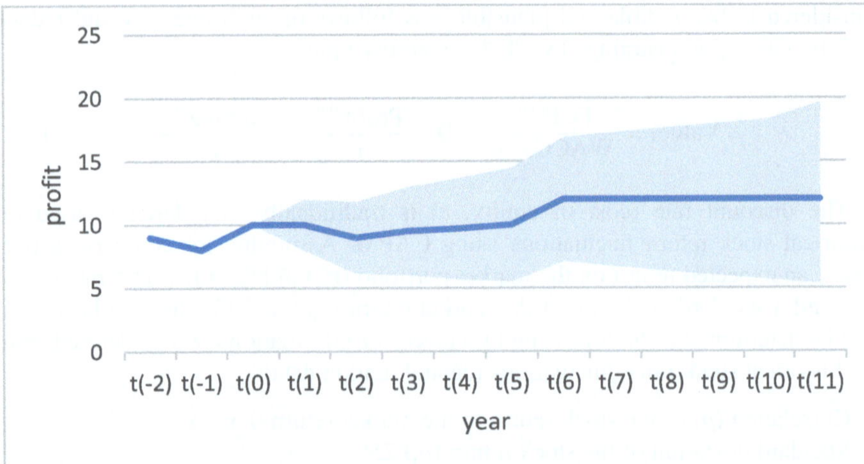

Fig. 13.1 Range of profit from Monte Carlo simulation (risk aggregation)

before implementation of the planned measure (outsourcing)) results in the following situation: The original planned value of the profit of US$10 million is not unbiased. This value does not show what profit can be expected "on average" across all risk-related possible scenarios (Gleißner, 2019; also see Chap. 5). We can easily derive the expected value of the profit as an average of all simulated scenarios from the risk aggregation. It amounts to US$9 million (note: the individual risks are not presented here). This means that an average of US$9 million can be expected for all risk-related possible future scenarios (as mentioned, this value is considered representative of the future below). Of course, it is also possible to look at the earnings of the detailed planning period independently (Gleißner & Ernst, 2019). Due to an existing risk overhang compared to the opportunities, the expected value relevant to valuation is lower than the planned value of US$10 million (see Fig. 13.1).

The expected return on assets, which strongly influences the credit rating in addition to the equity ratio (30%), is calculated as follows, assuming the time-variant expected value of profit (US$9 million), but the case with consideration of the simulation result and interest (US$1.5 million). EBIT is consequently US$10.5 million.

$$\mathrm{ROCE} = \frac{\text{US\$10.5 million}}{\text{US\$100 million}} = 10.5\% \tag{13.6}$$

Adequate consideration of the probability of insolvency p (of the credit rating), and the impacts of opportunities and threats (risks) relevant to the expected value of earnings or cash flows, is necessary in any proper company valuation, especially in strategy valuation. The probability of insolvency acts like a negative growth rate in the long term that means (see Chap. 10):

$$\text{Value} = \frac{\text{Earning}^e(1-p)}{c+p} \tag{13.7}$$

The insolvency probability is not a premium on the cost of capital, as it is in the build-up models. There is no double counting of a risk because p "only" captures the effect on expected earnings over time (just like a growth rate). Given a growth rate g, the (conditional) expected values of the earnings Earning^e, and a discount rate $\boldsymbol{c}$, the following equation results for the **shareholder value** in the going concern phase (terminal value) as a function of the insolvency probability p (i.e., after detailed planning phase), and a discount rate c results in Eq. (13.8) for the shareholder value in the going concern phase (terminal value) depending on the insolvency probability p (Franken et al., 2020; Gleißner, 2019; Saha & Malkiel, 2012):

$$\text{Value} = \sum\nolimits_{t=1}^{\infty} \frac{\text{earning}^e(1-p)^t \cdot (1+g)^t}{(1+c)^t} = \frac{\text{earning}^e(1-p)\cdot(1+g)}{r_e - g + p\cdot(1+g)} \tag{13.8}$$

This also applies if one wishes to derive the cost of capital (discount rates) based on the CAPM. So additionally, the rating is also considered (risk of insolvency/bankruptcy). This indicates the insolvency risk, which is expressed by the probability of insolvency. Credit rating and insolvency probability can be estimated using the Monte Carlo simulation (for simulation-based rating and evaluation procedures and an example using the "strategy navigator" software used here, see Gleißner (2019)). In a simplified form, the probability of insolvency can be estimated using financial ratios for the planned year equity ratio and ROCE, by means of the following "mini-rating" (Gleißner, 2022, pp. 433–434; alternatively, see Altman, 2000, Drobetz & Heller, 2014, or Krotter & Schüler, 2013, which includes approximate S&P ratings using a simple financial ratio system):

$$\begin{aligned} p &= \frac{0.265}{1+e^{-0.41+7.42\cdot\text{equity ratio}+11.2\cdot\text{ROCE}}} = \frac{0.265}{1+e^{-0.41+7.42\cdot 0.30+11.2\cdot 0.105}} \\ &= 1.3\% \end{aligned} \tag{13.9}$$

The insolvency probability derived from a simple financial ratio system can be estimated even more soundly using somewhat more complex ratio systems. For a supplementary plausibility check of the insolvency probability, considering the aggregated earnings risks neglected in financial ratios, risk aggregation with the Monte Carlo simulation can again be used. In this process, each simulation run checks of whether illiquidity or over-indebtedness occurs. Often, the company can already be assumed to be illiquid if either (a) covenants are breached in a simulation run or (b) a financial ratio rating of "B" is no longer guaranteed due to losses. In our case study, the risk simulation results in a fairly similar probability of insolvency. In the following, we will continue to calculate using an insolvency probability of $p = 1.3\%$ given in Eq. (13.9).

If the company is to be assessed from the perspective of a long-term committed investor (owner, shareholder) and it is assumed that the valuation-relevant risks of future earnings are not reflected in historical stock returns, the following derivation of the cost of capital rates based on earnings risks is recommended.

It is important to emphasize here that the risk-adequate valuation method can always be applied if the risk content of the cash flows or earnings (flow-to-equity) is captured by a risk measure, such as σ_{Earning} here. In the simplest case, the determination of the risk measure can simply be performed as an estimate or be based on a statistical evaluation of historical profit fluctuations (Gleißner et al., 2022).

However, it is recommended to use the best available information about the future risks of a company, which ultimately determines the level of the risk measure (i.e., the standard deviation). This is made possible using the simulation-based variant of the risk-adequate valuation of the company outlined here. The starting point here, as explained in Sect. 8.1, is a risk analysis plus risk aggregation using MCS (see Sect. 5.5). In this procedure, the main risks of a company are first systematically identified. For example, all of a company's uncertain planning premises are taken as a risk (e.g., assumptions about exchange rates, raw material prices, or the sales growth rate). The risks are described by suitable probability distributions, such as an exchange rate fluctuation with a normal distribution or the uncertain growth rate specifying (a) minimum value, (b) most probable value, and (c) maximum value (triangular distribution or beta-pert distribution). All risks are assigned to the integrated corporate planning items in which they can trigger deviations from the plan. Risk aggregation (Monte Carlo simulation) based on this risk analysis is then used to calculate a sufficiently large representative number of future scenarios. In this way, the expected value and, consistently, the risk measure of cash flows or flow-to-equity can be derived.

In the simple case study here, all of the outlined methods, including risk analysis and risk aggregation, lead to similar results in the standard deviation of return (flow-to-equity) as the risk measure to be used to determine the cost of capital (C).

The risk aggregation (risk simulation) allows quantification of the earnings risk, expressed by the standard deviation of earnings. This corresponds to the standard deviation of profit $\sigma_{\text{Earning}} =$ US\$3.1 million (the standard deviation of the past is US \$3.47 million and thus similar; see Fig. 13.2). The standard deviation of profit can be interpreted as a measure of planning certainty. This corresponds to the Value at Risk (e.g., at the 99% level) and in the case study is around US\$13 million (VaR).

The correlation of the earnings (or changes in earnings) of companies to the stock market index is $d = 0.5$, which thus corresponds to the degree of risk diversification d (see Gleißner and Ernst (2023) for derivation).

Equation (13.10) can be used to calculate the following risk-adjusted discount rate [derivation, e.g., in Gleißner (2019)]. The equation converts the coefficient of variation (VC) derived from risk analysis and risk aggregation into an expected return corresponding to this risk (i.e., a risk-adequate discount rate (c)). The derivation is based on the method of "imperfect replication" (see Chap. 10 and Dorfleitner and Gleißner (2018)).

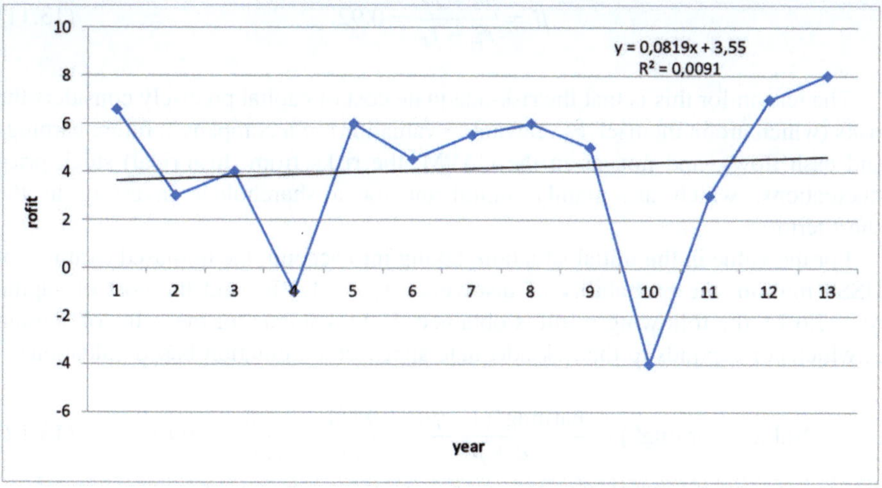

Fig. 13.2 Profit development in recent years (in US$ million; source: Gleißner, 2013)

In the case study, it is assumed that the correlation of earnings to the return (or earnings) of the market portfolio is as high as the correlation between the company's shares and the market portfolio (i.e., $d = \rho = 0.5$; see Eq. (13.10)). It is possible that some entrepreneurs who essentially own their companies will set $d = 1$ when determining subjective decision values (i.e., neglect risk diversification effects; see Kerins et al. (2004) and the total beta approach, which assumes $d = 1$).

$$c = \frac{1 + r_f}{1 - \lambda \cdot CV \cdot d} - 1 = \frac{1 + r_f}{1 - \lambda \cdot \frac{\sigma_{\text{Earning}}}{\text{Earning}_2^e} \cdot d} - 1 = \frac{1 + 3\%}{1 - 0.25 \cdot \frac{3.1}{9} \cdot 0.5} - 1 = 7.6\% \quad (13.10)$$

with $\lambda = \frac{r_m^e - r_f}{\sigma_{r_m}} = \frac{8\% - 3\%}{20\%} = 0.25$ and

$\text{CV} = \frac{\sigma_{\text{Earning}}}{\text{Earning}^e}$ as coefficient of variation.

As can easily be seen, the ratio λ (Sharpe ratio) is exclusively derived from information that is also used in the CAPM (specifically beta factor; see Eqs. (13.3) and (13.4)). λ is a measure of the risk-return profile of alternative investment opportunities. Accordingly, a λ of 0.25 expresses that an additional return of 0.25% can be expected on the capital market per unit of increased risk. When evaluating the company, its risk-return profile is compared with that of the selected alternative investment options, in this case, government bonds and a broad stock market index like the MCSI World.

In our case study, the risk-adjusted cost of capital deviates significantly from that determined using the CAPM. The "implied beta factor" β', which can be calculated for comparison purposes, is:

$$\beta' = \frac{r_e - r_f}{r_m^e - r_f} = 0.92. \tag{13.11}$$

The reason for this is that the risk-adequate cost of capital precisely considers the risks (which are in themselves relevant to valuation) of a company's future earnings and cash flows, and not, as in the CAPM, the risks from (historical) stock price fluctuations, which are mainly significant for a shareholder investing in the short term.

For the value in the initial situation, taking into account the unbiased earnings of US$9 million, the probability of insolvency ($p = 1.3\%$), and the cost of capital ($c = 7.6\%$), the following result is obtained. Value_2 stands for the value of Variant 2, which corresponds to the risk-adequate approach (simulation-based valuation).

$$\text{Value}_2\left(\text{Earning}_2^e\right) = \frac{\text{earning}_2^e(1-p)}{c+p} = \frac{9 \cdot (1-1.3\%)}{7.6\% + 1.3\%} = 99.8 \tag{13.12}$$

13.1.4 Strategy Valuation: Risk-Adequate Valuation of an Option for Action

So far, we have looked at the initial situation of the company. The calculated (risk-adequate) enterprise value of US$99.8 million is to be interpreted as a "benchmark" (or hurdle rate) for the strategy valuation (i.e., the strategic action to be evaluated). Such a course of action makes sense precisely if it increases the sustainable success of the company (i.e., leads to an improvement in the risk-return profile). The basis of the evaluation is now an alternative business plan, in which the effects of the planned measures on sales, costs, and capital commitment are taken into account ("what-if analysis"). In the case study, it is assumed that the "internal" measure in the value chain will have no impact on sales. The capital commitment is also considered to be essentially unchanged.

From discussions and negotiations with the potential outsourcing partners, a significant improvement in profitability of one million dollars is forecasted (Δ profit = one million dollars). A structured risk analysis, which is not presented in detail here, shows that outsourcing has advantages and disadvantages in terms of the risk position. The advantage is that production-related risks (e.g., due to machine failure) are eliminated within the company because the corresponding activities are no longer carried out. Another advantage is that previously largely fixed costs are substituted by variable costs based on sales. However, a quantitative risk analysis also shows the downsides of outsourcing. An on-site visit to the production facility of the potential outsourcing partner by a team of experts with specialists from production, quality assurance, and logistics showed that, due to a large lack of redundancy, the technical insolvency probabilities at the partner company are higher than those previously seen at the company itself. In addition, a credit rating analysis of this company's key financial figures reveals a non-negligible insolvency risk, which could lead to the loss of a key supplier that is virtually impossible to replace in the short term. From publicly available data on equity ratio and profitability, a "B" rating is estimated, which implies an insolvency probability of no less than 5% per year.

This and other information regarding the changes in opportunities and threats (risks) in the event of outsourcing are now taken into account in the alternative planning. The change in the realistic range of the company's earnings and cash flows is shown using Monte Carlo simulation and risk aggregation. This occurs if the measure being assessed is implemented. In the case study, the expected increase in earnings to US$10 million ($\text{earning}_3^e$) is initially confirmed because, in addition to risks, some opportunities (further cost-saving opportunities) are also identified in the risk analysis. In addition, however, the risk aggregation shows a significant increase in the standard deviation of earnings (the risk measure) from US$3.1 million to US $4.2 million. This increase is caused by possible additional costs and lost sales in the event of a technical production stoppage (interruption of operations) or even insolvency of the future key supplier. However, the effects will not be so extreme as to have a significant impact on the company's own insolvency probability and rating. This means that an insolvency probability of $p = 1.3\%$ is still assumed.

Based on the increased predicted profitability and the simultaneously increased level of risk, we can now calculate the risk-adjusted cost of capital (c′) that would result in the case of an outsourcing decision (also d, which is the share of risks to be borne, is assumed to be constant. This can be examined as part of a detailed analysis. For the derivation of d, see Gleißner and Ernst (2023):

$$c' = \frac{1 + r_f}{1 - \lambda \cdot \frac{\sigma_{\text{Earning}_3}}{\text{Earning}_3^e} \cdot d} - 1 = \frac{1 + 3\%}{1 - 0.25 \cdot \frac{4.2}{10} \cdot 0.5} - 1 = 8.7\% \tag{13.13}$$

and

$$\text{Value}_3\left(\text{Earning}_3^e\right) = \frac{\text{Earning}_3^e}{c' + p} = \frac{10 \cdot (1 - 1.3\%)}{8.7\% + 1.3\%} = 98.7 \tag{13.14}$$

Value_3 stands for the value of Variant 3, which corresponds to the risk-adequate approach taking into account the strategic option. Here, the effect of outsourcing on shareholder value as a measure of success can be seen directly. As we can see, the shareholder value falls from US$99.8 million to US$98.7 million. The reason for this is that the risk-return profile deteriorates slightly. The increase in aggregate total risk and thus in the cost of capital more than compensates for the expected increase in profitability as a result of outsourcing. As mentioned above, this measure would not unduly affect the company's security of tenure (credit rating). However, it does not make economic sense when weighing up return and risk (refer to the following summary in Table 13.1).

Table 13.1 Evaluation of a strategic option for action

	Status quo	Strategic option
Expected earning	US$9 million	US$10 million
Risk (coefficient of variation earning)	34%	42%
Cost of capital	7.6%	8.7%
Rating forecast (probability of default)	1.3%	1.3%
Rating (stress scenario)	BB	BB
Value (in million US$)	99.8	98.7
Strategic fitting		Yes, but worse risk-return profile

13.2 Case Study: Budget Inc.—Bandwidth Planning

13.2.1 Introduction into the Case

The aggregation of the various identified and quantified risks requires the use of simulation methods because, unlike costs, risks cannot be added together, at least if one disregards special cases (normal distributions; Radinger et al., 2022). These simulation methods are the further development of known scenario analysis techniques (for a discussion of the significance, see Grisar and Meyer (2015)). Using Monte Carlo simulation, a large representative number of possible future scenarios are analyzed during risk aggregation. In this way, frequency distribution and thus a realistic range of future cash flows and expenses/income are shown (i.e., the planning reliability or the scope of possible deviations from the plan is presented). In this way, planned values of income or cash flows that are true to expectations are determined, taking into account the risks. Ambitious or conservative planned values are reconciled with expected values (Behringer & Gleißner, 2021). The probability that covenants will be breached or that a required minimum rating will no longer be achieved in the future can also be derived directly, for example. The breach of covenants is usually a serious crisis. The insolvency risk can therefore also be derived directly from the risk simulation (e.g., expressed by the probability of danger and/or the probability of insolvency (rating)). To better illustrate this topic, we will use a numerical example below.

13.2.2 Starting Point

The case study company (Budget Inc.) is a medium-sized company in the mechanical engineering sector. Budget Inc. is on a course for growth. Therefore, a (gross) investment of US$7 million in an additional production hall is planned to expand capacity in the planning year (Year 2). There are also plans to enter new markets in Eastern Europe.

The left column of Table 13.2 shows the planned P&L. The basis here is the total cost method commonly used in Germany. The rudimentary structure of the

Table 13.2 Linking the income statement, balance sheet, and cash flow statement

Step 1: P&L statement	year 1	year 2
Revenues		17,467
- change in inventory	-	1,205
+ capitalized expenses		-
= *total output*		*16,262*
- cost of materiasls/purchased services (P)	-	4,427
- production wages/social costs (P)	-	2,214
- salaries & other wages/social costs (S)	-	2,509
- other production costs (P)	-	738
- general expenses(S)	-	2,463
- allocated pension provisions (S)		-
- allocations to other provisions	-	100
= EBITDA		3,811
- Depreciation (S)	-	850
= EBIT		2,961
- interest expenses	-	800
- income taxtes	-	648
= net income/profit of the year		1,513

Step 2: Balance sheet	year 1	year 2
property and real estate	1,200	5,050
machinery	1,200	3,700
Fixtures and Fittings	800	600
capitalized expenses	800	-
fixed assets	*4,000*	*9,350*
accounts receivables	3,000	1,439
Materials and supplies	2,000	369
finished/unfinished goods	6,600	5,395
Cash and cash equivalents	400	326
current assets	*12,000*	*7,529*
TOTAL ASSETS	16,000	16,879
	Jahr 1	Jahr 2
subscribed capital	3,500	3,500
retained earnings	855	855
Net income/profit	-	1,513
equity capital	*4,355*	*5,868*
Pension provisions	1,000	1,000
long-term debt	2,000	2,000
long-term debt capital	*3,000*	*3,000*
other provisions	445	545
short-term credits	5,300	5,800
advance payments	200	1,200
accounts payables	2,700	466
short-term debt capital	*8,645*	*8,011*
TOTAL EQUITY AND DEBT	16,000	16,879

	Step 3: cash flow statement	Jahr 1	Jahr 2
	Net income/profit		1,513
	+ Depreciaton		850
	+ decrease in accounts receivables		1,561
	+ decrease in materials and supplies		1,631
	+ decrease in finished/unfinished goods		1,205
	+ increase in advanced payments		1,000
	- decrease in accounts payables	-	2,234
	+ increase in pension provisions		-
	+ increase in othe provisions		100
	+ interest expense		800
	+ income tax expense		648
	- income tax paid	-	648
(1)	OPERATING CASH FLOW		6,426
	- increase in fixed assets	-	6,200
(2)	CASHFLOW FROM INVESTING ACTIVITIES	-	6,200
(1)+(2)	FREE CASHFLOW		226
	- decrease in long-term debt		-
	- interest expense	-	800
	+ increase in short-term debt		500
	- Dividends		-
(3)	CASHFLOW FROM FINANCING ACTIVITIES	-	300
(1)+(2)+(3)	Decrease in cash and cash equivalents	-	74

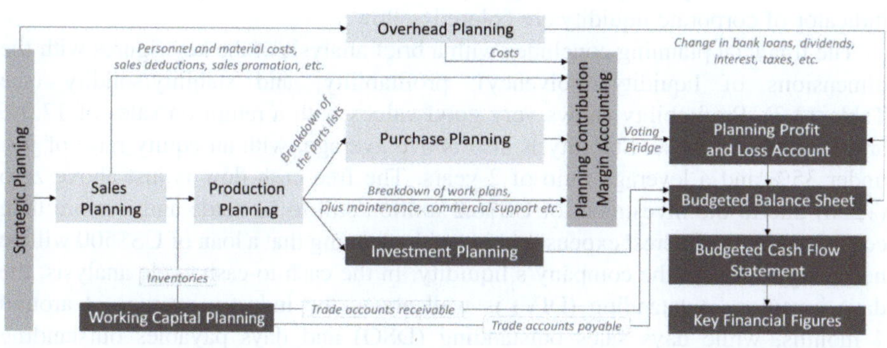

Fig. 13.3 Financial planning (black) is the final stage of the planning process

contribution margin accounting can still be recognized here. The items labelled with (P) represent **product costs** (variable/proportional/volume-dependent) according to the logic of contribution margins, those with an (S) represent **structural costs** (fixed/volume-independent).

The unlabeled P&L items are shown in the reconciliation bridge shown in Fig. 13.3.

To keep Fig. 13.3 clear but still show the diverse links between the three instruments, a color code was used for the most important items. The so-called **non-cash transactions** (i.e., balance sheet changes that have no effect on payments) are shown in blue. The depreciation of fixed assets and changes in provisions are

Table 13.3 Key figure analysis of financial planning

Key figures	
1. Liquidity	
$\text{DSO} = \frac{\text{Demands} \times 360}{\text{Sales}} =$	30 days
$\text{DIV} = \frac{\text{Stocks} \cdot 360}{\text{Sales}} =$	119 days
$\text{DPO} = \frac{\text{Liabilities from deliveries and services} \cdot 360}{\text{Material usage} + \text{Paid benefit}} =$	38 days
Cash-to-Cash-Cycle=DSO+DIV-DPO=	111 days
2. Profitability	
$\text{ROS} = \frac{\text{EBIT}}{\text{Sales}} =$	17.0 %
$\text{ROI} = \frac{\text{EBIT}}{\text{Average total assets}} =$	18.0 %
3. Stability	
$\text{Equity ratio} = \frac{\text{Equity capital}}{\text{Total assets}} =$	34.8 %
$\text{Leverage ratio} = \frac{\text{Net financial debt}}{\text{EBITDA}} =$	2.0

eliminated in the cash flow statement from the net profit for the year (shown in green as the final result of the income statement and also the starting basis for the cash flow statement). The items or changes in working capital, of which the changes in inventories of finished goods and work in progress appear in all three accounts, are colored red. Interest expense (colored gray) is assumed to be fully cash-effective. It is reclassified to cash flow from financing activities in the cash flow statement. **Cash and cash equivalents and changes in cash and cash equivalents** as a key indicator of corporate liquidity are colored yellow.

The financial planning concludes with a brief analysis of the key figures with the dimensions of liquidity (solvency), profitability, and stability/solidity (see Table 13.3). Profitability shows very good values with a return on sales of 17.0% and an ROI of 18.0%. Stability is also above average, with an equity ratio of just under 35% and a leverage ratio of 2 years. The free cash flow is just above zero (+226) due to the investment of US$6.2 million still to be made and is more than consumed by the interest expenses to be paid, meaning that a loan of US$500 will be necessary to secure the company's liquidity. In the cash-to-cash cycle analysis, the days inventory outstanding (DIV) is well above the industry average at around 4 months, while days sales outstanding (DSO) and days payables outstanding (DPO) are at an acceptable level.

13.2.3 Analyzing the Main Risks

Every assumption in corporate planning is uncertain, so this is the starting point for analyzing the underlying risks. In the case of Budget Inc., we will focus on the following key risks from a risk analysis:

Risk 1: fluctuations in demand—Sales are subject to normal market fluctuations in demand. To quantify this uncertainty, the typical fluctuations of a company in the mechanical engineering sector of 10% around the planned value are used (normal distribution). Market variables, such as demand or exchange rates, fluctuate in an approximately normally distributed manner. Based on the assumption of the distribution and the fluctuation range (standard normal distribution), the maximum fluctuation range can be estimated as three times the standard deviation. To simplify matters, sales are not broken down into price and quantity.

Risk 2: exchange rate risk (US dollar)—40% of planned sales are invoiced in US dollars. Corresponding payments on the purchasing side, on the other hand, only account for 20% of the cost of materials. A partial "natural hedging" therefore takes place. The typical fluctuation range of the USD in the budget year is estimated at around 7.5%.

Risk 3: inherent fluctuations in costs—In planning, costs are categorized into (volume-dependent) product costs and (volume-independent) structural costs. It is assumed that the product costs are 100% variable in relation to the fluctuations in demand. The product cost ratio initially remains constant with fluctuating sales volumes (true to margin). Structural costs, on the other hand, are not influenced by fluctuations in sales. However, this dependency (volume variability) does not yet represent an independent risk, but rather an (indirect) effect based on the uncertainty (risk) of sales revenues. Irrespective of the influence of other risks, there are still uncertainties for the cost items. These inherent fluctuations include risks such as price fluctuations in purchasing (use of materials) that cannot be passed on to the customer. In the case study, statistically analyzed historical fluctuations were used, which are considered representative of the future. The product costs fluctuate by 5% and the structural costs by a (relatively high) 10%.

Risk 4: risk from legal proceedings—Antitrust proceedings are currently underway against Budget GmbH for prohibited price fixing in sales. The probability of a negative outcome for the company is estimated at 25%, which is why no provision has been recognized to date. If the probability of occurrence of the risk is estimated at 50% or higher and a plan correction or provisions in the amount of the expected loss are recognized, there is a chance that the amount of the loss will be lower or that the risk will not occur at all. The empirical value from the past for the penalty in similar cases was (converted) 1000 plus procedural costs of 250. The maximum penalty is capped at 10% of turnover (i.e., 1750). A triangular distribution (Gleißner, 2022) is therefore assumed with a minimum value (250), most probable value (1250) and maximum value (2000).

Investment risk: There are further risks for the planned production hall, which in combination could have a significant impact on the financial situation. Such risks need additional risk analyses as well as valuing the possible impact on the company.

13.2.4 Risk Aggregation Using Monte Carlo Simulation: Bandwidth Planning

The main risks have now been analyzed, and each has been described with a distribution function. A dynamic planning model is required to be able to carry out risk aggregation. The planning or the individual planning items must be checked for further interdependencies, and the planning model must be expanded to include appropriate links (including assumptions to be made; planning logic).

Links between the income statement and balance sheet are shown above (e.g., via the net income for the year and the cash flow statement or the quantity variability of the cost items). The working capital items have not yet been considered. For the planning model, DSO, DIV, and DPO are kept constant (and assumed to be certain). Working capital therefore only fluctuates depending on sales and cost of materials/ services. For fixed assets and provisions, the (simplifying) assumption was made that these are safe (i.e., risk-free) and therefore remain unchanged (and thus also the depreciation and amortization and the expenses for the creation of provisions).

A Monte Carlo simulation is now carried out using the dynamic (integrated) planning model mapped in the software and the risks linked to the planning items. This means that a large number of random scenarios are generated and analyzed. In each scenario, a random characteristic is determined for each of the risks (the distribution functions are used for this), and the planning item on which the respective risks have an effect is recalculated. In accordance with the planning logic and risk effects, the planning is calculated once and saved. In the case study, 100,000 scenarios were calculated (which took less than five seconds). The planning model was created in Excel. The Excel add-in Crystal Ball was used to model the risks and carry out the risk aggregation using Monte Carlo simulation.

13.2.5 Simulation Results

Typical reasons for insolvency are a company's over-indebtedness on the one hand and (even imminent) inability to pay on the other hand. Critical variables in the planning model are therefore the net profit for the year and the cash flow in terms of the change in cash and cash equivalents. For reasons of clarity, the following analysis is limited to EBIT and net income. Table 13.4 shows the most important results resulting from the simulation-based risk aggregation.

The expected values (averaged values of all simulation results) of EBIT and net income show that a negative deviation from the plan is to be expected. This is due to the risk overhang of the risks. The cause is the risk from the legal proceedings (irrespective of the amount of loss), which represents a pure risk. The expected deviation from the plan is shown graphically in Fig. 13.4.

The **coefficient of variation** represents the fluctuation range of the net profit for the year and is a measure of planning reliability. Figure 13.4 shows the upper and

Table 13.4 Simulation results (expected values, EW)

Simulation results	Expected value	Δ to plan value
EBIT	2626.7	−334.3
Net income for the year	1257.9	−255.1
Coefficient of variation Net income for the year	82.8%	
Cost of capital (COC)	14.9%	
Equity ratio (ER)	33.1%	−1.7%
Return on sales (ROS)	15,0%	−1.9%
Return on investment (ROI)	15.5%	−2.5%
Rating forecast/probability of insolvency via		
1. Equity ratio; ROS	0.3%	
2. Equity ratio; ROI	0.6%	
1. and 2. averaged	0.5%	
Hazard if rating < B rating, i.e. PD >10%		
Probability of hazard	0.8%	
probability of default (PD) according to target rating	0.5%	
Equity requirement	1927.3	
Equity coverage	226.0%	

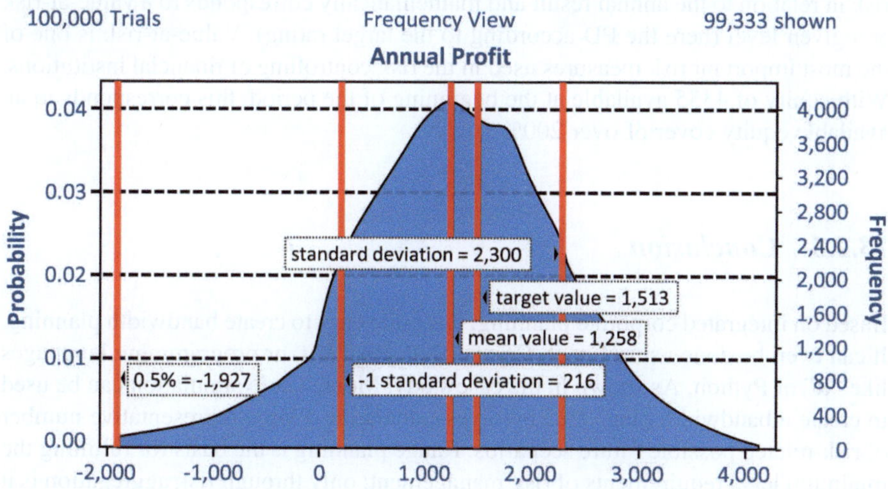

Fig. 13.4 Frequency distribution of net income from the simulation

lower limits of the fluctuation range as the upper and lower standard deviation. The standard deviation of 1042 divided by the expected value of 1258 results in a coefficient of variation of 82.8%. At around 83%, this is within an acceptable range for SMEs. The associated cost of capital (**cost of equity**) is just under 15% (for calculation see Gleißner, 2022).

Using a mini-rating system (Gleißner, 2022), the **probability of insolvency** can be predicted based on two financial ratios. This simulates the rating behavior of the banks. Two mini-rating systems are used for the case study and their results are averaged. Due to the very strong profitability (ROS, ROI) and the above-average stability (**equity ratio**), the predicted probability of default (PD) is 0.5% and therefore in the investment grade range. The PD was forecast using the expected values (i.e., the rating forecast was based on planning in line with expectations). The formulas for estimation can be found in Gleißner et al. (2022) and Berger and Kamaras (2020).

In addition to the PD, the **probability of missing covenants** should also be considered. This indicates the probability that a minimum rating required by the bank for granting a loan will not be achieved. The minimum rating to be achieved is usually a "B" rating, which corresponds to a PD of (on average) 10%. The probability of default is generally higher than the PD forecast on financial ratios and is 0.8% in our case. The probability of danger here only considers the granting of debt capital and no other options for covering liquidity requirements.

In its risk policy, the company has set itself the goal of achieving a probability of insolvency of less than or equal to 0.5% to obtain an investment grade rating. According to this target, the **equity capital requirement** (ECB) can be determined to be sufficient to cover losses (net loss for the year), in this case with a probability of 99.5% (= 1 – 0.5%). In the example case, the ECB is 1927. The ECB is a measure of risk in relation to the annual result and mathematically corresponds to a value-at-risk at a given level (here the PD according to the target rating). Value-at-risk is one of the most important risk measures used in the risk controlling of financial institutions. With equity of 4355 available at the beginning of the period, this corresponds to an available equity cover of over 200%.

13.2.6 Conclusion

Based on integrated corporate planning, it is quite easy to create bandwidth planning. It can even be done using Excel, Crystal Ball, Risk Kit, or programming languages like "R" or Python. As shown in the case study, Monte Carlo simulation can be used to create a bandwidth plan. This involves calculating a large representative number of risk-related possible future scenarios. Range planning is the basis for fulfilling the minimum legal requirements of risk management: only through risk aggregation is it possible to determine the degree to which a company's existence is at risk (probability of danger in accordance with the risk-bearing capacity concept). This type of range planning helps in specifying forecast values that are true to expectations, which are required for the preparation of business decisions (business judgement rule), especially for investment evaluation. The key figures derived from range planning also provide the information basis for implementing value-oriented corporate management: The key figure for the aggregated scope of risk, such as the coefficient of variation, can also be used to derive risk-adjusted cost of capital rates consistent with the expected values of cash flows and earnings (Gleißner, 2019).

The results show that risk analyses and risk simulation can be used to develop traditional planning to support corporate management in a world in which entrepreneurial activity is associated with opportunities, threats, and therefore uncertainties. The assessment of planning reliability and the risk-return profile of companies and their options for action are the basis for weighing up risk and return, particularly before making entrepreneurial decisions. Simulation-based bandwidth planning therefore helps to substantiate entrepreneurial decisions more effectively and thus contributes to the success of companies.

References

Altman, E. I. (2000). *Predicting financial distress of companies: Revisiting the Z-score and ZETA models*. New York University.

Behringer, S., & Gleißner, W. (2021). Unternehmensplanung als Grundlage für die Unternehmensbewertung: Die Perspektive der Wirtschaftsprüfer. *Die Wirtschaftsprüfung (WPg), 74*, 857–864.

Berger, T., & Kamaras, E. (2020). Ableitung eines Ratings mit Hilfe der Risikoaggregation. *Controller Magazin, 45*, 29–34.

Dorfleitner, G., & Gleißner, W. (2018). Valuing streams of risky cashflows with risk-value models. *Journal of Risk, 20*, 1–27.

Drobetz, W., & Heller, S. (2014). *What factors drive corporate credit ratings?: Evidence from German SMEs and large corporates*. http://ssrn.com/abstract=2392377. Accessed 4 March 2024.

Franken, L., Gleißner, W., & Schulte, J. (2020). Insolvenzrisiko und Berücksichtigung des Verschuldungsgrads bei der Bewertung von Unternehmen: Stand der Diskussion nach Veröffentlichung des IDW Praxishinweises 2/2018. *Corporate Finance, 11*, 84–96.

Gleißner, W. (2013). *Die risikogerechte Bewertung alternativer Unternehmensstrategien: ein Fallbeispiel jenseits CAPM*. Bewertungs Praktiker: 82–89.

Gleißner, W. (2019). Cost of capital and probability of default in value-based risk management. *Management Research Review, 42*, 1243–1258.

Gleißner, W. (2022). *Grundlagen des Risikomanagements: Handbuch für ein Management unter Unsicherheit* (Management competence) (4th ed.). Verlag Franz Vahlen.

Gleißner, W., & Ernst, D. (2019). Company valuation as result of risk analysis: replication approach as an alternative to the CAPM. *The Business Valuation OIV Journal, 1*, 3–18.

Gleißner, W., & Ernst, D. (2023). The simulation-based valuation of companies and their strategies: Classification, methodology and case study. *The European Business Valuation Magazine (EBVM), 2*, 4–16.

Gleißner, W., Günther, T., & Walkshäusl, C. (2022). Financial sustainability: Measurement and empirical evidence. *Journal of Business Economics, 92*, 467–516.

Grisar, C., & Meyer, M. (2015). Use of Monte Carlo simulation: An empirical study of German, Austrian and Swiss controlling departments. *Journal of Management Control, 26*, 249–273. https://doi.org/10.1007/s00187-015-0213-2

Kerins, F., Smith, J. K., & Smith, R. (2004). Opportunity cost of capital for venture capital investors and entrepreneurs. *The Journal of Financial and Quantitative Analysis, 39*, 385–405.

Krotter, S., & Schüler, A. (2013). Empirische Ermittlung von Eigen-, Fremd- und Gesamtkapitalkosten: eine Untersuchung deutscher börsennotierter Aktiengesellschaften. *Zfbf - Zeitschrift für betriebswirtschaftliche Forschung, 65*, 390–433.

Matschke, M. J., & Brösel, G. (2021). *Business valuation: Functions, methods, principles. Finance*. UVK Verlag; Narr Francke Attempto Verlag GmbH + Co. KG.
Radinger, G., Moecke, P., & Gleißner, W. (2022). Fallbeispiel zur Bandbreitenplanung. Risikoanalyse im Rahmen der Finanzplanung. *Controller Magazin, 47*, 25–31.
Saha, A., & Malkiel, B. G. (2012). DCF valuation with cash flow cessation risk. *The Journal of Applied Finance, 22*, 175–185.

Glossary of Important Terms

Agency Problem The conflict of interest that arises between managers (agents) and shareholders (principals). Agency problems can result in decisions that do not maximize shareholder value. (see Sect. 2.5)

At-Risk Metrics These are metrics such as Value at Risk (VaR) and Conditional Value at Risk (CVaR), which quantify the financial risk of losses. These metrics help in risk aggregation and are essential for financial risk management. (see Sect. 6.4)

Capital Asset Pricing Model (CAPM) A financial model that establishes a relationship between risk and expected return, primarily used to estimate the cost of capital. CAPM plays a crucial role in decision-making under risk. (see Sect. 2.7)

Conditional Value at Risk (CVaR) CVaR is an extension of Value at Risk (VaR) that accounts for the potential extreme losses beyond the VaR threshold. It provides a more complete picture of tail risk. (see Sect. 6.4)

Coefficient of Variation This is a standardized measure of risk, calculated as the ratio of standard deviation to the mean. It enables the comparison of risk across different investments or businesses. (see Sect. 6.3)

Cost of Capital The required return to compensate investors for the risks they take when providing capital to a company. This is a central concept in value-based management. (see Sect. 6.8)

Decision Trees A graphical tool that helps decision-makers map out different possible outcomes of decisions under uncertainty. It includes both risks and rewards. (see Sect. 4.3)

Economic Value Added (EVA) A performance measure that subtracts the cost of capital from net operating profit after tax (NOPAT) to determine if a company is creating value. It is closely linked to risk management. (see Sect. 6.8)

Enterprise Risk Management (ERM) ERM is a holistic framework used by organizations to identify, assess, and manage risks across all departments. It integrates risk management into the decision-making process. (see Chap. 1)

R. Rieg et al., *Enterprise Risk Management*, Springer Texts in Business and Economics, https://doi.org/10.1007/978-3-031-86425-4

Expected Utility Theory This theory suggests that people make decisions based on the expected utility (or satisfaction) of outcomes rather than their expected monetary value. It explains why risk preferences vary among individuals. (see Sect. 2.3)

Heuristics Heuristics are mental shortcuts or rules of thumb that simplify decision-making under uncertainty. They can lead to biases but are useful in situations where quick decisions are needed. (see Sect. 3.2)

Input-Oriented Valuation Focuses on the company's rating and financing constraints, treating risk as potential loss, often measured by Value at Risk (VaR). This method aligns with the "risk coverage approach" and considers the company's specific risk profile, integrating financing limitations into the valuation process. (see Sect. 10.6)

Insolvency Risk Describes the likelihood of insolvency due to uncertain future developments, impacting a company's ability to meet its obligations. Proper risk analysis and proactive risk management are essential to anticipate potential scenarios leading to insolvency. (see Sect. 10.6)

Liquidity Risk The risk that a company will not have enough cash to meet its short-term financial obligations. It is critical in understanding a firm's ability to operate smoothly. (see Sects. 6.5 and 8.2)

Monte-Carlo Simulation A technique that uses repeated random sampling to simulate the impact of risk and uncertainty on a model. It helps organizations estimate the probability of various outcomes. (see Sect. 5.5)

Net Present Value (NPV) A financial metric used to evaluate the profitability of an investment by comparing the present value of cash inflows and outflows. NPV helps in making capital budgeting decisions. (see Sect. 4.1)

Operational Risk The risk of loss due to inadequate or failed internal processes, people, systems, or external events. This type of risk is often difficult to quantify but can significantly impact a business. (see Chap. 1)

Output-Oriented Valuation A valuation approach based on deviations from expected values, often using measures like standard deviation to gauge risk. It is particularly suited for tradable investments, where uncertainties about future market behavior can be factored into valuation calculations. (see Sect. 10.5)

Portfolio Theory This theory emphasizes the benefits of diversification, suggesting that an optimal portfolio balances risk and return. It is foundational in financial decision-making. (see Sect. 2.6)

Principal-Agent Theory A framework for understanding the conflicts of interest between owners (principals) and managers (agents), focusing on how to align incentives and mitigate risks of misaligned interests. (see Sect. 2.5)

Rating A credit rating that reflects insolvency risk, often based on financial ratios, risk analysis results, and historical performance. It serves as an indicator of the company's financial health and its ability to handle future risks effectively. (see Sect. 10.7)

Risk-Adequate Valuation Determines the value of uncertain cash flows using risk measures like standard deviation or coefficient of variation. This method requires comprehensive risk analysis and aggregation to ensure that the financial model accurately reflects the company's unique risk landscape. (see Sect. 10.5)

Risk Aggregation The process of combining different types of risks to understand their overall impact on the organization. Tools such as Monte-Carlo simulation are commonly used for this. (see Sect. 5.5)

Risk Appetite The level of risk an organization is willing to accept to achieve its objectives. Risk appetite guides decision-making and is central to strategic planning. (see Chap. 7)

Risk Coverage Approach A valuation method used when capital market imperfections are significant, emphasizing potential losses. It highlights the importance of understanding a company's equity requirements to withstand risks, linking risk management directly to financial stability. (see Sect. 10.6)

Risk Paradox A phenomenon where companies simultaneously overestimate some low-probability risks while underestimating high-likelihood risks, leading to biased risk management decisions. (see Sect. 1.1.2)

Scenario Analysis A process of analyzing possible future events by considering alternative possible outcomes. It is a key tool in risk management to evaluate extreme cases. (see Sect. 4.2)

Semi-investment Theory Valuation Simplifies traditional investment theory for practical use, acknowledging the realities of imperfect capital markets. This approach bypasses complex optimization processes, focusing instead on practical risk-adjusted valuation strategies. (see Sect. 10.8)

Sensitivity Analysis An analysis technique used to determine how different variables impact a specific outcome. It helps identify which variables have the greatest influence on risk. (see Sect. 6.8)

Sharpe Ratio A ratio that measures risk-adjusted performance by comparing excess return over the risk-free rate to the standard deviation of returns. It is widely used in portfolio management. (see Sect. 6.6)

Simulation-Based Valuation Utilizes business risks and Monte-Carlo simulations to model uncertainty, providing a comprehensive picture of possible future outcomes. This method allows for scenario analysis and stress testing, ensuring robust decision-making even under uncertain conditions. (see Sect. 10.8)

Strategic Risk The risk that a company's business strategy may fail due to changes in the external environment or internal weaknesses. Strategic risk often affects long-term planning. (see Chap. 1)

Unbiased Plan Value Averages expected cash flows across possible future scenarios, based on a thorough risk analysis. Known as simulation-based plan values, these estimates often present a more realistic, less optimistic projection, helping in the development of resilient strategies. (see Sect. 10.8)

Value at Risk (VaR) VaR is a statistical measure that estimates the maximum loss a portfolio could face over a specified period at a given confidence level. It is essential for quantifying downside risk. (see Sect. 6.4)

Weighted Average Cost of Capital (WACC) The average rate of return a company is expected to pay to its security holders. It is a key factor in determining the cost of financing and impacts the value of a company. (see Sect. 6.8)

MIX
Papier aus verantwortungsvollen Quellen
Paper from responsible sources
FSC® C105338

If you have any concerns about our products,
you can contact us on
ProductSafety@springernature.com

In case Publisher is established outside the EU,
the EU authorized representative is:
Springer Nature Customer Service Center GmbH
Europaplatz 3, 69115 Heidelberg, Germany

Printed by Libri Plureos GmbH
in Hamburg, Germany